Financial System and Financial Institutions in India

Financial System and Financial Institutions in India

Reserve Bank of India □ Commercial Banks □ Development Finance Institutions (DFIs) □ State Level Financial Institutions □ Specialized Financial Institutions □ Investment Institutions □ Specialized Public Guarantee Institutions □ Regional Rural Banks (RRBs) □ Co-operative Banks □ Non-banking Financial Companies (NBFCs) □ Merchant Banking □ Venture Capital Companies □ Mutual Funds □ Lease Financing Companies □ Hire Purchase Companies □ Insurance Organizations

By

Dr. Benson Kunjukunju

Associate Professor,
Post-graduate and Research Department of Commerce,
St. Thomas College, Kozhencherry, Kerala

and

Dr. S. Mohanan

Associate Professor,
Department of Commerce,
V.T.M. N.S.S. College, Dhanuvachapuram,
Trivandrum, Kerala

New Century Publications
New Delhi, India

NEW CENTURY PUBLICATIONS
4800/24, Bharat Ram Road,
Ansari Road, Daryaganj,
New Delhi – 110 002 (India)

Tel.: 011-2324 7798, 4358 7398, 6539 6605
Fax: 011-4101 7798
E-mail: indiatax@vsnl.com • info@newcenturypublications.com
www.newcenturypublications.com

Editorial office:
LG–7, Aakarshan Bhawan
4754-57/23, Ansari Road, Daryaganj,
New Delhi – 110 002

Tel.: 011-4356 0919

First Published: **July 2012**

ISBN: **978-81-7708-314-9**

Published by New Century Publications and printed at Salasar Imaging Systems, New Delhi

Designs: Patch Creative Unit, New Delhi

PRINTED IN INDIA

Conversion Table

Unit Conversion

1 lakh	= 0.1 million
10 lakh	= 1.0 million
1 crore	= 10.0 million
100 crore	= 1.0 billion

Exchange Rate

The unit of currency in India is Indian Rupee, symbolized as ₹. As per reference rate of Reserve Bank of India (RBI) for May 22, 2012

US$ 1	= ₹ 54.88
UK£ 1	= ₹ 86.84
Euro (€) 1	= ₹ 70.20

Fiscal Year

Fiscal year in India runs from April 1 to March 31 of the following year.

About the Book

Finance is the mainstay of any development strategy. The financial system promotes savings by providing a wide variety of financial assets to the general public. Savings collected from the household sector are pooled together and allocated to various sectors of the economy for raising production levels. If the allocation of credit is judicious and socially equitable, it can help achieve the twin objectives of growth and social justice.

Financial institutions (intermediaries), which provide a meeting ground for the savers and the investors, form the core of India's financial sector. Through mobilisation of resources and their better allocation, financial intermediaries play an important role in the development process of underdeveloped countries.

The present book explains and examines at length the changes which have swept India's financial sector since Independence in 1947, with focus on post-1991 period. In the main, the book deals with the functioning of financial institutions, covering the following ones: Reserve Bank of India, Commercial Banks, Development Finance Institutions (DFIs), State Level Financial Institutions, Specialized Financial Institutions, Investment Institutions, Specialized Public Guarantee Institutions, Regional Rural Banks (RRBs), Co-operative Banks, Non-banking Finance Companies (NBFCs), Merchant Banking, Venture Capital Companies, Mutual Funds, Lease Financing Companies, Hire Purchase Companies and Insurance Organizations. Each chapter ends with two lists of questions: (a) short answer type questions and (b) essay type questions.

The book is designed to interest a cross-section of readers, viz. teachers and students of economics, commerce, law, public administration, business management, chartered accountancy and company secretaryship. It will also serve the needs of legislators, business executives, entrepreneurs and investors, and others interested in financial sector developments in India.

About the Authors

Dr. Benson Kunjukunju is presently Associate Professor in the Post-graduate and Research Department of Commerce, St. Thomas College, Kozhencherry, under Mahatma Gandhi University, Kottayam, Kerala. He did his M.Com., M.Phil. and Ph.D. from the University of Kerala, Trivandrum. He has more than 30 years of teaching experience at undergraduate and post-graduate levels. He is a recognized research guide of the Faculty of Commerce, Mahatma Gandhi University, Kottayam.

Dr. Kunjukunju has published 4 books and a good number of research articles in national and international journals of repute. His areas of specialization include financial accounting, financial institutions and financial markets.

Dr. S. Mohanan is currently Associate Professor, Department of Commerce, V.T.M. N.S.S. College, Dhanuvachapuram, Trivandrum, Kerala. He received his Ph.D. in Finance from the University of Kerala in 1992. He worked as Professor in the Department of Business Sciences, Universidad Catolica Del Norte, Antofagasta, Chile (2004-2006). He also worked as Associate Professor in Jimma University, Ethiopia (2002-2004) and in Dhofar University, Oman (2006-2008). He was a Senior Research Fellow at the University of Malaya, Kuala Lumpur, Malaysia (2010-2011).

Dr. Mohanan has published several research articles in Indian and international journals. His areas of research interest include corporate finance, bank management, and micro finance.

Contents in Brief

Contents in Detail

Preface

Financial system is the pivot around which the economy of a country revolves. The financial system promotes savings by providing a wide variety of financial assets to the general public. Savings collected from the household sector are pooled together and allocated to various sectors of the economy for raising production levels. If the allocation of credit is judicious and socially equitable, it can help achieve the twin objectives of growth and social justice.

In the context of relatively underdeveloped capital market and with little internal resources, economic entities depend largely on financial intermediaries for their fund requirements. A financial system performs the following functions, *inter alia*, for the smooth conduct of an economy:

1. It facilitates trading and hedging of risks. Risk mitigation reduces uncertainty and enables resources to flow towards most profitable projects. Such a situation raises the efficiency of investments and the rate of growth.
2. By acting as an efficient conduit for allocating resources, the financial system enables improvement in technical progress. Technological innovations take place when entrepreneurs exploit the best chances of successfully imitating technologies in their production processes and introducing new products.
3. To the extent that financial development leads to the creation of financial infrastructure and enables better and more efficient provision of goods and services, costs of transactions are lowered with positive spill over on development efforts.

Financial System Reforms in India

The environment in the financial sector of India up to the early 1990s was not particularly conducive for the development of financial institutions, financial markets and financial instruments. In fact, it had resulted in segmented and under-developed markets characterised by paucity of instruments, and limited number of participants. Banks and financial institutions functioned in a highly regulated environment, characterised by an administered interest rate structure, quantitative restrictions on credit flows, fairly high reserve requirements and pre-emption of significant proportion of lendable resources for the priority and Government sectors. While the quantitative restrictions resulted in credit rationing for the private sector, interest rate controls led to sub-optimal use of credit resulting in low levels of investment and growth. These, coupled with other factors such as the absence of proper accounting, transparency and prudential norms, resulted in a large build-up of non-performing assets in the banking system. All this led to erosion of profitability in the banking sector, besides decline in productivity and efficiency. The bank-based and highly controlled regime turned out to be inimical to financial market development.

In short, until the early 1990s, the role of the financial system in India was primarily restricted to the function of channelling resources from surplus to deficit sectors. Although the financial system performed this role reasonably well, its operations came to be marked by some serious deficiencies over the years. The Indian Government determined the quantum, allocation and the price of credit, a situation referred to as *financial repression* and marked by (a) high required reserve ratios, (b) subsidised or directed credit programmes, (c) credit rationing, (d) ceilings on deposit and (e) fixing maximum interest rates on loans.

It was in this backdrop, that wide-ranging financial sector reforms in India were introduced as an integral part of the economic reforms process initiated in the early 1990s.

Considering the strategic importance of the financial sector, the Government of India set up a Committee on Financial System (Chairman: M. Narasimham), 1991. It was asked to examine all aspects relating to the structure, organisation, functions and procedures of the Indian financial system. The Committee submitted its report in November 1991.

Pursuant to the recommendations of the Narasimham Committee, reforms in respect of financial intermediaries and financial markets have focused on creating a deregulated environment and enabling free play of market forces while at the same time strengthening the prudential norms and the supervisory system.

To achieve the above objectives, restrictions on pricing of assets have been removed, new instruments have been introduced, and technological infrastructure has been strengthened. Liberalisation of the financial sector has included, among others, the following measures:

1. Deregulation of interest rates.
2. Introduction of new products.
3. Relaxation in investment norms for financial intermediaries, especially banks.
4. Lowering of restrictions on specialisation/diversification of banks.
5. Emergence of new institutions such as primary dealers and mutual funds.
6. Withdrawal of reserve requirements on inter-bank borrowings.
7. Withdrawal of credit controls and excessively high reserve requirements.
8. Deregulation and development of markets.
9. Moves toward privatisation of financial services.
10. Easing of restrictions in respect of foreign currency investments of banks.
11. Easing of restrictions on current and capital account convertibility.
12. Lowering of entry barriers/limits on participation of foreign banks.

13. Granting operational autonomy to banks.
14. Reduction in statutory pre-emptions so as to release greater funds for commercial lending.

Thus, financial repression has eased substantially with the deregulation of interest rates and substantial removal of directed credit allocation. It has paved the way for integration among various segments of the financial system. It can be said that reduction/removal of financial repression has enhanced the efficiency and potential growth of the Indian economy.

Financial Institutions in India

Financial institutions (intermediaries) in India consist of Reserve Bank of India, Commercial Banks, Development Finance Institutions (DFIs), State Level Financial Institutions, Specialized Financial Institutions, Investment Institutions, Specialized Public Guarantee Institutions, Regional Rural Banks (RRBs), Co-operative Banks, Non-banking Finance Companies (NBFCs), Merchant Banking, Venture Capital Companies, Mutual Funds, Lease Financing Companies, Hire Purchase Companies and Insurance Organizations. These institutions, which provide a meeting ground for the savers and the investors, form the core of India's financial sector. Through mobilisation of resources and their better allocation, financial intermediaries play an important role in the development process of underdeveloped countries.

Financial institutions have transited since the mid-1990s from an environment of an administered regime to a system dominated by market-determined interest and exchange rates, and migration of the central bank from direct and quantitative to price-based instruments of monetary policy and operations. However, increased globalisation has resulted in further expansion and sophistication of the financial sector, which has posed new challenges to regulation and supervision, particularly of the banking system. In this context, the capabilities of the existing regulatory and supervisory structures also need to be assessed by benchmarking them against the best international practices.

The banking industry all over the world has undergone transformation since the early 1980s under the impact of deregulation, advances in information technology and globalisation. These forces have increased competitive pressures which have (a) unleashed the strong forces of restructuring and consolidation with the number of banks declining all over the world and (b) prompted banks to seek new sources of revenue beyond traditional products. These, in turn, have led to the blurring of distinctions among providers of various financial services and emergence of financial conglomerates. Although these developments have made institutions more efficient by lowering transaction costs, they have also challenged the traditional regulatory arrangements based on institutions. Also, heightened competitive pressures, by squeezing profit margins of institutions, could lead them to pursue riskier strategies, raising the possibility of failure. Financial instability can also impinge on a country's ability to pursue a prudent macroeconomic policy. The safety and soundness of financial institutions, therefore, have come to occupy a centre-stage in the policy making.

Setting up of Regional Rural Banks (RRBs) in the mid-1970s was a major initiative to meet credit requirements of rural people. The RRBs are specialized rural financial institutions for developing the rural economy by providing credit to small and marginal farmers, agricultural labourers, artisans and small entrepreneurs. During the 35 years of existence of RRBs, several Working Groups and Committees were set up at various points of time to deliberate on issues relating to RRBs and suggest measures to address the same. The focus has varied over time depending on the immediate concerns and the prevailing policy regime. While some of the issues relating to RRBs have lost their significance over time, others have become more relevant.

Reserve Bank of India has been initiating several measures from time to time for facilitating better access to financial services and credit for the rural population. The Regional Rural Banks (RRBs), since their inception, have played a vital role in taking banking to the rural masses, making available credit to weaker sections of society, mobilising and channelising rural savings towards productive activities and in generating employment opportunities in rural areas. RRBs have been provided greater flexibility in operations. Branch licensing norms have been made liberal and powers are delegated to the Regional Offices of the Reserve Bank. Further, the process of mergers of all RRBs of the same sponsor bank in the same State has been effected and the RRBs with negative net-worth are in the process of being re-capitalised.

The impact of reforms has not been so perceptible in the case of Urban Co-operative Banks (UCBs). No significant improvement has been observed either in the stability or efficiency parameters except that state co-operative banks and district central co-operative banks, which were incurring losses, have turned around and made some profits. The performance of scheduled urban co-operative banks in terms of asset quality and profitability has deteriorated. One reason for this appears to be that the reform process for co-operative banks started much later than the commercial banking sector and that too in a phased manner. It may, therefore, take some more time for the reforms to have their impact in the co-operative credit sector.

Reforms in respect of development finance institutions (DFIs) have focussed on imparting market orientation to their operations by withdrawing assured sources of funds. While there was some improvement in the stability parameters (capital and assets quality) of DFIs as a group, the asset quality of some of the DFIs was seriously impaired. Profitability of DFIs, in general, has also declined. The decline in profitability is due to increased competition on the asset side and increased cost of funds on the liability side after assured sources of funds were withdrawn. Thus, insofar as DFIs are concerned, overall there has been some deterioration in efficiency parameters. DFIs, which have traditionally played an important role in financing investment activity, are finding themselves at crossroads. In the initial phase of reforms, DFIs were able to sustain their business and profitability due to several factors, which worked to their advantage. However, on the whole, they have not been able to sufficiently reposition themselves in the changed operating environment.

Rapid expansion of non-banking financial companies (NBFCs) has taken place, providing avenues for depositors to hold assets and for borrowers to enhance the scale of funding of their activities. Various types of NBFCs have provided varied services that include equipment leasing, hire purchase and chit fund activities. More recently, NBFCs activity has picked up in the area of housing finance.

NBFCs have been witnessing significant changes. While the capital adequacy position of most of the NBFCs has improved in recent years, their profitability has been adversely affected due mainly to rise in the cost of funds. This, in turn, is due to decline in the share of public deposits and rise in the share of borrowings. In the coming years, the importance of deposits in their sources of funds is expected to decline further. This, however, should not be a cause of concern as in several other countries, borrowings are the main source of funds for NBFCs. Reform measures have brought asset side of NBFCs also under the regulation of the RBI.

In the case of mutual funds, although competition has increased with the increase in the number of mutual funds, their growth has slowed down sharply in recent years. This trend is partly due to the depressed market conditions and partly due to the problems faced by UTI. This should be a cause of concern as mutual funds in several countries play an important role in the development of the capital market.

Reforms have created competition in the insurance sector and given the customers a wide choice not only in the matter of insurance companies, but also in terms of insurance products. However, impact of increased competition is yet to be felt on insurance penetration. With banks having already been allowed to undertake insurance business, bancassurance market has also come up in a big way.

Financial sector reforms have supported the transition of the Indian economy to a higher growth path, while significantly improving the stability of the financial system. In comparison of the pre-reform period, the Indian financial system today is more stable and efficient. However, these gains need to be consolidated, so that these could be translated to drive the institutions, markets and practices into a mature financial system that can meet the challenges of sustaining India on a higher growth trajectory. The financial system would, therefore, not only need to be stable, but would also need to support still higher levels of planned investments by channelling financial resources more efficiently from deficit to surplus sectors. The banks would need to reassess their core banking business to view how best they could undertake maturity transformation to step up the lendable resources in support of real economic activity.

We are extremely thankful to New Century Publications, New Delhi for their valuable help in bringing out this volume within a short time and for the fine layout of the book. We welcome suggestions and comments for further improvement of the book.

June 2012
Kerala

Dr. Benson Kunjukunju
Dr. S. Mohanan

Abbreviations/Acronyms

ACU	Asian Clearing Union
ADRs	American Depository Receipts
ADs	Authorised Dealers
AIDBs	All India Development Banks
AIFIs	All India Financial Institutions
ALM	Asset Liability Management
AMC	Asset Management Company
AML	Anti-Money Laundering
AMS	Aggregate Measure of Support
APEC	Asia Pacific Economic Cooperation
APMC	Agriculture Produce Market Committee
ARC	Agricultural Refinance Corporation; Asset Reconstruction Company
ARDC	Agricultural Refinance and Development Corporation
ASEAN	Association of South East Asian Nations
ATMs	Automated Teller Machines
BCBS	Basel Committee for Banking Supervision
BCSBI	Banking Codes and Standards Board of India
BFRS	Board for Financial Regulation and Supervision
BFS	Board for Financial Supervision
BIFR	Board for Industrial and Financial Reconstruction
BIS	Bank for International Settlements
BPSS	Board for Payment and Settlement Systems
BSE	Bombay Stock Exchange
CAAP	Capital Adequacy Assessment Process
CAC	Capital Account Convertibility
CAMELS	Capital Adequacy, Asset Quality, Management, Earnings, Liquidity and Systems Control
CAR	Capital to Assets Ratio
CBLO	Collateralised Borrowing and Lending Obligations
CCFF	Compensatory and Contingency Financing Facility
CCIL	Clearing Corporation of India Ltd.
CDBMS	Centralised Data Base Management System
CDOs	Collateralised Debt Obligations
CDR	Corporate Debt Restructuring; Credit-Deposit Ratio
CDs	Certificates of Deposit

CFMS	Centralised Funds Management System
CFSs	Consolidated Financial Statements
CIBIL	Credit Information Bureau of India Limited
COC	Controller of Currency
CPC	Credit Planning Cell
CPR	Consolidated Prudential Reporting
CP	Commercial Paper
CPSS	Committee on Payment and Settlement Systems
CPSUs	Central Public Sector Undertakings
CR	Contingency Reserve
CRAR	Capital to Risk-Weighted Assets Ratio
CRISIL	Credit Rating Information Services of India Limited
CRR	Cash Reserve Ratio
CSF	Consolidated Sinking Funds
CVPS	Currency Verification and Processing Systems
DBD	Department of Banking Development
DBO	Department of Banking Operations
DBOD	Department of Banking Operations and Development
DBS	Department of Banking Supervision
DCA	Department of Company Affairs
DCCBs	District Central Cooperative Banks
DCM	Department of Currency Management
DEIO	Department of External Investment and Operations
DFIs	Development Finance Institutions
DIC	Deposit Insurance Corporation
DICGC	Deposit Insurance and Credit Guarantee Corporation
DM	Deutsche Mark
DPs	Depository Participants
DPSS	Department of Payment and Settlement Systems
DRI	Differential Rate of Interest
DRT	Debt Recovery Tribunals
DSB	Dispute Settlement Body
DSR	Debt Service Ratio
DSS	Debt Swap Scheme
ECBs	External Commercial Borrowings
E-commerce	Electronic Commerce
ECR	Export Credit Refinance
ECS	Electronic Clearing Service
EDMU	External Debt Management Unit

EFF	Extended Fund Facility
EFT	Electronic Funds Transfer
EMEs	Emerging Market Economies
E-money	Electronic Money
EMU	European Monetary Union
EXIM Bank	Export Import Bank of India
FCA	Foreign Currency Assets
FCCBs	Foreign Currency Convertible Bonds
FCNR(A)	Foreign Currency Non-Resident (Accounts)
FCNR(B)	Foreign Currency Non-Resident Accounts (Banks)
FDI	Foreign Direct Investment
FEMA	Foreign Exchange Management Act
FERA	Foreign Exchange Regulation Act
FIIs	Foreign Institutional Investors
FRBM	Fiscal Responsibility and Budget Management
FSQ	Free Sale Quota
GDRs	Global Depository Receipts
GIC	General Insurance Corporation of India
HDFC	Housing Development Finance Corporation Ltd.
HFCs	Housing Finance Companies
IBA	Indian Banks' Association
IBRD	International Bank for Reconstruction and Development
ICAI	Institute for Chartered Accountants of India
ICDs	Inter-Corporate Deposits
ICICI	Industrial Credit and Investment Corporation of India
ICRA	Information and Credit Rating Agency
IDBI	Industrial Development Bank of India
IDBs	India Development Bonds
IDFC	Infrastructure Development Finance Company Ltd.
IFC	International Finance Corporation
IFCI	Industrial Finance Corporation of India Ltd.
IMF	International Monetary Fund
IRDA	Insurance Regulatory and Development Authority
IRDP	Integrated Rural Development Programme
IRS	Interest Rate Swaps
ISDA	International Swap and Derivatives Association
ISQ	Internal Sale Quota
IT	Information Technology
ITES	Information Technology Enabled Services

ITEs	Intra-group Transaction and Exposures
KYC	Know Your Customer
LAF	Liquidity Adjustment Facility
LAN	Local Area Network
LERMS	Liberalised Exchange Rate Management System
LIBOR	London Inter-Bank Offered Rate
MFs	Mutual Funds
MNCs	Multinational Companies
MOU	Memorandum of Understanding
NABARD	National Bank for Agriculture and Rural Development
NAIS	National Agricultural Insurance Scheme
NBFCs	Non-banking Financial Companies
NBFIs	Non-banking Financial Institutions
NEER	Nominal Effective Exchange Rate
NFA	Net Foreign Assets
NFEA	Net Foreign Exchange Assets
NHB	National Housing Bank
NLR	Net Liquidity Ratio
NPAs	Non-performing Assets
NREGS	National Rural Employment Guarantee Scheme
NRI	Non-resident Indian
NSE	National Stock Exchange
NSSF	National Small Savings Fund
NSSO	National Sample Survey Organisation
ODs	Overdrafts
OGL	Open General License
OLTAS	Online Tax Account System
OMO	Open Market Operations
OMS	Open Market Sales
ORFS	On-line Return Filing System
OSS	Off-Site Surveillance System
OTC	Over the Counter
PACS	Primary Agricultural Credit Societies
PDS	Public Distribution System
PLR	Prime Lending Rate
PPP	Purchasing Power Parity
PSBs	Public Sector Banks
PSU	Public Sector Undertaking
RBI	Reserve Bank of India

RBIA	Risk-based Internal Audit
RBS	Risk-based Supervision
REER	Real Effective Exchange Rate
REPO	Repurchase Agreement
RRBs	Regional Rural Banks
RTGS	Real Time Gross Settlement
SBI	State Bank of India
SBS	Shredding and Briquetting System
SCBs	Scheduled Commercial Banks
SCBs	State Co-operative Banks
SCICI	Shipping Credit and Investment Company of India
SDRs	Special Drawing Rights
SEBI	Securities and Exchange Board of India
SENSEX	Sensitive Index
SFC	State Finance Corporation
SIDBI	Small Industries Development Bank of India
SLR	Statutory Liquidity Ratio
SPV	Special Purpose Vehicle
SRFAESI	Securitisation and Reconstruction of Financial Assets and Enforcement of Security Interest Act
SSIs	Small Scale Industries
STCI	Securities and Trading Corporation of India
TBs	Treasury Bills
TRAI	Telecom Regulatory Authority of India
UCBs	Urban Cooperative Banks
UTI	Unit Trust of India
WMA	Ways and Means Advances

1

Financial System: An Overview

1.1 Introduction

Financial system plays an important role in mobilizing savings and allocating them for the most profitable activities, and enables society to make use of its scarce resources for productive use. There is a close nexus between financial systems and the economic development of a nation. Financial system is a mirror, on which the economy gets reflected. It promotes saving habits of people and channels them to their most potent use. The system provides the principal means by which the savings are converted into investments. In other words, financial system may be said to be made up of all those channels through which savings becomes available for investment.

Financial system refers to a set of activities, which facilitates transfer of financial resources from the hands of savers to the borrowers. Financial system is defined as "a set of markets, individuals and institutions, which trade in those markets and the supervisory bodies responsible for their regulation". Financial system thus consists of individuals, institutions, borrowers, markets, practices, instruments and services that facilitate the transfer of financial resources from lenders to the borrowers. Financial institutions, financial markets and financial services together help to transfer financial resources from the savers to various sub sectors.

1.2 Various Options for Exchange of Funds

The end-users of the financial system are people and firms who wish to lend and borrow money. There are mainly three options in the financial system for exchanging of funds between the borrowers and lenders.

1.2.1 Direct Transfer of Funds: In the first option, the buyers and sellers can deal 'directly' with one another, with out being assisted by intermediaries. However, this type of deal is costlier, riskier and unattractive to the lenders when compared to the other two options.

1.2.2 Through Organized Markets: Secondly, for exchanging of funds, the borrowers and lenders of money have the option of using 'organized markets' viz. stock exchanges. In these markets, lenders buy the liabilities issued by borrowers. If the liabilities are newly issued, the issuer receives funds directly from the lender. This market also helps to buy an existing liability, instead of a new one, from one lender to another. In effect, this refinances the original loan, though the borrower is completely unaware of this secondary transaction. The organized markets are used by individuals as well as by financial and non-financial institutions.

1.2.3 Through Financial Intermediaries: In the third option, borrowers and lenders may decide to deal via financial institutions or intermediaries. Financial intermediaries obtain funds by issuing financial claims against themselves to market participants and then invest those funds. The investments made by financial intermediaries can be in the form of either loans or securities. For example, Commercial banks accept deposits and may use the proceeds to lend funds to consumers and businesses. An investment company pools the funds of investors and uses those funds to buy a portfolio of securities such as stocks and bonds.

1.3 Functions of Financial System

The most important and primary function of a financial system is channeling of surplus funds from savers to those who are in need of funds. Financial system helps in both mobilization of savings of the society and its allocation to the various sectors and sub sectors of the economy like industrial, agricultural, and service sectors. The investments of savings in various sectors facilitate capital formation, which in turn accelerate the process of economic growth. Since the industrial sector requires huge investment, bulk of the savings is allocated to these sectors. An efficient financial system also creates liquidity of money. In addition, a financial system also provides payment facilities and assortment of services such as insurance, pensions and foreign exchanges along with facilities, which allow people to adjust their existing wealth portfolios.

The banks and securities markets are two competing mechanisms in the financial system to channel savings for investment. The securities markets score over banks in allocation efficiency, as it allocates savings to those investments, which have a potential to yield higher returns. This inevitably leads to higher returns for savers from their savings and higher productivity on investments of enterprises.

1.4 Components of Financial System

The components of financial system assist in transfer of financial resources from lenders to the borrowers. The financial system comprises the following four major components:

1. Financial Markets,

2. Financial Institutions,
3. Financial Instruments, and
4. Financial Services.

1.4.1 Financial Markets: A market is a set of facilities that make it possible to exchange money for goods or goods for money, on a regular basis. Markets function by placing many interested buyers and sellers at one "place", thus making it easier for them to transact with each other. In economics a market is an organizational device which brings together buyers and sellers and many commodities are traded in the market place.

Financial or securities markets are the centres that provide facilities for buying and selling of financial assets. Securities are the goods exchanged in financial markets. Financial market includes buyers and sellers of securities and agencies/institutions, which help in the buying, and selling of securities of companies and government. Apart from enabling exchange of previously issued financial assets, financial markets also facilitate borrowing and lending by facilitating the sale of newly issued financial assets. Financial market is defined as an "an organizational frame work within which financial instruments can be bought and sold". It is an organized institutional structure or mechanism for creating and exchanging financial assets. In economics, a financial market is a mechanism that allows people to easily buy and sell financial securities (such as stocks and bonds), commodities (such as precious metals or agricultural goods), and other fungible items of value at low transaction costs and at prices that reflect the efficient market hypothesis.

The demand and supply side of money in the financial market determines the volume of business. The participants in the financial markets are borrowers, lenders, agents, brokers, financial institutions and intermediaries. Laws, contracts, communication networks prevailing in the financial market structure link the participants in the financial markets. Financial markets have evolved significantly over several hundred years and are undergoing constant innovation to improve liquidity.

A. Functions of Financial Markets: Financial markets are of great importance in the process of capital formation. Efficient and established financial markets are indispensable for speedy economic development of a nation. Financial markets perform many important functions, which are listed below briefly:

(a) Capital Formation: Efficient and developed financial markets are indispensable for the speedy economic development of a nation. The first task of the financial markets is the transfer of funds from suppliers to users for either investment or consumption purposes. The extent of growth of an economy depends on the rate of savings and investment. Financial markets mobilize savings from the peoplc and allocate them to the various sectors of the economy namely agriculture, service and industries sectors thereby help in capital formation.

(b) Liquidity: Another important function of financial markets is to provide a mechanism for an investor to sell a financial asset. Liquidity of the financial assets is an important characteristic, which attracts the investors. In the absence of liquidity, the owner must keep the financial instrument until it matures and an equity instrument until the company is voluntarily or involuntarily liquidated. Although all financial markets provide some liquidity, the degree of liquidity is one of the factors that differentiate various markets.

(c) Price Discovery for Securities: Third important function of financial market is that it helps in the 'price discovery processes' or determination of the price of a traded asset. Price discovery process is done both for newly issued financial assets as well as for the existing stock of financial assets. This is possible through the interaction of buyers and sellers in a financial market. The volume of transactions of buyers and sellers in a financial market determine the price of the traded asset or the required return on the asset. The inducement for firms to acquire funds ultimately depends on the required return that investors demand.

(d) Allocation of Resources: An important function of the financial market is the allocation of economic resources to various sectors of the economy. Investors compare the merits of different securities offered to them. These parties weigh yield, safety, growth, marketability, liquidity and other qualities that each bidder offers for his securities. Having evaluated these merits, suppliers of money buy some securities and reject others. While long-term and short-term funds flow to the successful bidders they are denied to those groups whose securities are not so attractive. Successful bidders use their funds to acquire material, labour and other factors of production.

(e) Low Search Cost: Another important function of a financial market is that it reduces the search and information cost of transacting. Search costs represent explicit costs such as the money spent to advertise the desire to sell or purchase a financial asset, and implicit costs, such as the value of time spent in locating counterparty. The presence of some form of organized financial market reduces the search and information cost of transacting.

In addition to the above functions financial markets allow transfer of risk from those who undertake investments to those who provide funds for investments. Financial markets also act as collectors and aggregators of information about financial asset values and the flow of funds from lenders to borrowers.

B. Classification of Financial Market: Financial markets are classified in different ways, which are given below:

1. On the Basis of Claim on Financial Assets.
2. On the Basis of Maturity of the Claims.
3. On the Basis of Existing Claim or New Claim.
4. On the Basis of Domicile.

(a) On the Basis of Claim on Financial Assets: The claims traded in a financial market may be for either a fixed amount or a residual amount. Based on claim on financial assets, financial markets are following two types: Equity market and Debt Market.

(i) Equity Market: Securities are conventionally divided into equities and debt securities. Financial markets in which equity instruments are traded are known as equity market. This market is also referred as the stock market. Two types of securities are traded in an equity market namely equity shares and preference shares. Preferred stock represents an equity claim that entitles the investor to receive a fixed amount of dividend. An important distinction between these two forms of equity securities lies in the degree to which they may participate in any distribution of earnings and capital and the priority given to each in the distribution of earnings.

(ii) Debt Market: Financial markets in which debt instruments are traded are referred as debt market. Debt instruments represent contracts whereby one party lends money to another on pre-determined terms and based on rate of interest to be paid by the borrower to the lender, the periodicity of such interest payment and the repayment of the principal amount borrowed. Debt securities are normally issued for a fixed term and are redeemable by the issuer at the end of that term. Debt securities include debentures, bonds, deposits, notes or commercial papers. Debt market is other wise called fixed income market. Generally, debt securities and preferred stock are classified as part of the fixed income market. That sector of the stock market which does not include preferred stock is called the common stock market.

(b) On the Basis of Maturity of the Claims: Another way of classifying financial markets is on the basis of maturity/period of the claims. Based on this, financial markets are following two types: Money market and Capital market.

(i) Money Market: A financial market for short-term financial assets is called the money market. It is a market for dealing in monetary assets of short-term nature. The traditional cut off period for short term and long term claim is one year. Financial asset with a maturity of one year or less than one year is considered short term and therefore part of the money market. It is the central wholesale market for short-term debt securities, or for the temporary investment of large amounts of short-term funds. Money market is a collective name given to various firms and institutions that deal with various grades of near-money. It includes trade bills, promissory notes and government securities. Money market instruments have the characteristics of quick liquidity and minimum transaction cost.

The instruments in money markets are relatively risk-free and the relationship between the lender and borrower is largely impersonal. Borrowers in the money market are the central government, state governments, local bodies, traders, industrialists, farmers, exporters, importers and the public. The money market comprises several sub-markets, which are listed below.

- **Call Money Market:** Call money means the amount borrowed and lent by commercial banks for a very short period i.e. for one day to a maximum of two weeks. It is also called as inter bank call money market, because the participants in the call money market are mostly commercial banks. Call money market is the core of the Indian money market, which supply short-term funds. Call money market plays an important role in removing the routine fluctuations in the reserve position of the individual banks and improving the functioning of the banking system in the country.
- **Treasury Bill Market:** For meeting its short-term financial commitments government issues these bills. The treasury bills market is a market, which deals in treasury bills issued by the Central Government for a short period of not more than 365 days. It is a permanent source of funds for the government. Regular treasury bills are sold to the banks and public, which are freely transferable.
- **Commercial Bill Market:** Commercial bills are important device for providing short-term finance to the trade and industry. Commercial bill market deals in commercial bills issued by the firms engaged in business. These bills are generally issued for a period of three months. After acceptance, the bill becomes a legal document. Such bills can be transferred from one person to another by endorsement. The holder of the bill can discount the bills in a commercial bank for cash.
- **Certificate of Deposit Market:** Certificate of deposit market deals with the certificate of deposits issued by commercial banks. A certificate of deposit is a document of title to a time deposit. The minimum amount of investment should not be less than Rs. one lakh and in the multiples of Rs. one lakh thereafter. The maturity period of CDs issued by banks should not be less than seven days and not more than one year. They are freely transferable by

endorsement and delivery. Certificate of deposits provide greater flexibility to an investor in the deployment of their short-term funds.

- **Commercial Paper Market:** Commercial paper refers to unsecured promissory notes issued by credit worthy companies to borrow funds on a short-term basis. Commercial papers will be issued in denominations of Rs. 5 lakh or multiples thereof. They are transferable by endorsement and delivery. Maturity period of commercial paper lies between 7 days and 365 days.
- **Collateral Loan Market:** This market deals with loans, which are backed by collateral securities. Commercial banks provide short-term loans against government securities, share and debentures of the government etc.

(ii) Capital Market: Capital market is a market that specializes in trading long-term and relatively high-risk securities. A financial asset with a maturity of more than one year is part of the capital market. It is a market for long-term capital. The capital market provides long-term debt and equity finance for the government and the corporate sector. Capital market comprises two segments namely the new issue market and secondary market. The various constituents of capital market are viz. equity market, debt market, government securities market, mutual funds etc.

(c) On the Basis of Existing Claim or New Claim: A third way of classifying financial markets is based on whether the financial claims are issued newly or not. On the basis of issue of a security financial markets are following two types: Primary market and Secondary market.

(i) Primary Market: The market for newly issued financial assets is called the primary market. Primary market provides opportunity to issuers of securities, Government as well as corporates, to raise resources to meet their requirements of investment and/or discharge some obligation. They may issue the securities at face value, or at a discount/premium and these securities may take a variety of forms such as equity, debt etc. They may issue the securities in domestic market and/or international market. Primary market consists of corporate securities, central and state government securities.

(ii) Secondary Market: The market where buying and selling of existing securities takes place is referred as secondary market. Secondary market, which is also referred as stock market predominantly, deals in stock or equity shares. The distinguishing difference between the primary and secondary markets is that in the primary market, the issuer of those securities from investors receives the money for the securities, whereas in the secondary market, the money flows from one investor to the other. The primary as well as the secondary markets is dependent on each other and changes in one market affect changes in the other.

(d) On the Basis of Domicile: Another way of classifying financial markets is on the basis of domicile. Based on domicile financial markets can be divided into two viz. International Market and Domestic Market.

(i) International Market: International market is also referred as the external market or offshore market or more popularly as the Euro market. International market is the markets were the issuances of securities are offered simultaneously to investors of a number of countries and are issued outside the jurisdiction of any single country. As a result of globalization, deregulation and liberalization of financial markets the companies and the investors in any country seeking to raise funds are not limited to the financial assets issued in their domestic market.

(ii) Domestic Market: Domestic market is that part of a nation's internal market representing the mechanisms for issuing and trading securities of entities domiciled within that nation. It is a market where issuers who are domiciled in the country issue securities and where those securities are subsequently traded. It is otherwise called national or internal market. Domestic financial markets can be divided into different sub types like:

- **Gilt-edged Market:** It is a market for government and semi government securities, which carries fixed interest rates. Major players in the gilt-edged securities market in India are the Reserve Bank of India, State Bank of India, private and public sector commercial banks, co-operative banks and financial institutions.
- **Housing Finance Market:** Housing finance market is characterized as a mortgage market, which facilitates the extent of credit, to the housing sector. National housing bank is an apex bank in the field of housing finance in India. It is a wholly owned subsidiary of the RBI. The primary responsibility of the bank is to promote and develop specialized housing finance institutions to mobilize resources and extent credit for house building.
- **Foreign Exchange Market:** Foreign exchange market or Forex-market facilitates the trading of foreign exchange. RBI is the regulatory authority for foreign exchange business in India. The foreign exchange market in India prior to the 1990s was characterized by strict regulations, restrictions on external transactions, barriers to entry, low liquidity and high transaction costs. Foreign exchange transactions were strictly regulated and controlled by the Foreign Exchange Regulations Act (FERA), 1973. With the rupee becoming fully convertible on all current account transactions in August 1994, the risk-bearing capacity of banks increased and foreign exchange trading volumes started rising.
- This was supplemented by wide-ranging reforms undertaken by the Reserve

Bank of India (RBI) in conjunction with the reforms by the Government to remove market distortions and strengthen the foreign exchange market. The reform phase ensued with the Sodhani Committee (1994) which, in its report submitted in 1995, made several recommendations to relax the regulations with a view to vitalizing the foreign exchange market. With the replacement of the Foreign Exchange Regulation Act (FERA) by the market friendly Foreign Exchange Management Act (FEMA), 1999, the Reserve Bank delegated powers to authorised dealers to release foreign exchange for a variety of purposes. Capital account transactions were also liberalized in a systematic manner.

- **Futures Market:** Futures markets provide a way for business to manage price risks. A futures contract is an agreement that requires a party to the agreement to either buy or sell something at a designated future date at a predetermined price. The basic economic function of futures market is to provide an opportunity for market participants to hedge against the risk of adverse price movements. Buyers can obtain protection against rising prices and sellers can obtain protection against declining prices through futures contracts. Futures contract can be either commodity futures or financial futures. Commodity futures involve traditional agricultural commodities and industrial commodities. Futures contract based on financial instruments or a financial index are known as financial futures. Financial futures can be classified as follows:

1. Stock index futures.
2. Interest rate futures.
3. Currency futures.
4. Commodity futures etc.

C. Factors Affecting Financial Market: Important factors, which affect the movement of prices of securities in the market are the following:

(a) Actions of Investors: Actions of individuals, institutions and mutual funds investors will instantly affect the prices of stocks, bonds, and futures in the securities market. For example, if a large number of people want to buy a certain stock its price will go up, similarly if many people were bidding on an item of stock, its price will crash.

(b) Business Conditions: Both the condition of an individual business and the strength of the industry will affect the price of its stock. Profits earned volume of sales, and even the time of year all will determine how much an investor wants to invest in stock.

(c) Government Actions: The government makes all kinds of decisions that affect both how much an individual stock may be worth (new regulations on a business) and what sort of instruments people want to buy. The government's interest rates, tax rates, trade policy and budget deficits all have an impact on prices.

(d) Economic Indicators: General trends that signal changes in the economy are watched closely by investors to predict what is going to happen next. Such indicators include the Gross National Product (GNP), the inflation rate, the budget deficit and the unemployment rate. These indicators point to changes in the way ordinary people spend their money and how the economy is likely to perform.

(e) International Events: Events around the world, such as changes in currency values, trade barriers, wars, natural disasters, and changes in governments will affect the price of securities, which ultimately influence the amount of investment.

1.4.2 Financial Institutions: Financial institutions play a vital role in providing finance for the economic development of a nation. The institutional framework, its structure and diversification of activities is an indicator of the efficiency and vibrancy of the financial system. However, financial intermediaries or institutions are better positioned than individuals to channel the funds into investments, which are more conducive to economic development. The nature and scope of financial intermediaries, their investment policies and operations affect substantially the process of capital formation.

A. Classification of Financial Institutions: Indian financial institutions can be classified into two types: On the Basis of Control and On the Basis of Function.

(a) On the Basis of Control: Based on control exercised by the RBI Indian financial institutions can be classified mainly into two categories: (a) Financial Institutions under the Organized Sector and (b) Financial Institutions under the Unorganized Sector.

(i) Financial Institutions under the Organized Sector: The organized financial institutions comprise a set of institutions, which are directly regulated and controlled by the Reserve Bank of India. Reserve Bank of India plays the lead role in the Indian financial system by creation of money and control of credit in the economy. The organized sector consists of the Reserve Bank of India, the State Bank of India and its subsidiaries, Nationalized Banks, Private Sector Banks, Foreign Banks, Regional Rural Banks, Co-operative Banks, Non-Banking Financial Institutions, National Bank for Agriculture and Rural Development, Exim Bank etc.

(ii) Financial Institutions under the Unorganized Sector: The unorganized sector comprises several institutions which are over the length and breadth of the country such as indigenous bankers, moneylenders, landlords, Nidhis, investment companies, chitty funds, traders etc. These institutions are categorized under the unorganized sector because their activities are not directly regulated and coordinated by the Reserve Bank of India. However, the institutions under the unorganized sector are also governed by the rules and regulations framed periodically by the monetary authorities of the country.

(b) On the Basis of Functions: Financial institutions are functionally classified into two: (a) Money Market Institutions and (b) Capital Market Institutions This classification is based on the term of credit i.e. whether the credit is supplied for short-term or long-term.

(i) Money Market Institutions: Money market is the market in which short-term funds are borrowed and lend. The money market, which is the market for short-term funds with maturity ranging from overnight to one year, provides an avenue for the central bank's intervention in influencing both the quantum and liquidity in the financial system. Money market institutions deal with marketable assets, which are relatively liquid and quick. Indian money market institutions are classified mainly in to three. They are the following:

- **Banking Institutions:** Banking institutions consists of RBI at the top as the leader of the financial system followed by commercial banks, cooperative banks, foreign banks, regional rural banks, post office savings bank etc.
- **Non-banking Financial Institutions:** Non-banking financial institutions are life insurance companies, general insurance companies, mutual fund companies, pension funds, lease finance companies, hire purchase companies etc.
- **Specialized Financial Institutions:** Specialized Financial Institutions are NABARD, Industrial Credit and Investment Corporation of India, which is now merged with ICICI Bank Ltd, Exim Bank, Industrial Development Bank of India which got merged with IDBI Bank, Industrial Finance Corporation of India, National Housing Bank etc.

(ii) Capital Market Institutions: Capital market provides long-term debt and equity finance for the central and state governments and the corporate sector. Capital market consists of new issues market and secondary market. Individuals, banks, financial institutions, mutual funds, non-resident Indians, employees, promoters etc. are the suppliers of money to the new issue market. Stockbrokers, mutual funds, financial institutions, foreign institutional investors and individual investors are the lead players in the secondary market.

1.4.3 Financial Instruments: Financial market is a market wherein some financial products or instruments are traded. Financial instruments are broadly classified into two. They are: money market instruments and capital market instruments.

A. Money Market Instruments: Money market instruments in India consists of Treasury bills, Call and Short notices, Certificates of deposits, Commercial papers, Commercial bills, Promissory notes, Term money etc.

B. Capital Market Instruments: The important capital market instruments are equity shares, preference shares, debentures and bonds.

1.4.4 Financial Services: In a narrow sense, a financial service otherwise called financial intermediation includes all types of financial activities which are carried on by financial institutions. In broader terms financial services mean the 'mobilization and allocation of savings' i.e. transformation of savings into investment.

Financial services institutions help in the mobilization of savings and allocation of savings to various sectors of the economy but mainly to the industrial sector. These institutions thus play a vital role in the economic development of a nation. The financial services industry includes both money market and capital market intermediaries. Since independence, commercial banks and non-banking financial institutions have been dominating the Indian financial services industry.

Financial services include a multiplicity of monetary activities namely factoring, merchant banking, lease and hire purchase financing, venture capital, consortium lending, underwriting and new issue marketing, bill discounting, investment advisory services, corporate advisory services, depositories, money market operations, insurance services, mergers, acquisitions and amalgamations, securitization, mutual funds, portfolio management services, technical consultancy and project preparation, forward contracts, options, features, swaps, derivative security etc.

A. Financial Intermediaries: A financial intermediary is defined as "an organization which borrows funds from lenders and lends them to borrowers on terms which are better for both parties than if they deal directly with each other". Financial intermediaries are financial institutions that engage in financial asset transformation. Financial intermediaries purchase one kind of financial asset from borrowers and sell a different kind of financial asset to savers. In addition, unlike brokers and dealers, financial intermediaries typically hold financial assets as part of an investment portfolio rather than as an inventory for resale. In addition to making profits on their investment portfolios, financial intermediaries make profits by charging relatively high interest rates to borrowers and paying relatively low interest rates to savers.

B. Types of Financial Intermediaries: Types of financial intermediaries include:

1. Depository Institutions namely commercial banks, savings and loan associations, mutual savings banks, credit unions etc;
2. Contractual Savings Institutions like life insurance companies, fire and casualty insurance companies, pension funds, government retirement funds; and
3. Investment Intermediaries includes finance companies, stock and bond mutual funds, money market mutual funds.

1.5 Indian Financial System

The performance of every economy including Indian economy is dependent on the efficiency and efficacy of the financial system. An inept financial system stands as an obstacle to growth. The financial sector in India remained a regulated one since independence. Of late Indian financial system has undergone speedy transitions and it comprises a net work of financial institutions, markets and instruments.

Up to 1990, the concept of an independent regulatory authority had no relevance. Following the global trend, the Indian financial system slowly entered into a market driven competitive system. The financial sector reforms of 1991 ushered in fundamental changes in the Indian financial system with innovative and novel financial products and market instruments for the growing needs of the economy and the divergent requirements of the investors.

In the emerging scenario, the financial sector reforms, characterized by increasing financial deregulation and liberalization has paved the way for the role of financial sector growing in the economy as a whole. The Indian financial system is thus passing through a period of structural adjustment and consolidation consequent to economic liberalization. Of late, it has become more market-oriented. There has been significant increase in financial institutions' market activities and exposures, and also participation by non-financial corporations and households in the markets.

1.5.1 Structure of Indian Financial System: The financial system in India comprises a large number of financial institutions, financial markets, financial instruments and financial services to cater to the requirements of finance for the various segments of society. These financial institutions differ not only in their corporate structure, size, sources of funds, but also in terms of purposes for which loans are extended and the targeted clientele. These institutions further differ in terms of indicators of financial soundness. The financial system in India has become more advanced in response to the various requirements of the economy.

The regulatory and supervisory powers of Reserve Bank of India vary over various sets of institutions. The responsibility of regulating and supervising banks including Urban Co-operative Banks (UCBs) is vested with the Reserve Bank of India under the Banking Regulation Act, 1949. However, urban co-operative banks are also regulated by the State Governments (by Registrar of Co-operative Societies in the case of UCBs operating in a single State and the Central Registrar of Co-operative Societies in the case of UCBs having presence in more than one State). The Reserve Bank of India Act, 1934 also empowers the Reserve Bank to regulate some of the financial institutions.

In the case of State and district central co-operative banks, and regional rural banks, the Reserve Bank is the regulator and their supervision is vested with the National Bank for Agriculture and Rural Development (NABARD). With the amendments to the RBI Act in 1997, a comprehensive regulatory framework in respect of non-banking financial companies (NBFCs) was effected into. Financial institutions, which are under the regulatory purview of the Reserve Bank of India, encompassed commercial banks, urban co-operative banks, regional rural banks, financial institutions and non-banking financial companies. The Reserve Bank closely monitors developments in the financial markets bearing in mind their critical role, and simultaneously takes measures to further develop the various segments of the financial market under its purview, *viz*., the money market, the Government securities market and the foreign exchange market. The SEBI regulates the capital market.

1.5.2 Indian Financial Institutions: Indian financial institutions comprise an impressive net work of:

1. Banking,
2. Non-banking, and
3. Specialized financial institutions.

Banking institutions in India comprises State Bank of India and its associate banks, nationalized banks, regional rural banks, private sector banks, foreign banks in India, state co-operative banks, state level land development banks, central co-operative banks, central land development banks, urban co-operative banks, primary agricultural credit societies, primary land development banks, farmers' service societies etc.

Non-banking financial institutions includes private and public sector mutual funds, unit trust of India, post office savings bank, employees provident fund, pension funds, public and private life and non-life insurance companies, investment companies, loan companies, hire purchase companies, equipment leasing companies, mutual benefit finance companies, merchant banking companies, factoring companies, credit rating agencies, miscellaneous finance companies, residuary non-banking companies, housing finance companies etc.

Specialized financial institutions consists of National Bank for Agricultural and Rural Development, Industrial Finance Corporation of India, Industrial Reconstruction Bank of India, Exim Bank, State Financial Corporations, Industrial Co-operatives, National Small Industries Corporation, Agricultural Finance Consultancy, Small Industries Development Bank of India, Industrial Investment Bank of India, National Housing Bank, Deposit Insurance and Credit Guarantee Corporation of India, Risk Capital and Technology Finance Corporation, Venture Capital Institutions, Export Credit Guarantee Corporation, Discount and Finance House of India, Tourism Finance Corporation of India etc.

1.5.3 Indian Financial Markets: Financial markets in India consist mainly of money market, capital market, gilt-edged market for government securities, housing finance market, foreign exchange market etc. Money market includes Call money market, Treasury bills market, Commercial bill market, Collateral loan market, Certificate of deposits and Commercial paper market. Capital market is inclusive of both primary market and secondary market.

1.5.4 Financial Instruments in India: Financial instruments in India are broadly classified into two, namely money market and capital market instruments. Money market instruments consist of call money, treasury bills, certificate of deposits, repos, collateral loans, commercial papers, money market mutual funds and commercial bills. Capital market instruments include equity shares, preference shares, debentures, bonds, derivative instruments etc.

1.5.5 Financial Services in India: Various financial services provided by banking and non-banking companies in the Indian financial system are viz. merchant banking and new issue marketing, leasing and hire purchase services, underwriting and loan syndication, investment advisory and consultancy service, factoring, portfolio management service, credit rating, insurance services, corporate asset management service, technical consultancy services, housing finance, depository services etc.

Stock Exchanges, Stock Holding Corporation of India, National Depository Corporation of India, Securities Trading Corporation of India Ltd., National Securities Depository Ltd., Indian Securities Depository Nominee Company Ltd., Central Depository Company, and Investor Services of India Ltd. are the institutions providing services in the capital market.

1.5.6 Recent Trends in Indian Financial System: Since 1990 Indian financial services industry has undergone a transformation. The Narasimham Committee recommended sweeping changes in the financial sector as per international norms to cater to the needs of the sector and to strengthen it. The system got transformed itself into a vibrant financial service sector with many innovative and technology driven services in their hand. A brief note on recent trends in Indian financial system is given below:

A. Expansion in the Number of Institutions: Since independence, there has been a steady increase in the number of financial institutions in India. Economic liberalization and financial sector reforms in the mid 1990s witnessed radical changes in the number and structure of financial institutions in the country. Financial sector reforms resulted in the entry of new financial institutions both Indian and foreign.

B. Diversification in Activities: Since 1990, Indian financial sector has witnessed drastic changes at the level of both activities and functions. One of the most important trends in financial markets in recent years has been the introduction of 'Universal Banking'. As far as India is concerned the concept of universal banking is of recent origin. Universal banking is a name accorded to banks, which are engaged in dispensing diverse kinds of banking services. Universal banks in general refers to those banks that offer a wide range of financial services, other than commercial banking and investment banking i.e. issuing, underwriting, investing and trading in securities. In a very broad sense, however, the term 'universal banks' refers to those banks that offer a wide variety of financial services.

C. Sound Financial System: The existence of sound and healthy financial system is a pre requisite for the economic development of a nation. The existence of a strong financial system comprising many institutions should be able to put pressure on investors and borrowers. During the last few years, Indian financial market has been regaining its buoyancy. Globally recognised vibrant economic fundamentals of the country and widely perceived robustness of the Indian economy have gradually and substantially restored the confidence of the investors both global and local in the Indian market.

D. Financial Innovations: Today, anything and everything is traded in the market. In recent years, innovation has been the key word behind the phenomenal success of many of the financial service companies. There is a huge scope for the structured and synthetic products in the Indian financial market. Financial innovation is becoming ubiquitous. Financial institutions now undertake a broader range of activities than the traditional ones of taking deposits and extending loans. Today, financial institutions are co-designing the products/services with their customers and striving to provide them with global solutions. Since the major objective of a financial institution is to broad-base its customer base these institutions give importance to financial innovations. Money market and Capital Market institutions are competing with each other to attract investors by offering innovative and attractive services and products.

E. Technological Advancement: Technology is also helping market players to redefine the way they have been operating in the market. Today, banks advise their customers to opt for ATM for cash requirements of a specified nature and for other minor transactions. Availability of the concepts like anytime banking, tele-banking, internet banking etc. has become possible only because of the recent technological developments.

F. Integration, Financial Liberalization and Internationalization: As a result of technological developments and increasing degree of cross-industry and cross-border integration, financial systems are also more integrated nationally as well as internationally. A large number of financial conglomerates have also emerged by way of mergers and acquisitions. The Indian economy until the nineties was subjected to regimentation because of control and regulation. The reforms initiated in 1991 transformed the economy from a controlled one to that of a market driven one. The financial market especially the securities market facilitates the internationalization of an economy by bonding it with the rest of the world. This linkage assists through the inflow of capital in the form of portfolio investment. This implies that the domestic economy gets opened to international competitive pressures, which in a way helps to raise its efficiency.

G. Fierce Competition: Today, businesses are no longer businesses; they have become battles of competencies. Indeed, there is competition for competence in the market. Success or failure of a market player in this battle for competence determines his potential for growth and the competitive differentiation. Hence, companies have to strategize and re-strategize almost on a continuous basis. They need to persistently fortify their existing knowledge base and acquire/create new knowledge, compatible with the existing one, as quickly and as inexpensively as possible, to continue their lead at the opportunity zones. Tomorrow, their competitive position in market place would depend on the speed with which they run on the learning curve, discover the new frontiers of knowledge in all dimensions of their operations and then think creatively and imaginatively of the strategic ways to transform this accumulated knowledge into value delivering propositions. It should be understood that the existence of knowledge does not ensure success; corporations must also possess the capabilities to leverage on that knowledge to create values.

H. Consolidation of Existing Institutions: Another important trend in financial markets in India is the consolidation of existing institutions, particularly the commercial banks. The recent years witnessed significant strides in the financial market. Speed and efficiency are the hallmarks of the current financial system.

To sum up, until the early 1990s, the role of the financial system in India was primarily restricted to the function of channeling resources from surplus to deficit sectors. Whereas the financial system performed this role reasonably well, its operations came to be marked by some serious deficiencies over the years. The Indian Government determined the quantum, allocation and the price of credit, a situation referred to as *financial repression* by some experts.

It was in this backdrop, that wide-ranging financial sector reforms in India were introduced as an integral part of the economic reforms initiated in the early 1990s.

Short Answer Type Questions

1. What is meant by financial market?
2. What is gilt-edged market?
3. What is Euro market?
4. Define investment.
5. What is domestic market?
6. What do you mean by financial system?
7. What are the various ways for exchange of funds?
8. What are the functions of financial system?
9. Define financial intermediary.
10. What do you mean by financial institution?
11. Write a short note on collateral loan market.
12. What is equity market?
13. Explain the functions of financial market.
14. What is forex-market?
15. What is meant by commercial bill market?
16. What do you mean by financial intermediation?
17. Differentiate physical assets and financial assets.
18. What is housing finance market?
19. List the financial institutions under the organized sector.
20. What are financial services?
21. What are the specialized financial institutions?
22. Name the different types of financial intermediaries.
23. What do you mean by offshore market?
24. What is a security?

Essay Type Questions

1. Explain the factors affecting the movement of prices of securities.
2. Describe the various components of financial system and bring out their features.

3. What is financial market? Explain briefly the functions of financial markets.
4. Discuss briefly the structure of Indian financial system.
5. What transformation services do financial institutions provide?
6. Discuss how financial sector reforms have changed the face of Indian financial system.
7. What do you understand by financial system and what are its functions?

2

Financial Institutions: An Overview

2.1 Introduction

The financial system of any country consists of a set of financial institutions, instruments, services and markets. The most important and primary function of financial system is channeling of surplus funds from savers to those who are in need of funds. Financial institutions, instruments, services and markets act together to transfer financial resources from the savers to the borrowers. Financial system thus provides the principal means by which the savings are converted into investments.

Financial system plays an important role in mobilizing savings and allocating them for the most profitable activities, and enables society to make use of its scarce resources for productive purposes. There is a close nexus between the financial system and the economic development of a nation. Financial system is a mirror, on which the economy gets reflected.

A financial institution is typically an intermediary that facilitates the channeling of funds from people who have extra money (savers) to those who do not have enough money to carry out a desired activity (borrowers). That is, savers give funds to an intermediary institution and that institution gives those funds to spenders. Financial institutions collect funds from the public and place them in financial assets, such as deposits, loans and other securities rather than in tangible properties. The classical example of a financial intermediary is a bank that transforms bank deposits into bank loans. A financial intermediary is defined as "an organization which borrows funds from lenders and lends them to borrowers on terms which are better for both parties than if they deal directly with each other".

Financial institutions are engaged in the transformation of financial asset i.e. purchase one kind of financial asset from borrowers and sell a different kind of financial asset to savers. In addition, unlike brokers and dealers, financial intermediaries typically hold financial assets as part of an investment portfolio rather than as an inventory for resale. In addition to making profits on their investment portfolios, financial intermediaries make profits by charging relatively high interest rates from borrowers and paying relatively low interest rates to savers.

Financial institutions play a vital role in providing finance for the economic development of a nation. The institutional framework (its structure and diversification of activities) is an indicator of the efficiency and vibrancy of the financial system. However, financial intermediaries or institutions are better positioned than individuals to channel the funds into investments, which are more conducive to economic development. The nature and scope of financial intermediaries, their investment policies and operations affect substantially the process of capital formation.

Financial intermediaries or institutions provide two important advantages to the savers. First, lending through an intermediary is usually less risky than lending directly. The major reason for reduced risk is that financial intermediaries can diversify their lending to multiple borrowers to spread the risk. It makes lot of loans to different activities and the losses will be largely offset by loans that are sound. In contrast, an average saver could directly make only a few loans, and any bad loans would substantially affect his wealth. Because an intermediary can put its "eggs" in many "baskets," it insures its depositors from substantial losses.

A second advantage the financial intermediaries give to savers is liquidity. Liquidity is the ability to convert assets into cash quickly. For example, if an individual saver has lent money directly to another person for house construction, the loan can be an illiquid asset. If the lender suddenly needs cash, he must either persuade the borrower to repay quickly, which may not be possible, or he must find someone else who will buy the loan from him, which may be very difficult. Although the intermediary may also use its funds to make illiquid loans, its size allows it to hold some funds idle as cash to provide liquidity to individual depositors.

2.2 Functions Performed by Financial Intermediaries

Financial intermediaries provide different functions which are:

1. **Channeling of Funds between Surplus and Deficit:** The basic function of financial institutions is to facilitate the channeling of funds between lenders and borrowers indirectly.
2. **Allocation of Funds into Productive Purposes:** Financial institutions are the intermediaries which help to mobilize financial surpluses of an economy and transfer them to areas of financial deficit. They allocate the mobilized savings effectively into the various productive purposes.
3. **Maturity Transformation:** Financial intermediaries deal with large number of lenders and borrowers and reconcile their conflicting needs by converting short term liabilities into long term assets.
4. **Risk Transformation:** Financial intermediaries convert risky investments

into relatively risk-free investments by lending to multiple borrowers to spread the risk. They create and sell assets with different risk characteristics.

5. **Lesser Transaction Cost:** Financial intermediaries reduce the time and money to be spent by individuals for carrying out financial transactions directly.
6. **Convenience of Denomination:** Financial intermediaries match small deposits with large loans and large deposits with small loans.

2.3 Classification of Financial Institutions

Financial institutions in India are classified mainly into three broad categories:

1. Banking Institutions.
2. Non-Banking Financial Institutions.
3. Development Financial Institutions.

2.3.1 Banking Institutions: Banking institutions constitute the core of the financial sector of the economy. Banking institutions in India consist of Reserve Bank of India (RBI) at the top as the leader of the financial system followed by Commercial Banks (CBs) and Regional Rural Banks (RRBs). In addition to commercial banks, there is a good network of co-operative banks and land development banks at state, district, block and village levels. Short term funds are mainly provided by commercial and co-operative banks. The banking system comprises of the following set of institutions:

1. Reserve Bank of India.
2. Commercial Banks.
3. Regional Rural Banks.
4. Co-operative Banks.

A. Reserve Bank of India: Reserve Bank of India is the apex monetary institution of the Indian financial system. It was established in the year 1935 with a view to organize the financial frame work and to facilitate fiscal stability in India. RBI supervises, regulates, controls and develops the monetary and financial system of the country. Reserve Bank of India has also been vested with immense responsibility of reviewing and reconstructing the economic stability of the country by formulating economic policies and ensuring a proper exchange of currency.

B. Commercial Banks: Commercial banks are financial intermediaries, which perform the dual functions of mobilization of deposits and deployment of surplus funds to the various sectors of the economy. The commercial banks indulge in varied activities such as acceptance of deposits, acting as trustees, offering loans for different purposes. Commercial banks usually carry out most of the banking activities in the country. These banks play an important role in the economic development of the country and thus form the core of the money market operations. Around two third shares in the total assets in the financial system are managed by the commercial banks.

C. Regional Rural Banks: Regional Rural Banks (RRBs) were established in 1975 to meet the excess demand for institutional credit in the rural areas, particularly among the economically and socially marginalized sections. The main objectives of Regional Rural Banks are to provide credit and other facilities especially to the small and marginal farmers, agricultural labourers, artisans and small entrepreneurs in rural areas. RRBs also provide assistance in the marketing of agricultural and other products through marketing organizations and also help in the overall development of the villages.

D. Co-operative Banks: Co-operative banks are an important constituent of the Indian financial system. Co-operative bank is a retail commercial banking institution which is organized on a co-operative basis. Co-operative Banks in India are registered under the Co-operative Societies Act. The co-operative banks are also regulated by the RBI. The co-operative credit structure of India was set up to serve the needs of short, medium and long term rural credit requirements. The structure of co-operative banking in India is federal or pyramidal in nature. The co-operative banking institutions in the country are divided into two categories: Rural Credit Co-operatives and Urban Credit Co-operatives.

(a) Rural Credit Co-operatives: The rural credit co-operative banks may be further divided into two: Short Term Credit Co-operative Banks and Long Term Credit Co-operative Banks.

(i) Short Term Credit Co-operative Banks: With regard to short-term credit co-operatives, at the grass-root level there are Primary Agricultural Credit Societies (PACS) dealing directly with the individual borrowers. At the central level (district level) District Co-operative Banks (DCB) function as a link between primary societies and State Co-operative Apex Banks (SCB). Short term credit is supplied in rural India by the following three set of institutions:

1. Primary Agricultural Credit Societies (PACS).
2. District Central Co-operative Banks (DCB).
3. State Co-operative Banks (SCB).

- **Primary Agricultural Credit Society (PACS):** Primary Agricultural Credit Society (PACS) at the grass root level constitutes the major retail outlet of short and medium term credit to the rural sector. The area of operation of a PACS is restricted to a compact area, preferably a village or a group of small villages where every person knows every other person of the locality. PACS provides short and medium term credit, supplies agricultural and other production requirements and undertakes marketing of agricultural produce.

- **District Co-operative Banks (DCB):** District Co-operative Bank (DCB) is in the middle level in the co-operative credit structure which links the Primary Agricultural Credit Societies and the State Co-operative Bank. The central co-operative banks are generally located at the district head quarters or some prominent town of the district. Branches can be opened at important centres of the district for serving the members.
- **State Co-operative Banks (SCB):** State Co-operative Bank (SCB) is the keystone of the co-operative moment in the state. State Co-operative Banks are the apex institutions in the three-tier co-operative credit structure, operating at the state level. State Apex Co-operative Bank is the federation of the District Co-operative Banks. Being the Apex Bank, it raises resources and channelises them through District Co-operative Banks for both agricultural and non-agricultural purpose. It also channelises the refinance provided by National Bank for Agriculture and Rural Development (NABARD) towards short term and medium term agriculture and allied sector loans to District Co-operative Banks. It is the top most co-operative bank in a state. In each state, there will be a State Co-operative Bank.

(ii) Long-term Credit: As against three-tier structure of short-term credit co-operatives, the long-term co-operative credit structure has two tiers in many states with Primary Co-operative Agriculture and Rural Development Banks (PCARDB) at the primary level and State Co-operative Agriculture and Rural Development Bank at the state level.

- **Primary Co-operative Agriculture and Rural Development Banks (PCARDB):** The Primary Co-operative Agricultural and Rural Development Banks (PCARDB) operate in important centres. The primary co-operative agriculture and rural development banks provide long term loan assistance to farmers with the period of repayment ranging from 5 to 15 years. They provide credit for developmental purposes like minor irrigation, cultivation of plantation crops and for diversified purposes like poultry, dairying and sericulture on schematic basis. They get requisite financial assistance from the State Co-operative Agriculture and Rural Development Bank.
- **State Co-operative Agriculture and Rural Development Bank (SCARD):** State Co-operative Agriculture and Rural Development Bank (SCARD) is the apex institution for all Primary Co-operative Agriculture and Rural Development Banks (PCARDBs) constituted for issuing long term loans for the purpose of developing agriculture and allied activities. The Primary Co-operative Agriculture and Rural Development Banks located at Taluk and

Block levels throughout the state are affiliated to the State Agriculture and Rural Development Bank. The main objective of the Co-operative Agriculture and Rural Development Bank is to provide long term loans to primary agriculture and rural development banks.

(b) Urban Credit Co-operative Banks: Urban Co-operative Banks (UCBs) are an important part of the financial system in India. Urban Co-operative Banks provide banking and credit facilities to urban and semi urban population. They mobilize deposits from the public and extend credit facilities for specified purposes. Their lending operations include provision of credit facilities to small traders, artisans and persons belonging to low and middle income group for purposes ranging from housing, business, education, consumer and other non-farm sector activities.

2.3.2 Non-banking Financial Institutions: Non-Banking Finance Companies (NBFCs) are heterogeneous set of financial institutions with differing financial intermediation. Non-banking finance companies are the intermediaries engaged in the business of accepting deposits and delivering credit. NBFCs provide banking services, but do not hold a banking license. These companies are providing an extensive range of financial services which are divergent in nature. These institutions play a vital role in the Indian financial system because they supplement the activities of banks in terms of deposit mobilization and lending.

These services rendered by non-banking finance companies are either fee based or fund based. The fee based services rendered by non-banking finance companies include portfolio management, stock broking, issue management, loan syndication, merger and acquisition, credit rating, depository services etc. Fund based activities include venture capital financing, housing finance, equipment leasing, hire purchase financing underwriting, factoring, forfeiting, discounting of bills etc. NBFCs consist of mainly eight categories of institutions, with differing financial intermediation viz.

1. **Hire Purchase Finance Company:** It is a class of company which carries on its principal business as hire purchase transactions.
2. **Investment Company:** These companies are primarily engaged in the acquisition of securities and trading in such securities to earn a profit.
3. **Loan Company:** These companies provide finance by making loans or advances, or otherwise for any activity other than its own, excluding equipment leasing, hire purchase and housing finance.
4. **Mutual Benefit Finance Company:** It is a type of non-banking finance company notified by the Central Government under Section 620 A of the Companies Act, 1956.
5. **Equipment Leasing Company:** It is a company which carries on its

principal business as leasing of equipments or the financing of such activity.

6. **Residuary Non-banking Company:** It is a class of Non-Banking Company in which the principal business is the receiving of deposits and does not advance any amount as loan or investment or asset financing.
7. **Miscellaneous Non-banking Company (Chit Fund Companies):** It is a company which collects money from specified number of subscribers periodically and in turn distributes the same as prizes amongst them. Any other form of chit is also included in this category.
8. **Housing Finance Company:** It is a type of company which advances money for the acquisition or construction of houses including the acquisition or development of plots of land.

2.3.3 Development Financial Institutions: The commercial banking network was expanded in the post-independence period, primarily to cater to the requirements of general banking and for meeting the short term working capital requirements of industry and agriculture. The development financial institutions in India were set up under the strong control of both Central and State Governments, and the Government utilized these institutions for the achievements in planning and development of the nation as a whole. These institutions are government undertakings that were set up to provide assistance to the different sectors and thereby cause overall development of the Indian economy.

Development Financial Institutions (DFIs) is an institutional mechanism in which they act as an active agent for the promotion of a balanced and viable economic development of the country. Development financial institutions or development banks provide medium and long term finance to the corporate sector and also take up promotional activities for economic development of the county. The main objective of Development Financial Institutions (DFIs) is to serve as an agent of development in various sectors of economy namely industry, agriculture and international trade. The primary tasks of these institutions are to accelerate the growth of the Indian economy and to provide support to rapid industrialization, particularly in the private sector and backward regions so as to create additional employment opportunities as well as to increase production. Development financial institutions in India commenced with the establishment of Industrial finance Corporation of India (IFCI) in the year 1948 and the State Financial Corporations (SFCs) in 1951. Then after regular intervals the government started new and different development financial institutions to attain the different objectives. The Development financial institutions can be classified according to their economic importance. They are:

1. National level Development Banks.

2. Specialized Financial Institutions.
3. Investment Institutions.
4. Specialized Public Guarantee Institutions.
5. State-level institutions.
6. Other institutions.

A. National Level Development Banks: National Level Development Banks consist of five development banks which are given below:

- Industrial Finance Corporation of India (IFCI).
- Industrial Development Bank of India (IDBI).
- Industrial Credit and Investment Corporation of India Ltd. (ICICI).
- Small Industries Development Bank of India (SIDBI).
- Industrial Reconstruction Bank of India (IRBI) now (Industrial Investment Bank of India).

(a) Industrial Finance Corporation of India (IFCI): Industrial Finance Corporation of India (IFCI) is the first development institution in India. It was incorporated immediately after Independence under the Industrial Finance Corporation Act of 1948 as a statutory corporation to pioneer institutional credit to medium and large-scale industrial units. The share capital of IFCI is contributed by Industrial Development Bank of India, scheduled commercial banks, insurance companies, investment trust and co-operative banks. IFCI is the first development financial institution in India to be converted from a statutory corporation into a company in 1993 under the Companies Act of 1956.

The main focus of IFCI is to provide long term finance to the various sectors in the economy. It provides credit to industrial units in the private, public and co-operative sector. IFCI also provides project finance and corporate advisory services. Under project finance scheme, assistance is available in the form of medium and long term loans to both existing and new industrial units for modernization, expansion and diversification in Indian rupees and foreign currencies. Under corporate advisory services, IFCI provides merchant banking, portfolio management services, corporate financial advisory, receivables financing, IPO management, loan syndication, corporate project and advisory services, lease financing, takeover of accounts from banks and financial institutions etc.

(b) Industrial Development Bank of India (IDBI): The Industrial Development Bank of India (IDBI) was established on July 1, 1964 under an Act of Parliament as a wholly owned subsidiary of the Reserve Bank of India. In 16 February 1976, the ownership of IDBI was transferred to the Government of India. IDBI is the apex financial institution in the field of development banking in the country. The main aim of the formation of the IDBI was to provide easy loans and financial support to the industrial sector in order to develop the industrial sector and also the Indian economy.

IDBI is vested with the responsibility of coordinating the working of institutions engaged in financing, promoting and developing industries. IDBI also undertakes and supports wide-ranging promotional activities including entrepreneurship development programmes for new entrepreneurs, provision of consultancy services for small and medium enterprises, upgradation of technology and programmes for economic upliftment of the underprivileged.

The IDBI (Transfer of Undertaking and Repeal) Act of 2003 passed by Parliament in December 2003 provides for repeal of IDBI Act. It facilitated the formation, corporatisation and registration of Industrial Development Bank of India Ltd. as a company under the Companies Act, 1956 and a deemed banking company under the Banking Regulation Act of 1949 and helped in obtaining requisite regulatory and statutory clearances, including those from RBI. The Reserve Bank of India issued the requisite notification on September 30, 2004 incorporating IDBI as a 'scheduled bank' under the RBI Act of 1934. IDBI was merged and transformed into a commercial bank viz. IDBI Bank. IDBI Bank would continue to provide the extant products and services as part of its development finance role even after its conversion into a banking company. In addition, the new entity would also provide an array of wholesale and retail banking products, designed to suit the specific needs cash flow requirements of corporates and individuals.

(c) Industrial Credit and Investment Corporation of India Ltd. (ICICI): Industrial Credit and Investment Corporation of India Limited (ICICI) was established in 1955 as a joint stock company to encourage and assist mainly private sector industrial units in the country. It was set up with the support from the Government of India, World Bank and other foreign institutions. ICICI was registered as a private limited company under the Indian Companies Act, with a view to support industries in the private sector.

The main objective of ICICI is to assist private industrial undertakings for new projects as well as expansion, modernization and diversification of existing units. It also encourages in the participation of internal and external capital in the private industrial sector. In the 1990s, ICICI transformed its business from a development financial institution offering only project finance to a diversified financial services group offering a wide variety of products and services, both directly and through a number of subsidiaries and affiliates like ICICI Bank. In October 2001, the Boards of Directors of ICICI and ICICI Bank approved the merger of ICICI and two of its wholly-owned retail finance subsidiaries, ICICI Personal Financial Services Limited and ICICI Capital Services Limited, with

ICICI Bank.

(d) Small Industries Development Bank of India (SIDBI): Small Industries Development Bank of India (SIDBI) was established in 1990 under the SIDBI Act of 1989, passed by the Indian Parliament. IDBI is the principal financial institution in India for promotion, financing and development of industries in the small scale sector. SIDBI provides both direct and indirect financial assistance and development and support services in the small scale sector. SIDBI also coordinates the functions of various institutions engaged in the promotion and financing of industries in the small scale sector. It was established as a wholly owned subsidiary of the Industrial Development Bank of India. . As a subsidiary of IDBI, it took over the administration of National Equity Scheme and Small Industries Development Fund (SIDF) from IDBI relating to small scale industries.

(e) Industrial Reconstruction Bank of India (IRBI): Industrial Reconstruction Corporation of India (IRCI) was established by the Government of India in 1973 with a view to overcome the problems of industrial sickness in the country. IRCI was established to provide financial assistance to the sick units for their rehabilitation and reconstruction. The financial resources of IRCI have been subscribed by the IDBI, IFCI, ICICI, LIC, SBI and nationalized banks.

Industrial Reconstruction Corporation of India Ltd. (IRCI) was reconstituted under the IRBI Act of 1984 to take over the functions of IRCI. With effect from March 20, 1985 Industrial Reconstruction Corporation of India Ltd. was renamed as Industrial Reconstruction Bank of India (IRBI). With a view to converting the institution into a full-fledged development financial institution, IRBI was converted in to a joint stock company in March 1997 by naming it as Industrial Investment Bank of India (IIBI). The bank offers wide range of products and services. It provides term loan assistance for project finance and working capital and other short-term loans to companies.

B. Specialized Financial Institutions: The specialized financial institutions are the following:

- Risk Capital and Technology Finance Corporation Ltd. (RCTC).
- Technology Development and Information Company of India Ltd. (TDICI).
- Tourism Finance Corporation of India Ltd. (TFCI).

(a) Risk Capital and Technology Finance Corporation Ltd. (RCTC): IFCI Venture Capital Funds Ltd. was originally set up by Industrial Finance Corporation of India (IFCI) in 1975 to provide institutional support to first generation professionals and technocrats for setting up their own ventures in the medium scale sector through soft loans under the Risk Capital Scheme. In 1988, Risk Capital Foundation (RCF) was converted into a company named as Risk

Capital and Technology Finance Corporation Ltd. (RCTC). The name of RCTC was changed to IFCI Venture Capital Funds Ltd. (IFCI Venture) in February 2000.

(b) Technology Development and Information Company of India Ltd. (TDICI): Venture Capital financing started in India in 1988 with the formation of Technology Development and Information Company of India Ltd. (TDICI). ICICI venture Funds Ltd. formerly known as Technology Development and Information Company of India Ltd. (TDICI) was promoted by ICICI in 1988 as a joint venture with the Unit Trust of India. Subsequently, ICICI bought out UTI's stake in 1998 and ICICI Venture became a fully owned subsidiary of ICICI. It is one of the largest and most successful private equity firms in India. ICICI Venture specializes in private equity, venture capital and mezzanine investments.

(c) Tourism Finance Corporation of India Ltd. (TFCI): Tourism Finance Corporation of India Ltd. (TFCI) was established by the Government of India in 1989 as a public limited company under the Companies Act of 1956. It was promoted by Industrial Finance Corporation of India Ltd. (IFCI), All-India Financial and Investment Institutions and nationalized banks. The objective of Tourism Finance Corporation of India Ltd. (TFCI) is to provide financial assistance to enterprises for setting up and development of tourism related projects, facilities and services.

C. Investment Institutions: The three investment institutions are given below:

- Unit Trust of India (UTI).
- Life Insurance Corporation of India (LIC).
- General Insurance Corporation of India (GIC).

(a) Unit Trust of India (UTI): Unit Trust of India was established in 1964 as a statutory corporation. The primary objective of UTI is to attract the savings of small investors for channeling them into productive investments. The formation of Unit Trust of India in 1964 marked the evolution of the Indian mutual fund industry. UTI was set up by the Reserve Bank of India and its capital was subscribed by RBI, Life Insurance Corporation of India, State Bank of India, commercial banks and financial institutions.

(b) Life Insurance Corporation of India (LIC): Life Insurance Corporation of India is the largest insurance company in India and also the country's largest investor. Life Insurance Corporation of India founded in 1956 is owned solely by the Government of India. LIC was formed through the take over and nationalization of the business of Indian and foreign insurers and provident societies. The main objectives of LIC are to spread life insurance cover widely in the country especially the socially and economically backward sections in the rural areas and to provide adequate financial coverage against death at a reasonable cost.

(c) General Insurance Corporation of India (GIC): General Insurance Corporation of India was established in 1973. GIC was formed for the purpose of superintending, controlling and carrying on the business of general insurance. As soon as GIC was formed, Government of India transferred all the shares it held in the general insurance companies to the GIC. After the formation of General Insurance Corporation of India (GIC), all the existing companies were merged and reorganized into four fully owned subsidiaries of GIC viz. (i) National Insurance Company Ltd., (ii) New India Insurance Company Ltd., (iii) Oriental Fire and General Insurance Company Ltd. and (iv) United India Insurance Company Ltd.

D. Specialized Public Guarantee Institutions:

- Export Credit Guarantee Corporation of India Ltd (ECGC).
- Deposit Insurance and Credit Guarantee Corporation (DICGC).
- Agricultural Insurance Company of India Ltd. (AIC).

(a) Export Credit Guarantee Corporation of India Ltd. (ECGC): Export Credit Guarantee Corporation of India Ltd. (ECGC) is a company owned wholly by the Government of India established in the year 1957. It was originally named as Export Risk Company Private Limited. ECGE is the fifth largest credit insurer of the world. It was transformed into Export Credit Guarantee Corporation of India Ltd. (ECGC) in 1964 and to Export Credit Guarantee of India in 1983. The primary objective of ECGC is to promote Indian export by providing export credit insurance and other trade related services to Indian exporters. The corporation provides guarantee to financial institutions for the benefit of the exporters.

(b) Deposit Insurance and Credit Guarantee Corporation (DICGC): Deposit Insurance Corporation was established in 1962. The main objective of Deposit Insurance Corporation is to give protection to the depositors. The corporation was set up to create confidence in the minds of the depositors and to discourage the withdrawal of deposits. The entire capital of the Deposit Insurance Corporation was contributed by RBI. Deposit insurance scheme provides automatic coverage for deposits received in India by all commercial banks including regional rural banks and co-operative banks.

(c) Agricultural Insurance Company of India Ltd. (AIC): Agriculture Insurance Company of India Ltd. (AIC) was set up in 2002. Agriculture Insurance Company of India Ltd. (AIC) is the largest agricultural insurance company in India and one of the biggest in the world. The main objective of AIC is to protect the interest of the farmers. Agricultural Insurance Company of India

Limited was promoted by General Insurance Corporation of India (GIC), NABARD and 4 public sector General Insurance Companies.

E. State-Level Institutions: At state level two institutions are working which are the following:

- State Financial Corporations and (SFCs).
- State Industrial Development Corporations (SIDCs).

(a) State Financial Corporations (SFCs): To meet the financial needs of the diversified small and medium-scale industries, Government of India passed the State Financial Corporation Act in 1951. The act empowered the State governments to establish separate financial corporations to operate for their respective state. State Financial Corporations (SFCs) are the state level financial institutions which play a crucial role in the development of small and medium enterprises in the concerned states. The main objective of SFCs is to provide finance to small and medium sized and cottage industrial units. They provide financial assistance by term loans, direct subscription of equity and debentures, discounting of bills of exchange and guarantees. The first State Financial Corporation was set up in Punjab in 1953. At present there are 18 state Financial Corporations in the country.

(b) State Industrial Development Corporations (SIDCs): State Industrial Development Corporation (SIDC) is the government agency for industrial and investment promotion in states. State Industrial Development Corporation has been established under the Companies Act of 1956, as wholly-owned undertakings of State Governments. SIDC acts as a promotional agency involved in catalyzing the development of physical and social infrastructure required for constant growth of industry in the State. They offer professional guidance and support for potential investors through a comprehensive set of services that include developing business ideas, identifying viable projects, providing financial assistance, guidance and assistance for implementation. The first State Industrial Development Corporation (SIDC) was established by the government of Andhra Pradesh followed by Bihar in the year 1960. At present 28 State Industrial Development Corporations are functioning in the country.

F. Other Financial Institutions: Important other financial institutions are given below:

- Export-Import Bank of India (Exim Bank).
- National Bank for Agricultural and Rural Development (NABARD).
- National Housing Bank (NHB).
- Discount and Finance House of India Ltd. (DFHI).
- Securities Trading Corporation of India Ltd. (STCI).
- Housing and Urban Development Corporation Ltd. (HUDCO).

- Stock Holding Corporation of India Ltd. (SHCIL).
- Powei Finance Corporation Ltd. (PFC).
- Indian Railways Finance Corporation Ltd. (IRFC).

(a) Export-Import Bank of India (EXIM Bank): Export-Import Bank of India is the premier export finance institution in the country. It was established in 1982. Exim bank is a statutory corporation wholly owned by the Government of India. The primary objective of the Export-Import Bank of India is to provide financial assistance to importers and exporters and function as the top financial institution. Exim Bank provides wide range of products and services offered at all stages of the business cycle, starting from import of technology and export product development to export production, export marketing, pre-shipment and post-shipment and overseas investment.

(b) National Bank for Agricultural and Rural Development (NABARD): National Bank for Agriculture and Rural Development (NABARD) was established in 1982. NABARD was set up as an apex development bank with a mandate for facilitating credit flow for promotion and development of agriculture, small-scale industries, cottage and village industries, handicrafts and other rural crafts. It has also the mandate to support all other allied economic activities in rural areas, promote integrated and sustainable rural development and secure prosperity of rural areas. NABARD also provides refinance for short-term, medium-term and long-term credit to eligible institutions.

(c) National Housing Bank (NHB): The National Housing Bank (NHB) was established in 1988 under the National Housing Bank Act of 1987 to function as a principal agency to promote Housing Finance Institutions and to provide financial and other support to such institutions. National Housing Bank (NHB) is an apex institution for housing finance. NHB is a wholly owned subsidiary of the Reserve Bank of India. The primary objective of NHB is to promote a network of highly efficient and dedicated housing finance institutions to cater to the needs of all segments of the population.

(d) Discount and Finance House of India Ltd. (DFHI): The Discount and Finance House of India Ltd. (DFHI) was set up in 1988. It was set up by the Reserve Bank of India jointly with public sector banks and all India financial institutions. The Discount and Finance House of India Ltd. has been established to deal in various money market instruments (viz. call and notice money, commercial bills, treasury bills, certificates of deposit and commercial paper) in order to ensure liquidity in the money market.

(e) Securities Trading Corporation of India Ltd. (STCI): Securities Trading Corporation of India Ltd. (STCI) is an important non-deposit taking non-banking financial company. Securities Trading Corporation of India Limited

(STCI) was promoted by Reserve Bank of India (RBI) in 1994 along with Public Sector Banks and All-India Financial Institutions with the objective of developing an active, deep and vibrant secondary debt market. The main objective of setting the STCI is to foster the development of an active secondary market for Government securities and bonds issued by public sector undertakings. STCI is a leading market maker of government securities.

(f) Housing and Urban Development Corporation Ltd. (HUDCO): Housing and Urban Development Corporation Ltd. (HUDCO) was incorporated on April 25, 1970. HUDCO was established with the object of assisting various agencies and authorities in upgrading the housing conditions in the country. It grants loans to State Governments, State Housing Boards and Local Authorities for housing and urban development projects.

(g) Stock Holding Corporation of India Ltd. (SHCIL): Stock Holding Corporation of India Limited (SHCIL) is the largest custodian and depository Participant Company in India. Stock Holding Corporation of India Limited (SHCIL) was incorporated at the special initiative of the Government of India as a Public Limited Company in 1986. It has been jointly promoted and owned by the All India Banks and Financial Institutions.

(h) Power Finance Corporation Ltd. (PFC): Power Finance Corporation Ltd. (PFC) is a financial institution owned by the Government of India. It is a financial institution specialized in lending to power projects. Power Finance Corporation Ltd. was established in 1986. PFC was established with a view to provide a range of fund based and non-fund based support to the Indian power sector. The main objective of Power Finance Corporation Ltd. is to provide financial aid to the power sector for the integral development of power based infrastructure.

(i) Indian Railways Finance Corporation Ltd. (IRFC): Indian Railway Finance Corporation Limited was established in 1986. The main objective of Indian Railways Finance Corporation Ltd. (IRFC) is to raise money from the market to part finance the plan outlay of Indian Railways. The money so made available is used for acquisition of rolling stock assets and for meeting other developmental needs of the Indian Railways.

Short Answer Type Questions

1. Define financial intermediary.
2. What do you mean by financial institutions?
3. What is meant by non-banking institutions?
4. Name the basic components of financial system.
5. What are specialized financial institutions?

6. What are urban credit co-operatives?
7. What do you mean by financial intermediation?
8. What is state co-operative bank?
9. Name the structure of banking institutions.
10. What is PACS?
11. What do you mean by development financial institutions?
12. What is a residuary non-banking company?
13. Name the specialized public guarantee institutions in India.
14. What are the investment institutions in India?

Essay Type Questions

1. What do you mean by financial intermediaries? What are the functions performed by financial intermediaries?
2. Explain the structure of Indian financial institutions.
3. Discuss the recent trends in the Indian financial institutions.
4. Explain the structure of non-banking financial institutions.
5. Discuss the structure of co-operative institutions in India.
6. Briefly explain the structure of banking institutions in India.

3

Reserve Bank of India

3.1 Introduction

The Reserve Bank of India (RBI) was established on April 1, 1935 in accordance with the provisions of the Reserve Bank of India Act of 1934. RBI is the central bank of the country. RBI is the apex institution of the Indian financial system. It is the apex monetary institution for supervising, regulating, controlling and developing the monetary and financial system of the country. RBI is entrusted with monetary stability, the management of currency and the supervision of the financial as well as the payment systems in the country. The bank has also been vested with immense responsibility of reviewing and reconstructing the economic stability of the country by formulating economic policies and ensuring a proper exchange of currency. The central office of RBI is located at Mumbai. RBI has 19 regional offices and most of them are located at State capitals. RBI is one of the oldest central banks among the developing countries.

3.2 History of Reserve Bank of India

The need for a central bank in India was felt during 18th century. The history of the Reserve Bank of India traces back to 1773 when Warren Hastings, the Governor of Bengal pointed out the need for a central bank in the country and recommended to establish the General Bank of Bengal and Bihar. The Chamberlin Commission in its report in 1913 also recommended for a central bank in the country. Subsequently to Chamberlin Commission report, Professor Keynes submitted a comprehensive report to the British Government for the formation of a central bank in India.

Historically Reserve Bank of India had its origin with the establishment of the Presidency Banks. "The Bank of Calcutta" began its banking business in the year June 1806. The Government of India did not realize the need for banks till 1809 and in that year, a royal charter re-designated the "The Bank of Calcutta" as the "The Bank of Bengal". Two other presidency banks namely "Bank of Bombay" and the "Bank of Madras" were formed in April 1840 and July 1843. These banks came to be known as the 'Presidency Banks', and the bankers bank for all Indian joint stock banks. These three banks were called the Presidency Banks, because they were partly financed by the East India Company.

'The Bank of Bengal', 'the Bank of Bombay' and 'the Bank of Madras' referred as 'Presidency Banks' got amalgamated into the "Imperial Bank of India", which came into existence on January 27, 1921 by the Imperial Bank of India Act of 1920. Although the Imperial Bank of India was created by the special Act of 1920, the liability of its shareholders was limited as that of shareholders of all other banks registered under the Indian Companies Act. The only difference is that the word limited does not form part of its name, as it does in the case of banks constituted under the Companies Act.

Though Imperial Bank of India performed certain central banking function, but the right of note issue was not given to Imperial Bank of India and Government of India performed the functions of control over currency of the country. However, Imperial Bank of India was allowed to hold government balances and to manage public debt and clearing houses till the establishment of the Reserve Bank of India in 1935.

The founding of' Central Bank in India was again stressed by the Royal Commission in Indian Currency and Finance (known as the Hilton Young Commission). The commission submitted its report in the year 1926. In 1931, Central Banking inquiry Committee also recommended for setting up of a Central Bank in India. In 1933, the 'Round Table Conference' also suggested to set up a Central bank free from political influence.

The Reserve Bank of India was actually set up on the basis of the recommendations of the Hilton Young Commission. Though the Commission submitted its report in 1926 but the Central Bank was not set up for nine years. After the submission of the report of Hilton Young Commission, a Bill to this effect was introduced in the Legislature Assembly in January 1926, but the Bill was dropped on constitutional grounds. In 1931, the Central Banking Committee made strong recommendations for the establishment of Reserve Bank of India. Hence a new Bill was introduced in the Indian Legislature Assembly on September 8, 1933. The Bill was passed and received the assent of the Governor General on March 6, 1934 and become the Reserve Bank of India Act of 1934.

The Reserve Bank of India as the central bank of the country was established on April 1, 1935 in accordance with the provisions of the Reserve Bank of India Act of 1934. RBI commenced its operations with Sir Osborne Smith as the first Governor of the bank with a share capital of ₹ 5 crore. The share capital was divided into shares of ₹ 100 each fully paid which was entirely owned by private shareholders. The Central Office of the Reserve Bank was initially established in Kolkata but was permanently shifted to Mumbai in 1937.

3.3 Objectives of RBI

The main objectives for the establishment of RBI as the Central Bank of India were as follows:

1. To regulate the issue of bank notes.
2. To operate and manage monetary and credit system in the country.
3. To develop an organized money market in the country.
4. To develop balanced and systematic development of banking system in the country.
5. To keep reserves with a view to securing monetary stability in India.
6. For proper management of public debts.
7. To provide finance to agriculture and industries.

The Bank began its operations by taking over from the Government, the functions which were being performed by the Controller of Currency and those of the Imperial Bank of India, which managed Government accounts and public debt. The existing currency offices at Calcutta, Bombay, Madras, Rangoon, Karachi, Lahore and Kanpur became branches of the Issue Department. Offices of the Banking Department were established in Calcutta, Bombay, Madras, Delhi and Rangoon.

RBI acted as the Central Bank for Burma and Pakistan till the invasion of Burma by Japan and the Independence of Pakistan. Burma (Myanmar) separated from the Indian Union in 1937 but the Reserve Bank continued to act as the Central Bank for Burma till Japanese occupation of Burma and later up to April, 1947. After Independence to make RBI more powerful, the Government of India took a decision to nationalize it. Hence, the Reserve Bank of India Act of 1948 (Transfer to Public Ownership) was passed and the Government took over the RBI from private shareholders by paying adequate compensation. Though originally privately owned, after nationalization the RBI is fully owned by the Government of India. On January 1, 1949, the RBI started functioning as a state owned central banking institution.

3.4 Administration

RBI is administered by a Central Board of Directors and Local Boards of Directors. The governor of Reserve Bank of India is responsible for formulating the policies of the Reserve Bank.

3.4.1 Central Board of Directors: The Reserve Bank of India's affairs is governed by a Central Board of Directors consisting of 20 members. The Central Board of Directors is appointed by the Government of India as per the Reserve Bank of India Act. The Board of Directors is appointed or nominated for a period of four years. The Board of Directors consists of both Official and Non-Official

Directors.

Official Directors in the Board consists of a full time Governor and not more than four Deputy Governors. The Governor and the Deputy Governors are full time officials of the RBI. Governor and the Deputy Governors of the bank are Government of India appointees. The Union Government nominates fifteen Non-Official Governors in the board. Of this, ten Directors are nominated by the Government from the experts in various fields to give representation to the important segments in the economic life of the country. The Government also appoints one government official in the board from the Ministry of Finance. Other four Directors are nominated to give representation to the four Local Boards.

The important function of the Board of Directors is the general supervision and direction of the affairs of the Reserve Bank. The RBI Act stipulates that there must be at least six meetings in a year and the gap between two meetings should not exceed three months. The Governor of RBI can call a meeting of the Central Board whenever necessary.

3.4.2 Local Boards: Local Boards are set up for each of the four regions in the country viz.

1. Western Region Office located at Mumbai.
2. Eastern Region Office at Kolkata.
3. Southern Region Office at Chennai.
4. Northern Region Office at New Delhi.

The local boards are advisory in nature. The local board consists of five members each who are appointed by the Union Government for a period of four years. One member from each local board is nominated by the Government of India to the Central Board.

3.4.3 Functions of Local Board: The important function of the Local Board is to advise the Central Board on local matters and to represent territorial and economic interests of local co-operative and indigenous banks and to perform such other functions as are delegated by the Central Board form time to time.

3.4.4 Legal Framework: Following are the Acts leading to the functions of the Reserve Bank of India and the financial sector:

A. Umbrella Acts: Umbrella Act consists of two important Acts which are given below:

1. Reserve Bank of India Act of 1934, which governs the functions of the Reserve Bank of India.
2. Banking Regulations Act of 1949, which governs the financial sector.

B. Acts Governing Specific Functions: Acts governing specific functions\markets are the following:

1. Public Debt Act of 1944/Government Securities Act, which governs government debt market.
2. Securities Contracts Regulation Act of 1956, which regulates securities market.
3. Indian Coinage Act of 1906, which governs currency and coins.
4. Foreign Exchange Regulation Act of 1973 and Foreign Exchange Management Act of 1999, which governs trade and foreign exchange market.

C. Acts Governing Banking Operations: Acts governing the banking operations in the country are as under:

1. Companies Act of 1956 which governs banks as companies.
2. Banking Companies (Acquisition and Transfer of Undertakings) Act of 1970 and 1980 which relate to the nationalization of banks.
3. Negotiable Instruments Act, of 1881.
4. Banking Secrecy Act.

D. Acts Governing Individual Institutions: These are as follows:

1. State Bank of India Act, 1954.
2. The Industrial Development Bank (Transfer of Undertaking and Repeal) Act, 2003.
3. The Industrial Finance Corporation (Transfer of Undertaking and Repeal) Act, 1993.
4. National Bank for Agriculture and Rural Development Act of 1981.
5. National Housing Bank Act of 1987.
6. Deposit Insurance and Credit Guarantee Corporation Act of 1961.

3.5 Functions of Reserve Bank of India

The Reserve Bank of India is the apex monetary institution, which supervises, regulates, control and develop the monetary and financial system of the country. The functions of the Reserve Bank of India are mainly divided into monetary functions and non-monetary functions.

3.5.1 Monetary Functions: The monetary functions are also known as the central banking functions. Monetary functions of the RBI are significant as they control and regulate the volume of money and credit in the country. Reserve Bank of India formulates, implements and monitors the monetary policy to ensure price stability and optimum flow of credit to productive sectors. Monetary functions are related to control and regulation of money and credit, i.e. issue of currency, control of bank credit, control of foreign exchange operations, banker to the Government and operations in the money market. Following are the monetary functions of RBI.

1. Issuing Currency Notes.

2. Acting as Bankers Bank and Lender of Last Resort.
3. Banker to the Government.
4. Custodian of Foreign Exchange.
5. Controller of Credit.

A. Issuing Currency Notes: Issue of currency notes is one of the important functions of the Reserve bank of India. As per the Reserve Bank of India Act of 1934, RBI has the sole right to issue bank notes of all denominations. The basic objectives of RBI are to issue bank notes, to maintain the currency and credit system of the country to utilize it in its best advantage, and to maintain the reserves. Under Section 22 of the RBI Act, the bank has the right of full control of issuing, circulating, exchanging or destroying unfit currency from time to time along with maintaining a fresh and adequate supply of currency notes and coins.

The Government of India issues rupee coins and subsidiary coins. The distribution of rupee coins and other small coins all over the country is undertaken by the Reserve Bank of India as an agent of the Government. Coins up to 50 paise are called small coins and one and above are called rupee coins. The printing of notes in the denominations of ₹ 1 and ₹ 2 has been discontinued as these denominations have been coinised. Coins can be issued only up to the denomination of ₹ 1,000. Major currency is in the form of RBI notes, such as five, ten, twenty, fifty, one hundred, five hundred, and one thousand. Earlier notes of higher denominations viz. five thousand and ten thousand were also issued. But these notes were demonetized to discourage users from indulging in black market operations. As per RBI Act 1934, denominations of higher than ten thousand are not permitted to issue.

The Reserve Bank of India manages currency in India. Reserve Bank of India co-ordinates with the Government in designing of bank notes, including the security features. The Currency Management Department of RBI is involved in the core statutory function of note and coin issue. Currency Department involved in forecasting the denomination-wise demand for fresh banknotes and coins. They place the indent with four printing presses and mints, receiving supplies against those indents and distributing them through its Issue Offices. The Department also keeps an account of banknotes in circulation and also the stocks at RBI offices and currency chests. The Department reviews various security features of the currency notes for incorporation in the banknotes from time to time. Notes received from banks and currency chests are examined by RBI. Notes fit for circulation are reissued and the others are destroyed so as to maintain the quality of notes in circulation.

B. Acting as Bankers Bank and Lender of Last Resort: The Reserve Bank of India acts as the bankers' bank. The Banking Regulations Act of 1949 gave to the Reserve Bank of India extensive powers of supervision and control of the banking system in the country. These regulatory powers include licensing of banks and branches, supervision and inspection of banks, audit and maintenance of accounts, methods of operation of banks, amalgamation, reconstruction and liquidation of banks, deposit insurance, approval of liquid assets, reserves and capital.

Reserve Bank maintains banking accounts of all scheduled banks in India. According to the provisions of the Banking Companies Act of 1949, every scheduled bank was required to maintain with the Reserve Bank a cash balance equivalent to 5 percent of its demand liabilities and 2 percent of its time liabilities in India. By the amendment of 1962, the distinction between demand and time liabilities was abolished and now banks are required to keep cash reserves equal to 3 percent of their aggregate deposit liabilities. RBI has the power to raise cash reserve ratio from 3 to 15 percent if it considers necessary. By an Amendment Act in 2006, this limit has been removed and so RBI is free to fix any CRR. Thus the minimum cash reserve requirements to be maintained by the commercial banks can be changed by the Reserve Bank of India as and when needed.

The scheduled commercial banks can borrow from the Reserve Bank of India on the basis of eligible securities in times of need. Scheduled commercial banks are also accommodated by RBI in times of financial stringency by rediscounting bills of exchange. RBI thus acts as a lender of last resort to commercial banks by way of giving financial accommodation in the form of rediscounting bills of exchange or through repo operation. Cash deposits and withdrawals of scheduled commercial banks are handled by the Banking Department of the RBI. Commercial banks always expect the help of Reserve Bank of India in times of financial crisis. Reserve Bank thus becomes not only the banker's bank but also the lender of the last resort.

C. Banker to the Government: Third important function of the Reserve Bank of India is to act as banker, advisor and agent to the Government. The Reserve Bank of India is the agent of the Central Government and of all State Governments in India except that of Jammu and Kashmir. The Reserve Bank of India has the obligation to transact Government business, viz. to keep the cash balances as deposits free of interest, to receive and to make payments on behalf of the Government and to carry out their exchange remittances and other banking operations. The bank is required to transact the general banking business of the Central Government and keep accounts in its books. It gives loans and advances to the States and local authorities. It acts as adviser to the Government on all monetary and banking matters.

The RBI is the debt manager for both the Central Government and State

Governments. The Reserve Bank of India helps both State and Central Governments to float new loans and to manage public debt. RBI is also the regulator of Government securities market. RBI also advises the Government at the time of formulation of annual borrowing programme. Under the RBI Act of 1934, RBI is the manager of Central Government debt by statute. RBI manages the debt of state governments based on separate agreements.

As a debt manager for both Central and State Governments, RBI in consultation with the Government, manages the maturity profile, timing of issue, composition of debt and the type of instruments issued. Operationally, RBI deals with the issue, servicing and repayment of government debt. The most significant development has been the elimination of the practice of automatic monetization of the Central Government budget deficit through Ad hoc Treasury Bills with effect from April 1, 1997 and the introduction of a new scheme of Ways and Means Advances (WMA). The Bank makes ways and means advances to the Governments for 90 days.

D. Custodian of Foreign Exchange: Reserve Bank of India is the custodian of Indian's foreign exchange reserves. Reserve Bank manages the foreign exchange to facilitate external trade and payment and promote orderly development and maintenance of foreign exchange market in India. The Reserve Bank of India has the responsibility to maintain the official rate of exchange of the rupee. The RBI fixes the selling and buying rates of foreign currencies. They also administer exchange control measures and other restrictions imposed by the government. According to the Reserve Bank of India Act of 1934, the Reserve Bank was required to buy and sell at fixed rates any amount of sterling in lots of not less than ₹ 10,000. After India became a member of the International Monetary Fund in 1946, the Reserve Bank has the responsibility of maintaining fixed exchange rates with all other member countries of the I.M.F.

Besides maintaining the rate of exchange of the rupee, the Reserve Bank has to act as the custodian of India's reserve of international currencies. The vast sterling balances were acquired and managed by the Bank. Further, the RBI has the responsibility of administering the exchange controls of the country.

E. Controller of Credit: The Reserve Bank of India is the regulator and supervisor of the financial system in the country. The Reserve Bank of India takes a leading role in formulating, implementation and monitoring the monetary policy. It prescribes broad parameters of banking operations within which the country's banking and financial system functions. RBI has the power to influence the volume of credit created by commercial banks in India.

As the central bank of the country, RBI has the responsibility of controlling credit in order to ensure the internal price stability and to promote economic growth. It also regulates the interest rates on loans, which it provides to other commercial banks in the country that allows it to restrict the flow of money or to relax the flow of currency as per the needs and requirements of the circumstances. The Reserve Bank regulates the money supply in accordance with the changing contours of the economy. RBI achieves credit control by changing the bank rate or through open market operations.

According to the Banking Regulation Act of 1949, the Reserve Bank of India can ask any particular bank or the whole banking system not to lend to particular groups or persons on the basis of certain types of securities. The Reserve Bank of India is armed with many more powers to control the Indian money market. Every bank has to get a license from the Reserve Bank of India to do banking business within India, the license can be cancelled by the Reserve Bank of certain stipulated conditions are not fulfilled. Every bank will have to seek the permission of the Reserve Bank prior to opening of a new branch. Each scheduled bank must send a weekly return to the Reserve Bank showing, in detail, its assets and liabilities. This power of the Bank to call for information is also intended to give it effective control of the credit system. The Reserve Bank has also the power to inspect the accounts of any commercial bank.

F. Powers of RBI as Controller of Credit: As the supreme banking authority in the country, the Reserve Bank of India has the following powers:

1. RBI has the power to hold the cash reserves of all the scheduled banks.
2. RBI controls the credit operations of banks through quantitative and qualitative measures.
3. RBI controls the banking system through the system of licensing, inspection and calling for information.
4. RBI acts as the lender of the last resort by providing rediscounting facilities to scheduled commercial banks.

3.5.2 Non-monetary Functions: In addition to its traditional central banking functions, the Reserve Bank of India has certain non-monetary functions. In the context of India's economic backwardness, the non-monetary functions of the Reserve Bank are very important. Non-monetary functions include promotional and developmental functions and regulatory and supervisory functions.

A. Promotional and Developmental Functions: Besides the monetary functions, the Reserve Bank of India also performs a variety of promotional and developmental functions. The Reserve Bank of India from its very inception is playing a special role in the context of development of the economy especially agriculture. The RBI now performs wide range developmental and promotional functions. These functions were performed by the Reserve Bank to meet the national objectives. They are:

1. To encourage commercial banks to expand their banking network in rural and semi-urban areas.
2. To promote banking habits among the people.
3. To increase the share of bank credit to small scale industries.
4. To develop and strengthen the co-operative credit movement to encourage savings, to eliminate moneylenders from the villages and to route its short-term credit to agriculture.
5. To establish and promote new specialized financing agencies. Accordingly, the Reserve Bank has helped in the setting up of the Deposit Insurance Corporation in 1962, the Unit Trust of India in 1964, the Industrial Development Bank of India (IDBI) in 1964, the Agricultural Refinance Corporation of India in 1963, the Industrial Reconstruction Corporation of India (IRBI) in 1972 and the Discount and Finance House of India in 1988. The RBI has set up the Agricultural Refinance and Development Corporation to provide long-term finance to farmers. These institutions were set up directly or indirectly by the Reserve Bank to promote savings habit and to mobilize savings, and to provide industrial finance as well as agricultural finance.

B. Regulatory and Supervisory Functions: In addition to its traditional central banking functions, the Reserve Bank has certain non-monetary functions of the nature of supervision of banks and promotion of sound banking system in the country. The Reserve Bank of India is the regulator and supervisor of the financial system. Its regulatory and supervisory powers prescribe broad parameters for banking operations within the country. By performing this function, the Reserve Bank is able to maintain public confidence in the banking system, protect depositors' interest and provide cost-effective banking services to the public.

The promotion of sound banking in India is an important objective of the Reserve Bank of India. The Reserve Bank of India Act of 1934 and the Banking Regulation Act of 1949 give extensive and drastic powers to RBI. According to these two Acts, RBI is empowered with the supervision and control of commercial and co-operative banks, relating to their licensing and establishments, branch expansion, liquidity of their assets, management and methods of working, amalgamation, reconstruction, and liquidation. RBI is authorized to carry out periodical inspections of the banks and to call for returns and necessary information from them. RBI also regulates the opening/installation of ATM (Automatic Teller Machines). It is trying to increase the density of the ATMs in rural areas.

The Banking Ombudsman Scheme has been formulated and implemented by the Reserve Bank of India (on 14th June, 1995) for the effective redressal of complaints by bank customers. If a bank does not solve a customer's problem they can approach the Reserve Bank of India through the Banking Ombudsman Scheme. The scheme facilitates settlement of disputes between a bank and their customers and between banks. The scheme envisages expeditious and satisfactory disposal of customer complaints in a time-bound manner through methods of conciliation, mediation and arbitration.

The RBI's powers of supervision have now been extended to non-banking financial institutions. In March 2006, RBI has issued know your customer guidelines for non-banking finance companies (NBFCs). The Reserve Bank of India also regulates the trade of gold. Currently, 17 Indian banks are involved in the trade of gold in India. RBI has invited applications from more banks for direct import of gold to curb illegal trade in gold and increase competition in the market.

Under RBI's supervision and inspection, the working of banks has improved spectacularly. Commercial banks have developed into financially and operationally sound and viable units. The nationalization of Indian scheduled banks has imposed new responsibilities on the RBI for directing the growth of banking and credit policies towards more rapid development of the economy and realization of certain desired social objectives. The supervisory functions of the RBI have helped a great deal in improving the standard of banking in India to develop on sound lines and to improve the methods of their operation.

3.6 Board for Financial Supervision

The Reserve Bank of India performs financial supervision under the guidance of the Board for Financial Supervision (BFS). The Board was constituted in November 1994 as a committee of the Central Board of Directors of the Reserve Bank of India. The primary objective is to undertake consolidated supervision of the financial sector comprising commercial banks, financial institutions and non-banking finance companies.

The Board is constituted by co-opting four Directors from the Central Board as members for a term of two years and is chaired by the Governor of RBI. The Deputy Governors of the Reserve Bank are ex-officio members. One Deputy Governor, usually, the Deputy Governor in charge of banking regulation and supervision, is nominated as the Vice-Chairman of the Board. The Board is required to meet normally once in every month. It considers inspection reports and other supervisory issues placed before it by the supervisory departments.

The Audit Sub-Committee in BFS aims at upgrading the quality of the statutory audit and internal audit functions in banks and financial institutions. The audit sub-committee includes Deputy Governor as the chairman and two Directors of the Central Board as members. The BFS oversees the functioning of Department of Banking Supervision (DBS), Department of Non-Banking Supervision (DNBS) and Financial Institutions Division (FID) and gives directions on the regulatory and supervisory issues.

3.6.1 Functions of BFS: Some of the functions of BFS include the following:

1. Restructuring of the system of bank inspections.
2. Introduction of off-site surveillance.
3. Strengthening of the role of statutory auditors.
4. Strengthening of the internal defences of supervised institutions.

3.7 Monetary Policy of RBI

Monetary policy is a macroeconomic tool used by RBI to influence interest rates, inflation and credit availability through changes in the supply of money available in the economy. Reserve Bank of India is responsible for formulating and implementing the monetary policy of the country. The monetary policy regulates the supply of money and the cost and availability of credit in the economy. It deals with both the lending and borrowing rates of interest for commercial banks. Monetary Policy aims at maintaining price stability, providing employment opportunities and rapid growth of the economy. Through monetary policy RBI can increase or decrease the supply of currency as well as interest rate, carry out open market operations, control credit and vary the reserve requirements.

The Reserve Bank of India Act of 1934 sets out broadly the objectives of monetary policy as "to regulate the issue of Bank notes and the keeping of reserves with a view to securing monetary stability in India and generally to operate the currency and credit system of the country to its advantage". Although there is no explicit mandate for price stability, the objectives of monetary policy in India have evolved as maintaining price stability and ensuring adequate flow of credit to the productive sectors of the economy to support economic growth. The relative emphasis placed on price stability and economic growth is modulated according to the circumstances prevailing at a particular point in time and is spelt out, from time to time, in the policy statements of the Reserve Bank. In the recent period, considerations of financial stability have assumed an added importance in view of increasing openness of the Indian economy.

Monetary policy formulation is carried out by the Reserve Bank in consultation with various stakeholders such as banks, market participants, and industry and trade associations. Reserve Bank prepares monetary and credit policy statement and is announced by the RBI four times in a financial year. The

Annual Policy (April) and its Second Quarter Review (October) consist of two parts i.e. Monetary Policy and Developmental and Regulatory Policies. The First Quarter Review (July) and the Third Quarter Review (January) of Monetary Policy comprise only Monetary Policy. The Monetary Policy has become dynamic in nature because RBI reserves its right to alter it from time to time, depending on the state of the economy.

The RBI holds the power to stabilize the situation of an economy or to satisfy its expansion needs by pumping in additional money or currency in the market. It also regulates the interest rates on loans, which it provides to other commercial banks in the country that allows it to restrict the flow of money or to relax the flow of currency as per the needs and requirements of the circumstances.

The Monetary Policy is different from Fiscal Policy as the former brings about a change in the economy by changing money supply and interest rate, whereas fiscal policy is a broader tool with the government. The Fiscal Policy can be used to overcome recession and control inflation. It may be defined as a deliberate change in government revenue and expenditure to influence the level of national output and prices. The annual Union Budget showcases the Government's Fiscal Policy.

3.7.1 Objectives of Monetary Policy: Important objectives of monetary policy are the following:

1. To maintain price stability and to prevent inflation.
2. To maintain stability of the national currency.
3. To strengthen the banking system of the country.
4. To ensure adequate flow of credit to the priority and neglected sectors of the economy.
5. To mobilize the savings of the community and to promote capital formation.
6. To promote steady growth in employment and income.

3.7.2 Tools Used for Monetary Policy: The Reserve Bank has multiple instruments at its command for implementation of monetary policy such as repo and reverse repo rates, cash reserve ratio, open market operations, including liquidity adjustment facility and market stabilization scheme, special market operations; sector-specific liquidity facilities and prudential tools. The tools used for credit control can be broadly classified in to Quantitative Tools and Qualitative Tools.

A. Quantitative Tools: Quantitative tools are used by RBI to control the volume of credit and inflation indirectly. The quantitative or general measures influence the total volume of the credit while the qualitative measures influence the selective or particular use of credit.

Following are the tools used for credit control under quantitative technique:

1. Bank Rate.
2. Cash Reserve Ratio (CRR).
3. Statutory Liquidity Ratio (SLR).
4. Repo/Reverse Repo.
5. Open Market Operations.

(a) Bank Rate: Bank rate is a tool used by RBI for controlling the credit. It is a tool, which is used by RBI for short-term purposes. The bank rate is the official interest rate at which RBI rediscounts the approved bills held by commercial banks. It is the minimum rate at which the RBI provides loans to the commercial banks. RBI advances money to commercial banks against approved securities or rediscounting eligible bills of exchange. The lending rates for these advances by the RBI is called bank rate, which is a traditional weapon for controlling money supply. It is also called the discount rate.

Any revision in bank rate by RBI is a signal to banks to revise deposit rates as well as Prime Lending Rate (PLR). An increase in bank rate discourages commercial banks to borrow money from the RBI. An increase in bank rate ultimately results in an increase in lending rate which decreases borrowings by the public from banks. Similarly a fall in the bank rate ultimately results in a fall in the interest rate. Fall in interest rate implies availability of cheap money, which ultimately increases borrowings by the public from banks. Changes in bank rate thus affect credit creation by banks through altering cost of credit. RBI has the power to change the bank rate from time to time to meet the changing conditions of the economy.

(b) Cash Reserve Ratio (CRR): Cash Reserve Ratio (CRR) is a quantitative tool used by RBI to regulate the supply of money in the economy. Cash reserve ratio refers to that portion of total deposits in commercial banks which it has to keep with RBI as cash reserves. This keeping of cash with RBI means that banks cannot lend that percentage of cash in the market.

Reserve Bank uses CRR either to impound the excess liquidity or to release funds requirements for the economy from time to time. CRR generally influences the country's economy, borrowing and interest rates. An increase in CRR affect the amount of free cash that banks can use to lend i.e. reducing the amount of money for lending cuts into overall liquidity, driving interest rates up, lowering inflation and sucking money out of markets.

The CRR is fixed as a percentage of totals of the net demand and time liabilities in India, on a fortnightly basis. Reserve Bank of India is empowered to increase this ratio between 3 to 15 percent. The Regional Rural Banks and State Co-operative Banks have been allowed to maintain a lower level of cash reserves i.e. 3 percent of its net demand and time liabilities. Similarly, non scheduled commercial banks have also been permitted to maintain a lower CRR of 3 percent of its net demand and time liabilities in India. Non scheduled commercial banks can maintain the cash reserve with themselves or current account with RBI or State Bank of India or any other institution notified by RBI.

(i) Objectives of CRR: CRR serves two purposes:

- CRR ensures that a portion of bank deposits is totally risk-free by maintaining it with RBI.
- Secondly it ensures liquidity in the banking system, and thereby controlling inflation.

When RBI increases CRR, banks are required to keep a higher amount of money as reserves and vice versa. When inflation is high (money supply is high), RBI increases the CRR rate, this will mean, commercial banks will have to keep more percentage of deposits with RBI. This in turn will reduce the commercial bank's lending capacity. When lending capacity is reduced, less money is available for individuals and corporate in the market. This causes aggregate demand to decrease and thus reducing inflation. On the other hand when RBI decreases CRR, banks have more funds to lend to people.

(c) Statutory Liquidity Ratio (SLR): As per Statutory Liquidity Ratio (SLR) banks in India are required to maintain certain percentage of their demand and time liabilities in the form of cash or gold or government securities or in approved securities. Approved securities mean bonds and shares of different companies. In terms of Section 24 of the Banking Regulations Act of 1949, all scheduled commercial banks are required to maintain a minimum proportion of their net demand and time liabilities as liquid assets in the form of gold, cash etc in addition to cash reserve requirements (CRR). The ratio of liquid assets to demand and time liabilities is known as Statutory Liquidity Ratio (SLR).

The Banking Regulation (Amendment) Act of 1962 provides for maintaining a minimum SLR of 25 percent by the bank against their net demand and time liabilities, however RBI is powered by this act to raise the SLR up to 40 percent. The Reserve bank of India (Amendment) Act 2005 which was approved by Lok Sabha on May 17, 2006 amends the Reserve Bank Act for providing flexibility to the Central Bank in Fixing the CRR.

For controlling the inflationary pressures in the economy, RBI generally increases the SLR. A rise in Statutory Liquidity Ratio reduces the availability of liquid cash in banks which ultimately reduces commercial banks' capacity of credit creation. When SLR is reduced more liquid cash is available in banks for lending purposes.

Commercial banks can maintain liquid assets in the following forms:

- Cash, or

- Gold valued at a price not exceeding the current market price, or
- Unencumbered approved securities valued at a price as specified by the RBI from time to time.

As on May 19, 2012, all Scheduled Commercial Banks are required to maintain a uniform SLR of 24 percent of the total of their demand and time liabilities in India as on the last Friday of the second preceding fortnight, which is stipulated under section 24 of the Banking Regulations Act, 1949.

Statutory Liquidity Ratio is determined as a percentage of total demand and time liabilities. Time Liabilities refer to the liabilities, which the commercial banks are liable to pay to the customers on demand. The liabilities that the banks are liable to pay within one month's time, due to completion of maturity period, are also considered as time liabilities. Deposits in fixed accounts are considered as time liabilities.

(i) Objectives of Maintaining SLR: There are some purposes behind introducing Statutory Liquidity Ratio. The main objectives of maintaining the Statutory Liquidity Ratio are the following:

- Statutory Liquidity Ratio is maintained by the Reserve Bank in order to control the expansion of bank credit. By changing the level of Statutory Liquidity Ratio, Reserve Bank of India can increase or decrease bank credit expansion.
- Statutory Liquidity Ratio is maintained by RBI for ensuring the solvency of commercial banks.
- By determining Statutory Liquidity Ratio, Reserve Bank of India, in a way, compels the commercial banks to invest in government securities like government bonds.

If any Indian Bank fails to maintain the required level of Statutory Liquidity Ratio (SLR), then it becomes liable to pay penalty to Reserve Bank of India. The defaulter bank pays penal interest at the rate of 3 percent per annum above the Bank Rate, on the shortfall amount for that particular day. But, according to the Circular, released by the Department of Banking Operations and Development, Reserve Bank of India, if the defaulter bank continues to default on the next working day, then the rate of penal interest can be increased to 5 percent per annum above the Bank Rate.

(d) Repo/Reverse Repo: A repo or repurchase agreement is an instrument of money market. It is a type of transaction in which two parties agree to sell and repurchase the same security. A repurchase agreement (repurchase repo) is an agreement between two parties whereby one party sells the other a security at a specified price with a commitment to buy the security back at a later date for another specified price. Similarly, the buyer purchases the securities with an agreement to resell the same to the seller on an agreed date in future at a predetermined price. Such a transaction is called a Repo when viewed from the prospective of the seller of securities (the party acquiring fund) and Reverse Repo when described from the point of view of the supplier of funds. In simple terms, it is recognized as a buy back arrangement. Repo and reverse repo are exactly the same kind of transaction, just described from opposite viewpoints.

RBI has been using repo and reverse repo effectively for its liquidity management, both for absorbing liquidity and also for injecting funds into the system. Thus, Repos and Reverse Repo are resorted to by the RBI as a tool of liquidity control in the system.

Market liquidity for repos is good, and rates are competitive and attractive for investors. A repo is equivalent to a cash transaction combined with a forward contract. The cash transaction results in transfer of money to the borrower in exchange for legal transfer of the security to the lender, while the forward contract ensures repayment of the loan to the lender and return of the collateral of the borrower.

Repo is a collateralized lending by which commercial banks borrow money from the Reserve Bank of India to meet their short-term needs by selling their securities to the Reserve Bank with an agreement to repurchase the same at a predetermined rate and date. Reserve bank charges some interest rate on the cash borrowed by banks. The rate at which RBI borrows money from the banks or banks lend money to the RBI is termed as repo or reverse rate. This rate is usually less than the interest rate on bonds as the borrowing is collateral. The interest rates depend on the demand and supply of the short-term surplus or deficit amongst the inter bank players.

(i) Instruments used in Repo Market: RBI extends several relaxations on repo transactions. Treasury Bills and all Central and State Government securities are also eligible for repo. In addition, all Dated Government securities are eligible for trading in the repo market. Repos have also been permitted in PSU bonds and private corporate debt securities provided they are held in dematerialized from in a depository and the transactions are done in a recognized stock exchange.

RBI uses this tool when it feels there is too much money floating in the banking system. If the reverse repo rate is increased, it means the RBI will borrow money from the bank and offer them a lucrative rate of interest. As a result, banks would prefer to keep their money with the RBI (which is absolutely risk free) instead of lending it out to the public (with a certain amount of risk). Consequently, banks would have lesser funds to lend to their customers. This is helpful in reducing the flow of excess money into the economy.

Internationally repos are versatile instruments and used extensively in money market operations. In India, repos were discouraged by clamping severe restrictions on their use on account of large-scale violations of the guidelines leading to the 'securities scam' in 1992. However, subsequently repo trading was permitted to be resumed after plugging all loopholes in their operation.

(e) Open Market Operations: Open market operations refer to direct sales and purchase of securities and bills in the open market by Reserve Bank of India. Open market operation is the primary and most frequent way by which RBI control monetary policy. The aim is to control volume of credit and the national money supply.

Open market operation involves buying and selling of short term gilts or government securities. It is method used by RBI to influence the volume of cash reserves with commercial banks and thus influences their loans and advances. This method may be different from others but the end result is the same i.e. controlling money supply in the economy. Compared to other methods of credit control, open market operations are highly flexible, easily reversible in time and their effect is immediate.

To increase the flow of credit, RBI starts purchasing government securities from commercial banks and it gives them money and keeps the securities with itself. To contract the flow of credit, RBI starts selling government securities to commercial banks. If the RBI sells securities in the open market, the amount of money that the purchasing bank holds decreases, thus effectively by keeping the money by the RBI itself. If interest rates are too high, it may bring them down by offering to buy government securities at a lower yield than what is available in the market.

Since most money is now in the form of electronic records, rather than paper records such as banknotes, open market operations are conducted simply by electronically increasing or decreasing ('crediting' or 'debiting') the amount of money that a bank has, e.g., in its reserve account at the central bank, in exchange for a bank selling or buying a financial instrument. Newly created money is used by the central bank to buy in the open market a financial asset, such as government securities, foreign currency or gold. Open market operations are considered very effective in developed countries.

B. Qualitative Tools: Qualitative tools are otherwise called as 'selective credit control' or 'direct credit control' measures which were introduced by RBI in 1956. Qualitative tools are used by RBI for directing the supply of money in selective productive sectors of the economy. The main objective of selective credit control is to prevent excessive speculative stock building of commodities and to prevent price rise.

RBI uses different selective credit controls to check speculative and inflationary pressures in the country and to divert credit to productive and developmental channels. In India, selective credit control means control over advances against the security of 'sensitive commodities' such as food grains, pulses, oilseeds, vegetable oils, sugar etc. RBI has fixed minimum margins to be maintained by commercial banks regarding their advances against the commodities subject to selective controls. RBI also fixed higher minimum lending rates for advances against commodities subject to selective control. Besides, Food Corporation of India (FCI) and State Trading Corporations (STCs) has been exempted from the use of selective credit control.

Main instruments of selective credit control in India are the following:

1. Directives.
2. Moral Suasion.
3. Credit Authorization Scheme.
4. Direct Action.

(a) Directives: As per Banking Regulations Act 1949, RBI is empowered to issue directions to commercial banks regarding their advances. These directions may relate to the following:

- RBI issues directions to commercial banks relating to the purpose for which advances may or not be made.
- Directions regarding the margins to be maintained by commercial banks in respect of secured advances.
- Ceilings on the levels of credit to any borrower.
- The maximum amount of guarantee that can be given on behalf of any firm.
- Charging discriminatory rate of interest on certain types of advances.
- Charging minimum rate of interest on advances against specified commodities.
- Specifies minimum margins for lending against specific securities.
- Ceiling on amount of credit for certain purposes to stern the flow of credit to speculative and non productive sectors.

(b) Moral Suasions: Through moral suasion, RBI can influence the investment and credit policies of the commercial banks and other financial institutions. Moral suasion refers to regular meetings and discussions with officials of banks, suggestions, advices, indications, letters, circulars etc. given by RBI in relation to lending and other operations with the objective of implementing it.

(c) Credit Authorization Scheme: Credit Authorization Scheme (CAS) is a selective credit control scheme which was introduced by RBI in 1965 as an additional measure to ensure the flow of credit to genuine productive purposes. It was introduced to align credit policies of the nation closely with its Five Year

Plans. The main object of Credit Authorization Scheme is to keep a close watch on the flow of credit to large borrowers. The scheme ensures that there is no undue channeling of credit to any single borrower or group of borrowers. Credit Authorization Scheme was introduced by RBI to prevent the problem of pre-emption of scarce bank resources by a few large borrowers and enforcing a measure of financial discipline on them. Under this scheme RBI regulates not only the amount of credit but also the terms on which credit flows to different large borrowers.

Under this scheme, commercial banks were required to obtain RBI's authorization before sanctioning fresh credit of ₹ 1 crore or above to a single party or any fresh limit which would take the total limits to a borrower from the entire banking system to ₹ 1 crore. This limit was raised to ₹ 6 crore in respect of borrowers in private as well as public sector. The scheme has been modified from time to time in the light of the prevailing economic situations.

(d) Direct Action: Direct Action involves step taken by the RBI against banks that don't fulfil conditions and requirements. RBI may refuse to rediscount their papers or may give excess credits or charge a penal rate of interest over and above the Bank rate, for credit demanded beyond a limit.

3.8 Departments of the Reserve Bank of India

When RBI started in 1935, there were just three departments, namely the Banking Department, the Issue Department and the Agricultural Credit Department. Today, RBI has 26 departments, 28 regional and field offices across the country and four subsidiaries. Following are the departments of RBI:

1. Banking Operations and Development Department.
2. Department of Currency Management.
3. Urban Banks Department.
4. Rural Planning and Credit Department.
5. Foreign Exchange Department.
6. Financial Markets Department.
7. Department of Banking Supervision.
8. Department of Non- Banking Supervision.
9. Internal Debt Management Department.
10. Department of External Investments and Operations.
11. Monetary Policy Department.
12. Department of Government and Bank Accounts.
13. Legal Department.
14. Department of Economic Analysis and Policy.
15. Department of Payment and Settlement Systems.

16. Customer Service Department.
17. Department of Information Technology.
18. Human Resources Development Department.
19. Department of Statistical Analysis and Computer Services.
20. Inspection Department.
21. Secretary's Department.
22. Department of Communication.
23. Department of Expenditure and Budgetary Control.
24. Rajbhasha Department.
25. Premises Department.
26. Department of Administration and Personnel Management.

Functions of important departments of RBI are given below:

3.8.1 Banking Operations and Development Department: The Department of Banking Operations and Development is entrusted with the responsibility of regulation of commercial banks under the provisions of various Acts. RBI exercised regulatory powers in commercial banks under the regulatory provisions contained in the Banking Regulations Act of 1949, the Reserve Bank of India Act of 1934 and other related statutes and development of banking policies.

The main function of the Department is to supervise, regulate and control the working of the banking institutions in the country. It is entrusted with the licensing of new banks, branch expansion of commercial banks and foreign banks, maintenance of statutory liquidity reserves, management and operations, amalgamation, reconstruction and liquidations of banking companies, setting up of subsidiaries and undertaking of new activities by commercial banks. The Department endeavours towards promoting and fostering a sound, multi-faceted and competitive banking system by laying down norms for prudential regulations of commercial banks relating to capital adequacy, income recognition, asset classification, provisioning for loan and other losses, investment valuation, accounting and disclosure standards, asset-liability management and risk management systems.

The other important activities of the Department include Corporate governance, Asset Reconstruction Company, Corporate debt restructuring, Amendment of Banking Regulation Act, Setting up international accounting standards for banks, Credit Information Bureau, Capital adequacy framework, Restructuring of weak banks, Entry of banks into insurance, Licensing norm for entry of new banks in private sector, Reduction of government equity in nationalized banks etc.

3.8.2 Department of Currency Management: The Department attends to the core statutory function of note and coin issue and currency management.

Currency Department involves in forecasting the demand for fresh banknotes and coins, placing the indent with four printing presses and mints, receiving supplies against those indents and distributing them through its 18 Issue Offices and one Sub office and a wide network of currency chests. The Department also keeps an account of banknotes in circulation and also the stocks at RBI offices and currency chests.

The Department reviews various security features of the currency notes for incorporation in the banknotes from time to time. It studies the features of the counterfeit banknotes detected and seized with a view to determining the steps needed to be taken to strengthen the integrity of the banknotes. The Department administers the Reserve Bank of India (Note Refund) Rules. The rules lay down the circumstances in which value of torn and mutilated banknotes can be refunded. Soiled banknotes, which are unfit for circulation is mopped up from circulation for destruction.

3.8.3 Urban Banks Department: The main function of the Urban Banks Department is to supervise, regulate, control and supervises the banking functions of Urban Cooperative Banks (UCBs) under the provisions of Banking Regulation Act of 1949. Urban Banks Department functions in close coordination with other regulators viz., Registrar of Cooperative Societies and the Central Registrar of Cooperative Societies.

The Reserve Bank has been vested powers to issues licence to Urban Cooperative Banks under Section 22 and 23 Banking Regulation Act of 1949 to carry on banking business and to open new places of business (branches, extension counters, etc.) respectively. As a regulator, the Reserve Bank of India has prescribed prudential norms in various areas, e.g. capital adequacy, income recognition, asset classification and provisioning, exposure to single/group borrowers, exposures to sensitive sectors, loans and advances, investments, liquidity requirements, etc. The Reserve Bank carries out on-site inspections and off-site surveillance of UCBs. It also issues directions and operational instructions to UCBs, wherever necessary to streamline the functioning and to protect the interests of the depositors.

3.8.4 Rural Planning and Credit Department: The Rural Planning and Credit Department formulates policies relating to rural credit and monitors timely and adequate flow of credit to the rural population for agricultural activities and rural employment programmes. It also formulates policies relating to the priority sector which includes agriculture, small-scale industries, tiny and village industries, artisans and retail traders, professional and self-employed persons, state sponsored organizations for Scheduled Castes and Scheduled Tribes and Government Sponsored credit-linked programmes like Swarnjayanti Gram

Swarojgar Yojana (SGSY), Prime Ministers Rojgar Yojana (PMRY) etc.

It implements and monitors the Lead Bank Scheme which is aimed at forging a coordinated approach for providing bank credit to achieve overall development of rural areas in the country. The department acts as regulators for Regional Rural Banks and State/Central Co-operative Banks. It gives financial and policy support to NABARD. The department also oversees implementation of the Banking Ombudsman Scheme.

3.8.5 Foreign Exchange Department: With the introduction of the Foreign Exchange Management Act 1999, (FEMA) with effect from June 1, 2000, the objective of the Foreign Exchange Department has shifted from conservation of foreign exchange to "facilitating external trade and payment and promoting the orderly development and maintenance of foreign exchange market in India". The Department ensures timely realization of export proceeds and reviews, on a continuous basis, the existing rules in the light of suggestions received from various trade bodies and exporters' fora. The Department collects data relating to forex transactions from authorized dealers on a daily basis for exchange rate management and on a fortnightly basis for monthly quick estimates of balance of payments and quarterly balance of payments compilation. The Department lays down policy guidelines for risk management relating to forex transactions in banks. The Department is also entrusted with the responsibility of licensing banks/money changers to deal in foreign exchange and inspecting them.

3.8.6 Financial Markets Department: The Financial Markets Department was constituted on July 6, 2005 with a view to providing an integrated market interface for the RBI and to bringing about integration in the RBI's conduct of monetary operations. The main function of Department is the monetary operations such as open market operations, liquidity adjustment facility, and market stabilization scheme. It also involved in the regulations and development of money market instruments such as call/term/notice money, market repo, collateralized borrowing and lending obligation, commercial paper and certificate of deposits. The department also monitors money, government securities and forex markets.

3.8.7 Department of Banking Supervision: The Reserve Bank of India has been entrusted with the responsibility of supervising the Indian banking system under various provisions of the Banking Regulation Act of 1949 and RBI Act of 1934. As regards commercial banks and financial institutions, this responsibility is discharged through the Department of Banking Supervision (DBS), which supervises 92 commercial banks and 9 select financial institutions (FIs), through its 16 Regional Offices.

The Department of Banking Supervision undertakes scheduled and special on-site inspections of banks, their off-site surveillance as also post inspection follow-up of compliance. The department also determines the criteria for the appointment of statutory auditors and special auditors and assessing audit performance and disclosure standards. It also deals with financial sector frauds and attending to the complaints received against the banks and financial institutions from public, banks, Government etc. It exercises supervisory intervention in the implementation of regulations which includes recommendation for removal of managerial and other persons, suspension of business, amalgamation, merger, winding up, issuance of directives and imposition of penalties.

A high powered Board for Financial Supervision (BFS), comprising the Governor of RBI as Chairman, one Deputy Governor as Vice Chairman, other Deputy Governors and four Directors of the Central Board of RBI as Members with the mandate to exercise the powers of supervision and inspection in relation to the banking companies, financial institutions and non-banking financial companies. Presently, BFS exercises supervision not only over banks but also over select Developmental Finance Institutions (DFIs), Non-banking Financial Companies (NBFCs), Primary Dealers (PDs) and Urban Cooperative Banks (UCBs).

3.8.8 Department of Non-banking Supervision: The Department of Non-banking Supervision is entrusted with the responsibility of supervising the Non-banking Finance Companies. The RBI Act was amended in January 1997 and provided entry norms for Non-banking Financial Companies (NBFCs), prohibition of deposit acceptance by unincorporated bodies with some exceptions, compulsory registration, maintenance of liquid assets, reserve fund, punitive action like cancellation of Certificate of Registration, prohibition from acceptance of deposits and alienation of assets, filing criminal complaints and winding up petitions in extreme cases, appointment of RBI observers etc.

The Department also involved in the supervisory framework for NBFCs comprising (a) on-site inspection (CAMELS pattern) (b) off-site monitoring through returns and (c) market intelligence. In co-ordination with State Governments the Department of Non-banking Supervision also developed appropriate State Legislations to curb unauthorized and fraudulent activities in this sector.

3.8.9 Internal Debt Management Department: The main activity of the Internal Debt Management Department is to manage the public debt of Government of India and State Governments. The Department also regulates and supervises the Primary Dealers System and has the responsibility for development of Government Securities Market. The Department prepares calendar for issuances of Government of India dated securities and Treasury Bills, introduction of new instruments for Governments and market borrowings. The Department also fixes limits on Ways and Means advances (WMA) for both Central and State Governments and monitoring the use of these limits on a daily basis.

3.8.10 Department of External Investments and Operations: The main function of External Investments and Operations Department is the management and investment of foreign exchange reserves of the Reserve Bank of India. The Department handles external transactions on behalf of Government of India (GOI) including transactions relating to IMF. The Department also deals with matters relating to gold policy, membership of the Bank for International Settlements (BIS), matters incidental to international cooperation, management and investment of the foreign currency and gold assets of the Reserve Bank of India and matters incidental to India's membership of the Asian Clearing Union.

3.8.11 Monetary Policy Department: Monetary Policy Department is entrusted with the responsibility of designing, formulating and implementing monetary policy of the Reserve Bank. Important functions of the Monetary Policy Department is to regulate the issue of Bank notes and the keeping of reserves with a view to securing monetary stability in the country and to operate the currency and credit system of the country to its advantage. The Department is entrusted with the preparation of Reserve Bank of India's Annual Policy Statement and its Reviews in each quarter. The department monitors and reviews the maintenance of CRR and SLR by scheduled commercial banks.

They conduct Technical Advisory Committee meetings on Monetary Policy in each quarter and pre-policy consultation meetings with the bankers, market participants, trade bodies, self-regulatory organizations and economists and journalists to facilitate the policy formulation process. They conduct Governor's meetings with banks to announce monetary policy. The department also monitors and reviews the developments in macroeconomic conditions, prices and inflation, key monetary and banking aggregates, financial markets including interest rates and sanctioning of refinance limits/utilization in respect of scheduled commercial banks.

3.8.12 Department of Government and Bank Accounts: The Department of Government and Bank Accounts (DGBA) is responsible for discharging certain core traditional central banking functions, viz., acting as bankers to the banks and governments and administering public debt of both, central and state governments. It is also responsible for maintenance of the Reserve Bank's internal accounts and compilation of its weekly statement of affairs and annual balance sheets. The Department also monitors disposal of the complaints received from the members of public regarding unsatisfactory services rendered by various departments of the Reserve Bank.

3.8.13 Legal Department: The main function of Legal Department is to tender legal advice on various matters referred by the operational departments, offices and associates of the Reserve Bank of India. These references mainly involve interpretation of the Constitution of India, provisions of the Reserve Bank of India Act, 1934, Banking Regulation Act, 1949, the Foreign Exchange Management Act, 1999, Government Securities Act, 2006 and various other central and state statutes. The department is also required to interpret the rules and regulations governing the Reserve Bank's staff and to deal with legal issues relating to industrial relations. The department is associated with legislative drafting on matters related to banking and finance including drafting of subordinate legislation such as rules, regulations and statutory notifications.

3.8.14 Department of Economic Analysis and Policy: Department of Economic Analysis and Policy studied and analyses the basic issues and problems (both domestic and international) affecting the Indian economy. The department prepares monetary and credit aggregates, balance of payments and external debt statistics, internal debt and government finance statistics, and flow-of-funds and financial saving. They also publish six major publications viz. Annual Report, the Report on Currency and Finance, the Report on Trend and Progress in Banking and Finances of State Governments), monthly (RBI Bulletin), Weekly (Statistical Supplement) and a tri-annual research journal (RBI Occasional Papers). In addition, research studies are published in a series of Staff Studies. The publications of RBI have established as the reference documents among the market participants, analysts, academics and international community.

3.8.15 Department of Payment and Settlement Systems: The Department of Payment and Settlement Systems is a new department in the Reserve Bank which was operational with effect from March 2005. The Department is responsible for regulation and oversight on the Payment and Settlement Systems which encompass the cheque based clearing systems managed by the Reserve Bank and other commercial banks, Electronic Clearing Service (ECS), Electronic Funds Transfer (EFT) System, the inter-institutional Government Securities clearing, the inter-bank foreign exchange clearing as also the RTGS.

The Department also provides secretarial support to the newly constituted Board for regulation and supervision of Payment and Settlement Systems (BPSS), which happens to be a Committee of the Central Board. The Department also formulates policies of payment and settlement systems, regulation and supervision of payment and settlement systems, implementation of the core principles relating to payment systems and monitoring the operations of payment and settlement systems.

3.8.16 Customer Service Department: The Customer Service Department was constituted to provide proper focus to the entire range of customer service related activities of banks and the Reserve Bank of India. The Department started functioning from July 1, 2006. The department is entrusted with the function of dissemination of information relating to customer service and grievance redressal by banks and Reserve Bank of India. They also administer the Banking Ombudsman (BO) Scheme. The department is acting as a nodal department for the Banking Codes and Standards Board of India (BCSBI). It ensures redressal of complaints received directly by RBI on customer service in banks. They also liaison between banks, Indian Banks Association, BCSBI, Banking Ombudsman offices and the RBI's regulatory departments on matters relating to customer services and grievance redressal.

3.8.17 Department of Information Technology: The Department of Information Technology (DIT) is entrusted with the responsibility of computerization in Regional and Central Offices of RBI. They design and develop projects for use of banks and financial institutions and monitor the progress of technology in banks.

3.8.18 Human Resources Development Department: Human Resources Development Department is involved in the process of Recruitment, Placement, Performance and Potential Appraisal, Promotion and Career Progression, Industrial Relations, Deputation, Retirement and Voluntary Vacation, Motivation, Training Establishments, Remuneration and Reward Mechanism, Staff Welfare, Organizational Development, Training and Skills Upgradation, Medical Facility etc.

3.8.19 Department of Statistical Analysis and Computer Services: Department of Statistical Analysis and Computer Services are involved in the collection, processing and dissemination of data on banking, credit, corporate and external sectors. The department undertakes studies in the areas of interest and relevance to the Reserve Bank. It also collects important statistics relating to various aspects of the economy.

3.8.20 Inspection Department: Inspection Department carry out inspections to examine, evaluate and report on the adequacy and reliability of existing systems and follow-up to ensure that Laws, Regulations, Internal Policies and Procedures are meticulously followed. The main objectives of this department is to assess in clear terms the achieved and achievable performance of the Offices/branches and Central Office Departments with the available resources and to suggest appropriate improvements so that performance level could be enhanced further.

3.9 Subsidiaries of RBI

1. National Housing Bank (NHB).
2. Deposit Insurance and Credit Guarantee Corporation of India (DICGC).
3. Bharatiya Reserve Bank Note Mudran Private Limited (BRBNMPL).
4. National Bank for Agriculture and Rural Development (NABARD).

The Bank was also instrumental in institutional development and helpful in establishing institutions like the Unit Trust of India, the Industrial Development Bank of India, the Discount and Finance House of India etc. to build the financial infrastructure of the country. RBI has divested the stake in the State Bank of India (SBI), Securities Trading Corporation of India Ltd. (STCI), and Discount and Finance House of India (DFHI).

3.10 Training Establishments

RBI owns six training establishments, namely:

1. College of Agricultural Banking, Pune.
2. Bankers Training College, Mumbai.
3. Reserve Bank of India Staff College, Chennai.
4. National Institute for Bank Management, Mumbai.
5. Indira Gandhi Institute of Development Research (IGIDR), Mumbai.
6. Institute for Development and Research in Banking Technology (IDRBT), Hyderabad.

Short Answer Type Questions

1. What do you mean by lender of last resort?
2. What do you mean by bankers bank?
3. What are the basic functions of RBI?
4. What are the subsidiaries of RBI?
5. Explain central board of directors of RBI.
6. What is local board of RBI?
7. What is central board of RBI?
8. What are the functions of local board of RBI?
9. What is SLR?
10. What is non-monetary function?
11. What is CRR?
12. What is open market operation?
13. What is the object of maintaining statutory liquidity ratio?
14. Name the important Acts governing banking operations in India.
15. What is monetary function?
16. What is repo?
17. What is department of currency management?

18. What are the objectives of monetary policy?
19. What are the instruments in used in repo?
20. What is bank rate?
21. What are the tools used for credit control?
22. What is the object of maintaining cash reserve ratio?
23. What do you mean by controller of credit?
24. What is credit authorization scheme?
25. What is financial supervision?
26. Name the functions of department of financial markets.
27. What is variable reserve ratio?
28. What is moral suasion?
29. What is direct action?

Essay Type Questions

1. Explain briefly the monetary functions of RBI.
2. What are the instruments of monetary control?
3. Give a brief history and management of RBI.
4. Explain the origin and organizational structure of RBI.
5. What are the important objectives and functions of RBI?
6. Explain briefly the role of RBI in issue of currency notes.
7. Explain briefly the promotional and developmental functions of RBI.
8. How do repo and reverse repo affect liquidity?
9. What are the qualitative tools are used by RBI to control the volume of credit in the country?
10. Discuss the tools used by RBI for regulating the money supply.
11. Mention the assumptions on the basis of which bank rate policy works.
12. Explain the function of RBI as the banker to the government.
13. Explain the function of RBI as the bank of issue.
14. Give the relation between bank rate and open market operation.
15. Explain how do SLR and CRR regulate money supply in the country?
16. Explain briefly the non-monetary functions of RBI.
17. Open market operation is the most frequently used tool for controlling monetary policy. Explain.
18. Analyze the monetary policy of RBI.
19. Open market operations as an instrument of credit control are superior to bank rate policy. Discuss.
20. What are the regulatory and supervisory functions of RBI?
21. What are the quantitative tools are used by RBI to control the volume of credit and inflation in the country?

22. Explain the functions of banking operations and development department
23. Distinguish between quantitative credit control and qualitative credit control.
24. Explain briefly the functions of different departments of RBI.
25. Explain the function of RBI as the bankers' bank and supervisor.
26. Give the importance of selective credit control.

4

Commercial Banks

4.1 Introduction

Banks are places where people can deposit their savings with the assurance that they will be able to withdraw money from the deposits whenever required. Banks lend money to individuals and business houses that need it. Banks acts as an intermediary between people having surplus money and those requiring money for various business activities. Banks promotes saving habits among the public. It encourages savings habit amongst people and thereby makes funds available for productive use. Banks are regarded as the nerve centre of the trade, industry and commerce of the country.

4.2 Evolution of Banking

The banking business in its oldest form originated in Italy where the early bankers were called moneychangers. They used to conduct their money changing business in streets seated on banca or benches. The name bank derived from the Italian word *banco* means 'desk or bench', used during the Renaissance by Florentine bankers, who used to make their transactions above a desk covered by a green table cloth. However, traces of banking activity can be found even in ancient times. In fact, the word traces its origins back to the Ancient Roman Empire, where moneylenders would set up their stalls in the middle of enclosed courtyards called '*macella*' on a long bench called a '*bancu*', from which the words '*banco*' and *bank* are derived.

The origin of the modern banker can be traced back to the merchant bankers, moneylenders and London Goldsmiths. The merchants accepted deposits from their clients to carry on their trade, the moneylenders lent their surplus money to goldsmiths, who accepted the money and other valuables for safe custody. They possessed special facilities to keep under safe lock and key valuables of many kinds. A modern commercial banker performs these three functions namely accept deposit; lend money and safe custody of valuables of customers.

4.3 History of Commercial Banks in India

Historically commercial banking in India had its origin in the seventeenth century with the establishment of trading centres by the East India Company.

Unable to depend on indigenous bankers for trading and banking purposes, the East India Company encouraged the establishment of agency houses, which carried on trading and banking operations. Western style banking in India began with the launching of banking operations by Calcutta agency houses and trading firms for the benefit of their business. Both Messer's Alexander & Co. and Ferguson & Co. combined their banking with other kinds of business. 'Bank of Hindoostan' which is considered as the first bank in India was established under the directions of the East India Company in the year 1770. However, this bank could not survive for long because of the failure of the parent firm in 1832. The Sholapur Bank Ltd. started by trading houses also went into liquidation in 1818 due to the unwise combination of banking business with trading operations by them. Faulty speculation and greedy profit motive by ignoring the principle of safety of banking operation was the reason for the failure of the agency houses that also led to the collapse of their banking department.

4.4 Presidency Banks

The second development in the banking sector happened with the establishment of Presidency Banks. "The Bank of Calcutta" began its banking business in the year June 2, 1806. The Government of India did not realize the need for banks in India till 1809. Three years later, bank received its charter and was re-designed as the Bank of Calcutta as the "The Bank of Bengal" (January 2, 1809). It was the first joint-stock bank of British India sponsored by the Government of Bengal. It was established with a capital of ₹ 50 lakh, one-fifth of which was contributed by the Government, which shared the privilege of voting and direction.

Two other presidency banks namely "Bank of Bombay" and the "Bank of Madras" were formed in 15th April 1840 and 1st July 1843. "Bank of Bombay" and the "Bank of Madras" were formed with a capital outlay of ₹ 52.25 and ₹ 30 lakh respectively. The Government had subscribed Rs.3 lakh as capital in each of these banks. These three banks were called the Presidency Banks, because they were partly financed by the East India Company. The banks were governed by royal charters, which were revised from time to time. The members of the board of directors, which managed the affairs of each bank, were mostly proprietary directors representing the large European managing agency houses in India. The rest were government nominees, invariably civil servants, one of whom was elected as the president of the board.

Banking business of these three banks was initially confined to discounting of bill of exchange or other negotiable instruments, keeping cash accounts and receiving deposits. Loans were restricted to one-lakh rupees and the period of accommodation was limited to three months. Thcy were given the right to issue notes in their own regions. The first legal tender currency was issued by these banks.

With the passing of the Paper Currency Act in 1860, the right of note issue of the Presidency Banks was abolished and the Government of India assumed the sole power of issuing paper currency with in British India from March 1, 1862. The management and circulation of the new currency notes was conferred on the Presidency Banks and the Government undertook to transfer the Treasury balances to the banks at places where the banks would open branches. None of these three banks had any branches till 1862. Then they embarked on branch expansion at a rapid pace.

'Allahabad Bank' was established in the year 1865 and for the next five years, no other bank was established. In 1881, the first purely Indian bank i.e. "Oudh Commercial Bank" came into existence. Fall in the gold price during 1871-1893 also resulted in the slow growth of joint stock banking. The "Punjab National Bank", began in 1895 with Lahore as its head office. The "Peoples Bank" was established in the year 1901 and the "City Union Bank Ltd" in 1904.

Following the Swadeshi Movement of 1905, many Indian entrepreneurs launched banking institutions. Later many more banks sprung up like mushrooms. The number of Indian Joint Stock banks also increased remarkably during the period of 1906-21. Important banking ventures started during these period were; Bank of India Ltd. (1906), The Corporation Bank Ltd. (1906), The Indian Bank Ltd. (1907), The Bank of Baroda Ltd. (1908), The Canara Bank Ltd. (1910), The Central Bank of India Ltd., The South Indian Bank Ltd. (1911), The Karur Vysya Bank Ltd. (1916), The Catholic Bank Ltd. and The Union Bank of India Ltd. (1920) and The Tamil Nadu Mercantile Bank Ltd. (1921).

The Bank of Bengal, the Bank of Bombay and the Bank of Madras referred as Presidency Banks with their 70 branches got amalgamated into the Imperial Bank of India, which came into existence on January 27, 1921 by the Imperial Bank of India Act of 1920. The new bank took on the triple role of a commercial bank, a banker's bank and a banker to the government.

During 1922- 48 the number of joint stock banks increased further. Andhra Bank Ltd. (1923), Karnataka Bank Ltd. (1924), Syndicate Bank Ltd. (1925), The Federal Bank Ltd. (1930), Viyaya Bank Ltd. (1931), Dhana Lakshmi Bank Ltd. (1935), Bank of Maharashtra Ltd. (1936), Indian Overseas Bank Ltd. (1937), Dena Bank Ltd. (1938), Lord Krishna Bank Ltd. (1940), Oriental Bank of Commerce Ltd. (1943) United Commercial Bank Ltd. (1943) etc. were established during this period.

The history of banking industry in India reveals that it evolved after passing through a number of crises and consequent bank failures. The years 1917, 1932 and 1939 were years of banking crisis in India. Following Second World War, there was a mushroom growth of banks characterized by inadequate capital and the issue of both preference and deferred shares in addition to ordinary shares, appointment of managing directors for long periods with high salaries and perquisites. As the number of banks increased, there arose a need for centrally regulating the banking system in India. This felt need gave birth to the Reserve Bank of India (RBI) in 1935. The Reserve Bank of India took over all the functions of the Imperial Bank of India.

4.5 State Bank of India

After Independence, there was a concerted demand for the nationalization of the Imperial Bank of India. However, the Government was not in favour of nationalization because of two reasons. First, the banks have branches outside India, which may create political problems and consequences of great magnitude. Secondly, it was thought that nationalization would devoid the banks of their useful commercial operations and functions. The 'Rural Banking Enquiry Committee' (1950) also recommended against nationalization. In August 1947, the Imperial Bank had a capital base (including reserves) of ₹ 11.85 crore, deposits and advances of ₹ 275.14 crore and ₹ 72.94 crore respectively and a network of 172 branches and more than 200 sub offices extending all over the country.

The State Bank of India came into being as result of the implementation of the recommendation of the 'Committee of Directors' of the "All India Rural Credit Survey" appointed by the Reserve Bank of India in 1951. The committee recommended the setting up of the State Bank of India as one strong integrated state sponsored and state partnered commercial banking institution with an effective network of branches spread throughout the country. An act was accordingly passed in Parliament in May 1955 and the State Bank of India was constituted on 1 July 1955. The Government of India nationalized Imperial Bank of India with the RBI taking 60 percent stake. In 2008, the Government of India took over the stake held by the Reserve Bank of India.

The SBI by further expansion of branches can be put in a position to take over cash from non- banking treasuries and to stimulate banking development by providing extended remittance facilities for co-operative and other banks and by following a policy consonant with the national policies adopted by the government and with out departing from the canons of sound banking business. Between October 1959 and May 1960, seven banks of the erstwhile princely states were also brought under the control and full or near-full ownership of the

State Bank of India. These banks were founded under princely patronage. Bhavanagar Durbar Bank was established in the year 1902 to which the 'State Bank of Saurashtra' owes its origin. Erstwhile Government of Mysore established 'State Bank of Mysore' in 1913. 'State Bank of Patiala' was founded by erstwhile Patiala State. 'State Bank of Hyderabad' was constituted as Hyderabad Bank in 1941 by the erstwhile State of Hyderabad. 'State Bank of Travancore' was originally established as Travancore Bank Ltd. in 1945 and was sponsored by the erstwhile Princely State of Travancore. 'State of Bikaner and Jaipur' were established by way of taking over of the business of Govind Bank Pvt. Ltd. in 1956.

In accordance with the provisions of the SBI Act of 1959, State Bank of India established its seven subsidiaries viz.

1. State Bank of Bikaner and Jaipur.
2. State Bank of Hyderabad.
3. State Bank of Indore.
4. State Bank of Mysore.
5. State Bank of Patiala.
6. State Bank of Saurashtra.
7. State Bank of Travancore.

The State Bank of India together with its subsidiaries is popularly known as the State Bank group. SBI is the largest commercial bank in India, in terms of branch network, resources and work force. Based on number of its branches it has the largest office net work of its kind in the whole world. State Bank of India had 100 percent stake in State Bank of Hyderabad and State Bank of Patiala, 98.3 percent in State Bank of Indore and 92.3 percent in State Bank of Mysore. It has 75 percent stake in State Bank of Travancore and State Bank of Bikaner & Jaipur.

In the world setting, State Bank of India is the only Indian bank, which is placed 82nd position among the hundred big banks of the world having big assets. It has a market share among Indian commercial banks of about 20 percent in deposits and advances, and SBI accounts for almost one-fifth of the nation's loans.

There has been a proposal to merge all the seven associate banks into SBI to create a "mega bank" and streamline operations. The first step along these lines occurred on 13 August 2008 when State Bank of Saurashtra merged with State Bank of India, which reduced the number of state banks from seven to six. SBI board also approved the merger of its subsidiary State Bank of Indore with SBI. The finance ministry is planning to merge unlisted State Bank of Hyderabad, State Bank of Indore and State Bank of Patiala in the first phase. Since SBI owns 100 percent shares in State Bank of Hyderabad and State Bank of Patiala and

98.3 percent in State Bank of Indore, the acquisition process can be carried through a Union Cabinet order sanctioning the 'scheme of acquisition' similar to the way SBI acquired its associate State Bank of Saurashtra. Acquisition of the three 'listed' associate banks viz. State Bank of Travancore, State Bank of Bikaner & Jaipur, and State Bank of Mysore are listed on stock exchanges, hence the government and SBI will have to work on the share-swap ratio and their valuation.

4.6 Social Control on Banks

The banking system and banking business grew by leaps and bounds after Independence by way of the number of offices and volume of bank deposits and bank credits. The banking institutions are considered as the custodians of private savings and as powerful instruments for giving credit. The commercial banks in India during the 1960s merely acted as financial agencies and failed to give any lead to the nation's development.

In 1960, there were persistent complaints about the functioning of Indian commercial banks and the main complaint was about the banks not discharging their functions in consonance with the aims of our socialistic democracy. They were directing a substantial portion of their advances to large and medium scale industries and established big business houses and paving the way for concentration of economic power, monopoly and misdirection of resources. The members of the big business houses were associated with the banks as their directors and they were mainly interested in advancing loans to their firms on easy terms and conditions.

There were complaints that commercial banks were not advancing credit to those sectors requiring priority such as agriculture, small-scale industries and exports and to the hitherto neglected and weaker section of the community. It was also observed that most of the commercial bank offices were concentrated in urban areas where the branches proved to be economically viable. Fear of losses due to unremunerative working results made rural banking unattractive.

Many political parties made a demand for the nationalization of commercial banks repeatedly and a vocal section of the ruling Indian National Congress strongly supported nationalization. It was felt that nationalization was the only remedy to cure the maladies of banking in the private sector. At the Bhuvaneswar session of the congress party in 1964, a twelve- point programme of possible achievements, as a result of nationalization of banks was placed and this included measures to eradicate the entire range of economic and social evils and to achieve all aspirations of the people.

The government was not opposed to the demand for bank nationalization.

However, the decision to nationalize the banks was not taken because of administrative difficulties and also the consequential effects on the economy of the country. Nationalization was disfavoured because it would severely strain and adversely affect the administrative and financial resources of the country and would weaken the structure of our mixed economy. As an alternative, the government from time to time tried to reform the commercial banking system through legislative and other measures. One such important measure was the social control of banks. As a matter of fact, the term 'social control' of banks was adopted for the first time by the then ruling Indian National Congress in its 1967-election manifesto, stating that " it is necessary to bring the banking institutions under social control in order to ensure socio- economic growth and to fulfil our social purposes more effectively and to make credit available to the producers in all fields where it is needed".

A comprehensive scheme for social control of banks was enforced through a legislative measure on 1 February 1969, to ensure the need for economic growth and to fulfil our social objectives more effectively. The aim of social control was to bring about changes in the management and the credit policy of the commercial banks.

The objective of social control over banks was "to ensure without active take-over of banks into public ownership, the achievements of those social ends that nationalization could conceivably secure. The major aim clearly was a more purposeful distribution of available credit in terms of accepted investment priorities and correspondingly more efficient mobilization of savings".

4.7 First Phase of Bank Nationalization

The scheme of social control initiated by the Government of India in December 1967 was found to be unsatisfactory and inadequate. There were complaints that the Indian commercial banks continued to direct their advances to large and medium scale industries and sectors demanding priority such as agriculture, small-scale industries and imports were not receiving the attention due to them from the banks.

Nationalization of banks began with the passing of the Reserve Bank (Transfer of Public Ownership) Act 1948 and it was a 'revolution' in the Indian banking system. This revolution did not merely signify a change of the ownership of these banks but it was the beginning of a coordinated endeavour to utilize an important segment of the financial mechanism for the country's economic development. It was stated that, in nationalizing the banks, Government was only putting into effect its programme for achieving the goal of a socialistic pattern of society and it was hoped that nationalization would effectively decentralize credits with the result that the priority sectors such as agriculture, small scale industries, exports, self employed entrepreneurs would be provided with liberal banking facilities and that banking units would be extended to rural areas. Nationalized banks are expected, to meet some of the demands of the public sector undertakings and to use the balance of the available resources for organized industries on the basis that new enterprises and those in backward areas will be given preference over the big business houses.

On July 19, 1969 fourteen major banks each having deposits of more than ₹ 50 crore and having between themselves aggregate deposits of ₹ 2,632 crore with 4130 branches were nationalized and taken over by the Government. Over 85 percent of the total deposits with the banking system passed into public control with the nationalization of these 14 banks. The total deposits with banks at the end of June 1969 were of the order of ₹ 4,600 crore and of this deposits amounting to ₹ 2,632 crore were accounted for by the 14 nationalized banks. The State Bank of India and its subsidiaries had deposits amounting to ₹ 1,300 crore. Following are the banks that were nationalized in 1969.

1. The Central Bank of India Ltd.
2. The Bank of India Ltd.
3. The Punjab National Bank Ltd.
4. The Bank of Baroda Ltd.
5. The United Commercial Bank Ltd. (UCO Bank).
6. The Canara Bank Ltd.
7. The United Bank of India Ltd.
8. The Dena Bank Ltd.
9. The Syndicate Bank Ltd.
10. The Union Bank of India Ltd.
11. The Allahabad Bank Ltd.
12. The Indian Bank Ltd.
13. The Bank of Maharastra Ltd.
14. The Indian Overseas Bank Ltd.

The United Commercial Bank Ltd. has been renamed as "UCO Bank" by the Banking Laws (Amendment) Act, 1985 so as to avoid confusion in the international operations of the Bank in view of the existence of a bank with the same name set up in Bangladesh.

4.8. Objectives of Nationalization of Banks

Following are some of the main objectives of bank nationalization.

1. To ensure provision of adequate credit to the neglected sectors such as agriculture, cottage and small-scale industries, retail trade, exports, artisans

and self-employed persons.
2. To prevent the diversion of bank finance to anti-social, less productive, low-priority sectors and to big industrialists and businessmen.
3. To give a professional bent to bank management.
4. To reduce regional imbalances in banking facilities by opening of branches in rural, remote and unbanked areas.
5. To develop banking habits among people.
6. To distribute economic power equitably by removal of the control of banks by a few big industrialists and business houses.
7. To provide adequate training as well as reasonable terms of service for bank staff.

4.9 Second Phase of Bank Nationalization

After eleven years of the first phase of banks' nationalization, an ordinance was promulgated on 15th April 1980, by the President of India for the acquisition and transfer of undertakings of six more private banking companies. In the second phase of nationalization, private banks having time and demand liabilities of not less than ₹ 200 crore each were nationalized. This further extended the area of public control over the country's banking system. In the second phase of nationalization only banks having deposits exceeding ₹ 50 crore each alone were nationalized. The objective of the second nationalization was to enhance the capacity of the banking system to meet more effectively the needs of the developing economy and to promote the welfare of the people in conformity with the national policy. Banks that were nationalized in the second phase were as follows:

1. The Andhra Bank Ltd.
2. The New Bank of India Ltd.
3. Vijaya Bank Ltd.
4. The Punjab and Sind Ltd.
5. Corporation Bank Ltd.
6. The Oriental Bank of Commerce Ltd.

Thus from 15th April 1980, the number of public sector banks increased to 28, including the State Bank of India and its 7 subsidiaries and excluding Regional Rural Banks. With the nationalization of six more banks in 1980, ninety-one percent of the entire banking system was brought under the public sector. The total deposits of six newly nationalized banks at the end of June 1980 were ₹ 2,773 crore and those of twenty nationalized banks were ₹ 22,854 crore. The total deposits of all scheduled commercial banks during this period stood at ₹ 33,377 crore. The New Bank of India got merged with the Punjab National

Bank in 1993, and this reduced the number of nationalized banks to 19.

4.10 Classification of Banks

Banks can be classified in to various types on the basis of their functions, ownership, domicile etc. On the basis of functions, the banking institutions in India can be divided into the following types:

1. **Central Bank:** A bank which is entrusted with the functions of guiding and regulating the banking system of a country is known as Central bank. It acts as banker to the Government and bankers bank. It maintains deposit accounts of all other banks, advances money to other banks when needed, issuance of currency notes, regulating their circulation in the country etc. The Reserve Bank of India is the central bank of our country.
2. **Industrial Banks:** Industrial or Development banks are established to cater the financial needs of the industrial undertakings. The primary objective is to extend long-term loans to industrial sectors. In addition to providing of long-term financial assistance, they guide industrial units on technical and managerial problems. The Industrial Development Bank of India and the Industrial Finance Corporation of India are the pioneers in the industrial banking system of the country.
3. **Agricultural Banks:** Agricultural banks are a type of banks which provide short-term as well as long-term finance to the agricultural sector. Examples are co-operative banks which provide short-term financial assistance to the people engaged in agriculture. Long-term agricultural loans are given by the Land Mortgage Banks. The National Bank for agriculture and Rural Development (NABARD) was established in 1982 to promote integrated rural development and to provide all sorts of credit to agriculture.
4. **Exchange Banks:** Exchange bank is a type of bank which provides finance to foreign trade in the country. They deal mainly in foreign exchange business by buying and selling of foreign currencies. They facilitates foreign remittances, accepting, collecting and discounting of foreign bills of exchanges.
5. **Co-operative Banks:** Co-operative banks are an important constituent of the Indian financial system. When a co-operative society engages itself in banking business it is called a Co-operative Bank. It is a retail banking institution which is organized on a co-operative basis. Co operative Banks in India are registered under the Co-operative Societies Act. These banks are under the overall supervision of the Registrar of Co-operative Societies of the State. The cooperative banks are also regulated by the RBI. As regards banking business, the society must follow the guidelines issued by the

Reserve Bank of India.

4.10.1 Types of Co-operative Banks: The co-operative banking institutions in the country are divided mainly into four categories:

1. **Primary Credit Societies:** Primary Agricultural Credit Society (PACS) formed at the village level constitutes the major retail outlet of short and medium term credit to the rural sector. The operations of each society are restricted to a small area so that the members know each other and are able to watch over the activities of all members to prevent frauds.
2. **Central Co-operative Banks:** District Co-operative Bank (DCB) operates at the middle level in the co-operative credit structure. The central co-operative banks are generally located at the district head quarters or some prominent town of the district. These banks provide loans to their members (i.e., primary credit societies) and function as a link between the primary credit societies and state co-operative banks.
3. **State Co-operative Banks:** These are the apex (highest level) co-operative banks in all the states of the country. They mobilize funds and help in its proper channelisation among various sectors. State Apex Cooperative Bank is the federation of the District Cooperative Banks. The money reaches the individual borrowers from the state co-operative banks through the central co-operative banks and the primary credit societies.
4. **Urban Credit Co-operative Banks:** Urban Co-operative Banks (UCBs) constitute an important place in the Indian financial system. Urban Cooperative Banks provide banking and credit facilities to urban and semi urban population. They mobilize deposits from the public and extend credit facilities for various purposes.

4.10.2 Post Office Savings Bank: Post offices extend banking facilities by post office savings bank. Post offices accept deposits from the people but do not grant loans like other commercial banks. They usually accept deposits in the form of savings deposit. They usually pay a high rate of interest as compared to other commercial banks. The main purpose of post office savings banks is to promote saving habits among the general public especially in the rural and remote areas.

4.10.3 Indigenous Banks: Before the establishment of commercial banks, private money lenders and country bankers played an important role as important sources of finance. These establishments were known as Indigenous Bankers. Their activities are not controlled and coordinated by the Reserve Bank of India. They charged high rate of interest and exploited the people who took financial assistance. These banks have lost their monopoly with the development of commercial banks in India. Now-a-days even though a large number of commercial banks act in the banking system, the indigenous bankers have played a significant role because some people depend on indigenous bankers for financial assistance.

4.10.4 Commercial Banks: Commercial banks are financial intermediaries, which perform the dual functions of mobilization of deposits and deployment of surplus funds to the various sectors of the economy. In addition to giving short-term loans, commercial banks also give medium-term and long-term loan to business enterprises. These banks perform all kinds of banking business. The main aim of commercial bank is to earn profit.

In addition to giving short-term loans, commercial banks also give medium-term and long-term loan to business enterprises. Commercial Banks also render many other useful services viz. collection of bills, cheques, safe-keeping of jewellery and other valuable items, certifying the credit-worthiness of business, and so on. It also helps in national development by providing credit to farmers, small-scale industries and self-employed people as well as to large business houses which lead to balanced economic development in the country.

4.10.5 Classification of Commercial Banks: As per the Reserve Bank of India Act of 1934, commercial banks in India are classified into two broad categories. They are:

1. Scheduled Commercial Banks.
2. Non-scheduled Commercial Banks.

A. Scheduled Commercial Banks: The Scheduled Commercial Banks are those banks which are included in the Second Schedule of the Reserve Bank of India Act of 1934. RBI includes only those banks in this schedule which satisfy the criteria laid down vide Section 42 (6) (a) of the Act. The scheduled banks have to keep minimum stipulated statutory cash reserves with the RBI. They are entitled to enjoy the facilities of borrowing from RBI.

They are also covered by the deposit insurance scheme and credit guarantee scheme in operation. The banks included in this schedule list should fulfil the following conditions.

1. The bank must have a minimum paid up capital and total reserves of ₹ 5 lakh.
2. It should ensure to the Reserve Bank of India that its operations are not detrimental to the interest of the depositors.
3. It must be either a company, or a corporation, or an institution notified by the Central Government in this respect or a state co-operative bank.
4. Every Scheduled bank enjoys the following facilities.
5. They are eligible for refinance or loans on bank rate from the RBI.
6. Such banks automatically acquire the membership of clearing house.
7. They are covered by the deposit insurance and credit guarantee scheme.

Scheduled Commercial Banks in India are categorized into five different groups according to their ownership and or nature of operation. These bank groups are as under:

1. Public Sector Banks.
2. Private Banks.
3. Foreign Banks.
4. Scheduled Co-operative Banks.
5. Regional Rural Banks.

(a) Public Sector Banks: These are banks owned and controlled by the government. In public sector banks majority of the shares are held by the Government or Reserve Bank of India. Public sector banks consist of Nationalized Banks and State Bank of India and its six associates. Examples of public sector banks are: State Bank of India, Punjab National Bank, Central Bank of India, Bank of Baroda, and Canara Bank etc.

(b) Private Sector Banks: These are banks owned and controlled by the private individuals or corporations. In the case of private sector banks majority of share capital of the bank is held by private individuals. These banks are registered as companies with limited liability. Federal Bank, Development Credit Bank Ltd, Axis Bank, ING Vysya Bank, HDFC Bank are examples of private sector banks.

(c) Foreign Banks: These banks are foreign in origin and have their registered office in a foreign country but operate their branches in other countries. Some of the foreign banks operating in India are Hong Kong and Shanghai Banking Corporation (HSBC), American Express Bank, Standard & Chartered Bank, Grindlays Bank, etc.

(d) Scheduled Co-operative Banks: State Co-operative Banks and Urban Co-operative Banks which are included in the Second Schedule of the Reserve Bank of India Act of 1934 are called scheduled co-operative banks.

(e) Regional Rural Banks: Regional Rural Banks are a type of bank which provides credit and other facilities to small farmers, agricultural labourers, small entrepreneurs and artisans of the rural areas. These are banks set up under the Regional Rural Banks Act of 1976. Regional Rural Banks are meant to operate as state sponsored, region based and rural oriented scheduled commercial banks.

B. Non-scheduled Commercial Banks: Those banks which are not included in the second schedule of the RBI Act of 1934 are called non-scheduled banks.

4.11 Functions of Commercial Banks

The functions of commercial banks are of following two types:

1. Primary functions.
2. Secondary functions.

4.11.1 Primary Functions: The primary functions of a commercial bank include the following:

1. Accepting deposits.
2. Granting loans and advances.

A. Accepting Deposits: The first and the most important function of commercial banks are to mobilize deposits from the public. People who have surplus income and savings find it convenient to deposit the amounts with banks. Bank deposits ensure both safety and security and a reasonable rate of return to the investors in the form of interest. Realizing the importance of savings in India's developing economy, several deposit schemes were evolved. To attract savings from all sorts of people banks began to offer innovative deposit schemes with wide range of options to suit the requirements of customers. To attract deposits from the various classes of people banks maintain different types of deposit accounts namely, current, savings bank, fixed deposit, recurring deposit and home-safe accounts. The following types of deposits are usually accepted by commercial banks:

1. Current Deposit.
2. Savings Deposit.
3. Fixed Deposit.
4. Recurring Deposit.
5. Miscellaneous Deposits.

(a) Current Deposit Account: A current deposit account is also called as 'demand deposit' or 'demand liabilities'. Current account is generally maintained by the traders and businessmen. Any amount can be withdrawn from this account any time without any notice. There are no restrictions on the number of withdrawals. Current accounts do not carry any interest, as the amount deposited in these accounts is repayable on demand without any restriction. Banks usually charge a small amount known as incidental charges on current deposit accounts depending on the number of transaction.

(b) Savings Bank Account: Savings deposit account is meant for individuals who wish to deposit small amount out of their current income. The middle class people usually hold savings deposit account. The rate of interest on this type of deposit is lower than interest on fixed deposits. Savings bank account can be opened with or without cheque book facility. There are restrictions on the number of withdrawals from this account. Savings account holders are also allowed to deposit cheques, drafts, dividend warrants, etc. drawn in their favour for collection by the bank. To open savings bank account, it is necessary for the depositor to be introduced by a person having a current or savings account with the same bank.

(c) Fixed Deposit Account: The term 'fixed deposit' means money deposited for a fixed period of time and repayable after the expiry of a specified period. It is also known as, 'time deposit' or 'time liabilities'. The rate of interest on fixed deposits depends upon the period of deposits. The longer the period, the higher is the rate of interest offered. In this type of deposit, amount cannot be withdrawn before the fixed future date. However, premature withdrawal is permitted, which results in loss of interest to the depositor. Fixed deposits are most useful for commercial banks. Since they are repayable only after a fixed period, the bank may invest these funds more profitably by lending at higher rates of interest and for relatively longer periods.

(d) Recurring Deposit: This is a type of deposit, in which the depositor is required to deposit a fixed amount of money every month for a specific period of time. The purpose of this account is to encourage small savings of the pubic especially fixed income group. After the completion of the specified period, the customer gets back all his deposits along with the cumulative interest accrued on the deposits. The rate of interest on these deposits is nearly the same as on fixed deposits. Recurring Deposits are gaining wide popularity these days.

(e) Miscellaneous Deposits: Banks have introduced several deposit schemes to attract deposits from different types of people, like home safe deposit account, children's gift plan, old age pension scheme, public provident fund account etc.

B. Granting of Loans and Advances: The second important function of a commercial bank is to grant loans and advances to the public. The success of banking business primarily depends upon the confidence of the depositors on the bank. Thus the banks keep adequate amount of cash to meet the demand from the depositors. In order to meet the demand of depositors, banks usually keep a certain percentage of the deposits received as cash reserves. After maintaining sufficient amount as cash reserves the banks lend the balance amount of deposits to the needy persons. The banks should invest its excess funds in such a way that it earns maximum income with minimum cost. Loans and advances are given to the customers at a higher rate of interest than that allowed by banks on various types of deposit accounts. The difference between the rate of interest allowed on deposits and the rate charged on the loans is the main source of a bank's profit. The rate of interest charged on loans and advances varies depending upon the purpose, period and the mode of repayment.

Generally, commercial banks grant short-term loans. Sometimes, medium and long-term loans are also granted. Various types of credit facilities are term loans, cash credit and overdraft, money at call and short notice, and discounting of negotiable instruments. They also provided packing credit, export credit, housing, educational, consumer and vehicle loan, loan for self-employment, agricultural loans etc. Loans are also granted against approved securities such as gold, silver, government securities, shares, stocks, national saving certificates, marketable goods etc.

(a) Loans: A specified amount sanctioned by a bank to the customer is called a 'loan'. It is granted for a fixed period. The specified amount is put on the credit of the borrower's account. The borrower may be given the entire amount in lump sum or in instalments. Interest is charged on the full amount even if the borrower does not utilize it. The rate of interest on loans is low as compared to cash credit. Loans are generally granted against the security of certain assets. The loan may be repaid in lump sum or in instalments. Every bank has its own procedure of granting loans. Hence, a bank is at liberty to grant loan depending on its own resources.

(b) Advances: Advances are short term loans provided by the bank to its customers. It differs from loan in the sense that loans may be granted for longer period, but advances are normally granted for a short period. The rate of interest charged on advances is comparatively higher than loans and it varies from bank to bank. Interest is charged only on the amount withdrawn and not on the sanctioned amount. Following are the different types of advances granted by commercial banks.

1. Cash Credit.
2. Bank overdraft.
3. Discounting of Bills.

(i) Cash Credit: A cash credit is an arrangement whereby the bank allows the borrower to draw amounts up to a certain limit. In this type of advance money is granted by the bank for a short period against pledge, hypothecation or personal guarantee. In cash credit the bank opens the account in the name of the borrower and the amount of advance is credited to the account. The customer can withdraw this amount as and when he requires. Interest is charged on the amount actually withdrawn from the account. Cash Credit is granted as per agreed terms and conditions with the customers.

(ii) Bank Overdraft: Overdraft is a type of short term advance granted by a bank to its customers. Overdraft facility is more or less similar to cash credit facility. It is a temporary arrangement granted only to the current account holders. A customer who has a current account with the bank is allowed to withdraw more than the amount of credit balance in his/her account. Overdraft facility is generally granted by bank on the basis of a written request by the customer. The customer is permitted to withdraw the amount as and when he/she needs it and to repay it through deposits in his account as and when it is convenient to him/her. Interest is charged on actual amount withdrawn by the customer. The rate of interest on overdraft is higher than that of term loans. Overdraft facility with a specified limit is allowed either on the security of assets or on personal security or both.

(iii) Discounting of Bills: Apart from granting cash credit, loans and overdraft, banks also grant financial assistance to customers by discounting bills of exchange. It is a short term advance by which the bank makes payment of the amount before the due date of the bill after deducting a certain rate of discount. In discounting, bank purchases the bill of exchange at face value minus interest at current rate of interest for the period of the bill. The party gets the funds without waiting for the date of maturity of the bills. The bank recover the full amount of the bill on due date from the person liable to make payment. In case any bill is dishonoured on the due date, the bank can recover the full amount of the bill from the customer.

4.11.2 Secondary Functions: Besides the primary functions of accepting deposits and lending money, banks perform a number of non-banking or secondary functions. These services supplement the main activities of the banks. Secondary or ancillary functions of commercial banks are of following two types:

1. Agency Services.
2. General Utility Services.

A. Agency Services: Agency services are those services, which are rendered by commercial banks as agents of their customers which include:

1. Collection and payment of cheques and bills on behalf of the customers.
2. Collection of dividends, interest and rent, etc. on behalf of customers.
3. Payment of rent, interest, insurance premium, subscriptions etc. on behalf of customers.
4. Acting as banker to issue.
5. Purchase and sale of various types of securities such as shares, stocks, bonds and debentures on behalf of customers.
6. Acting as a trustee or executor.
7. Collection of electricity, water and telephone bills.
8. Acting as agents, correspondents or representative on behalf of customers for other banks and financial institutions at home and abroad.
9. Income tax consultancy services.
10. Transferring money from one place to another and from one branch to another branch of the bank.

B. General Utility Services: General utility services are those services, which are rendered by commercial banks not only to the customers but also to the general public. These are available to the public on payment of a fee or charge.

1. Issuing letters of credit and travellers' cheque etc.

2. Safe keeping of valuables and important documents in safe deposit locker.
3. Providing customers with facilities of foreign exchange.
4. Standing guarantee on behalf of its customers, for making payments for purchase of goods, machinery, vehicles etc.
5. Collecting and supplying business information.
6. Providing remittance facilities like issuing of DD, TT, MT, EFT etc.
7. Acting as referee with respect to the financial standing, business reputation and respectability of the customers.
8. Advisory services.
9. Providing reports on the credit worthiness of customers.
10. Underwriting of shares, debentures etc.
11. Underwriting loans floated by government and public bodies.

4.12 Difference between Primary and Secondary Function

1. Primary functions are the main activities of a commercial bank whereas secondary functions are less important activities of a commercial bank.
2. Major source of income of a commercial bank is derived from primary activities, whereas the incomes from secondary services constitute only a small share of the total income.
3. It is obligatory for the commercial banks to render primary functions to their customers' whereas secondary functions are not obligatory on part of banks to perform. In order to attract and retain the customers generally all commercial banks perform these activities.

4.13 Number of Commercial Banks and Branches

At the end of March 2011, there were 163 scheduled commercial banks in India. The scheduled commercial banks consisted of 26 public sector banks, 21 private sector banks, 83 Regional Rural Banks (RRBs) and 33 foreign banks. Public sector banks comprise of State Bank of India and its 6 subsidiaries and 20 nationalized banks, and the IDBI Bank Ltd. classified as 'other public sector bank'. Private sector banks comprise 7 new private sector banks and 14 old sector private banks.

Apart from these, there are 4 non-scheduled commercial banks (Local Area Banks) also. The commercial banks in India achieved tremendous progress in branch expansion. The number of bank branches of commercial banks increased from 8,262 at the end of June 1969 to 99,523 at the end of March 2011.

4.14 Off-shore Banking

Off-shore Banking Unit (OBU) is a branch or subsidiary in Offshore Banking

Centre (OBC) that is specifically established according to the legislation of Offshore Banking Centre (OBC) to accept deposits and provide loans to the non-residents of Offshore Banking Centre. At the same time off shore banking units are prohibited to provide banking services to the residents of OBU in order to eliminate potential competition between domestic and offshore banking sectors. These units obtain funds from international money markets and invest them in the country, where they set up the units or in various projects started by the said country elsewhere. These units provide finance to those projects, which are of a capital-intensive nature and for importing costly capital equipments. In all other aspects OBUs are free to conduct any legal operations and offer any legal banking service.

The sources for raising foreign currency funds would be only external. Funds can also be raised from those resident sources to the extent such residents are permitted under the existing exchange control regulations to invest and maintain foreign currency accounts abroad. Deployment of funds would be restricted to lending to units located in the SEZ and SEZ developers. Foreign currency requirements of corporates in the domestic area can also be met by the OBUs.

A commercial bank has both domestic banking unit and offshore banking unit. Domestic banking unit is designed to serve residents, while offshore banking unit conducts offshore banking services. Domestic banking unit and offshore banking unit are integral parts of a commercial bank, simply their accounting records are kept separately. Generally, offshore banking units are exempted from some monetary controls, legal obligations, capital requirements and investment controls imposed by financial supervisor.

The functions of the Off-shore Banking include raising funds in convertible foreign currency as deposits and borrowing from non-resident sources, transacting in foreign exchange with residents in India who are eligible to do so under the Foreign Exchange Act, opening foreign currency accounts abroad as well as other OBUS in India and trading in foreign currencies in the overseas market.

The OBUs would operate and maintain balance sheet only in foreign currency and would not be allowed to deal in Indian Rupees except for having a special Rupee account out of convertible fund to meet their day to day expenses. These branches would be prohibited to participate in domestic call, notice, term, etc. money market and payment system. Operations of the OBUs in rupees would be minimal in nature, and any such operations in the domestic area would be through the Authorized Dealers (distinct from OBUs), which would be subject to the current exchange control regulations in force. The OBUs would be required to maintain separate Nostro accounts with correspondent banks, which would be distinct from Nostro accounts maintained by other branches of the same bank.

Banks operating in India viz. public sector, private sector and foreign banks authorized to deal in foreign exchange are eligible to set up OBUs. Such banks having overseas branches and experience of running OBUs would be given preference. Each of the eligible banks would be permitted to establish only one OBU which would essentially carry on wholesale banking operations. However, the banks can set up more than one OBU, but not in the same Special Economic Zone (SEZ). Off-shore Banking units will be regulated and supervised by RBI through its Exchange Control Department, Department of Banking Operations and Development and Department of Banking Supervision.

4.15 Guideline for Setting up of Off-shore Banking Units

Following the announcement in the EXIM Policy of 2002-07 by the Government of India, the Reserve Bank of India issued guidelines in November 2002 allowing banks operating in India to set up Off-shore Banking Units (OBUs) in Special Economic Zones (SEZs) which would virtually be foreign branches of Indian banks located in India. They provide finance to SEZ units and SEZ developers at international rates. The salient features of the scheme for setting up Off-shore Banking Units in Special Economic Zones are the following::

1. Banks would be required to obtain prior permission of the RBI for opening an OBU in a SEZ under Section 23 (1)(a) of the Banking Regulation Act, 1949.
2. All commercial banks operating in India, authorized to deal in foreign exchange, are eligible to set up OBUs, with a preference for banks having overseas branches and experience of running OBUs.
3. Since Off-shore Banking Units would be branches of Indian banks, no separate assigned capital for such branches would be required. However, with a view to enable them to start their own operations, the parent bank would be required to provide a minimum of US$ 10 million to its OBU.
4. The Reserve Bank would grant exemption from CRR requirements to the parent bank in respect of its OBU branch.
5. All prudential norms applicable to overseas branches of Indian banks would apply to the OBUs. The OBUs would be required to follow the best international practice of 90 days payment delinquency norms for income recognition, asset classification and provisioning.
6. The sources of raising foreign currency funds would only be external.
7. The OBUs would be required to follow scrupulously 'Know Your Customer' and other anti-money laundering instructions issued by the Reserve Bank.

8. Deposits of Off-shore Banking Units will not be covered by deposit insurance.
9. The loans and advances of OBUs would not be considered as net bank credit for computing priority sector lending obligations.

Short Answer Type Questions

1. What is the meaning of bank?
2. Write a note on commercial bank?
3. What is public sector bank?
4. What are the functions of commercial banks?
5. What is bank overdraft?
6. What are the features of a bank?
7. Distinguish between fixed deposit and savings deposit.
8. What is discounting of bills?
9. Name the primary functions of commercial banks.
10. What is non-scheduled commercial bank?
11. What is current account?
12. What are the different types of banks?
13. What is fixed deposit?
14. Explain cash credit.
15. What is meant by scheduled commercial banks?
16. What are foreign banks?
17. What is off-shore banking?
18. What is recurring deposit?
19. What is social control on banks?

Essay Type Questions

1. Give a brief history of the origin and development of commercial banks in India.
2. Explain the features of commercial banks.
3. Give the primary functions of commercial banks.
4. What are the advantages of bank nationalization?
5. Discuss the various achievements of banks in the post-Nationalization period.
6. Discuss the secondary functions of commercial banks. Differentiate the primary and secondary functions of commercial banks.
7. What are the guidelines for opening off shore banking units in India?
8. Discuss the general utility services rendered by commercial banks.
9. What is a bank? What are the important functions performed by a modern bank?

10. What are the objectives of bank nationalization?
11. What are the agency services rendered by commercial banks?

5

Innovations in Banking Services

5.1 Introduction

The banking sector in India remained a regulated one and rigid since the nationalization of banks in 1969. Up to 1990, the concept of an independent regulatory authority had no relevance. With the liberalization of the Indian Economy, the Indian banking system also followed the suit and slowly entered into a market driven competitive system. Technological changes have entered Indian banks well before the nationalization of major banks in 1969. But the banks introduced the mechanization and automation only in selected operations and in a very slowly manner. Computers were nowhere in picture at that time. The most important developments through computerization came following the recommendations of the Rangarajan Committee.

The Rangarajan Committee was appointed in July 1983 to review the scope of mechanization in banks and to draw up a roadmap for mechanization especially computerization. The committee made an in depth study of the problems and after a thorough study spanning more than a year, the recommendations came at the end of 1984. The Rangarajan Committee recommended mechanization in a phased manner at all levels viz. Branch, Zonal, and Regional office level. After the recommendations of the Rangarajan Committee, a high-level committee headed by Executive Director Mr. Ratnagar, was constituted to implement the programme of computerization.

Changes have taken place in the banking sector only from the time of then Finance Minister of India, Dr. Manmohan Singh who unveiled the New Economic Policy through his maiden Budget for the year 1991 of the Government of India. The much-debated New Economic Policy was the outcome of acute financial crisis faced by the country in mid 1991 caused primarily by the political uncertainty, which got aggravated with the Gulf War. During this period, the country was passed through an unprecedented economic crisis following the strain on balance of payment, galloping inflation, depleting condition of foreign exchange reserves and many other macroeconomic imbalances. The new economic policy was based on a combination of measures aimed at economic stabilization and structural reforms to overcome the short comings of a socialistic pattern of economy pursed by India for the past 40 years. The overall package was aimed at enhancing the productivity and efficiency of the economy as a whole and to make it competitive internationally.

The new economic policy is structured on the pillars of deregulation, liberalization, privatization and globalization. Close on the heels of announcement of the National Economic Policy, the Government appointed a high level committee on financial sector reforms under the Chairmanship of Mr. Narasimham. The committee was to examine exhaustively all aspects relating to the structure, organization functions and procedures of the system. The committee submitted its first report in November 1991 and its second one in 1998. Second generation reforms meant to strengthen the banking sector in India and to make it globally competitive. Government of India accepted most of the major recommendations of the Narasimham Committee and many of its recommendations were implemented by the Reserve Bank of India.

The Narasimham Committee (I&II) made several recommendations to improve the productivity, efficiency and profitability of the banking and financial systems. The Narsimham Committee suggested that there should be functional autonomy, flexibility in operations and loosening of banking regulations. The committee envisaged major changes in banking sector by way of reduction in cash reserve ratio and statutory liquidity ratio requirements, deregulation of interest on deposits and advances. Its other recommendations were recapitalization of weak public sector banks, merger of banks to prune their numbers, adequate financial infrastructure in terms of supervision, audit, and sophisticated technology for improving customer service, operational efficiency and voluntary retirement scheme.

The Narsimham Committee also proposed introduction of prudential norms such as income recognition, asset classification, provisioning and capital adequacy norms, and transparency in operations and improvement in productivity, efficiency and profitability of banking operations. The committee recommended entry of foreign banks, new private sector banks and local area banks. The committee further advocated the introduction of universal banking, setting up of special recovery tribunals, introduction of banking ombudsman scheme etc.

In September 1990, RBI set up another committee on customer services, under the chairmanship of Sri. M.N. Goiporia, Chairman, State Bank of India to examine the problems related to customer services in India and suggested measures to improve the situation. The Rangarajan Committee on Computerization in banks and Saraf Committee (1994) on technology issues made several recommendations and RBI implemented many of the recommendations.

The liberalization and economic reforms in 1991 unleashed stiffer competition among banks. The financial sector became intensely competitive with several new competitors like new private banks, foreign banks, non-banking financial companies, merchant bankers, mutual fund and insurance companies. The new generation private sector banks rapidly expanded their operations by opening branches mainly in the metros and cities by providing state of the art services and facilities to their customers. New generation and foreign banks operate in a highly sophisticated environment by offering up-to-date products and services with enhanced personnel efficiency attracting many new clients.

The banks in India have flourished not just in numbers but also in their services, products and client base. The commercial banks in India offer a variety of new products and services like ATM, investment advisory services, tax advisory services, demat of shares, consultancy services, cash management services, debit cards, credit cards, international cards, smart cards, telephone banking, electronic fund transfer, net banking, personal, educational, housing, vehicle and consumer durable loan etc. On account of the knowledge of the financial market of India the financial companies are attracted towards them to act as trustees to take the responsibility of the security for the financial instrument like a debenture. The Indian Government presently hires the commercial banks for various purposes like tax collection and refunds, payment of pensions etc.

5.2 Virtual Banking

The growing universalisation and internationalization of banking operations, driven by a combination of factors, such as, the continuing deregulation, heightened competition and technological advancements, have altered the face of banks from one of mere intermediator to one of provider of quick, efficient and consumer friendly services.

The practice of banking was subjected to a significant transformation in the nineties. Banks and other financial entities in India entered the world of information technology and computer networking only very recently. The introduction of liberalization measures in the banking sector and the emergence of new private sector and foreign banks equipped with latest technology, led to increased competition in the banking sector. With the introduction of the new technology in banking sector, customers are fast moving away from the traditional branch-banking system to the convenience and comfort of remote electronic banking services or virtual banking. With E-Banking, the brick and mortar structure of the traditional banking gets converted into a click and portal model thereby giving real shape and form to the concept of virtual banking. In virtual banking, brick and mortar structure or physical bank branch is no more required for rendering banking services.

Virtual banking denotes the rendering of banking and related services through extensive use of information technology without direct physical recourse to the bank by the customer. The services are delivered to the customers by relying solely on information technology. The origin of virtual banking in the developed countries can be traced back to the seventies when the Automated Teller Machines (ATMs) got installed for the first time. The most important types of virtual banking services are Automated Teller Machines (ATMs), Shared ATM networks, Debit card, Credit card, Smart cards, Stored-value cards, Mobile banking, Phone-banking, Internet banking, Electronic Funds Transfer (EFT), Electronic Clearing Services (ECS) etc.

5.3 Core Banking

Core Banking Solutions (CBS) is new jargon frequently used in banking circles. The advancement in technology, especially internet and information technology has led to new ways of doing business in banking. These technologies have cut down time, working simultaneously on different issues and increasing efficiency. Core banking is one of the recent developments in the field of banking and is very effective in bringing a radical change in the filed of banking.

Core Banking is a general term used to describe the services provided by a group of networked bank branches. Core banking is a facility provided by banks in which a person, having an account in one branch, can operate his account in another branch. Bank customers may access their funds and other simple transactions from any of the member branch offices. This has become possible because each account holder is given a specialized computerized and unique account number.

In simple terms core banking is a type of banking in which a person, who opens a bank account in a particular branch of a bank, will be a customer of the bank, rather than being a customer of a particular branch. Therefore, the customer can transact anywhere at any time. Core Banking is defined as "the business conducted by a banking institution with its retail and small business customers". Many banks treat the retail customers as their core banking customers, and have a separate line of business to manage small businesses. Larger businesses are managed via the Corporate Banking division of the institution.

The platform where communication technology and information technology are merged to suit core needs of banking is known as Core Banking Solutions. Here computer software is developed to perform core operations of banking like recording of transactions, passbook maintenance, and interest calculations on loans and deposits, customer records, balance of payments and withdrawal are done. This software is installed at different branches of bank and then interconnected by means of communication lines like telephone, satellite, internet etc. It allows the user (customers) to operate accounts from any branch if it has installed core banking solutions. This new platform has changed the way banks are working.

Core banking services include mainly deposit of money, loans, mortgages and payments. Core banking services include the following services:

1. Make enquiries about the account balance.
2. To obtain cash payment out of his account by tendering a cheque.
3. To deposit cheque in to the account.
4. To deposit cash in to the account.
5. To deposit cash and cheque in to the account of some other person who has account in a CBS branches.
6. To transfer funds from the account of the customer to the account of some other person who maintains an account in the CBS branches.
7. To get statement of account.
8. To obtain Demand Drafts or Bankers Cheques from any branch on CBS.

The coverage of the number of branches providing Core Banking Solutions (CBS) has been increasing steadily over the years. Many banks have covered 100 percent of their business of the bank under CBS. The total number of branches of public sector banks which have implemented CBS increased from 35,464 as on March 31, 2008 to 44,304 as on March 31, 2009.

5.4 Automated Teller Machine (ATM)

Automated teller machine (ATM) is a modern device introduced by the banks to enable the customers to have access to money day in and day out without visiting the bank branches in person. An automated teller machine (ATM) is a computerized telecommunications device that provides the customers of a bank with access to financial transactions in a public space without the need for a human cashier. Through this facility, customers of the bank are not restricted to remain a customer of the branch where the account is maintained.

The first ATM was developed and installed in USA in 1939. Thereafter, the history of ATMs paused for over 25 years until the first electronic ATM which was installed in UK. ATMs first came to wide use in UK only in 1973. Till the beginning of 90s, banks in India had only one delivery channel which was the branch. By the end of 1990, private and public sector banks in India came up with their own ATM networks under the initiative of the Indian Banks Association in Mumbai. The Bank of India was the first nationalized bank to render ATM facilities to its customers in Mumbai. ATM has become the most popular and convenient delivery channel used by people in the rural and in urban areas. ATM is the most accepted and popular user-friendly technology for even the rural customers.

Using an ATM, the customers can access their bank accounts in order to make cash withdrawals, check their account balance and other information and services. In ATMs, the customer is identified by inserting a plastic ATM card/Debit card with a magnetic stripe that contains unique card number and some security information. Authentication is provided by the customer entering a Personal Identification Number (PIN).

ATMs have now become popular in India and they enable the customers to withdraw their money 24 hours a day, 7 days a week and round the year. ATM is known as 'Any Time Money' or 'Any Where Money', because it allows the customers to withdraw money from the bank from any of its ATMs round the clock even on Sundays and National holidays. ATM is also called as 'automated banking machine' or 'money machine' or 'cash point'.

The services of ATMs are placed not only near or inside the premises of banks (on premises), but also in convenient locations (off premises) such as shopping centres/malls, airports, grocery stores, petrol/gas stations, restaurants, or any place where large number of people may gather. These represent two types of ATM installations viz. 'on-site ATMs' and 'off-site ATMs'. In some banks on-site ATMs are typically more advanced and multi-function machines that complement an actual bank branch's capabilities and are more expensive. Depending upon the volume of business, banks install required number of ATMs for their customers at convenient places in the same town.

Most ATMs are connected to interbank network, enabling people to withdraw and deposit money from machines not belonging to the bank where they have their account or in the country where their accounts are held (enabling cash withdrawals in local currency).

Banks generally supply ATM card to their customers free of cost. However, banks now levy a nominal annual usage fee on customers for using Automated Teller Machines. In some cases, these fees are charged solely from users who are not customers of the bank where the ATM is installed, in other cases, they apply to all users. Certain banks also impose fees on customers for using ATMs under the shared network scheme. Some banks however restricted the number of withdrawals in other banks ATMs, above which they are chargeable. Now most banks direct their customers to withdraw cash up to a certain limit through ATM, rather than through the bank counter. The upper limit of withdrawal per day from ATM varies from bank to bank.

ATMs are beneficial to the banks in many respects. ATM can help the banks to reduce the number of people thronging at bank's counters. With regard to cash vending, ATMs are faster and accurate than manual operations. Use of ATMs brings down the load of voucher preparation, and its upkeep by the banks. ATM also enables the banks to redeploy their existing staff for other services and thereby making savings in salary. ATMs can also provide a number of value added services to their customers. ATM has brought about a great change for the better in the quality of banking service. It will also enable the banks to widen their customer base by obliterating the geographical constraints. ATM helps banks to retain their customer loyalty because convenience acts as tremendous psychological boost to customers at all time.

Indian banks are now planning to install Rural Automated Teller Machines (Rural ATMs), in order to encourage its use in a rural environment by rural customers. Rural ATMs can be operated without owning an ATM card. Small farmers can now use their Kissan Credit Cards to access ATMs. The deployment of rural ATMs will help in lowering the cost of transaction and carrying out banking transactions from non-branch locations. The under mentioned services can be carried out through rural ATMs. Viz. cash deposits and withdrawals, payment of utility bills, payment of insurance premium, collection of loan EMIs, account information, mini statement, balance inquiry, product information etc. At the end of the year 2006, City Bank launched biometric ATMs with multi language voice navigation features for the use of City Bank Pragati customers, which is its no-frills savings account facility for micro- finance customers.

From April 1, 2009, entire ATM network is available to customers from any bank for transactions without any fee at all, irrespective of the banks in which they have their accounts. With effect from April 2009, cash withdrawals from Automated Teller Machines of the banks are made free of charge. This will in turn increase usage of ATMS in India. Further, banks have been advised to reimburse to the customers, the amount wrongfully debited on account of failed ATM transactions within a maximum period of 12 days, from the date of receipt of customer complaint and effective from July 17, 2009, for any failure to re-credit the customer's account within the stipulated period, the bank shall pay compensation of ₹ 100 per day, to the aggrieved customer.

In total 74,505 ATMs were installed by commercial banks by the end of March 2011. Nationalized banks accounted for the largest share of installed ATMs (24,836) followed by SBI Group (24,651), the new private sector banks (23,651), old private sector banks (4126) and foreign banks (1,367). Of all the ATMs installed in the country at end-March 2011, new private sector banks had the largest share of 55 percent in off-site ATMs, while nationalized banks had the largest share of 63 percent in onsite ATMs. While, the ATMs installed by new private sector banks (204 percent) and foreign banks (431 percent) were more than 2 times of their respective branches, the ATM branch ratio was much lower for SBI Group (138 percent) followed by old private sector banks (86 percent) and nationalized banks (56 percent).

5.5 Debit Card

Debit card is a prepaid card with some stored value, which optimizes conveniences for the customers. A customer possessing a Debit Card need not carry cash. It is like carrying cash from the bank account, without the inconvenience or risk of carrying liquid cash. In other words, Debit card allows 'anywhere any time accesses' to the customers with their savings or current account.

The word debit means 'subtract' and, as the name suggests, debit card will subtract money from the card holder's account each time when it is used. Debit card is also known as 'bank card'. It is card made of plastic which provides an alternative payment method to cash when making purchases. Functionally, it can be called an electronic cheque, as the funds are withdrawn directly from either the bank account or from the remaining balance on the card.

The use of debit cards has become widespread in many countries and has overtaken the cheque and in some instances cash transactions by volume. Consumers and merchant establishments all over the world changed their attitude from one of transacting in hard cash and to one in its place of electronic cash. Like credit cards, debit cards are used widely for internet purchases, and unlike credit cards the funds are transferred from the bearer's bank account instead of having the bearer to pay back on a later date. Debit cards allow for instant withdrawal of cash, acting as the ATM card for withdrawing cash and as a cheque guarantee card. Merchants can also offer 'cash back'/'cash out' facilities to customers where a customer can withdraw cash along with their purchase.

To receive a Debit Card an individual needs only to open an account, either current or savings with the issuing bank. However, debit card facility does not extent to cash credit and other loan accounts. The banks should issue cards to its customers only having good financial standing, with satisfactory records of accomplishment for at least six months. A Personal Identification Number (PIN) will be issued to the customers for using the Debit Card. Debit card can be used at all outlets that accept such cards for payment viz. department stores, petrol pumps, jewellery shops, restaurants, textile shops, hospitals, airlines, railways etc.

A debit card has several of the advantages of a credit card in terms of convenience and reducing the use of cash and cheques. Furthermore, customers can use it as an ATM card as well, to withdraw cash from the accounts and carry out other ATM transactions. Also, customers do not have to worry about making regular payments or paying interest rates and penalties if forgot to make payments. In that sense, a debit card is more convenient than a credit card. However, debit card holders are not permitted to obtain credit facility by using a debit card.

5.5.1 Working of Debit Card: Debit Card works in the same way as a credit card for purchase transactions at merchant outlets. The only difference is that the transaction amount is directly debited to the bank account of the customer. After finishing the purchases, submit the card to the business outlet. Then cardholder has to enter the personal identification number on the shop's PIN pad. The merchant on an Electronic Data Capture Terminal for authorization will swipe the Debit card. When the card is swiped through the electronic terminal, it dials the acquiring bank system, which validates the PIN and finds out from the issuing bank whether to accept or not the transaction. The terminal will seek an approval regarding the availability of balance in the account from the card-issuing bank. After a successful authorization or an approval from the bank, the terminal will print a charge slip.

The transaction generated by the point of sale will be conclusive and binding on the cardholder. The customers account will subsequently be debited for the transacted amount. The bank has the authority to debit the designated account of the cardholder for all withdrawals effected by the card holder by using the card. Like Credit Cards, signature verification is a must for all Debit Card transactions. Hence, presence of the cardholder in person with the card at the time of every purchase is unavoidable and cardholder has to check the amount on the charge slip and sign on the same. The business establishment will return a copy of the charge slip and the card after verifying the holder's signature.

Presence of the cardholder in person along with the card at the time of every purchase is very essential therefore debit card cannot be used for mail order, telephone order. Debit Card seldom permits a customer to spend over and above his cash balance in the bank.

5.6 The Point of Sale

The Point of Sale (POS) terminal is a machine that facilitates merchant transactions through Swipe of a card in an online environment. Merchant business establishments operate point of sale in their premises in order to accept plastic cards. The POS terminals facilitate electronic funds transfer. The points of sale devices are connected as backend to interface with the main servers where the immediate authentication of the transaction is made. POS system identifies the cardholder and check whether the customer's account has sufficient funds to cover the purchase. The POS machine has a display screen, keypad and a printer with the facility to transact both online and offline. Any of the available communication medium can be used for networking. The terminals can be integrated with magnetic stripe or smart card interface for authentication of the customer. The customized POS terminals can support both debit and credit cards and can also be made to support different kinds of plastic including magnetic and smart chip based cards to make the merchant transaction possible without making use of cash.

5.7 Credit Card

Credit card is a card entitling its holder to buy goods and services from the business establishments without using money. It authorizes the holder to charge goods or services to his account for which he is billed. Credit card is a cute card made of plastic. Credit card is otherwise called 'plastic money'. Credit card is a convenient medium of exchange. Credit cards are designed to reduce the use of either cash or cheque for transactions. It enables a customer to purchase goods or services within prescribed limits from certain authorized retail and service establishments without making immediate cash payments. The customer thus possessing a credit card need not carry any cash and is empowered to spend wherever and whenever he wants goods or services with his credit card within the limits prescribed by his banks. It reduces the physical movement of cash and enables bankers to transfer money electronically.

Credit cards began to be used in USA as early as 1920's and their use began to increase after 1950. Diners Club introduced their credit card in 1950 and the American Express Company in 1958 and Bank of America in 1959. In India Commercial banks, introduced the credit card facility in the early eighties. In India, the Central Bank of India was the first bank to introduce the credit card known as 'Central Card' in the middle of 1981. Credit card facility became immensely popular among customers in India only by 1990. With the introduction of credit card system, the concept of everywhere and any time banking became a reality. Convenience and easy acceptability of credit cards and technological advancement have paved the way for continuous rise in credit card-based of payments and transactions.

Credit cards are generally issued by banks only to those prompt customers having either savings or current account. The banks should issue cards to its customers only having good financial standing, with satisfactory records of accomplishment. The credit limit or purchasing power is fixed by the bank issuing the card. On the basis of credit limits bank issues different types of credit cards to its customers. The credit limits of card vary from bank to bank. The bank assumes the risk and responsibility of collecting the dues from the customers and they permit cardholders a 'cash advance facility' from its branches. The upper limit of the cash advance facility will be fixed by the bank.

Certain banks issue credit card free of cost to their customers, while some other banks charge a small amount from the customers as annual service charge. Loyalty bonus is also given by banks to their customers for encouraging bulk purchases using credit card by them. Usually the card issuing institution supply a guide or booklet with the card containing detailed terms and conditions, risks on the account when the card is lost or misused and other relevant information with regard to the usage of the card.

The main benefit of credit card to a customer is its convenience. Compared to debit cards, a credit card allows small short-term loans to be quickly made to a customer who need not calculate a balance remaining before every transaction.

5.7.1 Grace Period: Credit card purchases normally become payable after a free credit period, during which no interest or finance charge is imposed. Grace periods vary, but usually range from 20 to 50 days depending on the type of credit card and the issuing bank. Every month the bank sends a statement of all the credit purchases to the credit card holder and the latter has to remit the amount either by cash or cheque. Credit card statement will be dispatched on a particular date in every month free of cost in the mailing address of the cardholder or online. Interest is charged on the unpaid balance after the payment is due. Cardholders may pay the entire amount due and save on the interest that would otherwise be charged. Alternatively, they have the option of paying any amount, as long as it is higher than the minimum amount due, and carrying forward the balance.

5.7.2 Payment of Bill: The monthly bill amount can be remitted to the bank branch either in total or in instalments known as revolving credit facility. Banks usually waive interest charges if the balance is paid in full each month. Usually, if a customer is late paying the balance, finance charges will be calculated and the grace period does not apply. In other words, the bank will charge full interest on the entire outstanding balance from the date of each purchase if the total balance is not paid. If revolving credit facilities are granted by the bank for the payment of the bill amount, the bank charges interest only for the outstanding balance.

5.7.3 Working of Credit Card: The customers can avail the credit card facility only in those establishments, which accepted them. Credit card has a method of identification of users by means of either signature identification or a stamp size photo of the cardholder. After purchase of goods or services, the customer will hand over the card to the supplier/seller who swipes the card in an electronic terminal, which reads the cardholders name, card number etc. On accepting the card by the machine, the supplier records the amount of the transaction in the machine. The imprinter of the machine prints a sales voucher showing the card holder's name, card number, card type, name of the business establishment, transaction ID, invoice number, amount of transaction etc. The holder signs the voucher and the signature is cross checked by the supplier with that of the specimen signature on the card. The business establishments will receive the money from the institution operating the plan either on the same day or the next day.

5.7.4 Parties Involved in Credit Card: Following are the parties involved in credit card operation:

1. **Cardholder:** The holder of a credit card is known as card holder who uses such card to make a purchase. Card holder is the customer of a bank or a financial institution.
2. **Card-issuing Bank:** The bank or financial institution that issues the credit card to the cardholder.
3. **Merchant:** The individual or business accepting credit card payments for products or services sold to the cardholder.
4. **Acquiring Bank:** The bank or financial institution accepting payment for the products or services on behalf of the merchant.
5. **Credit Card Issuing Companies**

There are many different credit cards companies in existence today. Hundreds of credit cards are offered every day to potential new customers from all the different companies. They are marketed credit card through various banks and other financial institutions. Banks and financial institutions, which issue credit cards, tie up with the international organizations like Master, Visa, Maestro, Cirrus, American Express, Diners, Discover etc. that issue credit cards. Card issuing banks give a service charge to the card issuing international organizations. One of the leading credit cards is VISA which is known all over the world. Visas have grown into a largest and most widely used payment brand in the world. Visa card is issued by Visa International operated through more than 21,000 member financial institutions. There is more than one billion visa branded cards with cardholders in more than 150 countries. Master Card and American Express Credit Cards are also leading and accepted all over the world.

5.7.5 Difference between Credit Card and Debit Card: While credit cards and debit cards may seem similar but they are quite different in the way they work and the services they offer. The most important difference between a Credit card and a Debit card is that while credit card is a 'post paid' card, the latter is a 'pre paid' card. A credit card allows borrowing money when making purchases.

The money borrowed is not directly debited to the card holder's bank account at the time of purchase, instead, bank sends a bill every month for the sum total of purchases whereas in the case of debit card when goods or services are purchased, the amount of the bill is immediately deducted from the customers' account.

5.7.6 Issue of Credit Cards: In India all major commercial banks and leading non banking financial institutions both Indian and foreign in origin are issuing credit cards viz. HDFC, ICICI Bank, Axis Bank, SBI, Bank of Baroda, Canara Bank, Kotak Mahindra, Vijaya Bank, Punjab National Bank, Union Bank of India, Indian Overseas Bank, HSBC, RBS, Macquarie Bank, Deutsche Bank, Barclays Bank etc.

5.7.7 Guidelines for Issuing of Credit Card: Banks in India can undertake credit card business either departmentally or through a subsidiary company set up for the purpose. Prior approval of the Reserve Bank is not necessary for banks desirous of undertaking credit card business either independently or in tie-up arrangement with other card issuing banks. Banks can do so with the approval of their Board of Directors. However, only banks with net worth of ₹ 100 crore and above should undertake credit card business. Banks desirous of setting up separate subsidiaries for undertaking credit card business would, however, require prior approval of the Reserve Bank.

The Reserve Bank of India has initiated several steps to encourage the use of credit card transactions in an efficient and a safe manner. In order to ensure best international practices in credit card operations, the Reserve Bank of India in October 26, 2004, constituted a Working Group under the chairmanship of Shri R. Gandhi to study the 'Regulatory Mechanism for Cards'.

Based on the recommendations of this Working Group and the feedback received from card issuing banks, non banking finance companies and the public, guidelines on credit card operations of banks were issued by the RBI in November 2005. The most important features of the guidelines are given below:

1. Each bank/NBFC must have a well documented policy and a Fair Practices Code for credit card operations. The Banking Codes and Standards of India (BCSBI) has released a "Code of Bank's Commitment to Customers" (Code) in July 2006 as also a Guidance Note in December 2006, which have been adopted by most of the banks with the approval of their Boards.
2. Before issuing a credit card, the issuing institution must independently assess the applicant based on self-declaration or credit information supplied by the customer. Based on the information received the institution must assess the credit risk and fix the credit limit for the credit card holder.
3. The card issuing institution would be solely responsible for the fulfilment of

the conditions of Know Your Customer (KYC) requirements.

4. Add-on cards (i.e. those that are subsidiary to the principal card) will be issued to the principal cardholder, only on the condition that the liability will be that of the principal cardholder.
5. While applying for the credit card, the terms and conditions such as credit limit, cash withdrawal limit, joining fees for primary card holder and for add-on card holder, annual membership fees for primary and add-on card holder, billing statements-periodicity and mode of sending, Cash advance fee, Service charges levied for certain transactions, interest free (grace) period, prevailing rate of interest should be communicated to the card holder in clear and simple language. They should also furnish to the card holder charges in case of default, methods of computation of overdue, overdue interest charges, finance charges for both revolving credit and cash advances, renewal and termination procedures. Contact particulars of 24 hour call centres of card issuer, particulars of officers to be contacted, grievance redressal, Procedure to be followed in case of loss, theft and misuse of card- mode of intimation to card issuer and all other valid information which the customer requires to operate the card effectively should be furnished to them.
6. Card issuer should ensure that there is no delay in dispatching monthly bills. Sufficient time for payment of bill i.e. at least 10 days should be given to the customer before the interest starts getting charged. The issuer should charge interest only after the last date mentioned for payment.
7. The card issuer should not levy any charge that was not clearly indicated to the credit card holder at the time of issue of the card. They must obtain the prior consent of the cardholder for levying fresh charges. They need not obtain such consent of the cardholder in case of service taxes, which are levied by the Government or any other statutory authority from time to time.
8. Changes in charges other than interest rate should be effected in to only with prior notice of at least one month.
9. If a customer has any dispute on any bill, the card issuer should provide explanation and, if necessary, documentary evidence to the customer within a maximum period of sixty days in a spirit of amicable redressal of grievances.
10. To avoid frequent complaints of delayed billing, the credit card issuing institution should consider providing bills and statements of accounts on-line.
11. Credit card issuer should be extremely careful in the appointment of service providers while outsourcing, ensuring that they seldom compromise on quality of customer service.
12. Card issuer will be responsible for all acts of omission and commission of their direct sales marketing and recovery agents with regard to customer's

rights like their personal privacy, preservation of customer records, maintaining confidentiality of customer information and fair practices in debt collection.

13. Card issuing institution should not reveal the information regarding customers received at the time of opening the account or issuing the credit card to any other person or organization without obtaining their specific consent.
14. Before reporting the default position of a card holder to CIBIL or any other credit information company authorized by the Reserve Bank, the credit card issuer must serve advance notice to the card holder of its intention of reporting. While reporting they should stick on to a procedure duly approved by their boards.
15. In the matter of recovery of dues, card issuer should ensure that they and their agents adhere to the instructions on Fair Practice Code for lenders as recommended by the Reserve Bank as also the IBAs Code for collection of dues and repossession of security.
16. Card issuer or their agents should not resort to threats or harassment of any kind, either verbal or physical, against any person in their debt collection efforts.
17. Card issuer should constitute grievance redressal machinery for credit cards and give wide publicity to it through electronic and print media. The name and contact number of designated grievance redressal officer of the bank/ NBFC should be mentioned on the credit card bills. The designated officer should ensure that genuine grievances of credit card subscribers are redressed promptly without involving delay.
18. If the customer does not get a satisfactory reply for their complaints from the card issuer within a maximum period of thirty days from the date of his lodging the complaint, he will have the option to approach the office of the concerned Banking Ombudsman for redressal of his grievance.
19. Card issuers should quote Annualized Percentage Rates (APR) on card products (separately for retail purchase and cash advance, if they are different). The method of calculation of APR should be given with one or two examples for better comprehension. The APR charged and the annual fee should be shown with equal prominence. The late payment charges including the method of calculation of such charges and the number of days should be prominently indicated. The manner in which the outstanding unpaid amount will be included for calculation of interest should also be specifically shown with prominence in all monthly statements. Even when the minimum amount indicated to keep the card valid has been paid, it should be indicated boldly that the interest will be charged on the amount due after the due date of

payment.

20. The card issuing institution should obtain prior consent of the card holder for upgrading credit cards, enhancing credit limits and for any other changes in the terms and conditions.

5.8 Smart Card

A smart card is a plastic card, with an embedded microchip that can be loaded with data, used for telephone calling, electronic cash payments, and other applications, and then periodically refreshed for additional use. Smart cards look like a plastic card and contain a small microprocessor or computer chip on the face of the card. A smart card is a mini-computer without the display screen and keyboard. Smart cards contain a microchip with an integrated circuit capable of processing and storing thousands of bytes of electronic data.

Smart card is actually a debit card loaded with a sum of money. A smart card contains the properties of a credit card and debit card. It can be used for both small payments and prepaid telephone card. Such a card facilitates small purchases with exact change viz. a cup of coffee or tea, a newspaper, bus, railway fare etc. Information in the microchip can instantaneously verify the cardholder's identity and any privileges to which the cardholder may be entitled. Information such as withdrawals, sales, and bills can be processed immediately and if/when necessary, those records can be transmitted to a central computer for file updating.

The merchant establishments need a special device to transfer the money from the smart card. The moment the card is inserted into the machine, money gets transferred from the smart card to the merchant. There is no need of waiting for an authorization or signing a receipt to settle with the bank as in debit card/credit card.

The major boom in smart card use was started in the 1990s, with the introduction of the smart-card-based SIM used in GSM mobile phone equipment in Europe. With the ubiquity of mobile phones in Europe, smart cards have become very common. Progress is being made towards developing standards for newer payment instruments like SMART cards in India. A pilot project on SMART Card technology in India titled 'SMART Rupees System (SMARS)' was initiated by the Indian Institute of Technology, Mumbai to find out the viability and use of SMART cards as retail payment instruments within the country. It came out with a set of recommendations on SMART cards standards. With a view to examine these recommendations and to determine the standards for the Indian banking industry, the Reserve Bank in September 1999 set up a 'Working Group' to study and recommend 'SMART card based Payment System

Standards'. The Working Group submitted its Report to the Reserve Bank in January 2000 and they were accepted by the Reserve Bank.

5.9 Internet Banking

Internet banking is a new delivery channel for banks in India. Economic integration within and across countries, deregulation, advances in telecommunications, and the growth of the internet and wireless communication technologies are changing dramatically the structure and content of financial services. Banks have traditionally been in the forefront in making use of technology to update their products, services and efficiency. They began using electronic and telecommunication networks for delivering a wide range of value added products and services for a long time. With the popularity of personal computers, easy and better access to internet and world wide web (www) it is being used increasingly by banks as a channel for receiving instructions and delivering their products and services to their customers. Now, in most of the branches it is seen that computers are being used for recording banking transactions.

Internet banking is nothing more than traditional banking services delivered through an electronic communication device viz. the internet. Net banking is defined as "the application of the internet that allows customers to dial into bank networks or their websites, using their own telephones and computers, and to get a host of banking services directly on their home or office PCs". Internet banking is a product of e-commerce in the field of banking and financial services. Net banking is also known as 'electronic banking' or 'on-line banking'. Banking activity carried on through computers and other electronic means of communication is called 'electronic banking' or 'e-banking'.

Net banking offers armchair convenience to the customers and access the account information from anywhere in the world, at any time of the day or night. It means that, as long as the customer has a computer, a modem, a phone line and an internet account, the customer need not worry about bank holidays or taking time to go to the bank, or standing in long queues for a simple transaction. Net banking demolishes the traditional geographical barriers and thus reaches out to customers across the world. It is an efficient and cost effective delivery mechanism for banking services. Through internet banking, banks are in a position to offer extensive range of products and services of varied content and sophistication.

5.9.1 Development of Internet Banking in India: The financial reforms that were initiated in the early 1990s and the globalization and liberalization measures brought in a completely new operating environment to the banks in India. The process started when Reserve Bank of India (RBI) set up a high-level committee formed under the chairmanship of Dr. C. Rangarajan, then Governor of RBI, to draw up a phased plan for computerization and mechanization in the banking industry over a five-year time frame of 1985–1989. The committee made an in depth study of the problems and after a thorough study spanning more than a year, the recommendations came at the end of 1984. The focus by this time was on customer service and two models of branch automation were developed and implemented.

The second Rangarajan committee constituted in 1988 drew up a detailed perspective plan for computerization of banks and for extension of automation to other areas such as funds transfer, e-mail, BANKNET, SWIFT, ATMs, internet banking, etc. The Government of India enacted the Information Technology Act, 2000 (generally known as IT Act, 2000), with effect from 17 October 2000 to provide legal recognition to electronic transactions and other means of electronic commerce.

5.9.2 Working Group to Study Issues Relating to Internet Banking: In order to promote safety and reliability of e-banking activities, the Reserve Bank of India constituted a Working Group to examine the different issues relating to internet banking. The Group was headed by Shri S.R. Mittal, Chief General Manager in Charge of the Department of Information Technology, RBI and comprised experts from the fields of banking regulation and supervision, commercial banking, law and technology. The Group had focused on three major areas of internet banking such as 'technology and security issues', 'legal issues' and 'regulatory and supervisory issues'.

Working Group examined different aspects of internet banking viz. legal, regulatory, security, technology, supervisory and operational. RBI had accepted the recommendations of the 'Working Group', and accordingly issued guidelines on internet banking in India. The Reserve Bank of India (RBI) has created a comprehensive document which lays down security-related guidelines, types of risks associated with internet banking, technology standards, legal issues involved, regulatory and supervisory concerns and strategies for banks to follow in order to offer internet banking.. Any bank that wants to offer internet banking must follow these guidelines and adhere to them as a legal necessity.

5.9.3 Facilities Available from Internet Banking: Internet banking in India is currently at a nascent stage. While there are scores of companies specializing in developing i-banking software, security software and website designing and maintenance. A number of banks have set up banking portals, which enable their customers to access facilities like eliciting information, querying on their accounts etc. Banks now introduce newer and larger products and services to their customers. ICICI bank is the first one to have introduced internet banking for a limited range of services such as access to account information, correspondence and, recently, funds transfer between its branches. ICICI is also getting into e-trading, thus offering a broader range of integrated services to the customer.

All commercial banks in India both private and public are now providing online banking account. However, many scheduled commercial banks in India still remain in the initial stage of internet banking operations. ICICI Bank, HDFC Bank, Axis Bank. SBI, Citibank, Federal Bank, IDBI Bank etc. are pioneers in the field on internet banking. The following services are made available and accessible through internet banking:

1. Request for opening of accounts.
2. Pay bills.
3. Know account balances.
4. Forward loan applications.
5. View and print copies of cheque book and deposits.
6. Transfer funds.
7. Direction for stop-payment of cheques.
8. Reorder cheque books and statements.
9. Receive banking industry news.
10. Transfer of funds within the same bank.
11. Instructions for opening of Letters of Credit and Bank Guarantees etc.

Banks, which provide Internet banking services, enter into agreements with their customers and set out the terms and conditions of the services. These include information on the access through user-id and secret password, minimum balance and charges, authorization to the bank for carrying out transactions performed through the service, liability of the user and the bank, disclosure of personal information for statistical analysis and credit scoring, non-transferability of the facility, notices and termination, etc.

5.9.4 Benefits of Net Banking: Internet banking, as a medium of delivery of banking services and as a strategic tool for business development has gained wide acceptance internationally and is fast catching up in India with more and more banks entering the fray. India can be said to be on the threshold of a major banking revolution with the unleashing of net banking.

1. Internet banking is a cost effective delivery channel to banks: Of the various delivery channels available, internet banking is the most cost effective delivery channel to banks. The cost-conscious banks in the country have actively considered and accepted use of the internet as a medium for providing services. Costs of banking services through the internet are only a

fraction of costs incurred in conventional methods. Rough estimates assume cost of teller at ₹ 1 per transaction, ATM transaction costs at 45 paisa, phone banking at 35 paisa, debit cards at 20 paisa and internet banking at 10 paisa per transaction.

2. Internet banking enables greater reach to customers by removing the traditional geographical barriers as it could reach out to customers of different countries and legal jurisdiction.
3. Internet banking is more efficient and reliable and thus it creates greater customer loyalty.
4. Internet banking enables banks to introduce new products and services quickly and successfully.
5. Customers are given access to information easily across any location.
6. It poses a strategic risk of loss of business to those banks who do not respond in time to this new technology.

5.10 Mobile Banking Services

Mobile banking is relatively a new form of electronic banking product and it is gaining ready acceptance from the customers. With the rapid growth in the number of mobile phone subscribers in India, banks have been exploring the feasibility of using mobile phones as an alternative channel of delivery of banking services.

Mobile banking is a service that allows the customers to do banking transactions through mobile phone without making a call by using the SMS facility. Mobile banking is defined as "a provision and availment of banking and financial services with the help of mobile telecommunication devices. The scope of offered services may include facilities to conduct bank and stock market transactions, to administer accounts and to access customized information".

Mobile banking has become one of the customer-friendly facilities, which can have far-reaching implications for the financial sector as a whole. It is cost effective and assists the rural customers in reaching the customer and banker instantly. It takes the bank to the customer's cell phone. In this system, a customer can access his/her account details on a mobile phone via Short Messaging Service (SMS) or the Mobile Internet technology through which select data is entered into the mobile device. Mobile banking is otherwise called as 'M Banking' or 'SMS Banking'.

On-line banking is now moving into the mobile mode, giving everybody with a mobile phone access to real time banking services, irrespective of their location. The potential for mobile banking is endless with the scope for introduction of new services and products on a large scale. With mobile banking, the concept of 'anywhere anytime banking' is at the fingertips of the customer literally. Mobile banking addresses the fundamental limitation of Internet Banking, as it reduces the customer requirement to just a mobile phone. The main reason that Mobile Banking scores over Internet Banking is that it need not access to a computer terminal to access their bank accounts.

In India banks with the facility of mobile banking services at present provide only limited number services to their customers. Some banks have started offering information based services like balance enquiry, stop payment instruction of cheques, transactions enquiry, and location of the nearest ATM/branch etc. Acceptance of transfer of funds instruction for credit to beneficiaries of same/or another bank in favour of pre-registered beneficiaries have also commenced in a few banks.

Presently, 65 banks have been approved for conduct of mobile banking out of which 47 banks have commenced offering these services. Transactions in mobile banking have been showing an uptrend. During February 2012, more than 2.8 million transactions for close to ₹ 1961.23 million were transacted. A little over 12.23 million bank customers have so far registered for mobile banking services.

5.10.1 RBI Guidelines for Mobile Banking: In order to ensure a level playing field and considering that the technology is relatively new, Reserve Bank has brought out a set of operating guidelines for adoption of Mobile Banking by banks.

1. Only banks which are licensed and supervised in India and have a physical presence in India will be permitted to offer mobile banking services.
2. Banks wishing to provide mobile banking services shall seek prior one time approval of the Reserve Bank of India, by furnishing full details of the proposal.
3. The services shall be restricted only to customers of banks and holders of debit or credit cards issued as per the extant Reserve Bank of India guidelines.
4. Only Indian Rupee based domestic services shall be provided.
5. Use of mobile banking services for cross border transfers is strictly prohibited.
6. Banks can use the services of Business Correspondent appointed in compliance with RBI guidelines, for extending this facility to their customers.
7. The guidelines issued by Reserve Bank on "Know Your Customer (KYC)", "Anti Money Laundering (AML)" and Combating the Financing of Terrorism (CFT) from time to time would be applicable to mobile based banking services also.
8. Only banks who have implemented core banking solutions would be

permitted to provide mobile banking services.

9. Banks shall put in place a system of document based registration with mandatory physical presence of their customers, before commencing mobile banking service.
10. Technology used for mobile banking must be secure and should ensure confidentiality, integrity and authenticity.
11. Banks offering mobile banking service must ensure that customers having mobile phones of any network operator is in a position to avail of the service. Restriction, if any, to the customers of particular mobile operator(s) is permissible only during the initial stages of offering the service, up to a maximum period of six months subject to review.
12. Approval of the Board of Directors (Local Board in case of foreign banks) for the product as also the related security policies must be obtained before launching the scheme.
13. Banks are required to make mandatory disclosures of risks, responsibilities and liabilities of the customers on their websites and/or through printed material.
14. The existing mechanism for handling customer complaints and grievances may be used for mobile banking transactions as well.
15. Customer's complaints and grievances arising out of mobile banking facility would be covered under the Banking Ombudsman Scheme, 2006.

5.10.2 Services Available from Mobile Banking: Customers can carry out a number of conventional transactions by remaining in their office, or home, in fact from anywhere with a mobile phone. The following services are made available and accessible through mobile phone:

1. Details of account balance.
2. Request for a cheque book.
3. Stop payment of a cheque.
4. Inquire about a cheque status.
5. Mobile alerts such as Debits and Credits to the account.
6. Get fixed deposit details.
7. Paying of utility bills and giving details for Electricity, Mobile phone and Telephone services.
8. Statement of last few transactions (get details of last 3 transactions).
9. Password change for mobile banking.
10. Suspension of mobile banking services.
11. Transfer of funds from one account to another etc.

5.10.3 Benefits of Mobile Banking: Mobile banking is certainly beneficial to the customers. It enables the customers to carry on certain routine business transactions without personally visiting the branch or ATM counters of a bank. Customers can make use of this facility from anywhere in India. When a customer comes to a branch for a routine transaction viz. checking a balance or for getting a cheque book, he has to wait for a while in the bank. Mobile banking is doubly beneficial to the customers i.e. by way of savings in both time and money. Another advantage of mobile banking to the customers is that they can avail reliable information quickly and in easy manner.

Mobile banking is advantageous to the banks also. Mobile banking reduces the number of visits of customers to bank branches and thereby reduces their physical presence. When there are no queues or no waiting of customers in the bank it brings down considerably the cost of banking services for the customer over a period of time. The bank also benefits because mobile banking helps them to increase their productivity. It also enables banks to deliver speedy and quality services, which are ultimately beneficial to the banks by way of increasing and retaining their customer base. Thus, Mobile banking dissuades customers from visiting branches personally and they can instead 'hook' on to the convenience of armchair banking.

5.10.4 Procedure for Availing Mobile Banking Services: To avail mobile banking services the customer must:

1. Have an account in a bank that offers mobile banking service.
2. Be a subscriber to any of the cellular service providers who have tie up with the selected bank.
3. Apply for mobile banking through an appropriate application form with the bank.

Bank Customers can adopt any of the following methods of registration for mobile banking services.

A. Registration through ATM: A customer can register for mobile banking service through ATM by inserting the ATM card and by selecting the 'Other Services Menu', and thus select mobile banking registration option, by entering their mobile number and in return receive a receipt as acknowledgement of registration.

B. Direct Submission of Application Form: Application form for mobile banking services is available in most of the bank branches and their ATM counters. A customer has to fill up and submit the application form for mobile banking at any of the bank branches or drop in at an ATM.

C. Opt for On-line Registration: A customer can also register for mobile banking service online. Click on to the website and select the mobile banking registration option by submitting the details of the customer.

The mobile will be activated by the bank for mobile banking after 48 hours from the time of registration through any of the above options. Bankers charge a nominal fee per quarter as service charge for providing mobile services. Most of the banks offer Mobile Banking service absolutely FREE, although SMS charges for outgoing messages would be charged as usual by the mobile phone service provider.

HDFC Bank is the first bank in India, which introduced mobile banking service in Mumbai. ICICI Bank, Axis Bank and SBI followed the lead given by the HDFC Bank. A good number of commercial banks in our country have already started offering the mobile phone technology to extend banking facilities, which has become a convenient, economical and efficient way of transacting the banking business.

5.11 Telephone Banking

Telephone banking is another innovative form of electronic banking service introduced by banks to their customers. Telephone banking is a service provided by a bank which allows its customers to perform banking transactions over the telephone. A customer can access his/her bank account through the telephone at anytime or at any place throughout the country with the same Tele banking PIN they desire. Customers can carry on a number of transactions from their own home or office; in fact, from anywhere they have access to a phone and in a very convenient and comfortable manner. It is definitely one of the most convenient modes of transacting banking business.

A bank which operates mostly or exclusively by telephone is known as phone banking or Tele banking. Telephone banking is offered by the banks through a technology known as Interactive Voice Response Service (IVRS). Telephone banking generally uses an automated phone answering system with phone keypad response or voice recognition capability. Basically this system, accept only 'tone' dialled input from callers telephone instruments and provides suitable voice response messages and information to the caller. Tele-banking service is available 24 hours a day and 7 days of a week. In other words, it provides "round the clock banking. The potential of Tele-banking is limitless and it is often projected as a future potential growth area.

5.11.1 Facilities Available from Telephone Banking Services: With the obvious exception of cash withdrawals and deposits, telephone banking offers virtually a number of services relating to the customers account. Banks provide the following facilities under telephone banking service.

1. Account balance information.
2. List of latest transactions.
3. Information on deposit interest rates.

4. Electronic bill payment.
5. Request cheque book.
6. Stop payment of a cheque.
7. Funds transfer between customers account.
8. Information on locations of branches and ATM.
9. Receiving of following forms by fax or e-mail:

- *i c*onnect Registration and declaration form.
- Debit Card application form.
- Travel Currency Card Application form.
- Registration form for LIC Premium payment through ATM.
- BSNL bill payment registration form.

Usually, customers can also speak to a live representative located in a call centre or a branch, although this feature is not guaranteed to be offered always. In addition to the self-service transactions listed earlier, telephone banking representatives are usually trained to do what was traditionally available only at the branch such as loan applications, investment purchases and redemptions, cheque book orders, debit card replacements, change of address, etc.

Now many banks in India provide this facility to their customers to carry on their transactions with the banks. Phone Banking service is currently available at Ahmedabad, Bangalore, Chandigarh, Chennai, Coimbatore, Gurgaon, Hyderabad, Indore, Jaipur, Kochi, Kolkata, Lucknow, Ludhiana, Mumbai, Mysore, Nagpur, Noida, New Delhi, Patna, Pune, Raipur, Trivandrum, Vadodara and Visakhapatnam.

5.12 Payment of Utility Bills

Over the last few years, the banking sector witnessed a proliferation in the use of IT based delivery channels and internet banking activity. Some of the new facilities provided are funds transfer options, utility bill payments and other regular periodical payment facilities and integration with e-commerce transactions such as bookings for rail and air tickets. With electronic banking, customers now in a position to deal with banks and get many of their requests serviced through desktop computers, telephones and Automated Teller Machines of banks.

Payment of utility bill and other regular periodical payment facilities is a novel technique adopted by banks since 1994 to attract new customers and to retain their existing customers. Under this system, the bank facilitates the speedy and instant payment of utility bills of customers of electricity, water, telephone, mobile phone, insurance premium, tuition and hostel fees of wards etc. For availing this facility, a customer is required to register with the bank branch or its

ATM for the payment of utility bills and insurance premium.

5.13 Accounts

Banks undertake to purchase and sell shares and debentures of joint stock companies on behalf of its customers. Only members of the stock exchanges can do the function of purchase and sale of securities. The amendment in the stock exchange regulations Act permits the banks to become members in the stock exchange.

Internet banking provides banks with an opportunity to enter the world of e-broking, made possible by the SEBI's approval of internet trading in stocks. Internet banking account, electronically records holdings of dematerialized shares. An e-investment account for equity trading enables trading in shares on the internet. In internet banking payments and share transfers are handled automatically and seamlessly without separate paper work.

In January 1998 Securities and Exchange Board of India initiated Demat Accounts system to regulate and improve stock investing. This is done through Depository Participants (DP) with National Securities Depositories Ltd., (NSDL) as the co-coordinator. The investor opens an account called Demat Accounts with the depository participants. These depositories transact business through electronic media. They get shares in electronic form. Then they send the actual sales to the investor. The banker should strictly follow the customer's instructions, use skill, and care in execution of sale and purchase of order.

When the customer gives an order for purchase of securities, the banker should ensure that sufficient funds are available in the account of the customer. The investor has to pay charges for opening and maintaining of demat account. There are certain advantages and benefits in this system. There is less paper work, no loss of share certificates, and lower transaction costs. It facilitates the banks in enlarging the non-interest income and their overall profitability. A few banks provide the customer the facilities through internet to enquire into his demat account holding details, transaction details and status of instructions given by him. These websites do not allow online transactions for their customers.

5.14 Doorstep Banking

Under traditional banking, a customer needs to visit the bank branch in person for each and every service. Under doorstep banking, there is no need for the customer to visit the branch for getting services or products from the bank. Doorstep banking means banking services and products made available to a customer at his\her place of residence or work. Banks thus become proximity to the customer's place of residence or work. In order to increase the customer base and to improve their income, banks now offer various products and services at the doorstep of their customers.

In order to ensure transparency in respect of the rights and obligations of customers, uniformity in approach and to clearly delineate the risks involved, RBI has laid down general principles and broad parameters to be followed by banks while offering "doorstep" services to their customers. RBI also advises banks to offer 'doorstep' banking services to their customers only with the prior approval of their Board of Directors and in accordance with the guidelines issued by the RBI. They are also advised to review the operation of doorstep banking by its board on a half yearly basis, during the first year of its operation and subsequently on an annual basis.

5.14.1 Services Provided on Doorstep Banking: RBI issued new guidelines on February 21, 2007 in connection with the delivery of door step banking services. As per RBI guidelines banks can offer Doorstep Banking services either through their own employees or by hiring agents. Detailed Guidelines for Doorstep Banking are given below:

1. Banks can offer the banking services like collection of cash and instruments from corporate clients, public sector units and departments of Central and state governments and individual customers at their doorstep. Cash collected from the customer should be acknowledged by issuing a receipt on behalf of the bank. Cash collected from the customer should be credited to the customer's account on the same day or next working day, depending on the time of collection. The customer should be informed of the date of credit by issuing a suitable advice.
2. Delivery of cash services to corporate clients, public sector units and departments of Central and State governments against the receipt of cheque at the branch, and not based on telephonic requests. Individual customers cannot, however, avail of this facility.
3. Delivery of demand drafts for both individual and corporate customers account will be done by debiting the account on the basis of requisition in writing or cheque received and not against cash collected at the doorstep.

For providing doorstep banking services an agreement should be entered into between the customer and the bank. The services can be offered at either the residence or office of the customer, the address of which should be clearly and explicitly mentioned in the agreement. Charges, if any, to be levied on the customer for doorstep services should be incorporated in the policy approved by the Board and should form part of the agreement entered into with the customer. The charges should be prominently indicated on brochures offering doorstep services.

It may be ensured that the agreement entered into with the customer does not entail any legal or financial liability on the bank for failure to offer doorstep services under circumstances beyond its control. The services should be seen as a mere extension of banking services offered at the branch and the liability of the bank should be the same as if the transactions were conducted at the branch. The "Scheme" should not be restricted to any particular client/customer or class of customers. The agreement should not provide any right to the customer to claim the services at his doorstep.

The RBI has, however, cautioned banks about risks arising out of these services and asked them to prescribe cash limits. Banks are advised to take into account the various risks that may arise on account of offering doorstep banking services to customers directly or through agents and take effective steps to manage the same. Banks may specifically consider prescribing cash limits for their agents and customers in this regard.

The agreement with the customer shall clearly specify that the bank will be responsible for the acts of omission and commission of its 'agent'. Banks will have to prepare their own schemes based on the guidelines with the approval of their Director Board. The RBI has also asked banks to appoint grievance redressal machinery for redressing complaints about services rendered by its `agents.' The name and the telephone number of the designated officer should be made available to the customers on the bank's website. If a customer feels that his complaint has not been satisfactorily addressed, he will have the option to approach the Office of the concerned Banking Ombudsman for redressal of his grievance.

5.15 Single Window Service

Single window service in banks is a novel technique adopted by commercial banks to attract and retain the customers. Before the introduction of single window service system, there were separate counters for each service of a bank. The customer, who required more than one banking service at a time, had to approach different counters. The customers used to wait and stand in a queue before each counter when he needs more than one service in a day.

Under single window service system, the banks provide all required banking services through a single counter. These services are cash and cheque deposits, withdrawal of money, issuing of demand drafts, transfer of funds, issue of cheque book etc. Under this scheme, a customer need not approach different counters for these banking services.

Many commercial banks in India have already introduced single window service to their customers. However, most of the banks in India still provide only limited banking services under single window system to their customers. These services mainly pertain to mainly deposit and withdrawal of money, issue of demand draft, MT, electronic funds transfer, issue of cheque book etc. The services provided through single window system are thus inadequate in every respect when compared to those available in foreign banks.

5.16 Clearing and Settlement Systems

Payment and settlement systems play a pivotal role in the development of an economy. Adoption of an efficient, modern and global electronic payment and settlement system is beneficial to everyone viz. the customers, business undertakings, bankers, the government and to the economy as whole. Electronic Payment and settlement systems are cheaper because they have lesser production cost than paper-based instruments. The clearing operation can also be carried out faster in comparison with paper-based transactions. The increased use of electronic payments enhances the efficiency of the payment and settlement system. It helps the process of capital formation and money management.

The evolution of electronic payment system can be traced back to 1950's, with the introduction of ERMA (Electronic Record Method of Accounting) and MICR (Magnetic Ink Character Recognition) based cheque-clearing systems in USA. Thus, these systems are considered as the initial innovations in the field of electronic clearing. Stanford Research Institute and Bank of America developed and introduced ERMA in 1951 for automation and recording of transactions in accounts. Several countries implemented these two systems in different forms and it remains as the backbone for payment systems. Later, many payment systems came into existence.

A Payment System is a mechanism that facilitates transfer of value between a payer and a beneficiary by which the payer discharges the payment obligations to the beneficiary. Payment system enables two-way flow of payments in exchange of goods and services in the economy. Payment systems are used by individuals, banks, companies, governments, etc. to make payments to one another. In other words, any body who has to make a payment to any one else can use one or the other form of payment system to make such a payment.

Payments can be made in India in the form of cash, cheque, demand drafts, credit cards, debit cards and also by means of giving electronic instructions to the banker who will make such a payment on behalf of his customers. Electronic payments can be made in the form of Electronic Funds Transfer (EFT), Electronic Clearing Service (ECS) for small value repetitive payments and through Real Time Gross Settlement (RTGS) System for large value payments. A few banks in India have begun to offer certain banking services through Internet that facilitate transfer of funds electronically.

5.17 Electronic Fund Transfer

Payments can be made between two or more parties by means of electronic instructions without the use of cheques. Retail payment mechanisms available to facilitate such payments are the Electronic Funds Transfer, Electronic Clearing Service, Credit/Debit cards etc. EFT system means a system established by RBI for carrying out inter bank and intra-bank funds transfers within India, through EFT centres connected by a network, and providing for settlement of payment obligations arising out of such funds transfers, between participating banks or institutions. Payment and Settlement Systems Department of Reserve Bank is responsible for implementation, administration and supervision of the EFT System.

Electronic Funds Transfer system (EFT) is one of the important electronic banking services offered by commercial banks to attract and retain their customers. Electronic funds transfer system is an easy and speedy mechanism to facilitate the transfer of funds from one place to another. Compared to all other existing systems of funds transfer, EFT is the most convenient system, which facilitates the instant transfer of funds from one end to the other. Electronic Fund Transfer system enables the customers to transfer money instantly from one bank account to another one of the same or another customer, from one branch or the other of the same bank or a different bank not only within the country but also within anywhere else of the world through electronic message. The objectives of RBI EFT System is to facilitate an efficient, secure, economical, reliable and expeditious system of funds transfer and clearing in the banking sector throughout India, and to relieve the stress on the existing paper based funds transfer and clearing system.

Electronic Funds Transfer (EFT) is a system whereby anyone who wants to make payment to another person, company etc. can approach his bank and make cash payment or give instructions, authorization to transfer funds directly from his own account to the bank account of the beneficiary. A bank customer (i.e. sender) availing of the remittance facilities offered by a sending bank shall submit an EFT Application Form authorizing the sending bank to debit the sender's account and transfer funds to the beneficiary specified in the EFT Application Form. Complete details such as the receiver's name, bank account number, account type (savings or current account), bank name, city, branch name etc should be furnished to the bank at the time of requesting for such transfers so that the amount reaches the beneficiaries' account correctly and faster.

With the introduction of EFT system, the existing systems of funds transfer namely Cheque, Demand Draft (DD), Mail Transfer (MT) and Telegraphic Transfer (TT) and Money Order (MO) have lost their significance. These traditional systems of funds transfer viz. demand drafts, cheques, money order or other means have their own limitations. These transactions can take several days to complete. EFT system offers many advantages to the bankers as well as the customers.

EFT system enables the beneficiary to receive money on the same day or on the next day of money transfer. Because money is transferred instantly, EFT system minimizes the loss of interest as far as the customer is concerned. More over Mail Transfer (MT) and Telegraphic Transfer (TT) systems do not facilitate the transfer of money from one bank branch to another branch of a different bank. EFT eliminates paper cheques and late payments. It also liberates the customer from worry and fear of theft or loss of money during transit.

It is also beneficial to the banks that it helps to reduce their cost of administration by around forty percent. Electronic Fund transfer is a completely paperless transaction mechanism, which accelerates the speed of transfer or exchange of money.

The banks generally charge some processing charges for EFT just as in the case of other services like demand drafts, pay orders, etc. The actual charges depend upon the amount and the banker-customer relationship. However, for the present, the RBI has waived all its charges on EFT that were being recovered from the banks for processing such funds transfer transactions at the clearing houses run by RBI. This has certainly reduced the processing cost for the banks also.

The Electronic Fund Transfer system was introduced on the basis of the recommendations of the 'Saraf Committee' appointed by RBI on 'Technology Issues' in 1994. The scheme has been in operation since February 1996. The scheme was originally intended for small value transactions. The electronic funds transfer was extended during the year 2002, to 15 centres of the country viz. Ahmedabad, Bangalore, Bhopal, Bhubaneshwar, Chandigarh, Chennai, Guwahati, Hyderabad, Jaipur, Kanpur, Kolkata, Mumbai, Nagpur, New Delhi and Thiruvananthapuram. All banks and branches in these locations are mandatory participants. The maximum limit for any single transaction under the EFT, which was ₹ 5.00 lakh, was enhanced during the year to ₹ 2.00 crore. Some banks for security reasons impose limit on the amount per transaction and per day transactions. There are faster and simpler ways to transfer money safely through use of RBI supported electronic funds transfer systems such as NEFT and RTGS.

5.18 National Electronic Funds Transfer (NEFT)

The Reserve Bank of India introduced a payment system called the "RBI National Electronic Funds Transfer System" which is referred as "NEFT. The operationalisation of the NEFT in November 2005 was a major step in the direction of setting up and operating a national level payment system. The NEFT is a secured network, which uses the Structured Financial Messaging Solution (SFMS) messaging format with Public Key Infrastructure (PKI) enabled digital signatures retail electronic payment system having a nation-wide network.

National Electronic Funds Transfer (NEFT) is a nation-wide system that facilitates individuals to electronically transfer funds from any bank branch to any other bank branch in the country. As of January 2012, there is no limit–either minimum or maximum–on the amount of funds that could be transferred using NEFT. However, maximum amount per transaction is limited to ₹ 50,000 for cash-based remittances. However, Reserve Bank of India has instructed banks that they should not use RTGS for amounts below ₹ 2 lakh. For small transactions, RBI has asked banks to offer National Electronic Fund Transfer (NEFT) which provided T+0 and T+1 settlement system (depending on the time a customer gives instruction to the bank for transferring the fund).

Presently, the clearing and settlement for NEFT takes place at RBI in hourly batches–there are eleven settlements from 9 am to 7 pm on weekdays (Monday through Friday) and five settlements from 9 am to 1 pm on Saturdays. Any transaction initiated after a designated settlement time would have to wait till the next designated settlement time.

Contrary to this, in RTGS, transactions are processed continuously throughout the RTGS business hours from 9 am to 4.30 pm on week days and 9 am to 1.30 pm on Saturdays for settlement at the RBI end. If the money cannot be credited for any reason, the beneficiary's bank has to return the money to the remitting bank within 2 hours. Once this amount is received back by the remitting bank, the amount is credited to the remitter's account by the remitting bank branch.

NEFT brings greater efficiency in the movement of funds and reduction in risks relating to the transfer of funds.

Individuals, firms and corporates maintaining accounts with a bank branch can transfer funds using NEFT. Even such individuals, firms or corporates who do not have a bank account can also deposit cash at the branch with instructions to transfer funds using NEFT. Such customers have to furnish full details including complete address, telephone number etc. NEFT, thus, facilitates originators or remitters to initiate funds transfer transactions even without the need for having a bank account.

Individuals, firms and corporates maintaining accounts with a bank branch can receive funds through the NEFT system. It is, therefore, necessary for the beneficiary to have an account with the destination bank branch in the country.

The NEFT system takes advantage of the core banking system in banks. Accordingly, the settlement of funds between originating and receiving banks takes places centrally at Mumbai, whereas the branches participating in NEFT can be located anywhere in the country.

For being part of the NEFT funds transfer network a bank branch has to be NEFT-enabled. As at end of April 2012, 127 banks were participating in NEFT. Steps are being taken to further widen the coverage both in terms of banks and branches.

5.18.1 Service Charges for NEFT: Reserve Bank of India waived the processing or service charges for member banks till March 31, 2010. As of January 2012, service charges to be levied by the member banks from their customers have also been rationalized by Reserve Bank of India. They are as under:

1. Inward transactions at destination bank branches (for credit to beneficiary accounts) Free, no charges to be levied from beneficiaries.
2. Outward transactions at originating bank branches (charges for the remitter):

- For transactions up to ₹ 1 lakh–charges not exceeding ₹ 5 + service tax.
- For transactions above ₹ 1 lakh and up to ₹ 2 lakhs–charges not exceeding ₹ 15 + service tax.
- for transactions above ₹ 2 lakhs–charges not exceeding ₹ 25 + service tax.

5.19 Special Electronic Fund Transfer (SEFT)

To provide for transfer of funds electronically across a large number of bank branches in the country as a forerunner to the nation-wide funds transfer system (NEFT), the Special Electronic Fund Transfer (SEFT) System was introduced from April 1, 2003. SEFT is a system with the settlement being centralized at Mumbai and providing for same day funds settlement with multiple settlements (three settlement cycles per day) during the day. This scheme facilitated the introduction of the T+2-settlement system by the capital markets. While inward SEFT is mandatory for all banks outward, SEFT is optional.

In order to ensure that the benefits of electronic modes of funds transfer are available across almost all the locations of the country and to provide for transfer of messages relating to EFT in a safe and secure manner, it is proposed to commence a National EFT using the facilities available under the SFMS over the INFINET. This would result in EFT being available from any branch of a bank, which has connectivity to INFINET with the settlement-taking place in the books of account of the RBI at a single location.

In November 2005, banks were advised to develop appropriate delivery channels of electronic payment services using the payment systems developed by the Reserve Bank such as RTGS, ECS, Electronic Fund Transfer (EFT) and National Electronic Fund Transfer (NEFT) with no further delay. Banks, which fulfil the eligibility criteria for participation in RTGS, were invited to participate in the NEFT. RBI made it mandatory to migrate all the SEFT banks to NEFT by 15 December 2005. With the implementation of NEFT, the SEFT system was discontinued from February 2006.

5.20 Real Time Gross Settlement

RTGS system is the fastest possible inter bank money transfer facility available through secure banking channels in India. Real Time Gross Settlement (RTGS) system is a funds transfer mechanism where transfer of money takes place from one bank to another on a "real time" and on "gross" basis. Real Time Gross Settlement (RTGS) is large values funds transfer system whereby financial intermediaries can settle inter bank transfers for their own account as well as for their customers. There is no definition of low value' or 'large value' for the purpose of RTGS transaction.

Real Time Gross Settlement system facilitates transfer of funds from accounts in one bank to another on a "real time" and on "gross settlement" basis. Settlement in 'real time' means payment transaction is not subjected to any waiting period. The transactions are settled as soon as they are processed. 'Gross settlement' means the transaction is settled on one to one basis without bunching with any other transaction. The system effects final settlement of inter bank funds transfers on a continuous, transaction- by-transaction basis throughout the processing day.

Under normal circumstances the beneficiary branches are expected to receive the funds in real time as soon as funds are transferred by the remitting bank. The beneficiary bank has to credit the beneficiary's account within two hours of receiving the funds transfer message. If it is unable to credit the amount of the remittance to the account of the beneficiary for any reason, the beneficiary's bank has to return the money to the remitting bank within 2 hours. Once this amount is received back by the remitting bank, the amount is credited to the Remitter's account by the remitting bank branch.

Customers can access the RTGS facility between 9 am to 4:30 pm on week days and 9 am to 1.30 pm on Saturday. The remitting bank receives a message from the Reserve Bank that money has been credited to the receiving bank. Based on this the remitting bank can advise the remitting customer that money has been delivered to the receiving bank. Considering that money transfer takes place in the books of the Reserve Bank of India, the payment is taken as final and irrevocable. The minimum amount to be remitted through RTGS is ₹ 2 lakh. There is no upper ceiling for RTGS transactions.

5.20.1 Features of RTGS: The RTGS System has several unique features. It is a single, all-India system, with the settlement being effected in Mumbai. The payments are settled through a transaction-by-transaction method. The settlement of funds is final and irrevocable. The settlement is done in near real time (maximum of 2 to 4 hours), the funds settled can be further used immediately. RTGS enables business enterprises and companies to transfer outstanding funds between banks in real time, thus allowing them to settle payments instantaneously and manage their working capital better. It is also expected to save significant amounts of money in interest payments on floating funds lying in banks.

5.20.2 Service Charge for RTGS: Banks may levy charges for such funds transfers at their discretion and based on the customer-bank relationship. Fees for RTGS vary from bank to bank. As on January-end, 2012, the following charges exist:

1. Inward transactions-free, no charge to be levied.
2. Outward transactions:

- ₹ 2 lakh to ₹ 5 lakh-not exceeding ₹ 30 per transaction.
- ₹ 5 lakh and above-not exceeding ₹ 55 per transaction.

A customer who desires to use this facility should approach his bank to find out whether his own bank branch as well as the beneficiary's bank branch is enabled to transfer funds through RTGS system. The remitting customer has to furnish the following information to a bank for effecting an RTGS remittance:

1. Amount to be remitted.
2. Account number which is to be debited.
3. Name of the beneficiary bank.
4. Name of the beneficiary customer.
5. Account number of the beneficiary customer.
6. Sender to receiver information, if any.
7. The IFSC Number of the receiving branch.

The RTGS system is maintained and operated by the RBI and provides a means of efficient and faster funds transfer among banks facilitating their financial operations. Real Time Gross Settlement (RTGS) system has been in operation in banks since March 2004. All the bank branches in India are not RTGS enabled. As on end-April, 2012, 127 banks across the country were RTGS enabled with outward remittances standing at ₹ 49,945 billion.

5.21 Difference between NEFT and RTGS

The key difference between RTGS and NEFT is that RTGS is on gross settlement basis, while NEFT is on net settlement basis. RTGS facilitates real-time transfer, NEFT involves specific number of settlement cycles a day. Electronic Fund Transfer (EFT) and National Electronic Funds Transfer (NEFT) are electronic fund transfer modes that operate on a Deferred Net Settlement (DNS) basis which settles transactions in batches.

In DNS, the settlement takes place at a particular point of time. All transactions are held up till that time. Any transaction initiated after a designated settlement time would have to wait till the next designated settlement time. Contrary to this, in RTGS, transactions are processed continuously throughout the RTGS business hours.

NEFT payment settlement takes place 11 times a day (between 9 am to 7 pm) and 5 times on Saturdays (9 am to 1 pm). RTGS settlement takes place between 9.00 am to 4.30 pm on week days and from 9.00 am to 1.30 pm on Saturdays. Thus, if a customer has given instruction to its bank to transfer money through NEFT to another bank in the morning hours, money would be transferred the same day, but if the instruction is given later during the day, money would be transferred next day. Thus, NEFT is a bit delayed process and it usually takes 24 to 72 hrs. for the funds transfer to take place. The minimum transaction value for RTGS is ₹ 2,00,000, whereas there is no minimum value for NEFT.

5.22 Electronic Clearing Services

Indian Banks are competing with one another to offer new products and services to their customers. Banking service and products in India witnessed transformation on a large scale in the last few years. Technology has played a significant role in facilitating the transformation in the banking sector. Electronic Clearing Services (ECS) is one of the new electronic banking services.

Electronic Clearing Service (ECS) is a non-paper based movement of funds, which is encouraged by the Reserve Bank of India on a wide scale. Electronic Clearing Service (ECS) is a retail payment system that can be used to make bulk payments of a similar nature especially where each individual payment is of a repetitive nature and of relatively smaller amount. This facility is meant for companies and government departments to make receive large volumes of payments rather than for funds transfers by individuals.

In November 2005, banks were advised to develop appropriate delivery channels of electronic payment services using the payment systems developed by the Reserve Bank such as RTGS, ECS, EFT and NEFT with no further delay. Emphasis on widespread usage of Electronic Clearing Services (ECS) is being prescribed by the Reserve Bank of India to encourage non-paper based funds movement. The prime thrust areas forming part of this vital activity include the extension of ECS to more centres, inclusion of more customers under the ambit of the scheme and provision of a centralized facility for making payments.

As at the end of September, 2011 the ECS facility is available in 91 centres across India operated by RBI at places where it manages the clearing houses and by SBI and its associates and other public sector banks in other centres. Settlement cycle has been reduced to T+1 from earlier T+3 across the country. To widen the geographical coverage of ECS beyond the existing ECS centres and to have a centralized processing capability, the National Electronic Clearing Service (NECS) was operationalised with effect from September 29, 2008. The NECS is a nationwide system leveraging on core banking solutions (CBS) of member banks. As at the end of April, 2011 as many as 116 banks with 50,647 branches participated in NECS.

The ECS is further divided into two types ECS (Credit) to make bulk payments to individuals/vendors and ECS (Debit) to receive bulk utility payments from individuals.

1. Electronic Credit Clearing Service.
2. Electronic Debit Clearing Service.

5.22.1 Electronic Credit Clearing: RBI introduced the Electronic Credit Clearing Services in April 1995. At the time of introduction, the facility was available only at National Clearing Centre Mumbai and Chennai and later it was extended to New Delhi and Kolkata. However, at present this facility is available across the country at 58 centres. All banks and branches in these locations are mandatory participants.

Electronic Credit Clearing Service is a reliable device used for bulk and repetitive payments such as salary, pension, dividend, commission, IPO refunds, interest etc. ECS facility is largely utilized by the public and private limited companies and Government departments which make bulk and recurring payments. Electronic Credit Clearing Services brings down administration cost and ensures more profitability and productivity to the bank.

Under ECS (Credit) an entity or a company would make payments from its bank account to a number of recipients by direct credit to their bank accounts. For instance, companies make use of ECS (Credit) to make periodic dividend/interest payments to their investors. Similarly, employers like banks, government departments, etc make monthly salary payments to their employees through ECS (Credit).Payments of repetitive nature to be made to vendors can also be made through this mode.

Organizations, which desire to make bulk payments frequently to a large number of beneficiaries, can avail the ECS facility by registering for it with their bank. The bank will forward a copy of the registration form to RBI after allotting a register number. For this purpose, the company or entity making the payment has to have the bank account details of the individual beneficiaries. Institutions availing this facility have to prepare the credit instructions on the magnetic media and submit the same to RBI, through their bankers. Bank would present the payment data for clearing through its local service branch. Clearing house debits its account and credit the account of the banks where the beneficiaries of the transactions maintain their accounts. RBI processes the data arrived at inter-bank settlement and provides bank and branch wise reports containing the details of payments to facilitate fast payment to the beneficiaries. The maximum limit for ECS credit clearing facility is limited to ₹ 5,00,000 and below. It is an electronic bulk transfer, using the values in T+3-process cycle.

5.22.2 Electronic Debit Clearing: Electronic Debit Clearing service was introduced by RBI to facilitate the payment of credit-pull transactions such as payment of utility bills, insurance premium and repayment of loan instalments. ECS (Debit) is mostly used by utility companies like telephone companies, electricity companies etc. to receive the bill payments directly from the bank account of their customers. Instead of making electricity bill payment through cash or by means of cheque, a consumer (individuals as well as companies) can opt to make bill payments directly into the account of the electricity provider/company/board from his own bank account.

Under this scheme, on receipt of the bill from the utility or service providing company the customer can approach his banker and authorize the bank branch to debit his account for the amount of the bill and transfer the amount to the bank account of the utility company. For this purpose, the consumer has to give an application to the utility company [provided the company has opted for the ECS (Debit) scheme], providing details of bank account from which the monthly/bi-monthly bill amount can be directly deducted. Such details have to be authenticated by the bank of the customer who opts for making payments through this mode. Once this option is given, the utility company would advise the consumer's bank to debit the bill amount to his account on the due date of the bill and transfer the amount to the company's own account. This is done by crediting the account of the sponsor bank which again is generally the bank with whom the company receiving the payments maintains the account with. The actual bill would be sent to the consumer as usual at his address as before.

In this scheme, the branch has to prepare a floppy file through a table top MICR Reader of all such transfer advices and this floppy is received by the service branch, which would consolidate it for onward submission to the clearing house. The RBI would debit the individual bank and credit the sponsor bank of the utility company. The system facilitates electronic transfer of bulk amounts using T+3-process cycle.

Electronic Debit clearing facility was initially introduced by the RBI at Chennai in August 1994 and at Mumbai in March 1996 and later was extended to New Delhi and Kolkata. At present, this facility is available at 43 centres across the country and all banks and branches in these locations are mandatory participants. In terms of the guidelines issued on October 17, 2005, banks were advised to provide details to the customers in their Pass book/Account Statement regarding the credits affected through ECS.

5.23 MICR Cheque Clearing Facility

Magnetic Ink Character Recognition (MICR) technology is used for automatic listing and sorting of cheques and arriving at a settlement position of the member banks. Magnetic Ink Character Recognition is a character recognition system that uses special ink and characters.

Before the introduction of MICR technology cheques were cleared manually. MICR cheques were introduced with a view to automate the labour intensive business of clearing cheques and to facilitate, strengthen and speed up the payment and settlement system in the economy. MICR system is beneficial as it minimizes chances of error, clearing of cheques becomes easy and transfer of funds becomes faster in order to facilitate operations.

Banks, which intent to avail the automated cheque clearing facility, would issue MICR cheques to their customers. In MICR technology the information is printed on the instrument with a special type of ink which is made up of magnetic material. MICR instruments are made of special quality paper and have a number of specifications, which the MICR equipment can read. The code line at the bottom of MICR cheques contains a lot of information, which are in the code line and are printed in magnetic ink enabling the machine to read it instantly. On insertion of the instrument in the machine, the printed information is read by the machine.

Following are the pieces of information in the MICR cheques:

1. First Six numbers indicate the serial number of the cheque followed by a delimiter. The alpha numeric prefix to the serial number usually used by banks should be printed outside the code line is close proximity, just above the read band in normal ink.
2. Next Three numbers each indicate city code.
3. Next Three numbers indicate bank code.

4. Next three numbers indicate branch code.
5. Account type code viz. savings or current account.

The conversion or transaction period from a non-MICR based cheque system to MICR based clearing usually takes several years because member banks continue to issue the available stock of non-MICR cheques. In order to speed up the MICR based clearing facility all over India RBI advised banks to issue MICR cheques irrespective of whether cheque clearing centres use MICR cheque format or not.

MICR based clearing system was initially introduced in USA in 1959. Different countries have implemented this system in various forms and it remains the main mode of payment systems in many of those countries. Even though, a lot of other, which are highly advanced systems, come into existence, MICR based payment system continues to be a prime payment option.

The first phases of mechanized cheque clearing using Magnetic Ink Character Recognition technology has been completed in June 1986 with the introduction of high-speed reader sorter system for processing local as well as inter city MICR cheques at the clearing house managed by Reserve Bank of India. MICR cheque clearing facility was introduced by RBI initially in four Metropolitan cities namely Mumbai (1986), Chennai, New Delhi (1987) and Kolkata (1989).

Currently, 1064 clearing houses are operational in the country. Of these, at 66 centres the clearing and settlement process has been mechanized by the introduction of 'Magnetic Ink Character Recognition (MICR)' based sorter machines. More than eighty percent of the total cheque clearing volume and value in the country are accounted for by these centres. To further bring in efficiency and automating the settlement obligation Magnetic Media Based Clearing System (MMBCS) is being implemented at centres with more than 15 banks, where currently the process is being carried out manually.

5.24 Cheque Truncation System

The Reserve Bank of India has made several reforms for a safe and efficient electronic mode of payment, along with improved efficiency in the paper based mode of payments. The latest electronic payment product introduced by the RBI is the Cheque Truncation System In order to foster faster cheque processing the Reserve Bank has implemented Cheque Truncation system in India on a test basis in the National Capital Region in February 1, 2008 with the participation of 10 banks.

At present all the banks are participating in the system. Amendments to the Negotiable Instruments Act and the Informational Technology Act have been made to facilitate the smooth functioning of the new technology.

The Working Group appointed by RBI under the Chairmanship of Dr. R. B. Barman on "Cheque Truncation and e-cheques" recommended Cheque Truncation System (CTS) at the presenting bank. Cheque Truncation is a system of cheque clearing and settlement between banks based on electronic data/images or both without physical exchange of instrument. Under CTS, paper instruments do not travel beyond the presenting bank.

The system would entail the physical cheques being truncated within the presenting bank to derive maximum efficiency. It is up to banks to take a decision on the point of truncating the cheque–at the branch or service branch or gateway level. Electronic images would be used for payment processing. Grey Scale technology for image capture would be used for imaging.

The main objective of the Cheque Truncation System is to improve the efficiency and substantially reduce the cheque processing time in the system. The traditional clearing system requiring the physical presentation of cheques in the clearing house for payment and settlement, inevitably entails consequential inefficiencies in terms of clearing time and infrastructure required.

The main advantage of cheque truncation is that it obviates the physical presentation of the cheque to the clearing house, instead, the electronic image of the cheque would be sent to the clearing house. The CTS would enable the realization of cheques on the same day, and provide a more cost-effective mode of settlement than manual and MICR clearing. Smaller banks, which may find it unviable to set up the infrastructure, could utilize the services of service bureaus set up for this purpose by a few larger banks.

Customers also enjoy the benefit of encashing their cheques faster. The bank customers would get their cheques realized faster as T+0 local clearing and T+1 inter-city clearing are possible in Cheque Truncation System.

Moreover, with CTS, banks also have the additional advantage of getting reduced their reconciliation problems and incidents of clearing frauds. In order to ensure that banks gear up with the desired infrastructure well in time, detailed guidelines were issued to banks regarding the hardware communication requirements.

The preservation period of paper instruments would be one year and that of the electronic images would be eight years. Settlement will be generated based on the current structure of the MICR fields. A Centralized Agency per clearing location would act as an image warehouse for the banks. Minimum entry norms recommended for Warehouse Agency are technical competency, efficiency orientation and size of resources.

Short Answer Type Questions

1. What is RTGS?
2. What is MICR technology?
3. What is SEFT?
4. What is electronic clearing service?
5. What is core banking?
6. What is the difference between NEFT and RTGS?
7. What is credit card?
8. What is NEFT?
9. What is meant by innovative banking?
10. What is mobile banking?
11. What is door step banking?
12. What is telephone banking?
13. What is debit card?
14. What is virtual banking?
15. What is demat account?
16. What is cheque truncation system?
17. What is internet banking?
18. What is smart card?
19. What is the difference between debit card and credit card?
20. What is ATM?
21. What is payment of utility bill?

Essay Type Questions

1. What are the benefits of mobile banking?
2. What is telephone banking? What are the services provided through telephone banking?
3. Write a note on clearing and settlement system.
4. What is door step banking? What are the services rendered on door step banking?
5. What is ATM? Discuss its advantages to the customers and the bank.
6. Discuss the working of RTGS.
7. What are the advantages of debit and credit card?
8. Discuss briefly the electronic funds transfer facility.
9. Explain working of RBI EFT system.
10. Explain the electronic debit and credit clearing service.
11. Explain briefly the innovations in banking services.
12. Distinguish between MICR cheque clearing and cheque truncation system.
13. Explain national electronic funds transfer system.

14. What is mobile banking? What are the facilities available from mobile banking?
15. What is internet banking? What are the advantages of internet banking?

6

Development Finance Institutions (DFIs)

6.1 Introduction

The concept of Development Finance Institutions (DFIs) is not very much old. The concept of Development Financial Institutions in India arises only after the Second World War and after the depression in 1930s. After the World War chronic poverty was the main issue in many underdeveloped economies especially in Asia, Africa and Latin American countries. For the reconstruction of the economy and the rapid growth of industries these countries established special institutions for supplying capital, knowledge and entrepreneurship. This concept has also been widened all over the world and resulted in setting up of large number of banks around the world.

At the time of Independence in 1947, India had a fairly well-developed banking system. The adoption of bank dominated financial development strategy was aimed at meeting the sectoral credit needs, particularly of agriculture and industry. The commercial banking network was expanded to cater to the requirements of general banking and for meeting the short-term working capital requirements of industry and agriculture. Specialized Development Financial Institutions (DFIs) with majority ownership of the Reserve Bank were set up to meet the long-term financing requirements of industry and agriculture. The first development bank was incorporated immediately after independence in 1948 under the Industrial Finance Corporation Act as a statutory corporation to pioneer institutional credit to medium and large-scale industries. Then after at regular intervals the government started new and different development financial institutions to attain the different objectives.

6.2 Meaning and Definition

Development Financial Institution (DFI) is an institutional mechanism, which functions as an active agent for promoting a balanced and viable process for economic development. Types, functions and ownership of DFIs vary from country to country according to the socioeconomic setup. The variations are so large that it is difficult to define Development Financial Institutions. However, J.T. Dock Houk in his book "Financing and Problems of Development Banking" defines Development Financial Institutions as "an institution which undertakes to perform banking functions as well as development functions".

Banking functions include providing medium and long-term capital to economic development projects, investment in equity of borrowers, guaranteeing of loans, underwriting of issue of debentures and shares and financial contract both within and outside the country. But the development functions included overcoming shortage of viable projects, development of business skills, fostering capital market etc.

William Diamond considers development bank as "a promotional agency which promotes, encourages and stimulates entrepreneurial environment through entrepreneurial efforts to foster entrepreneurial and development spirit among the dormant and fledgling entrepreneurs".

Development banks differ from commercial banks in the sense that they do not mobilize savings from people and invest their own resources in a productive manner. These banks provide all the development services so as to accelerate the growth of the country. Thus development banks are those financial institutions which provide term finance, promote entrepreneurship, enhance organizational effectiveness and upgrade knowledge. They provide either loans or equity capital or both as also advisory, promotional and entrepreneurial services.

6.3 Objectives of Development Financial Institutions

The main objective of Development Financial Institutions (DFIs) is to serve as an agent of development in various sectors of economy namely industry, agriculture and international trade. The primary tasks of Development Financial Institutions are to accelerate the growth of the Indian economy and to provide support to rapid industrialization, particularly in the private sector and backward regions so as to create additional employment opportunities as well as increased production. Besides, development of entrepreneurial skills, development of backward areas, rural development, financing projects which are of great importance to the economy and financing small scale industries are the basic objectives of establishing DFIs. The financial institutions in India were set up under the strong control of both Central and State Governments, and the Government utilized these institutions for the achievements in planning and development of the nation as a whole.

6.4 Development Banking in India

Development banking in India is almost old as our independence. Today there are more than sixty development financial institutions in the country. Industrial Finance Corporation of India (IFCI) is the first Development Financial Institution established in India immediately after the independence. The Industrial

Investment Bank of India is one of oldest banks in India. IDBI is the most prominent Development Financial Institution in India. The national level financial institutions can be classified under six major heads according to their economic importance. They are:

1. National level Development Banks.
2. Specialized Financial Institutions.
3. Investment Institutions.
4. Specialized Public Guarantee Institutions.
5. State level Institutions.
6. Other Financial Institutions.

6.4.1 National Level Development Banks: National level Development Banks consist of five development banks which are given below:

1. Industrial Finance Corporation of India (IFCI).
2. Industrial Development Bank of India (IDBI).
3. Industrial Credit and Investment Corporation of India Ltd. (ICICI).
4. Small Industries Development Bank of India (SIDBI).
5. Industrial Reconstruction Bank of India (IRBI), presently known as Industrial Investment Bank of India.
6. National Bank for Agriculture and Rural Development (NABARD).
7. Export-Import (EXIM) Bank of India.
8. National Housing Bank (NHB).

A. Industrial Finance Corporation of India (IFCI): The Industrial Finance Corporation of India (IFCI) was incorporated on July 1, 1948 by the Government of India as an institution to provide financial assistance to industrial units engaged in manufacturing and other specified industrial activities. IFCI is the first Development Financial Institution in the country to provide impetus to industrial development through medium and long-term loans. IFCI played a pioneering role in the economic development of India and made significant contribution to the modernization of Indian industries. The main object of IFCI is to make credit more readily available to the medium and large sized industries in the country. It provides credit to industrial units in the private, public and co-operative sector.

(a) Origin of IFCI: At the time of Independence in 1947, Indian capital market scenario was relatively underdeveloped. Although there was significant demand for new capital, there was a dearth of providers. Besides, merchant bankers and underwriting firms were almost non-existent in India. At the time of independence commercial banks in India were not equipped to provide long-term industrial finance in any significant manner. It is against this backdrop the Government of India decided to establish IFCI under the Industrial Finance

Corporation of India Act of 1948.

IFCI is the first Development Financial Institution (DFI) in the country to cater to the medium and long-term financial requirements of the industrial units. Initially industries in the public sector and in the co-operative sector are only eligible for assistance. As per the IFCI Act of 1948, industries established in the private sector are not eligible for financial assistance. With the amendment of the IFCI Act in 1972 industrials in the private sector are also included for financial assistance from IFCI. However, small scale industries are not eligible for assistance from IFCI. The newly-established Development Financial Institution was provided access to low-cost funds through the Central Bank's Statutory Liquidity Ratio. This Statutory Liquidity Ratio enabled the corporate borrowers to take loans and advances at concessional rates.

The policies of Industrial Finance Corporation of India (IFCI) are integrated with the objectives of the Five Year Plans of the country and broad national policies announced by the Government of India from time to time. IFCI extents financial assistance to large and medium-scale industries engaged in the manufacture, preservation, processing of goods or in shipping or in mining or in the generation of electricity or other types of industries which are listed by the government periodically. For the provision of finance, the IFCI Act specifies that the industry eligible for assistance should be registered in India as a limited company. Financial assistance will be provided to medium and large-scale industries in the private, public, joint or co-operative sector.

(b) Management of IFCI: Management of IFCI is vested in the Board of Directors, which include Chairman, Managing Director and 10 Directors. Board of Directors comprises experienced persons from finance, banking, insurance, industry, administration and other professionals. The day to day affairs of IFCI are supervised by its Chairman and Managing Director and a full time Director. The head-office of IFCI is situated in New Delhi.

(c) Industries Eligible for Assistance: The IFCI had made a wide range of contributions in various sectors in Indian economy. Industrial units that have directly benefited from IFCI's disbursals include:

1. Consumer goods industry (textiles, paper and paper products, sugar).
2. Service industries (hotels, hospitals).
3. Basic industries (iron and steel, fertilizers, petroleum refining, basic chemicals, cement).
4. Capital and intermediate goods industries (electronics, synthetic fibers, synthetic plastics, miscellaneous chemicals).
5. Infrastructure (power generation, telecom services, bridges).

(d) Conversion of IFCI into a Company: Till 1993, Industrial Finance Corporation of India (IFCI) continued to be a Development Financial Institution (DFI). During the early 1990s, the Government of India realized that the financial system of the country needs more flexibility. The Government also felt that the Industrial Finance Corporation of India (IFCI) needs to access directly to the capital market for any kinds of funds or other financial issues. It is with this objective that the constitution of Industrial Finance Corporation of India was changed in 1993 from a statutory corporation to a company under the Indian Companies Act of 1956. Subsequently, the name of the institution was also changed to "IFCI Limited" with effect from October 1999.

After becoming a company IFCI went public by issuing equity shares totalling ₹ 250 million including premium, which increased the number of shareholders form 232 to over 1 million and the private holding increased to about 42 percent. IFC's shares are listed on six stock exchanges in India viz. NSE BSE, Delhi, Calcutta, Ahmedabad and Madras. IFCI's total equity as on March 2011 amounted to ₹ 1001.68 crore. The total income of IFCI for the year 2010-11 stood at ₹ 2,486 crore. Since 1948 IFCI has evaluated more than 4,800 projects, with a well diversified sector portfolio of over ₹ 400 billion. IFCI has branches in 16 important locations in the country. IFCI has been rated as world's top 500 global financial companies. IFCI is becoming a financial supermarket by offering a wide range of financial services to corporate clients.

(e) Functions of IFCI: IFCI has been instrumental in translating the Government's development priorities into a reality. IFCI provides noteworthy contributions to the Indian industries by providing a host of advisory services in the areas of project appraisal, risk analysis, credit syndication, corporate restructuring etc. IFCI has also been undertaking export promotion, entrepreneurship development, pollution control measures, energy conservation and generation of both direct and indirect employment. Functions of IFCI can be broadly classified into two broad categories viz. project financing and corporate advisory services:

(f) Project Financing: Project financing of IFCI include the following:

1. Providing medium and long term loans to both existing and new industrial units for modernization, expansion and diversification in Indian rupees and foreign currencies.
2. Underwriting the issue of shares and debentures of medium and large scale industrial units.
3. Subscribing the issue of shares and debentures of medium and large scale industrial units.

(g) Corporate Advisory Services: Corporate advisory services of IFCI include the following activities:

1. Merchant Banking and Portfolio Management Services.
2. Corporate Financial Advisory.
3. Receivables Financing.
4. Mergers and Acquisitions.
5. IPO Management.
6. Loan Syndication.
7. Corporate Project and Advisory Services.
8. Financial Consultancy.
9. Lease financing.
10. Purchase of Standard Assets and NPAs.
11. Takeover of accounts from Banks/Financial Institutions.
12. Industrial Finance.
13. Industry Research.
14. Legal Advisory Services.
15. Infrastructure Advisory Services.

(h) Institutions Promoted by IFCI: Apart from promoting and financing industries and creating capacities, IFCI has played a pivotal role in institution building. Through specialized subsidiaries and associate organizations IFCI has emerged as a major player providing comprehensive financial solutions ranging from merchant banking, insurance broking, venture capital, asset reconstruction and securitization, depository and factoring services to education. IFCI promoted the following type of institutions:

1. **Technical Consultancy Organizations:** IFCI has promoted Technical Consultancy Organizations (TCOs), primarily in less developed States to provide necessary services to the promoters of small-and medium-sized industries in collaboration with other banks and institutions.
2. **Investment Information and Credit Rating Agency of India (ICRA):** Investment Information and Credit Rating Agency of India (ICRA) was established on 16th of January 1991. Industrial Finance Corporation of India (IFCI) is the main promoter (26 percent) of ICRA. Other shareholders are UTI, LIC, GIC, Punjab National Bank, Central Bank of India, Bank of Baroda, UCO Bank, State Bank of India and financial service companies. It is an independent and professional investment information credit rating agency.
3. **Tourism Finance Corporation of India (TFCI):** Tourism Finance Corporation of India (TFCI) has been promoted for the hotel and tourism industry in India.
4. **IFCI Venture Capital Funds Ltd.:** IFCI Venture Capital Funds Ltd. is

established for promoting entrepreneurship by providing institutional support to first generation technocrats and entrepreneurs for setting up their own ventures in the medium scale sector.

5. **IFCI Financial Services:** IFCI Financial Services is incorporated to carry on merchant banking activities of IFCI. Other activities include stock brokerage, investment advisory services, portfolio management services, insurance broking and depository services.
6. **IFCI Factors Ltd.:** IFCI Factors Ltd. has been established for providing domestic and export factoring services.
7. **Institute of Labour Development (ILD):** Institute of Labour Development (ILD) has been promoted for rehabilitation and training of displaced and retrenched labour force.
8. **Rashtriya Gramin Vikas Nidhi (RGVN):** Rashtriya Gramin Vikas Nidhi (RGVN) is established by IFCI for promoting, supporting and developing voluntary agencies engaged in uplifting rural and urban poor in east and northeast India.
9. **Assets Care Enterprises Ltd.:** Assets Care Enterprises Ltd. is an Asset Reconstruction and Securitization Company incorporated for focused management of distressed and non performing assets.
10. **IFCI Infrastructure Development Ltd.:** IFCI Infrastructure Development Ltd. is promoted by IFCI to leverage its expertise in the infrastructure sector.
11. **Institute of Leadership Development:** Institute of Leadership Development aims to develop leadership talent in different spheres of the economy and society.
12. **MPCON Ltd**.: MPCON Ltd is a technical consultancy organization promoted by IFCI in 1979.

IFCI, along with other institutions, has also promoted the following institutions:

- Stock Holding Corporation of India Ltd. (SHCIL).
- Discount and Finance House of India Ltd. (DFHI).
- National Stock Exchange (NSE).
- Over the Counter Exchange of India (OTCEI).
- Securities Trading Corporation of India (STCI).
- LIC Housing Finance Ltd.
- GIC Grih Vitta Ltd.
- Bio-tech Consortium Ltd. (BCL).

IFCI has also set up Chairs in reputed educational/ management institutions and universities. A major contribution of IFCI has been in the early assistance provided by it to some of today's leading Indian entrepreneurs who may not have been able to start their enterprises or expand without the initial support from IFCI.

B. Industrial Development Bank of India (IDBI): The Industrial Development Bank of India (IDBI) is one of the well known public financial institutions in India. IDBI is the apex financial institution in the field of industrial finance. It is the apex financial institution for coordinating the activities of institutions engaged in financing, promoting and developing industries in the country. The main aim of the formation of the IDBI was to provide easy loans and financial support to the industrial sector in order to develop the industrial sector and also the Indian economy.

(a) Origin and History of IDBI: The Industrial Development Bank of India (IDBI) was established on July 1, 1964 under an Act of Parliament as the principal financial institution for industrial development in the country. IDBI was established as a wholly owned subsidiary of the Reserve Bank of India. As a subsidiary of the Reserve Bank of India, in the beginning both RBI and IDBI had common board of directors. However, it was de-linked from the Reserve Bank of India with effect from 16 February 1976. By its delinking, IDBI was made an autonomous corporation fully owned by the Government of India and has its own independent board representing the Government, Commercial Banks and Financial institutions and industries. In March 1982, International Finance Division of IDBI was transferred to the Export-Import Bank of India.

Over the years, (1964-91) IDBI has enlarged its basket of products and services, covering almost the entire spectrum of industrial activities, including manufacturing and services. IDBI provides financial assistance, both in rupee and foreign currencies, for green-field projects as also for expansion, modernization and diversification purposes. IDBI has given special attention to better regional development and innovational and promotional activities. It has conducted surveys of backward regions. It has given special help to backward regions on concessional terms. IDBI is playing a more dynamic role in promoting growth of industries as an innovator in the area of industrial finance. The financial resources are being diverted into socially more desirable channels. Emphasis is being placed on assistance to small and new entrepreneurs and units located in underdeveloped regions in the country.

(b) Management: The IDBI is managed by a Board of Directors. The maximum number of directors in the board is twenty two. At present there are in all eighteen directors in the board of directors. The head-office of IDBI is situated in Mumbai.

(c) Restructuring of IDBI: In the wake of financial sector reforms unveiled by the government since 1992, IDBI evolved and array of fund and fee-based services with a view to providing an integrated solution to meet the entire demand of financial and corporate advisory requirements of its clients. IDBI also provides indirect financial assistance by way of refinancing of loans extended by state level financial institutions and banks by way of rediscounting of bills of exchange arising out of sale of indigenous machinery on deferred payment terms.

Narasimham Committee recommended that IDBI should give up its direct financing functions and concentrate only in promotional and refinancing role. But this recommendation was rejected by the government. Latter RBI constituted a committee under the chairmanship of S.H. Khan to examine the concept of development financing in the changed global challenges. This committee is the first to recommend the concept of universal banking. The committee wanted to the development financial institution to diversify its activity. It recommended to harmonise the role of development financing and banking activities by getting away from the conventional distinction between commercial banking and developmental banking.

In January 1992, IDBI accessed domestic retail debt market for the first time with innovative Deep Discount Bonds. The IDBI Act was amended in October 1994 by giving greater operational flexibility and allowed to access capital market through public issue of equity shares. Public issue is subjected to the condition that the government holding shall be retained at a level not below 51 percent. As per the amendment, IDBI launched its first public issue of equity shares in the month of July 1995. The first issue was for an aggregate amount of ₹ 2,371 crore and thereby the government holding was reduced to 72.14 percent. However, even after further issue the majority of the share was still owned by the government, which is currently 52.3 percent.

(d) Functions of IDBI: IDBI is vested with the responsibility of coordinating the working of institutions engaged in financing, promoting and developing industries. It has evolved an appropriate mechanism for this purpose. IDBI also undertakes/supports wide-ranging promotional activities including entrepreneurship development programmes for new entrepreneurs, provision of consultancy services for small and medium enterprises, upgradation of technology and programmes for economic upliftment of the underprivileged. Various functions or types of assistance provided by IDBI can be classified in to five broad categories.

1. Direct Financial Assistance.
2. Indirect Financial Assistance.
3. Development Assistance.

4. Promotional Activities.
5. Technical Consultancy.

(i) Direct Financial Assistance: IDBI finances all types of industrial concerns covered under the provisions of the IDBI Act. IDBI provides direct financial assistance in the following ways:

1. In the form of term loans for the establishment of new projects as well as for expansion, diversification, modernization and technology upgradation of existing industrial enterprises both in rupees and foreign currencies.
2. Providing financial assistance to certain selected industries for modernizing and renovating their plant, machinery and equipments.
3. Direct subscription of the issues of shares, debentures and bonds.
4. Underwriting the issues of shares, debentures and bonds.
5. Seed capital assistance.
6. Guaranteeing of loans and deferred payment of industrial units.

(ii) Indirect Financial Assistance: IDBI provides indirect financial assistance to the industrial units in the following ways:

1. Refinances term loans given by Co-operative Banks, Regional Rural Bank, Commercial Banks and state level financial institutions such as State Finance Corporations and State Industrial Development Corporations to the small and medium industrial units. IDBI has playing a vital role in extending assistance to the small scale industries through its refinancing scheme.
2. Discounts/rediscounts bills of exchange and promissory notes arising out of sale or purchase of machinery and equipments.
3. Subscribing the shares, debentures and bonds of other financial institutions engaged in providing term loans to the industrial units.
4. Offer financial assistance to leasing and hire purchase companies both in rupees and foreign currencies for the import of capital goods and equipments.
5. Provide financial assistance to selected capital goods industries for the adaptation of imported technology.
6. Provide financial assistance to projects for the development and use of indigenous technology.
7. IDBI also extends financial support to various organizations in conducting studies or surveys which are relevant to industrial development.

(iii) Development Assistance: Industrial Development Bank of India provides development assistance to certain industries which require huge investments. IDBI established a special fund for this purpose called 'Development Assistance Fund'. Development Assistance Fund is created specifically for providing financial assistance to those industries which are not easy to obtain funds from other financial institutions due to its high risk and low rate of returns.

(iv) Promotional Activities: IDBI undertakes a wide range of promotional activities relating to:

1. Developmental programmes for new entrepreneurs.
2. Consultancy services for small and medium enterprises.
3. Extends financial support to various organisations in conducting studies or surveys of relevance to industrial development.
4. Programmes designed for accredited voluntary agencies for the economic upliftment of the underprivileged. These include entrepreneurship development, self-employment and wage employment in the industrial sector for the weaker sections of society through voluntary agencies.
5. Support to Science and Technology Entrepreneurs' Parks, Energy Conservation, Common Quality Testing Centres for small industries.
6. Providing financial as well as non-financial assistance to promote industries in the industrially backward areas of the country.
7. Establishment of Entrepreneurship Development Institutes.
8. Realising that entrepreneurship development is the key to industrial development; IDBI played a prime role in setting up of the Entrepreneurship Development Institute of India for fostering entrepreneurship in the country. It has also established institutes in Maharastra Bihar, Orissa, Madhya Pradesh and Uttar Pradesh.

(v) Technical Consultancy: IDBI in collaboration with other national level Financial Institutions set up a network of Technical Consultancy Organizations (TCOs) covering the entire country. TCOs offer consultancy and advisory services at low cost to new small and medium entrepreneurs. They provide diversified services to entrepreneurs in the form of selection, formulation and appraisal of projects and their implementation and review.

(e) Financial Resources of IDBI: Important financial resources of IDBI are the following:

1. Share Capital.
2. Issue of bonds.
3. Loan from Central Government.
4. Loan from Reserve Bank of India. The IDBI is authorized to take loan from the Reserve Bank of India on its securities for a period of 90 days.
5. Loan in Foreign Currency.
6. Reserve Fund.
7. Other Sources like public deposits, grants etc.

(f) IDBI Bank: In view of the changes in the operating environment, following initiation of reforms since the early nineties, Government of India has decided to transform IDBI into a commercial bank without eschewing its secular development finance obligations. The migration to the new business model of commercial banking, with its gateway to low-cost current, savings bank deposits, would help overcome most of the limitations of the current business model of development finance while simultaneously enabling it to diversify its client/ asset base.

IDBI Bank, with which the parent IDBI was merged, was a vibrant new generation Bank. On July 29, 2004, the Board of Directors of IDBI and IDBI Bank accorded in principle approval to the merger of IDBI Bank with the Industrial Development Bank of India Ltd. to be formed incorporated under the Companies Act of 1956 pursuant to the IDB (Transfer of Undertaking and Repeal) Act, 2003 (53 of 2003), subject to the approval of shareholders and other regulatory and statutory approvals. Subsequently, the Reserve Bank of India issued the requisite notification on September 30, 2004 incorporating IDBI as a 'scheduled bank' under the RBI Act of 1934.

Although IDBI Bank is owned by the Government of India, there is a popular misconception that IDBI bank is a private entity. Subsequently, the Reserve Bank of India categorized, the IDBI Bank under a new sub group as "other public sector bank". As on March 31, 2012, the bank had a network of 973 branches and 1542 ATMs. The Bank's total business, during 2011-12, reached ₹ 3,91,651 crore.

IDBI would continue to provide the extant products and services as part of its development finance role even after its conversion into a banking company. In addition, the new entity would also provide an array of wholesale and retail banking products, designed to suit the specific needs cash flow requirements of corporates and individuals. IDBI's transformation into a commercial bank would provide a gateway to low-cost deposits like current and savings bank deposits. This would have a positive impact on the Bank's overall cost of funds and facilitate lending at more competitive rates to its clients.

(g) Subsidiaries of IDBI: Following are the subsidiary companies promoted by IDBI.

(i) Small Industries Development Bank of India: Small Industries Development Bank of India (SIDBI) was established in April 1990 as a wholly owned subsidiary of IDBI to cater the demands of small scale industries. As per the amendment of the IDBI Act in September 2000, IDBI divested 51 percent of its shareholding in SIDBI to various commercial banks and financial institutions in the first phase. Subsequently IDBI divested a total of 79.3 percent of its holding in SIDBI.

(ii) IDBI Capital Market Services Ltd.: IDBI Capital Market Services Ltd. was established by IDBI in December 1993 as a wholly owned subsidiary. IDBI Capital Market Services Ltd. was established with the object of providing various financial services viz. corporate advisory services, equity broking, depository services, pension fund management, debt management services etc. IDBI Capital Ltd. is currently a leading primary dealer in the country. IDBI Capital Market Services Ltd. has launched its trading portal on July 2005.

(iii) IDBI Home Finance Limited: The IDBI Home Finance Limited is also a subsidiary of the Industrial Development Bank of India. In September 2003, IDBI diversified its business domain further by acquiring the entire shareholding of Tata Finance Limited in Tata Home finance Ltd., signalling IDBI's foray into the retail finance sector. The fully-owned housing finance subsidiary has since been renamed 'IDBI Home finance Limited'. It is used for the purpose of providing long term loans and other financial benefits to various companies of the industrial sector.

(iv) IDBI INTECH Limited: IDBI INTECH Limited was established for system support and implementation, applications, server hosting, system integration and other related services. IDBI INTECH Limited is the sole consultant for IDBI Bank Ltd. and forms the IT backbone for the bank.

(v) IDBI Gilts Limited: IDBI Gilts Limited was set up as a wholly owned subsidiary of IDBI Bank Ltd. to undertake Primary Dealer business. IDBI Gilts Limited was set up to transfer Primary Dealer business from IDBI Capital Market Services Ltd.

The company with its headquarters was incorporated in December 2006 with an authorized capital of ₹ 200 crore and subscribed capital of ₹ 100 crore. The company focused on bond trading, underwriting in auctions of primary issuance of government dated securities and treasury bills. In addition, IDBI Gilts also plans to be a major player in the interest rate and credit derivative market.

(vi) IDBI Fortis Life Insurance: In the year 2008, the IDBI went into a joint venture with Fortis Insurance International and the Federal Bank for making the IDBI Fortis Life Insurance programme. The IDBI Bank owns 48 percent of the shares in the new venture and the balance 26 percent being held by Federal Bank Ltd, and Fortis International.

IDBI also played a significant role in the setting up of several Financial Institutions. They are the following:

1. Export-Import Bank of India (Exim Bank).
2. The National Stock Exchange (NSE).
3. The National Securities Depository Services Ltd. (NSDL).
4. Stock Holding Corporation of India (SHCIL).

5. Credit Analysis and Research Ltd. (CARE).
6. Clearing Corporation of India Ltd. (CCIL).
7. Asset Reconstruction Company (India) Ltd. (ARCIL).
8. North Eastern Development Finance Corporation Ltd. (NEDF).
9. Entrepreneurship Development Institute of India (EDII).
10. Jawaharlal Nehru Institute of Development Banking (JNIDB).

C. Industrial Credit and Investment Corporation of India Ltd. (ICICI): During the post independence period, industrial finance was provided mainly by the institutions such as the Industrial Finance Corporation of India (IFCI) and State Financial Corporations (SFCs). There was felt need for more institutions providing capital for the rapid growth of industries in private sector. World Bank cum American Investment Mission during their visit in 1954 also highlighted the need for such institutions providing finance to private sector industries in India. World Bank Mission recommended for the establishment of a special institution for the purpose of assisting industries in the private sector. Industrial Credit and Investment Corporation of India Limited (ICICI) was incorporated at the initiative of World Bank, the Government of India and representatives of Indian Industry.

The Industrial Credit and Investment Corporation of India Limited (ICICI) were registered as a private limited company under the Indian Companies Act with a view to support industries in the private sector. It was established in January 5, 1955. Initially the entire share capital of ICICI was held by individuals, Indian commercial banks and private insurance companies. With the nationalization of major commercial banks and insurance companies a major portion of share capital was held by these nationalized institutions. As a joint sector company, it had greater flexibility in operations. After the public issue in 1994, the number of individuals holding shares has increased significantly. Initially ICICI was established to provide financial assistance to private industrial units only but later they changed their scope by providing financial assistance to industrial concerns in the public, joint and co-operative sectors.

(a) Objectives of ICICI: The main objectives of ICICI are the following:

1. Assist private industrial undertakings for new projects as well as expansion, modernization, diversification of existing units.
2. To encourage the participation of internal and external capital in the private industrial sector.

(b) Functions of ICICI: ICICI performs the following functions:

1. Provide medium and long-term project financing to Indian private businesses.
2. Provide term loans in foreign currencies.
3. Providing special attention to riskier heavy industries such as chemicals,

petroleum, heavy engineering etc.

4. Direct subscription of shares of industrial units.
5. Underwriting of capital issues.
6. Guaranteeing the payment for credits.
7. Extent guarantee for deferred payments.
8. Merchant banking, equipment leasing and project counselling.
9. Provide technical and managerial assistance to industries.

(c) ICICI Bank: In the 1990s, ICICI transformed its business from a development financial institution offering only project finance to a diversified financial services group offering a wide variety of products and services, both directly and through a number of subsidiaries and affiliates like ICICI Bank. ICICI Banking Corporation was originally promoted in 1994 by ICICI Limited. It was a wholly-owned subsidiary of Industrial Credit and Investment Corporation of India Limited. Later, ICICI Banking Corporation was renamed as 'ICICI Bank Limited'. ICICI's shareholding in ICICI Bank was reduced to 46 percent through a public offering of shares in India in the year 1998. In 1999, ICICI become the first Indian company and the first bank or financial institution from non Japan Asia to be listed on the New York Stock Exchange (NYSE).

After consideration of various corporate structuring alternatives in the context of the emerging competitive scenario in the Indian banking industry and the move towards universal banking, the managements of ICICI and ICICI Bank formed the view that the merger of ICICI with ICICI Bank would be the optimal strategic alternative for both entities, and would create the optimal legal structure for the ICICI group's universal banking strategy. In October 2001, the Boards of Directors of ICICI and ICICI Bank approved the merger of ICICI and two of its wholly-owned retail finance subsidiaries, ICICI Personal Financial Services Limited and ICICI Capital Services Limited, with ICICI Bank.

(d) Mergers and Acquisitions: ICICI Bank acquired Bank of Madura Limited in the year 2001. In the year 2002, the Board of Directors of ICICI and ICICI Bank approved the reverse merger of (i) ICICI, (ii) ICICI Personal Financial Services Ltd. and (iii) ICICI Capital Services Ltd. into ICICI Bank. After receiving all necessary regulatory approvals, ICICI integrated the group's financing and banking operations, both wholesale and retail, into a single entity.

In the year 2005 ICICI acquired Investitsionno-Kreditny Bank (IKB), a Russian bank with about US$ 4mn in assets, head office in Balabanovo in the Kaluge region, and with a branch in Moscow. ICICI renamed the bank ICICI Bank Eurasia. In the year 2007, ICICI amalgamated Sangli Bank, which was headquartered in Sangli in Maharashtra State, and which had 158 branches in Maharashtra and another 31 in Karnataka State. ICICI Bank acquired Bank of

Rajasthan in the year March 2010.

At present ICICI Bank has a network of 2,752 branches and about 9,225 ATMs in India and presence in 19 countries. ICICI Bank offers a wide range of banking products and financial services to corporate and retail customers through a variety of delivery channels and through its specialized subsidiaries and affiliates in the areas of investment banking, life and non-life insurance, venture capital and asset management. The Bank currently has subsidiaries in the United Kingdom, Russia and Canada, branches in United States, Singapore, Bahrain, Hong Kong, Sri Lanka, Qatar and Dubai International Finance Centre and representative offices in United Arab Emirates, China, South Africa, Bangladesh, Thailand, Malaysia and Indonesia.

ICICI Bank is the largest private sector bank in India in terms of market capitalization. It is also the second largest bank in India in terms of assets with a total asset of ₹ 4,062.34 billion (US$ 91 billion) as on March 31, 2011. ICICI Bank's equity shares are listed in India on Bombay Stock Exchange and the National Stock Exchange of India Limited and its American Depositary Receipts (ADRs) are listed on the New York Stock Exchange (NYSE).

(e) Subsidiaries of ICICI: ICICI floated number of institutions successfully which include the following:

1. ICICI Venture Funds Management Company Ltd.
2. ICICI Prudential Life Insurance Company Ltd.
3. ICICI Lombard General Insurance Company Ltd.
4. ICICI Trusteeship Services Ltd.
5. ICICI Securities Ltd.
6. ICICI International Management Company Ltd.
7. Credit Rating Information Services India Ltd.
8. ICICI Mutual Fund.

D. Small Industries Development Bank of India (SIDBI): Small Industries Development Bank of India (SIDBI) is a state run bank aimed to aid the growth and development of micro, small and medium scale industries in India. It is the principal Development Financial Institution (DFI) in India for the promotion and development of small scale industries. Small Industries Development Bank of India (SIDBI) was established in April 2, 1990 under the SIDBI Act of 1989, passed by the Indian Parliament. SIDBI Act 1989 envisaged SIDBI as the principal financial institution for promotion, financing and development of industries in the small scale sector. SIDBI also coordinate the functions of various institutions engaged in the promotion and financing of industries in the small scale sector. As a subsidiary of IDBI, it took over the administration of National Equity Scheme and Small Industries Development Fund (SIDF) from

IDBI relating to small scale industries.

Small Industries Development Bank of India Act 1989, defines the objective of SIDBI as: "the principal financial institution for the promotion, financing and development of industry in the small scale sector and to co-ordinate the functions of the institutions engaged in the promotion and financing or developing the industry in the small scale sector and for the matters connected therewith or incidental thereto."

(a) Share Capital: Small Industries Development Bank of India (SIDBI) was established as a wholly owned subsidiary of Industrial Development Bank of India (IDBI). After the amendment of SIDBI Act, which changed the provisions relating to capital structure, shareholding pattern, management, business, borrowing etc., the bank has been de-linked from IDBI with effect from 27.3.2000. In accordance with the amendment in SIDBI Act, the authorized share capital has been raised to ₹ 1000 crore equity shares of ₹ 10 each and 25 crore redeemable preference shares of ₹ 10 each.

Of the total Rs. 450 crore subscribed by IDBI, while setting up of SIDBI, 19.21 percent has been retained by it and balance 80.79 percent has been transferred or divested in favour of public sector banks, the General Insurance Corporation, the Life Insurance Corporation and other institutions owned or controlled by the Central Government. A total of 36 institutions owned or controlled by the Government of India are the shareholders of the Bank. While IDBI continues to be the single largest shareholder, the State Bank of India and Life Insurance Corporation of India follow as the next two largest shareholders in that order. The Registered office of SIDBI is located at Lucknow. SIDBI has 6 Zonal Offices at Chennai, Kolkata, Mumbai, New Delhi, Varanasi and Guwahati. The operations of the bank are carried out through more than 50 offices spread across the Country.

(b) Financial Resources: The initial share capital of Rs. 450 crore was provided by IDBI and the outstanding portfolio under small industries development fund of ₹ 450 crore was transferred to SIDBI upon its formation. Besides share capital, SIDBI mobilizes funds from open market through the issue of deep discount bonds, happy return bonds, floating rate bonds and unsecured bonds. Moreover, SIDBI also mobilizes external resources from leading international lending agencies.

(c) Financial Assistance by SIDBI: SIDBI provide financial assistance to all forms of organizations viz., proprietary, partnership firms and limited companies. SIDBI assistance flows to export, industrial manufacturing, and transportation, health care and tourism sectors and also to the professional and self-employed persons setting up small-sized professional ventures. Since its inception, SIDBI has been assisting the entire spectrum of SSI Sector including the tiny, village and cottage industries through suitable schemes tailored to meet the requirement of setting up of new projects, expansion, diversification, modernization and rehabilitation of existing units.

Beginning as a refinancing agency to banks and state level financing bodies for their credit to small industries, it has diversified into many activities, including direct credit to the Small and Medium Enterprises (SME) through more than 100 branches in all major clusters of SME in India. Besides, it has been playing the development role in several ways such as support to micro-finance institutions for capacity building and on lending. SIDBI schemes can broadly be divided into three categories:

1. Direct Financial Assistance.
2. Indirect Financial Assistance.
3. Development and Support Services.

(i) Direct Financial Assistance: The prime objective of SIDBI is to provide direct financial assistance to small scale industries. Assistance is provided directly under different schemes through 100 branches of SIDBI. The assistance is extended directly for setting up of new SSI units, small hotels, hospitals, discounting of bills, technology upgradation, modernization, expansion and diversification, marketing of SSI products, development of infrastructure for the SSI sector etc. In addition, SIDBI's assistance also flows to the transport, health care and tourism sectors and also to the professional and self-employed persons for setting up small-sized professional ventures.

(ii) Indirect Financial Assistance: SIDBI's indirect assistance include credit to small scale industries through a large network of around 1000 various primary lending institutions spread across the country through a network of over 65,000 branches. Indirect assistance is also provided by way of refinance to State Level Finance Corporations, State Industries Development Corporations and banks. SIDBI also rediscounts bills and provide resource support in the form of short term loans.

(iii) Development and Support Services: SIDBI extents development and support services in the form of loans and grants to different agencies working for the promotion and development of small scale industries and tiny industries. The support is given for rural industrialization, human resource development to suit SSI sector, technology upgradation, marketing promotion, environment management, dissemination of information etc.

(d) Subsidiaries of SIDBI:

(i) SIDBI Venture Capital Ltd.: SIDBI Venture Capital Ltd. (SVCL) is a wholly owned subsidiary of SIDBI. The company acts as Asset Management

Company of the National Venture Fund for Software and Information Technology.

(ii) SIDBI Trustee Co. Ltd.: SIDBI Trustee Co. Ltd. (STCL) has been set up to carry out trusteeship functions for Venture Capital Funds. Presently STCL is acting as Trustee of National Venture Fund for Software and Information Technology.

(e) Associated Organizations of SIDBI:

(i) Credit Guarantee Fund Trust Scheme for Small Industries: Credit Guarantee Fund Trust Scheme for Small Industries (CGTSI) was promoted jointly by the Government of India and SIDBI in 2000. Credit Guarantee Fund Trust Scheme for Small Industries was floated for providing guarantees to banks for collateral free loans extended to the new and existing industrial units in SSI sector. Member lending institutions include scheduled commercial banks, select Regional Rural Banks and such of the institutions as may be approved by Government of India. CGTSI is widely being used by many public sector banks and private sector banks.

(ii) Technology Bureau for Small Enterprises: Technology Bureau for Small Enterprises (TBSE) was set up by SIDBI in 1995 in collaboration with United Nations Asian & Pacific Centre for Transfer of Technology. The bureau aims at helping SSI units to attain international competitiveness through transfer of latest available technologies from both within and outside the country.

(iii) SME Rating Agency of India Ltd.: SME Rating Agency of India Ltd. (SMERA) provides composite ratings to small scale industries. SME Rating Agency of India Limited (SMERA) is a joint initiative by Dun & Bradstreet Information Services India Private Limited (D&B), SIDBI and several leading banks in the country. SMERA is the country's first rating agency that focuses primarily on the Indian SME segment. SMERA's rating facilitates greater and easier flow of credit from the banking sector to SMEs.

E. Industrial Reconstruction Corporation of India Ltd. (IRCI): In India, during 1970s there has been a serious problem relating to the sickness of major industries especially textiles, mining and engineering. The industrial sickness was due to varied reasons viz. inadequacy of finance, managerial inefficiency, labour related problems, lack of demand of products etc. Closing of industrial units create many problems in the economy especially unemployment. Considering the seriousness of the problem of industrial sickness, the Government of India has decided to provide assistance to the sick units for their rehabilitation and reconstruction. For providing assistance to sick units the government decided to establish a special institution called Industrial Reconstruction Corporation of India (IRCI).

The Industrial Reconstruction Corporation of India Ltd. (IRCI) was initially set up in 1971 for rehabilitation of sick industrial units in India. The IRCI was set up with an authorized capital of ₹ 25 crore. The share capital has been subscribed by Industrial Development Bank of India (IDBI), Industrial Finance Corporation of India (IFCI), Industrial Credit and Investment Corporation of India ((ICICI), Life Insurance Corporation (LIC), State Bank of India (SBI) and other nationalized banks.

(a) Objective of IRCI: The Industrial Reconstruction Corporation of India Ltd. (IRCI) was set up by the government to prevent the problems relating to industrial sickness. Industrial Reconstruction Corporation of India was established with the specific objective of providing finance for industrial rehabilitation and revival of sick industrial units by way of rationalization, expansion, diversification and modernization and also to co-ordinate the work of other institutions for this purpose.

(b) Industrial Reconstruction Bank of India (IRBI): Industrial Reconstruction Corporation of India Ltd. (IRCI) was reconstituted under the IRBI Act of 1984 to take over the functions of IRCI. With effect from March 20, 1985 Industrial Reconstruction Corporation of India Ltd. was renamed as Industrial Reconstruction Bank of India (IRBI).

(c) Industrial Investment Bank of India (IIBI): The Industrial Investment Bank of India is one of oldest banks in India. With a view to converting the institution into a full-fledged development financial institution, IRBI was converted into a joint stock company in March 1997 by naming it as Industrial Investment Bank of India. IIBI offers a wide range of products and services, including the following:

1. Term loan assistance for project finance.
2. Short duration non-project asset-backed financing.
3. Working capital and other short-term loans to companies.
4. Subscription of equity shares of companies.
5. Investments in capital market and money market instruments.

In view of certain structural and financial problems adversely impacting its long-term viability, IIBI submitted a financial restructuring proposal to the Government of India on July 25, 2003. IIBI received certain directives from the Government of India, which, inter alias, include restricting fresh lending to existing clients, restrictions on fresh borrowings, an action plan to reduce the overhead expenditure, disposal of fixed assets and a time-bound plan for asset recovery/reconstruction. The Government of India has also given its approval for the merger of IIBI with IDBI and the latter has already started the due diligence process.

F. National Bank for Agriculture and Rural Development: National Bank for Agriculture and Rural Development (NABARD) is an apex development bank for financing agriculture and rural development. NABARD is one of the premier agencies to provide credit in rural areas. It was set up under the recommendations of Committee to Review Arrangement for Institutional Credit for Agriculture and Rural Development (CRAFICARD). The Committee to Review Arrangement for Institutional Credit for Agriculture and Rural Development was set up by RBI under the Chairmanship of Shri B Sivaraman in its report submitted to Governor, Reserve Bank of India on November 28, 1979 recommended the establishment of NABARD.

The Committee after reviewing the arrangements came to the conclusion that a new arrangement would be necessary at the national level for achieving the desired focuses and thrust towards integration of credit activities in the context of the strategy for integrated rural development. Against the backdrop of the massive credit needs of rural development and the need to uplift the weaker sections in the rural areas within a given time horizon the arrangement called for a separate institutional set-up. The Reserve Bank had onerous responsibilities to discharge in respect of its many basic functions of central banking in monetary and credit regulations and was not therefore in a position to devote undivided attention to the operational details of the emerging complex credit problems. This paved the way for the establishment of NABARD.

It was set up under the NABARD Act of 1981 by replacing the Agricultural Credit Department (ACD) and Rural Planning Cell (RPCC) of RBI and took over the entire functions of Agriculture Refinance and Development Corporation (ARDC). The Parliament through the Act in 1981 approved its setting up.

As per the preamble of the NABARD Act of 1981 "NABARD is established as a development bank, for providing and regulating credit and other facilities for the promotion and development of agriculture, small scale industries, cottage and village industries, handicrafts and other rural crafts and other allied economic activities in rural areas with a view to promoting integrated rural development and securing prosperity of rural areas and more matters connected therewith or incidental thereto".

(a) Objectives of NABARD: NABARD is set up as an apex development bank with a mandate for facilitating credit flow for promotion and development of agriculture, small-scale industries, cottage and village industries, handicrafts and other rural crafts. It has also the mandate to support all other allied economic activities in rural areas, promote integrated and sustainable rural development and secure prosperity of rural areas. The main objectives of NABARD are the following.

1. To facilitate the flow of credit for agriculture, rural infrastructure and rural development.
2. To promote policies, practices and innovations conducive to rural development.
3. To strengthen rural credit delivery system through institutional development.
4. Supervise Rural Financial Institutions (Cooperative Banks and Regional Rural Banks).
5. To provide consultancy services.

(b) Share Capital: National Bank for Agriculture and Rural Development (NABARD) was established on July 12, 1982. It was set up with an initial capital of ₹ 100 crore contributed by the Central Government and RBI. The aggregate assets held by NABARD rose to ₹ 1,82,300 crore as on 31 March 2012, an increase of ₹ 23,500 crore compared to the position as on 31 March 2011.

(c) Financial Resources: NABARD's resource base comprises the following:

- Share capital and free reserves.
- Rural Infrastructure Development Fund.
- National Rural Credit Fund
- Deposits.
- Borrowings from Government of India.
- Foreign currency loans.
- Market borrowings etc.

(d) Management: The management of NABARD is entrusted to a Board of Directors appointed by the Government of India in consultation with the RBI. Board of Directors consists of Chairman, Managing Director, four Executive Directors and Directors. Deputy Governor of RBI is appointed as Chairman of the NABARD. Three Directors are from amongst experts in rural economics, rural development, village and cottage industries, small scale industries or persons having experience in the working of cooperative banks, regional rural banks or commercial banks or any other matter the special knowledge or professional experience which is considered useful to NABARD.

Three directors are appointed by the government as representatives of Reserve Bank of India. Three directors are appointed as officials of the Central Government and four directors from amongst the officials of the State Government. Such number of directors elected in the prescribed manner by share holders other than RBI and Government of India.

NABARD has its head office at Mumbai. NABARD operates throughout the country through its 30 Regional Offices and one Sub-office, located in the capitals of all the states/union territories. It has 391 District Offices across the country, one Sub-office at Port Blair and one special cell at Srinagar. Each Regional Office has a Chief General Manager as its head.

(e) Institutions Eligible for Refinance: NABARD is a refinancing agency for financial institutions offering production credit for promoting agriculture and development activities in rural areas. NABARD provide refinance support to the following set of institutions:

1. Commercial Banks (CBs).
2. State Co-operative Banks (SCBs).
3. Regional Rural Banks (RRBs).
4. State Co-operative Agricultural and Rural Development Banks (SCARDBs).
5. Scheduled Primary Urban Co-operative Banks.
6. Non Banking Financial Companies.
7. Other Financial Institutions approved by RBI.

(f) Functions of NABARD: NABARD provides refinance for short medium and long-term credit to eligible institutions. NABARD maintains expert staff to study all problems relating to agriculture and rural development and be available for consultation to the Central Government, the Reserve Bank, the State Governments and the other institutions engaged in the field of rural development. It also provides technical, legal, financial, marketing and administrative assistance to any person engaged in agriculture and rural development activities. NABARD may provide consultancy services in the field of agriculture and rural development and other related matters in or outside India. The functions of NABARD can be classified into 6 major heads:

1. Financial Services.
2. Credit Planning and Monitoring.
3. Development and Promotional Functions.
4. Supervisory Functions.
5. Institutional and Capacity Building.
6. Training.

(i) Financial Services: Under financial services, NABARD refinances commercial, co-operative and regional rural banks for lending to on farm and non-farm activities. This includes farm activities like minor irrigation, animal husbandry, farm mechanization, forestry, fisheries, land development, horticulture, plantation and medicinal crops and non-farm like rural industries, artisans, handicrafts, handlooms, rural housing, rural tourism and agro processing. Financial services cover mainly the following activities:

1. NABARD refinance by way of short, medium and long term credit to State Co-operative Banks, Regional Rural Banks, Co-operative Agricultural and Rural Development Banks and Commercial Banks for its investment in

agriculture and other allied activities.

2. Give short term loans to State Co-operative Banks for seasonal agricultural operations, marketing of crops, distribution of fertilizers etc.
3. Give medium term loans to State Co-operative Banks and Regional Rural Banks for purchasing shares of processing societies.
4. Providing loans to State Government/NGOs/Panchayati Raj Institutions for developing rural infrastructure.
5. Providing long term loans to State Governments for subscribing the share capital of co-operative institutions.

(ii) Credit Planning and Monitoring: Credit Planning and Monitoring involves the following functions:

1. Preparation of annual potential-linked credit plans for all districts for identification of credit potential in agriculture, allied sectors and non farm sectors.
2. Monitoring the flow of ground level credit to agricultural and allied sectors.
3. Formulation of policies and operational guidelines for rural financial institutions.
4. Coordinate the operations of rural credit institutions.
5. Coordination with various government agencies and departments at district, state and national level.

(iii) Development and Promotional Functions: In order to reinforce the credit functions and to make credit more productive, NABARD has been undertaking a number of developmental and promotional activities such as the following:

1. Helping co-operative banks and Regional Rural Banks to prepare development action plans for themselves.
2. Providing financial assistance to cooperatives and Regional Rural Banks for establishment of technical, monitoring and evaluations cells.
3. Providing financial support for the training institutes of cooperative banks.
4. Providing financial assistance to cooperative banks for building improved management information system, computerization of operations and development of human resources.
5. Providing facilities for training, research and dissemination of information in rural banking and development etc.
6. Providing recommendations to Reserve Bank of India on opening of new branches by State Co-operative Banks and Regional Rural Banks.
7. Supporting Farmers Club and promotes credit linkage for SHGs.
8. Promotion of rural non-farm sector.
9. Supporting research and development.

10. Promotion of micro credit innovations.
11. Promotion of Kisan Credit Card (KCC) scheme.
12. Consultancy services.

(iv) Supervisory Functions: NABARD acts as a regulator for Co-operative Banks and Regional Rural Banks (RRBs). NABARD has been entrusted with the statutory responsibility of conducting inspections of State Co-operative Banks, District Co-operative Banks and Regional Rural Banks under the provision of the Banking Regulation Act 1949. Objectives of Inspection are as under:

1. To protect the interest of the present and future depositors.
2. To ensure that the business conducted by these banks is in conformity with the provisions of the relevant acts/rules, regulations/bye-laws, etc.
3. To ensure observance of rules, guidelines, etc. formulated and issued by NABARD/RBI/Government.
4. To examine the financial soundness of the banks.
5. To suggest ways and means for strengthening the institutions so as to enable them to play more efficient role in rural credit.

Supervisory functions include the following activities:

1. To undertake inspection of State Co-operative Banks, District Central Co-operative Banks and Regional Rural Banks on a voluntary basis.
2. To undertake inspection of State Co-operative Agricultural and Rural Development Banks, Apex Weavers Societies, Marketing Federations etc.
3. To act as agent to Government and RBI in transaction of business in relevant areas.
4. To undertake off-site surveillance of co-operative banks and Regional Rural Banks.

(v) Institutional and Capacity Building: Under institutional and capacity building NABARD performs the following functions:

1. Helps co-operative banks and RRBs to prepare development actions plans for themselves.
2. Enters into MoU with state governments and co-operative banks specifying their respective obligations to improve the affairs of the banks in a stipulated timeframe.
3. Helps RRBs and the sponsor banks to enter into MoUs specifying their respective obligations to improve the affairs of the RRBs in a stipulated timeframe.
4. Monitors implementation of development action plans of banks and fulfilment of obligations under MoUs.
5. Provides financial support for the training institutes of co-operative banks.
6. Provides training for senior and middle level executives of commercial banks.

Regional Rural Banks and cooperative banks.

(vi) Training: To enable the client financial institutions, viz., RRBs and Cooperative Banks, to diversify their loan portfolio and accelerate the credit flow to rural non-farm sector, training programmes are supported and funded by NABARD. For developing the expertise to deal with agricultural and rural problems, NABARD establishes the following institutions in the country:

1. National Bank Staff College, Lucknow.
2. National Bank Training Centre, Lucknow.
3. Zonal Training Centre, Hyderabad.
4. Regional Training Centre, Mangalore.
5. Regional Training Centre, Bolpur.
6. Bankers Institute of Rural Development, Lucknow.

(g) Subsidiaries of NABARD:

(i) NABARD Consultancy Services Pvt. Ltd (NABCONS): NABARD Consultancy Services Pvt. Ltd (NABCONS) was registered as a wholly owned subsidiary of NABARD in November 2003. It is now an established professional consultancy service provider in the field of agriculture and rural development and allied activities. The affairs of NABCONS are professionally managed and its board has the Managing Director of NABARD as Chairman. The services of NABCONS are contracted by various agencies including Government of India, State Governments, banks, international bodies, corporate entities and individuals in a wide range of fields and purposes.

(ii) Agriculture Insurance Company of India Ltd. (AICI): Agriculture Insurance Company of India Ltd. (AICI) was established in December 2002 with an authorized capital of ₹ 1500 crore. Thirty percent of the paid up capital of ₹ 200 crore has been subscribed by NABARD and the remaining by five public sector general insurance companies.

(iii) Multi-commodity Exchange (MCX) and National Commodities and Derivatives Exchange (NCDEX): To strengthen the marketing infrastructure in the country, NABARD has been an equity partner in the major national level commodity exchanges, viz., Multi-Commodity Exchange (MCX) and National Commodities and Derivatives Exchange (NCDEX).

G. Export-Import Bank of India (Exim Bank): Export-Import Bank of India also known as Exim Bank of India is the premier export finance institution in the country. The EXIM bank of India was established by Government of India for providing financial assistance to exporters and importers, and for functioning as the principal financial institution for coordinating the working of institutions engaged in financing export and import of goods and services with a view to promoting the country's international trade.

Exim bank is a financial institution in the public sector wholly owned by the Government of India created by an Act of the India Parliament. The bank was established on January 1, 1982 (started functioning w.e.f. March 1, 1982) under the Export-Import Bank of India Act of 1981. Exim Bank was established with an initial authorized capital ₹ 200 crore (increased to ₹ 500 and then to ₹ 2,000 crore).

The Government of India established the Export-Import Bank of India with an aim to augment exports from India and also to combine the country's foreign trade and investment with the overall economic growth. The primary objective of the Export-Import Bank of India is to provide financial assistance to importers and exporters and function as the top financial institution. Commencing operations as a purveyor of export credit, Exim Bank of India has, over the period, evolved into an institution that plays a major role in partnering Indian industries, particularly the Small and Medium Enterprises, in their globalization efforts, through a wide range of products and services offered at all stages of the business cycle, starting from import of technology and export product development to export production, export marketing, pre-shipment and post-shipment and overseas investment.

(a) Management: Exim Bank of India is managed by a Board of Directors which has representatives from Ministries of Finance, Commerce, External Affairs and Industry of Government of India, Reserve Bank of India, Industrial Development Bank of India, State Bank of India, Export Credit Guarantee Corporation of India, public sector banks, business community, policy makers, players in industry and international trade, professionals in export, import etc.

The Board of directors of Exim Bank consists of 16 directors. Chairman and Managing Director of the banks is appointed by the Government of India. Five Directors are appointed by the Government as representatives from Ministry of Finance, Commerce, External Affairs and Industry. 3 Directors as appointed by the Government as representatives of public sector banks. Representatives of business community, professionals in import, export etc. consists 4 Directors which are also appointed by the Government of India. Of the remaining three Directors one nominated by the Reserve Bank of India (RBI), one by Industrial Development Bank of India (IDBI) and another one by Export Credit Guarantee Corporation of India (ECGC). The Registered Office of Exim Bank of India is located at Mumbai. As of 2012, Exim Bank of India has 10 regional offices and 7 overseas offices.

(b) Objectives of Exim Bank: The Exim Bank Act of 1981 describes the basic objectives of Exim Bank as "for providing financial assistance to exporters and importers, and for functioning as the principal financial institution for coordinating the working of institutions engaged in financing export and import of goods and services with a view to promoting the country's international trade."

(c) Sources of Finance: The main sources of finance of Exim Bank are the following:

1. Issue of bonds and debentures.
2. Loans from RBI, Central Government or other institutions.
3. Grants from RBI and Central Government.
4. Lines of credit from foreign institutions.
5. Raising foreign deposits.

(d) Functions of Exim Bank: Government of India established the Exim Bank with a mandate, not just to enhance exports from India, but to integrate the country's foreign trade and investment with the overall economic growth. Important functions of Exim Bank are the following:

(i) Finance for Export Oriented Units: This program was introduced by EXIM Bank in 1984 to provide term finance to export oriented units. Under this program, EXIM bank offers financial assistance to export oriented units on concessional terms with a view to enhance their competitiveness in overseas markets. Export oriented units set up in Free Trade Zones (FTZ)/Export Processing Zone (EPZ) and export units recognized by the Government of India as 100 percent export oriented is eligible for financial assistance under this program. Under this scheme Exim Bank provide finance for the following purposes.

(ii) Project Finance: Under project finance Exim Bank provides direct financial assistance to export oriented companies by way of term loans in Indian rupees and foreign currencies for setting up new production facility, expansion, modernization and upgradation of existing facilities and for acquisition of business, production equipment, technology etc. Direct finance is also provided for software exports and consultancy services.

1. Equipment Finance: Exim Bank also offers loans to export oriented units for import of technology and related services and for purchase of equipments both imported as well as indigenous.
2. Working Capital Finance: Exim Bank provides working capital finance to export oriented Indian companies for enhancing the export capabilities.
3. Underwriting of shares, bonds and debentures of Indian companies engaged in export or import.

(iii) Term Loans for Overseas Investment: Overseas Investment Finance programme of Exim Banks offers a variety of facilities for Indian investments and acquisitions in overseas. Under Overseas Investment Finance Exim Bank provide finance for the following purposes:

1. Loan to Indian companies for equity participation in the overseas joint venture and wholly owned subsidiary.
2. Direct working capital finance to the overseas joint venture and wholly owned subsidiary.
3. Finance for overseas joint ventures and construction projects.

(iv) Export Marketing Finance: Exim Bank provides assistance to Indian companies, to enable them to establish their products in overseas markets through its export marketing services, starting from identification of prospective business partners to facilitating placement of final orders. Term loans are extended to important strategic marketing plan covering mainly, overseas market research, participating in international trade fairs, promotion of product, brand positioning, international quality certification, mirror product adaptation, pre-operative expenses for overseas offices, prospective buyer's visits to India etc.

(v) Small and Medium Enterprises Finance: Exim Bank of India has been providing a suite of services to export oriented Small and Medium Enterprises (SME) clients. Exim Bank supports Small and Medium Enterprises in their export marketing efforts including financing the soft expenditure relating to implementation of strategic and systematic export market development plans, capacity building in niche areas such as quality, safety, financial advisory services such as loan syndication etc. The Bank also extends lines of credit to overseas financial institutions, foreign governments and their agencies, enabling them to finance imports of goods and services from Indian SME exporters on deferred credit terms.

(vi) Advisory Services: Exim Bank offers value-added information, advisory and support services to Indian exporters which enable exporters to evaluate international risks, exploit export opportunities and improve competitiveness, thereby helping them in their globalization efforts. Exim Bank's international network comprising overseas office, co-operation partners, correspondent banks and financial institutions is leveraged to provide export information on the following:

1. Overseas markets and market segments.
2. Direct marketing of product.
3. Overseas business opportunities.
4. Information on export and import regulations, finance.
5. Internal Audit, Management Information Services, Information Technology, Legal, Human Resources Management and Corporate Affairs.

(vii) Agriculture Finance: Under Agri Finance scheme term loans with varying maturities are provided for setting up processing facilities, expansion, modernization, import of equipment and technology, pre-shipment/post-shipment credit, overseas buyers' credit and guarantees to the needs of export oriented companies dealing in agricultural products. The Bank has strong linkages with other stakeholders in agri sector such as Ministry of Food Processing Industries, Government of India, NABARD, APEDA, Small Farmers' Agri-Business Consortium (SFAC), and National Horticultural Board. Apart from financing, the Bank also provides a range of advisory services to agri exporters.

(viii) Finance for Research and Development: Exim Bank also provides finance for Research and Development activities for facilitating exports.

(ix) Export Lines of Credit: Lines of credit are a financing mechanism that provides a safe mode of non-recourse financing option to Indian exporters, especially to SMEs, and serves as an effective market entry tool. The Exim Bank extends lines of credit to overseas financial institutions, foreign governments and their agencies, enabling them to finance imports of goods and services from India on deferred credit terms. The Indian exporters can obtain payment of eligible value from Exim Bank, without recourse to them, against negotiation of shipping documents.

(x) Export Bills Rediscounting: Under this scheme commercial banks in India which are eligible to deal in foreign exchange are allowed to rediscount their short term export bills with EXIM bank for unexpired usance period of not more than 90 days. This enables banks to fund post-shipment export credit to Indian exporters. The limit authorized by the RBI for the program is ₹ 50 crore.

(e) Operating Groups in Exim Bank: The Exim Bank's functions are segmented into eight operating groups which are given below:

1. **Corporate Banking Group:** Corporate Banking Group handles a variety of financing programmes for Export Oriented Units (EOUs), importers, and overseas investment by Indian companies.
2. **Project Finance Group:** Project Finance handles the entire range of export credit services such as supplier's credit, pre-shipment credit, buyer's credit, and finance for export of projects and consultancy services, guarantees, forfeiting etc.
3. **Lines of Credit Group:** Lines of Credit (LOC) is a financing mechanism that provides a safe mode of non-recourse financing option to Indian exporters, especially to SMEs, and serves as an effective market entry tool.
4. **Agri Business Group:** This group spearheads the initiative to promote and support Agri-exports. The Group handles projects and export transactions in the agricultural sector for financing.
5. **Small and Medium Enterprises Group:** Small and Medium Enterprises Group handles the specific financing requirements of export oriented SMEs. The group handles credit proposals from SMEs under various lending

programmes of the Bank.

6. **Export Services Group:** Export Services Group offers variety of advisory and value-added information services aimed at investment promotion.

(f) Fee based Export Marketing Services: Bank offers assistance to Indian companies, to enable them establish their products in overseas markets.

(g) Support Services Groups: Support Services Groups include Research and Planning, Corporate Finance, Loan Recovery, Internal Audit, Management Information Services, Information Technology, Legal, Human Resources Management and Corporate Affairs.

H. National Housing Bank (NHB): The Sub-Group on Housing Finance for the Seventh Five Year Plan (1985-90) identified the non-availability of long-term finance to individual households on any significant scale as a major lacuna impeding progress of the housing sector and recommended the setting up of a national level financial institution. A High Level Group was then appointed by RBI under the chairmanship of Dr. C. Rangarajan, to examine the proposal and the Group recommended the setting up of National Housing Bank as an autonomous housing finance institution. The recommendations of the High Level Group were accepted by the Government of India. The Government of India on February 28, 1987 announced its decision to establish the National Housing Bank (NHB) as an apex institution for housing finance.

The National Housing Bank (NHB) was established on July 9, 1988 under the National Housing Bank Act of 1987 to function as a principal agency to promote Housing Finance Institutions and to provide financial and other support to such institutions. NHB is wholly owned by Reserve Bank of India, which contributed the entire paid-up capital. The general superintendence, direction and management of the affairs and business of NHB vest under the Act in a Board of Directors.

The National Housing Bank Act of 1987 describes the basic functions of NHB as "to operate as a principal agency to promote housing finance institutions both at local and regional levels and to provide financial and other support to such institutions and for matters connected therewith or incidental thereto".

The Head Office of NHB is located at New Delhi. NHB has its office in all the major cities such as Mumbai, Hyderabad, Bangalore, Chennai, Kolkata, Lucknow and Ahmedabad. With trained professionals and proficient experts working at different levels, NHB is dedicated in the quest for excellence through modernism, work culture and contemporary work practices assisted by technology intervention.

(a) Regulations: As per the National Housing Bank Act of 1987, National Housing Bank is expected in the public interest, to regulate the housing finance system of the country to its advantage or to prevent the affairs of any housing finance institution being conducted in a manner detrimental to the interest of the depositors or in a manner prejudicial to the interest of the housing finance institutions.

National Housing Bank has been empowered to determine the policy and give directions to the housing finance institutions. Besides the regulatory provisions of the National Housing Bank Act of 1987, National Housing Bank has issued the Housing Finance Companies (NHB) Directions, 2001 as also Guidelines for Asset Liability Management System in Housing Finance Companies. These are periodically updated through issue of circulars and notifications. As part of the supervisory process, NHB is empowered to grant Certificate of Registration to companies for commencing or carrying on the business of a housing finance institution.

(b) Objectives of NHB: To promote a network of highly efficient and dedicated housing finance institutions to cater to the needs of various regions and different income groups.

1. To integrate the housing finance system with the overall financial system.
2. To make housing finance loans more affordable.
3. Direct and regulate the functioning of housing finance institutions for fair practices.
4. To increase the supply of housing property and building materials, thereby upgrading the housing stock in the country.

(c) Sources of Finance: The main sources of finance of NHB are the following:

1. Raising finance by issuing bonds or debentures.
2. Borrowing from Reserve Bank of India and other Financial Institutions.

(d) Functions of NHB: Important functions of NHB are the following:

1. Direct lending to scheduled commercial banks, state housing boards, development authorities, or any authority established by or under any Central, State or Provincial Act.
2. NHB provides refinances to major housing finance institutions. These include scheduled commercial banks, scheduled state cooperative banks, scheduled urban cooperative banks, specialized housing finance institutions, apex co-operative housing finance societies and agriculture and rural development banks. All the housing finance companies registered with the National Housing Bank are eligible for refinance from NHB if they have net owned funds of minimum ₹ 10 crore.
3. Provides loans and advances to banks and housing finance institutions for slum improvement.

4. Project finance for large-scale housing projects.
5. NHB has been playing the promotional role by issuing guidelines for participating in the equity of housing finance companies and guaranteeing the bonds to be issued by the housing finance companies. National Housing Bank has contributed in equity capital in 5 housing finance companies.
6. Mortgage backed securitization and development of secondary mortgage market in India.
7. Mortgage credit guarantee scheme for protection of lenders against any default.
8. Conducting training programs in areas relating to housing and housing finance for development of management capabilities of officials working in the sector.

It also provides financial assistance to people affected by natural calamities like earthquake, flood, cyclones etc.

Short Answer Type Questions

1. What is EXIM Bank?
2. What are development banks?
3. Define development bank.
4. What are the functions of ICICI?
5. What is NHB?
6. What are the sources of finance for the IDBI?
7. What is Small Industries Development Bank of India?
8. What are the functions of IFCI?
9. Write a note on IDBI.
10. What are the subsidiaries of IDBI?
11. What are the objectives of development banking?
12. Write a note on IFCI.
13. What is SIDBI?
14. Write a note on IDBI Gilts Limited.
15. Write a note on promotional activities of IDBI.
16. Explain direct financial assistance by SIDBI.
17. What are the objectives of EXIM Bank?
18. What are the sources of finance for the IFCI?
19. Write a note on Industrial Reconstruction Bank of India.
20. What is NABARD?

Essay Type Questions

1. What is National Housing Bank? What are the objectives of NHB?

2. Outline the organization and functions of EXIM Bank.
3. Write a note on the functions and achievements of NABARD.
4. Give a brief history of IDBI.
5. Explain the development and promotional functions of NABARD.
6. Give a brief history of the origin and development of EXIM Bank.
7. Explain the features and functions of National Housing Bank.
8. Outline the structure of development banks in India.
9. Explain the objectives, functions and financial resources of IFCI.
10. Clearly bring out the functions and importance of IDBI.
11. What are the objectives and functions of NABARD?
12. Give a brief history of the origin and development of ICICI.
13. Explain the IDBI's role in industrial financing.
14. Explain the financial assistance provided by Small Industries Development Bank of India.
15. What are the objectives and functions of ICICI?
16. Explain the role of ICICI in industrial development.

7

State Level Financial Institutions

7.1 Introduction

Several financial institutions have been set up at the State levels which supplement the financial assistance provided by the all India financial institutions. They act as a catalyst for promotion of investment and industrial development in their respective States. The state level institutions are of two types:

1. State Financial Corporations.
2. State Industrial Development Corporations.

7.2 State Financial Corporations (SFCs)

The Industrial Finance Corporation of India (IFCI) was established in 1948 to make credit available to the medium and large sized industries in the country. The Industrial Development Bank of India (IDBI) was established in 1964 with the objective of meeting the financial requirements of large scale industries in the public and co-operative sector. Small and medium-scale and cottage industries are excluded from the purview of IDBI and IFCI. In order to meet the financial needs of the diversified small and medium-scale industries, there was a need for special type of financial institutions. With this view, the Central Government passed the State Financial Corporation Act of 1951, which empowered the state governments to establish financial corporations to operate for their respective state.

As per the provisions in the State Financial Corporation Act, SFCs can formulate their policies and can function only in consultation with the respective State Government, Reserve Bank of India and Industrial Development Bank of India. The scope of the activities of State Financial Corporations is wider than that of the IDBI and IFC. With a view to enable SFCs to finance or undertake the new industrial business activities, definition of industrial concern under section 2(c) of SFCs Act has been modified by the government.

The first State Financial Corporation was set up in Punjab in 1953. At present there are 18 State Financial Corporations in the country of which 17 were set up under the SFCs Act of 1951. Tamil Nadu Industrial Investment Corporation Ltd. established in 1949 under the Companies Act as Madras Industrial Investment

Corporation also functions as a SFC.

7.2.1 Objectives of State Financial Corporations: State Financial Corporations (SFCs) are the State level financial institutions which play a crucial role in the development of small and medium enterprises in the concerned states. SFCs are established with the following specific objectives:

1. To provide finance to small and medium sized and cottage industrial units.
2. To provide incentives to new industries.
3. To achieve a balanced regional development.
4. To generate employment opportunities.
5. To widen the ownership base of industries.
6. To develop regional financial resources.

7.2.2 Management: State Financial Corporations (SFCs) is governed by a Board of Directors consisting of 18 directors in all, duly elected by the share holders and nominated by the government.

7.2.3 Functions of State Financial Corporations: State Financial Corporations are state level financial institutions, operating as regional development banks playing a crucial role in the development of small and medium enterprises in the states concerned in tandem with national priorities. Following are the important functions of SFCs:

1. To provide term loans for a period not exceeding 20 years to small, medium, cottage and tiny industrial units. SFCs should not be permitted to give a loan to an industrial unit not exceeding 10 percent of its paid up capital or ₹ 30 lakh which ever is lower. The maximum amount of financial assistance to an industrial unit has been fixed as ₹ 30 lakh in the case of limited company and ₹ 15 lakh for other industrial units. However, SFCs are not permitted to give loan on the security of the shares of industrial units.
2. Underwrite the issue of shares, debentures and bonds of industrial units. (SFCs are not permitted to purchase shares and stocks directly of an industrial unit or limited public company).
3. Subscribing the debentures of industrial units.
4. To give guarantee to loans taken by industrial units from commercial banks for a period not exceeding 20 years.
5. To guarantee the loans taken by industrial concerns from market and co-operative societies for a period not exceeding 20 years.
6. To make payment of capital goods, plant and machinery etc. purchased in India by industrial units.
7. To guarantee the deferred payments for the purchase of machinery etc. within the country.
8. Provide seed and special capital to the industrial units.

9. Discounting of bills of exchange.
10. To act as an agent of the Central and State governments and all India industrial financial institutions for sanction and disbursement of loans to small industries.
11. To do all such acts as may be incidental of its duties under the State Financial Corporation Act.

State Financial Corporations has also started providing assistance to newer types of business activities like floriculture, tissue culture, poultry farming, commercial complexes and services related to engineering, marketing etc. The SFCs operate a number of schemes of refinance and equity type assistance on behalf of IDBI/SIDBI in addition to special schemes for artisans and special target groups such as SC/ST, women, ex-servicemen, physically handicapped etc. SFCs have also started offering facilities such as equipment leasing and have entered the field of consultancy, merchant banking, debenture trusteeship and capital related services.

7.2.4 Financial Resources: The main sources of finance of State Financial Corporations are the following:

1. **Share Capital:** The share capital of a State Financial Corporation is ranging from ₹ 50 lakh to ₹ 5 crore. It can be increased up to ₹ 10 crore with the prior sanction of the Central Government. The capital structure of a State Financial Corporation is fixed by the State Government. The shares of the corporation are offered to the public, state government, IDBI and other approved financial institutions. The shares of the corporation are to be regarded as trustee securities under the Indian Trust Act and as an approved security for the purpose of the Banking Companies Act.
2. **Issue of Bonds and Debentures:** State Financial Corporation can issue bonds and debentures to supplement their working capital. However, the total amount of the issue of bonds and debentures in any case should not exceed ten times of the amount of paid up capital and reserves of a State Financial Corporation. The payment of principal and interest is guaranteed by the respective state governments.
3. **Public Deposits:** State Financial Corporation accepts public deposits for a maximum period of 5 years. However, the total amount of deposits received by way public deposits should not exceed twice its paid up capital. SFCs are not permitted to accept public deposit for period not less than 5 years.
4. **Borrowings from RBI and Government:** State financial Corporations can also borrow money from the state government and the Reserve bank of India.
5. **Refinance from IDBI:** Refinance from the Industrial Development Bank of India (IDBI) is a major source of finance to State Financial Corporations.

7.2.5 Arguments against the Working of SFCs: With the liberalization of the financial sector, State Financial Corporations' future business is likely to face tough competition from commercial banks and other financial institutions. However. several studies revealed that SFCs are working in accordance with the financial needs of the small, cottage and tiny industrial units. There are some limitations on the working of SFCs, which are given below:

1. Inadequate financial assistance to the industrial units.
2. Undue delay in sanctioning and disbursement of loans.
3. Shortage of technical experts.
4. Indifferent attitude towards new business enterprises.
5. Cumbersome and unwanted formalities in sanction of loans.
6. The financial resources of SFCs are inadequate for financing.
7. Mounting overdue.
8. High rate of interest on loans.
9. Lack of trained employees.
10. Inadequate underwriting.

7.3 State Industrial Development Corporation (SIDC)

State Industrial Development Corporation (SIDC) is the government agency for industrial and investment promotion in the states. State Industrial Development Corporation has been established under the Companies Act of 1956, as wholly-owned undertakings of State Governments. Even though these corporations are fully owned by the government some of the Industrial Corporations in some states are set up by the state government as statutory companies under special status while some others are incorporated as public or private limited companies under the Companies Act of 1956.

SIDC acts as a promotional agency involved in catalyzing the development of physical and social infrastructure required for constant growth of industry in the State. They offer professional guidance and support for potential investors through a comprehensive set of services that include developing business ideas, identifying viable projects, providing financial assistance, guidance and assistance for implementation.

State Industrial Development Corporations are entrusted with the task of accelerating the speed of industrial development in their respective states. These corporations are assigned to provide financial assistance in the form of loan and capital participation for rapid industrial development. State Industrial Development Corporation provides term loans to industrial units have normally lower paid up capital. They are also entrusted with the task of administering the state incentive schemes for attracting and developing industries especially in the backward areas.

The first State Industrial Development Corporation (SIDC) was established by the government of Andhra Pradesh followed by Bihar in the year 1960. The State of Kerala and Utter Pradesh established their State Industrial Development Corporations in 1961 followed by Maharashtra, Orissa and Gujarat in 1962 and Tamil Nadu and Madhya Pradesh in 1965. Over the years all the state governments established their own State Industrial Development Corporations. At present 25 State Industrial Development Corporations are functioning in the country. Andhra Pradesh and Rajasthan Industrial Development Corporations occupy the top position in promoting the largest number of joint sector industrial units in the country.

7.3.1 Objectives: State Industrial Development Corporations have been set up with the objective of promoting industrial development in the respective States and providing financial assistance to small entrepreneurs.

They are also involved in setting up of medium and large industrial projects in the joint sector in collaboration with private entrepreneurs or wholly-owned subsidiaries.

7.3.2 Functions: The main function of State Industrial Development Corporations is the promotion, improvement and development of industries in the states. State Industrial Development Corporations undertake a variety of promotional activities such as:

1. Provide financial assistance to small industrial units.
2. Underwriting the issues of shares and debentures issued by small industrial units.
3. Subscription of shares and debentures issued by small industrial units.
4. Preparation of feasibility reports.
5. Providing guarantee for loans and deferred payments.
6. Promotion and management of industrial concerns.
7. Conducting industrial potential surveys.
8. Entrepreneurship training and development programmes.
9. Developing industrial areas or estates.
10. Provision of technical assistance.
11. Provision of risk capital to entrepreneurs in the form of equity participation.

Short Answer Type Questions

1. What are the sources of finance for the State Financial Corporations?
2. What is SIDC?
3. Write are the objectives of State Financial Corporations?

Essay Type Questions

1. What are functions of State Financial Corporations?
2. What are the functions of State Industrial Development Corporations?

8

Specialized Financial Institutions

8.1 Introduction

Specialized Financial Institutions are set up mainly by the government for providing medium and long term financial assistance to certain types of industries specified by the government. These institutions receive funds for their financing operations primarily from the government or other public institutions. The specialized financial institutions are the following:

1. Tourism Finance Corporation of India Ltd. (TFCI).
2. IFCI Venture Capital Funds Ltd. (IFCI Venture) (Risk Capital and Technology Finance Corporation Ltd.).
3. Technology Development and Information Company of India Ltd. (TDICI).
4. Discount and Finance House of India Ltd. (DFHI).
5. Securities Trading Corporation of India Ltd. (STCI).
6. Housing and Urban Development Corporation Ltd. (HUDCO).
7. Stock Holding Corporation of India Ltd. (SHCIL).
8. Power Finance Corporation Ltd. (PFC).
9. Indian Railways Finance Corporation Ltd. (IRFC).

8.2 Tourism Finance Corporation of India Ltd. (TFCI)

Tourism Finance Corporation of India Ltd. (TFCI) was established by the Government of India on February 1, 1989. TFCI was set up as per the recommendations of the Yunus Committee (1988) appointed by the Planning Commission of India to promote a separate National Level Specialized Financial Institution for catering to the financial needs of tourism related activities. In accordance with the recommendations, the Government of India decided to set up a specialized financial institution for providing financial assistance to the tourism sector.

Industrial Finance Corporation of India Ltd. (IFCI), other national level Financial and Investment Institutions and nationalized banks are the promoters of TFCI. Tourism Finance Corporation of India Ltd. was incorporated as a public limited company under the Companies Act of 1956 on January 27, 1989. The Registered Office of TFCI is at New Delhi. The objective of setting Tourism Finance Corporation of India Ltd. (TFCI) was to provide financial assistance to enterprises for setting up and development of tourism related projects, facilities and services.

8.2.1 Functions of TFCI: The functions of TFCI are classified mainly into two categories viz. direct assistance and project related assistance.

A. Direct Assistance: TFCI provides direct financial assistance for the development of tourism related projects:

1. Hotels and Restaurants.
2. Holiday Resorts.
3. Amusement and Safari Parks.
4. Rope-ways.
5. Cultural Centres.
6. Convention Halls.
7. Travel and Tour Operating Agencies.
8. Sports Facilities.
9. Transport.
10. Entertainment Centres.
11. Air Service.

B. Project Related Assistance: TFCI's project related assistance includes the following:

1. Site evaluation studies.
2. Techno-economic feasibility studies.
3. Market potential assessment.
4. Loan syndication services.
5. Financial restructuring of project proposals.
6. Project implementation and monitoring services.
7. Evaluation of properties.
8. Arrangements for lease transfer of management and franchise tie-ups.
9. Design selection and architectural consultancy.
10. Direct subscription of shares and debentures issued by tourism related undertakings.
11. Underwriting of public issues of shares and debentures issued by tourism related undertakings.
12. Guarantee of deferred payments and credit raised abroad.
13. Equipment finance.
14. Equipment leasing.
15. Takeover financing.
16. Advances against credit card receivables.
17. Working capital financing.

The working capital assistance would be provided to concerns in the tourism sector with proven track record of at least 3 years and assisted concerns of TFCI with satisfactory credit record.

8.2.2 Eligibility for Assistance: TFCI provides financial assistance to projects with capital cost of ₹ 3 crore and above. In respect of projects costing between ₹ 1 crore and ₹ 3 crore, TFCI will consider financial assistance to the extent of unavoidable gap, if any, remaining after taking into account assistance from state level institutions and banks. Unique projects, which are important from the tourism point of view and for which assistance from state level institutions and banks is not available, may be considered on exceptional basis even though their capital cost is below ₹ 1 crore. Financial assistance is considered on similar lines for heritage and restaurant projects. Projects with high capital cost may be financed along with other national level financial and investment institutions. TFCI considers assistance even if the total cost is less than ₹ 3 crore for existing concerns with satisfactory performance for renovation and upgradation. The minimum promoters' contribution for the projects is 30 percent. The general norm of repayment is 8 years allowing moratorium of 2 years after full commercial operations.

8.3 IFCI Venture Capital Funds Ltd. (IFCI Venture)

IFCI Venture Capital Funds Ltd. (IFCI Venture) was originally set up by Industrial Finance Corporation of India (IFCI) as a society by the name of Risk Capital Foundation (RCF) in 1975 to provide institutional support to first generation professionals and technocrats setting up their own ventures in the medium scale sector through soft loans under the Risk Capital Scheme. In 1988, Risk Capital Foundation (RCF) was converted into a company named as Risk Capital and Technology Finance Corporation Ltd. (RCTC).

Based on IFCI Venture's credentials and strengths, UTI entrusted it with the management of a new venture capital fund named Venture Capital Unit Scheme (VECAUS-III) in 1991. The size of VECAUS-III was ₹ 80 crore, contributed by UTI and IFCI. To reflect the shift in the company's activities, the name of RCTC was changed to IFCI Venture Capital Funds Ltd. (IFCI Venture) in February 2000.

IFCI Venture Capital Funds Ltd. was promoted with the objective of broadening entrepreneurial base in the country by facilitating funding to ventures involving innovative product/process/technology. Initially, it started providing financial assistance, later it provides expertise and experience of investing in technology oriented innovative projects. IFCI Venture Capital Funds Ltd. is providing finance to ventures and supported commercialization of technologies. It has pioneered its effort for widening entrepreneurial base in the country and catalyzed the introduction of Venture Capital activity in India.

IFCI Venture Capital Funds Limited has launched three new funds in the emerging sectors of the economy namely:

1. **India Automotive Component Manufactures Private Equity Fund-I:** This Fund was dedicated for investment mainly in Indian Automotive Component Companies and in other related and emerging sectors. India Automotive Component Manufacturers Private Equity Fund was set up with a target corpus of Euro 60 million equivalents to ₹ 396 crore.
2. **India Enterprises Development Fund:** India Enterprises Development Fund was set up with the object of investing in knowledge based projects in key sectors of Indian economy with outstanding growth prospects. The fund was set up with target corpus of ₹ 250 crore.
3. **Green India Ventures Fund:** It is venture capital fund set up with the object of investing in commercially viable Clean Development Mechanism (CDM), energy efficient and other commercially viable projects with an aim to reduce negative ecological impact, efficient usage of resources such as energy, power etc and other related sectors and projects. Green India Venture Fund (GIVF) was setup with a target corpus of Euro 50 million (approx. ₹ 330 crore).

8.4 Technology Development and Information Company of India Ltd. (TDICI)

Venture Capital (VC) financing started in India in 1988 with the formation of Technology Development and Information Company of India Ltd. (TDICI). ICICI venture Funds Ltd. formerly known as Technology Development and Information Company of India Ltd. (TDICI) was promoted by ICICI in 1988 as a joint venture with the Unit Trust of India. Subsequently, ICICI bought out UTI's stake in 1998 and ICICI Venture became a fully owned subsidiary of ICICI.

ICICI Venture established in 1989 is headquartered in Bangalore, with an additional office in Mumbai. ICICI venture Funds Ltd. is one of the largest and most successful private equity firms in India. It specializes in private equity, venture capital and mezzanine investments. In private equity, the firm invests mainly in secondary transactions. The firm provides mezzanine financing for buyout opportunities by financial sponsors as well as leveraged acquisition by companies and towards mid-market growth capital. It provides finance to invest in manufacturing, information technology, healthcare, pharmaceuticals, biotechnology, media, financial services, and retail sectors. It also assists industrial units in the fields of computer, chemicals, polymers, biotechnology, environment engineering, drugs, diagnostics and vaccines.

ICICI venture Funds Ltd. seeks to exit its investments through the following routes:

1. Selling off the stake to strategic investors.
2. Initial public offering in India or overseas.
3. Sale to any other private equity fund or venture capital fund.
4. Secondary sale on stock markets.
5. Merger with an existing listed company.
6. Management or company buy-backs.

The firm typically exits its investments between 18 months and 5 years, depending upon the stage of investment and the performance of the sector and the company. The firm may take a minority or a controlling stake in its portfolio companies. It invests in listed and unlisted companies.

ICICI Venture also has an affiliation with the Trust Company of the West (TCW), which provides it a platform for networking Indian companies with global markets and technology. Strong parentage and affiliates for ICICI Venture also translates into access to a broad spectrum of financial and analytical resources thus enabling a keen understanding of the Indian financial markets and entrepreneurial ethos.

8.5 Discount and Finance House of India Ltd. (DFHI)

The Discount and Finance House of India Ltd., (DFHI) a unique institution of its kind, was set up in April 1988. It was set up by the Reserve Bank of India jointly with public sector banks and all India financial institutions. The Sukhamony Chkravarthy committee on monetary reforms in its report in 1985 examined various aspects for the development of money market. A Working Group on money market chaired by Vaghul recommended the need for a specialized institution for the development of the secondary money market.

On the basis of the recommendations of the Vaghul Committee to activate the secondary money market RBI took a decision on April 1988 to set up a Discount and Finance House. DFHI was incorporated on March 8, 1988 under the Companies Act of 1956 with an authorized share capital of ₹ 100 crore. The RBI (₹ 51 crore), Public Sector Banks (₹ 33 crore) and All-India Financial Institutions (₹ 16 crore) subscribed to the capital. The company received the certificate of commencement of business on April 25, 1988. The initial paid-up capital of ₹ 100 crore was increased to ₹ 150 crore in 1989-90 and further to ₹ 200 crore during 1991-92.

The Discount and Finance House of India Ltd. has been established to deal in money market instruments in order to ensure liquidity in the money market. The main objective of DFHI is to facilitate the smoothening of short-term liquidity imbalances by developing an active money market and integrating the various segments of the money market. In the initial stage of its operation, Discount and Finance House of India concentrated its operation mainly in 182-day treasury bills and rediscounting of short-term commercial bills. The operations of DFHI was increased periodically since its inception by actively trading in all the money market instruments viz. call/notice/term money, commercial bills, treasury bills, certificates of deposit and commercial paper and its business turnover has grown progressively over the years.

With effect from the year 1992-93, DFHI has been authorized to deal in Dated Government Securities also. After DFHI was accredited as a primary dealer in February 1996, its operations significantly increased particularly in Treasury Bills and Dated Government Securities. During these years, DFHI opened its branches in Ahmedabad, Bangalore, Kolkata, Chennai, New Delhi and Hyderabad with a view to cater to the requirements of the small and medium sized institutions operating at these centres and at the same time integrating the markets at these regional centres with the main money market at Mumbai.

8.5.1 Objectives of DFHI: The specific objectives of DFHI are given below:

1. To improve the liquidity imbalances in the banking system i.e. to balance the demand with the supply for short term finance in the money market.
2. To promote secondary market in short term money market instruments i.e. to be an active trader in money market instruments rather than a mere repository, and thereby, impart improved liquidity to short-term money market instruments.
3. To provide greater liquidity to money market instruments.

8.5.2 Functions of DFHI: The main functions of DFHI are as follows.

1. To discount, rediscount, buy, sell and underwrite marketable securities and negotiable instruments.
2. To facilitate money market transactions for small and medium sized institutions who are not regular participants in the market.
3. To provide safe and risk-free short-term investment avenues to various institutions.
4. To integrate markets at regional centres with the main market at Mumbai, through its network.
5. To undertake buy-back arrangements in treasury bills and other securities issued by government as well as local authorities and public sector institutions.
6. To advise the government, banks, financial institutions and business houses for their development, growth, and expansion of the money market.
7. To provide the 'Constituent SGL' Account facility which enables even those

entities which otherwise do not have an SGL Account facility with the RBI to reap the full benefits of investing in government securities.

DFHI being an institution promoted by the public sector banks/financial institutions and RBI, enjoys excellent credit rating in the market. At present DFHI's activities are restricted to the following types of money market instruments/products:

1. Treasury Bills.
2. Call (overnight) Money.
3. Notice Money.
4. Term Money.
5. Rediscounting short-term Commercial Bills.
6. Commercial Paper.
7. Certificates of Deposit.
8. Dated Government Securities.
9. Derivative Usance Promissory Notes of Commercial Banks.
10. Interest Rate Swaps/Forward Rate Agreements.

A. Treasury Bills: Treasury bills are issued by Reserve bank of India on behalf of the Government of India. DFHI deals in treasury bills of 91 days and 364 days maturity. Such bills are sold at fortnightly auctions. The Discount House regularly participates in such auctions. Moreover, it provides a ready market to other institutions/individuals to buy or sell the Treasury Bills. It purchases the same either as outright purchase or on repos basis. Repos mean the right to re-purchase the same bills again. For this purpose the DFHI quotes two way prices with fine spread. Such operations in Treasury Bills impart greater flexibility to banks in their funds management. Moreover, with the creation of a secondary market for treasury Bills, corporate bodies and other institutions could also invest their short-term surplus funds in such bills.

B. Call Money Market and Term Deposit: DFHI has been permitted by the Reserve bank of India to operate in the inter-bank call money market, both as lender and borrower of overnight call and notice money up to 14 days. DFHI also renders service to banks in the call money market by arranging or placing funds for banks.

C. Re-discounting of Commercial Bills: The Discount House aims at imparting liquidity to commercial bills, which have already been discounted by banks and financial institutions. It further re-discounts them and also enables banks and other eligible institutions to re-discount such bills. For this purpose of rediscounting DFHI announces its bid and offers re-discount rates on a fortnightly basis. The minimum value of the bill should be ₹ 10 lakh. The maturity of the bill should not exceed 90 days.

D. REPO: DFHI is also an authorised institution to undertake 'REPO' transactions in Treasury Bills and all Dated Government Securities to further facilitate money transactions by participants in the money market and at the same time impart greater liquidity to Treasury Bills and Dated Government Securities.

E. Constituent SGL Account: DFHI has opened a 'Constituent SGL' account with the RBI. Customers of DFHI can open Constituent SGL Accounts with DFHI. It enables even those entities, which are not eligible to have an SGL Account facility with the RBI to enjoy the benefits of investment in Government securities. It is possible for corporates, provident fund and co-operative banks to purchase and sell or hold Government securities through such an account.

When a purchase is made from DFHI, the corresponding security will be transferred from DFHI's normal SGL Account to the 'Constituents SGL' Account. A certificate of holding will be issued by the DFHI for the records of the investor. As and when maturity proceeds and interest (if any) are received, the same will be passed on to the constituent.

In case the constituent desires to disinvest, the same can be done and DFHI will transfer the security from its Constituents Account on receipt of authorization from the holder.

F. SBI Discount and Finance House of India: SBI DFHI Ltd. came into existence in April 2004 with the amalgamation of the two leading players in the domestic Money and Debt markets viz. Discount and Finance House of India (DFHI), a subsidiary of RBI and SBI Gilts Ltd, a subsidiary of SBI. The share holding pattern of SBI DFHI Ltd. is as follows. State Bank Group holds 67 percent, nationalized banks 22 percent, All India Financial Institutions 6 percent and Asian Development Bank 5 percent.

SBI Discount and Finance House of India is an important participant in the wholesale debt market in both the primary and secondary market segment with an outright turnover of Government Securities and Treasury Bills in 2007-08 at ₹ 54,919.39 crore and ₹ 5,428 crore respectively. It is a market leader in the Primary Dealer segment of the domestic debt market, with a net worth of ₹ 1059 crore (as on 31st March 2008) and a presence in all major financial centres of the country. SBI DFHI posted a post-tax profit of ₹ 85.68 crore for the year 2007-08.

G. Management of the Company: The Company is led by a team of experienced professionals, backed by strong research capabilities and driven by core-values. Board of Directors comprises reputed market professionals and eminent academicians. A Managing Director under the overall supervision of the Board of Directors manages the affairs of the Company. The Board is represented by very senior persons or Chief Executives from Reserve Bank of India, Nationalized Banks and Public Financial Institutions. By virtue of SBI being a major shareholder, it has been lending the services to one of its Chief General Managers who functions as the Managing Director of the Company. The Managing Director is assisted by a team of senior executives with rich experience in treasury activities. Officials on deputation from RBI/SBI assist the company.

H. Sources of Funds of SBI DFHI: DFHI mobilizes funds from commercial and cooperative banks, financial institutions and corporate entities having lendable resources. The corporates, provident fund and co-operative banks regularly invest in Government securities either to meet their statutory obligations or to invest their surplus funds. Public sector undertakings and corporates are allowed to lend their surplus resources through SBI DFHI in money market, subject to approval of RBI.

I. Types of Securities Traded by SBI DFHI: SBI DFHI, as a primary dealer, trade in Treasury Bills, Government securities, State Development Loans, Corporate Bonds, Certificates of Deposit, Commercial Paper, Inter-Corporate Deposits, Call and Notice Money Deposits. SBI DFHI is also active in retailing of Government securities, including small lots, and the distributors of mutual fund products of all leading funds. SBI DFHI also actively participates in the domestic interest rate derivatives and equities/equity futures markets. Individuals, corporates regional rural banks, co-operative banks, provident funds, pension funds, gratuity funds, trusts, insurance companies, mutual funds, banks etc. deal with the SBI DFHI.

8.6 Securities Trading Corporation of India Ltd. (STCI)

Securities Trading Corporation of India Ltd. is an important non-deposit taking non-banking financial company. STCI is a leading market maker of government securities. Securities Trading Corporation of India Limited (STCI) was promoted by Reserve Bank of India (RBI) in 1994 along with Public Sector Banks and All-India Financial Institutions with the objective of developing an active, deep and vibrant secondary debt market. The main objective of setting the STCI is to foster the development of an active secondary market for Government securities and bonds issued by public sector undertakings.

The Company was incorporated in May 1994 under the Companies Act, 1956 with an authorized and paid up capital of ₹ 500 crore of which RBI contributed 50.18 percent. Subsequently, being a regulator, RBI divested its equity in STCI to banks and financial institutions in a phased manner. In 1997, RBI divested part of its holding and the share holding came down from 50.18 percent to 14.41 percent of the total paid up capital. In 2002, RBI sold the remaining holding in the company to the existing shareholders. Bank of India is the largest shareholder of the company.

STCI was one of the first two institutions to be accredited by RBI as a Primary Dealer in Government securities. In 1996, Securities Trading Corporation of India Ltd. was authorized by RBI as one of the first Primary Dealer in India. As a Primary Dealer, the Company undertook trading in government securities, public sector bonds, Non-SLR instruments and money market instruments. The Company also carried out proprietary equity trading. Other lines of activities included trading in Interest Rate Swaps—both for hedging and market making.

8.6.1. Functions of STCI: STCI's core functions comprise participation, underwriting, market making and trading in Government Securities. Important functions of STCI are the following:

1. STCI focuses primarily on loan activities. STCI provide loans against the collateral security of shares subject to condition that such shares are included in the approved list of the company.
2. Funding for equity trading.
3. Funding for subscription to shares offered by companies under IPOs.
4. Underwriting of Government of India securities and treasury bills.
5. Participation in the auctions of Government of India securities and treasury bills.
6. Market-making and trading in Government of India securities and treasury bills.
7. Trading in both in the cash and futures and options segment in equity market.
8. Trading in public sector bonds and other corporate debt instruments.
9. Trading in fixed income securities viz. commercial papers, certificates of deposits.
10. Participation in Repo Market of government of India securities and treasury bills.
11. Participation in the Inter-Bank Call/Notice/Term money market, both as a borrower and as a lender.
12. Portfolio management services.
13. Equity trading business.
14. Distribution of insurance products.

In the near future, the company proposes to extend the scope of lending business to areas such as Promoter funding, Margin funding, Factoring, bill discounting, Private Equity etc.

STCI has diversified its activities into the PSU/Corporate Bond Market. It has already commenced participating in the primary issues of bonds of Development Finance Institutions (DFIs), PSUs and corporates and dealing in these bonds in the secondary market in order to provide liquidity to it. Having achieved the status of the largest Primary Dealer in Government securities, STCI now gears itself to become the future 'Debt House' of India.

A. STCI Primary Dealer Limited (STCI PD): STCI Primary Dealer Limited (STCI PD) was incorporated in October 2006 as a wholly owned subsidiary of Securities Trading Corporation of India Limited (STCI) undertaking Primary Dealership business. STCI Primary Dealer Ltd commenced operations with effect from June 25, 2007 in line with the Reserve Bank of India guidelines on diversification of business activities by Primary Dealers. STCI was one of the first accredited Primary Dealers in the Indian government securities market and has contributed immensely to the development of the Indian fixed income market.

8.7 Housing and Urban Development Corporation Ltd. (HUDCO)

Housing and Urban Development Corporation Ltd. (HUDCO) was incorporated on April 25, 1970. HUDCO was established with the object of assisting various agencies and authorities in upgrading the housing conditions in the country. It grants loans to state governments, state housing boards and local authorities for housing and urban development projects. HUDCO also finances schemes of housing co-operatives. HUDCO lays special emphasis on the development of housing facilities or HUDCO Nivas Yojana for the lower income group and the economically weaker sections of the society. HUDCO was established initially with an initial equity base ₹ 2 crore. It had a net worth of ₹ 5,521 crore as on March 31, 2011.

8.7.1 Financial Resources of HUDCO: HUDCO mobilizes financial resources from various institutions viz.

1. Financial assistance form institutions like LIC, GIC and banking institutions.
2. Financial assistance from international financial institutions.
3. Raising money by issuing debentures.
4. Issue of bonds both taxable and tax-free.
5. Accepting deposits from the public.

8.7.2 Functions of HUDCO: HUDCO is providing financial assistance for housing development and for overall infrastructure development. Following are the functions of HUDCO:

1. Urban housing.
2. Rural housing.
3. Staff rental housing.
4. Repairs and renewal of building.
5. Shelter and sanitation facilities for footpath dwellers.
6. Housing through private builders and joint sector.
7. Individual HUDCO housing loans.

8. Land acquisition.
9. Project for the development of real estates.
10. Valmiki Ambedkar Awas Yojana (VAMBAY).
11. Jawahar Lal Nehru National Urban Renewal Mission (JLNNURM).
12. Consultancy in housing, urban development and infrastructure.

8.8 Stock Holding Corporation of India Limited. (SHCIL)

Stock Holding Corporation of India Limited (SHCIL) is the largest custodian and depository Participant Company in India. Stock Holding Corporation of India Limited (SHCIL) was incorporated at the special initiative of the Government of India as a Public Limited Company in 1986. It has been jointly promoted and owned by Banks and Financial Institutions, viz., IDBI Bank Ltd, ICICI Bank, SU-UTI, IFCI Ltd., LIC, GIC, NIA, NIC, UIC, and TOICL all leaders in their fields of business. Stock Holding Corporation of India Limited is having its registered office in Mumbai and branches across the country. SHCIL Services Limited (SSL) is the broking arm of SHCIL.

8.8.1 Services Offered by SHCI: Stock Holding Corporation of India Ltd. is offering the following services:

1. Custodial services.
2. Depository services.
3. Securities lending.
4. PF fund accounting.
5. SGL constituent account services.
6. Distribution of mutual fund and other capital market instruments.

8.9 Power Finance Corporation Ltd. (PFC)

Power Finance Corporation Ltd. (PFC) is a financial institution owned by the Government of India. PFC is under the administrative control of Ministry of Power, Government of India. Power Finance Corporation Ltd. is a financial institution specializing in lending to power projects. Power Finance Corporation Ltd. was established in July 1986 to provide exclusive focus for financing and development of the power sector in the country. In the year 1990, the Power Finance Corporation Ltd. was notified as a public financial institution under the Companies Act of 1956.

The organization is registered by the Reserve Bank of India as a non-banking financial company. The company issued an IPO in January, 2007. The issue was oversubscribed by over 76 times, which is the largest for an IPO of any Indian Company in recent times. Today, PFC is the single largest lender to the Indian power sector and support about 23 percent of the countries installed power.

8.9.1 Objectives: PFC was established with a view to provide a range of fund based and non-fund based support to the Indian power sector. The main objective of Power Finance Corporation Ltd. is to provide financial aid to the power sector for the integral development of power based infrastructure.

8.9.2 Organization: The Corporation is run by a Board of Directors which is the highest decision making body. The Corporation is headed by the Chairman and Managing Director. The company has three wings, each headed by a Functional Director namely (i) Institutional Development and Administration Division (ii) Projects Division and (iii) (Finance and Financial Operations division. The Institutional Development and Administration Division looks after the credit appraisal and categorization of borrower entities, power sector reforms, review and analysis. The Projects Division controls the operation in various states and project appraisal. Finance and Financial Operations Division looks after the Fund Mobilization and Disbursement. PFC is a lean organization.

8.9.3 Functions: The function and duties of the corporation in relation its customer and clients include providing a range of services and products in the area of:

1. Providing financial and fund based assistance to State Electricity Boards, State sector power utilities, Central sector power utilities and Private sector companies for generation, transmission and distribution.
2. Institutional development services.
3. Financing other infrastructure projects which have backward linkages to the power sector like coal mine development, fuel transportation, oil & gas pipelines etc.
4. Fee based consultancy services.
5. Rating different state Power Utilities on its performance.

A. Subsidiary Companies: PFC presently has seven subsidiary companies:

1. PFC Consulting Ltd. (PFCCL) is a wholly owned subsidiary handling fee based services.
2. Coastal Karnataka Power Limited.
3. Coastal Tamil Nadu Power Limited.
4. Coastal Maharashtra Power Limited.
5. Orissa Integrated Power Limited.
6. Jharkhand Integrated Power Limited.
7. Agarthla Power Limited.

8.10 Indian Railways Finance Corporation Ltd. (IRFC)

Indian Railways Finance Corporation Ltd. (IRFC) is a dedicated financing arm of the Ministry of Railways in India. Indian Railway Finance Corporation

Limited was founded in 1986 and is based in New Delhi. IRFC play a crucial role in financing the plan outlay of Indian Railways. IRFC's funding has supported technology infusion in railways and has enabled Ministry of Railways in enhancing its assets base.

8.10.1 Objectives: The sole objective of Indian Railways Finance Corporation Ltd. (IRFC) is to raise money from the market to finance the plan outlay of Indian Railways. The money so made available is used for acquisition of rolling stock assets and for meeting other developmental needs of the Indian Railways.

8.10.2 Sources of Finance: The company raises fund by issuing:

1. Taxable and tax free bonds.
2. Term loans from banks and financial institutions.
3. Off shore borrowings.

New generation locomotives from General Motors USA along with transfer of technology and new generation coaches from Germany for use in high speed trains have been funded by the IRFC. Till March 31, 2010, rolling stock assets-locomotives, coaches and wagons-valued at ₹ 60,163 crore have been added to the asset base of the Indian Railways with funding assistance from IRFC.

Short Answer Type Questions

1. Write a note on Indian Railways Finance Corporation Ltd.
2. What do you mean by specialized financial institutions?
3. What are the objectives of Discount and Finance House of India Ltd.?
4. List out important specialized financial institutions.
5. What is 'Constituent SGL' account?
6. Explain STCI Primary Dealer Limited.
7. What is HUDCO?
8. What is SBI DFHI LTD?

Essay Type Questions

1. Explain the organization and functions of Discount and Finance House of India Ltd.
2. What are the functions of Securities Trading Corporation of India Ltd.?
3. Outline the organization and functions of Housing and Urban Development Corporation Ltd.
4. Explain the organization and functions of Power Finance Corporation Ltd.
5. What is SHCIL? Explain the services rendered by Stock Holding Corporation of India Ltd.?

6. What are objectives and functions of Tourism Finance Corporation of India Ltd.?
7. Explain the organization and working of IFCI Venture Capital Funds Ltd.

9

Investment Institutions and Specialized Public Guarantee Institutions

9.1 Introduction

Investment Institutions are financial institutions that facilitate the process of capital accumulation by transferring resources from savers to investors. Investment institutions occupy important place in the well-integrated structure of financial institutions. They are financial intermediaries selling their customers financial assets in order to build up savings for retirement or for other customer uses.

9.2 Investment Institutions in India

The three important investment institutions in India are given below:

1. Unit Trust of India (UTI).
2. Life Insurance Corporation of India (LIC).
3. General Insurance Corporation of India (GIC).

9.2.1 Unit Trust of India (UTI): Unit Trust of India (UTI) was a statutory corporation created under the Unit Trust of India Act of 1963 which was passed by the Indian Parliament. UTI commenced its operations from February 1, 1964. The formation of Unit Trust of India in 1964 marked the evolution of the Indian mutual fund industry. UTI was a public sector investment institution constituted as a result of the collective efforts taken by the Reserve Bank of India and the Government of India.

The primary objective of UTI at that time of establishment was to attract the savings of small investors for channeling them into productive investments. UTI was set up by the Reserve Bank of India and it continued to operate under the regulatory control of the RBI until the two were de-linked in 1978 and the entire control was transferred in the hands of Industrial Development Bank of India (IDBI).

Unit Trust of India was set up with an initial capital outlay of ₹ 5 crore. Of this fifty percent of the capital was subscribed by RBI (₹ 2.5 crore). The capital contributions by Life Insurance Corporation of India (LIC) and State Bank of India (SBI) accounted 15 percent each. Balance 20 percent was subscribed by commercial banks and financial institutions. Unit Trust of India is controlled by

Board of Trustees, comprising Chairman and nine other trustees.

A. Functions of UTI: Following are the functions of Unit Trust of India:

1. Mobilize the savings of small and medium investors through the sale of units.
2. Investing the money collected through the sale of units in securities issued by corporates.
3. Distributing income from these investments to subscriber in the form of dividend.

For more than two decades UTI remained the sole vehicle for investment in the capital market by the Indian citizens. In mid-1980s public sector banks were allowed to open mutual funds. The real vibrancy and competition in the mutual fund industry came with the setting up of the Regulator SEBI and its laying down the Mutual Fund Regulations in 1993.

UTI launched its first scheme in 1964, named as Unit Scheme 1964 (US-64), which attracted the largest number of investors in any single investment scheme over the years. UTI launched more innovative schemes in 1970s and 80s to suit the needs of different investors. It launched ULIP in 1971, six more schemes during 1981-84, Children's Gift Growth Fund and India Fund (India's first offshore fund) in 1986, Mastershare (India's first equity diversified scheme) in 1987 and Monthly Income Schemes (offering assured returns) during 1990s. By the end of 1987, UTI's assets under management grew ten times to ₹ 6700 crore.

The Indian mutual fund industry witnessed a number of public sector players entering the market in the year 1987. In November 1987, SBI Mutual Fund from the State Bank of India became the first non-UTI mutual fund in India. SBI Mutual Fund was later followed by Canbank Mutual Fund, LIC Mutual Fund, Indian Bank Mutual Fund, Bank of India Mutual Fund, GIC Mutual Fund and PNB Mutual Fund. However, UTI remained to be the leader with about 80 percent market share.

UTI maintained its pre-eminent place till 2001, when a massive decline in the market indices and negative investor sentiments after Ketan Parekh scam created doubts about the capacity of UTI to meet its obligations to the investors. This was further compounded by two factors; namely, its flagship and largest scheme US 64 was sold and re-purchased not at intrinsic NAV but at artificial price and its Assured Return Schemes had promised returns as high as 18 percent over a period going up to two decades.

In February 2003, the UTI Act was repealed and UTI was stripped of its special legal status as a trust formed by an Act of Parliament. The primary objective behind this was to bring all mutual fund players on the same level. UTI was bifurcated into two parts.

They are the Specified Undertaking and the UTI Mutual Fund.

Presently Unit Trust of India operates under the name of UTI Mutual Fund and its past schemes (like US-64, Assured Return Schemes) are being gradually wound up. UTI Mutual Fund was created as a SEBI registered fund like any other mutual fund. The assets and liabilities of US-64, Assured Return Schemes where Government had to come out with a bail-out package were taken over directly by the Government in a new entity called Specified Undertaking of UTI.

Besides running domestic MF Schemes UTI AMC is also a registered portfolio manager under the SEBI (Portfolio Managers) Regulations. It runs different portfolios for institutional clients. It is also running a Sharia Compliant portfolio for its offshore clients. UTI tied up with Shinsei Bank of Japan to run a large size India-centric portfolio for Japanese investors.

For its international operations UTI has set up its 100 percent subsidiary, UTI International Limited, registered in Guernsey, Channel Islands. It has branches in London, Dubai and Bahrain. It has set up a Joint Venture with Shinsei Bank in Singapore. In the area of alternate assets, UTI has a 100 percent subsidiary called UTI Ventures at Bangalore. This company runs two successful funds with large international investors being active participants. UTI has also launched a Private Equity Infrastructure Fund along with HSH Nord Bank of Germany and Shinsei Bank of Japan.

UTI Bank (now Axis Bank) was the first of the new private banks to have begun operations in 1994, after the Government of India allowed new private banks to be established. The Bank was promoted jointly by the Administrator of the specified undertaking of the Unit Trust of India, Life Insurance Corporation of India and General Insurance Corporation Ltd. As on March 31, 2012, the Bank is capitalized to the extent of ₹ 413.20 crore with public holding at 54.08 percent.

9.2.2 Life Insurance Corporation of India: Life Insurance Corporation of India is the largest insurance company in India and also the countries largest investor. Life Insurance Corporation of India was founded in 1956 by the Government of India. The role of life insurance funds in the national economy can not be over-emphasized since they form an integral part of the national finance. Over its existence of around 50 years, Life Insurance Corporation of India, which command a monopoly of selling insurance in India, created huge surpluses, and contributed around 7 percent of India's GDP in 2007.

A. History of LIC: The first 150 years of the British Rule in India were characterized by turbulent economic conditions. The World Wars 1 and 2 (1914 - 1918 and 1939-45) and India's national struggle for freedom in between had adverse effect on the economy. In addition to this the period of world wide economic crisis in between the two World Wars termed as the period of great depression led to the high rate of bankruptcies and liquidation of most life insurance companies in India that existed during that time. These occurrences led to loss of faith in insurance of the people of India.

Life insurance in the modern form was first set up in India through a British company called the Oriental Life Insurance Company in 1818 followed by the Bombay Assurance Company in 1823 and the Madras Equitable Life Insurance Society in 1829. All these companies operated in India targeted Europeans but did not insure the lives of Indians. They were insuring the lives of Europeans living in India.

The Indian Assurance Companies Act and the Provident Fund Act passed in 1912 was the first statute meant to regulate the life insurance business in India. The Indian Insurance Companies Act of 1928 authorized the government to obtain statistical information from companies operating in both life and non-life insurance areas. The subsequent Insurance Act of 1938 was the first comprehensive legislation in India intended to control the business of insurance companies in all its totality. In 1937, the Government of India set up a consultative committee. Mr. Sushil C. Sen, a well known solicitor of Calcutta, was appointed as the chair of the committee. He consulted a wide range of interested parties including the industry. Finally, in 1938, the Insurance Act was passed. This piece of legislation was the first comprehensive one in India. It covered both life and general insurance companies.

The first half of the 20th century witnessed heightened struggle for India's independence. The aggregate effect of these events led to a high rate of bankruptcies and liquidation of life insurance companies in India. This had adversely affected the faith of the general public in the utility of obtaining life cover. The failure of insurance business was mainly due to lack of control over the business by the Government because of its absence of legislative measure. However, the situation changed after the country's independence and through a series of legislative and regulatory measures.

In 1955, parliamentarian Feroz Gandhi raised the matter of insurance fraud by owners of private insurance companies. In the ensuing investigations, one of India's wealthiest businessmen, Ram Kishan Dalmia owner of Times of India newspaper, was sent to jail for two years. Eventually, the Parliament of India passed the Life Insurance of India Act. The Life Insurance Corporation of India was established by an Act of Parliament, which received the President's assent on June 19, 1956. The Act came into force on July1, 1956 and the Corporation became functional on September 1, 1956.

LIC was formed through the take over and nationalization of the business of Indian and foreign insurers and provident societies. When the life insurance business was nationalized in 1956, there were 154 Indian life insurance companies. In addition, there were 16 non-Indian insurance companies and 75 provident societies issuing life insurance policies. Most of these policies were centered in the metropolitan areas like Bombay, Calcutta, Delhi and Madras. The assets and liabilities pertaining to the life business of 245 existing insurance companies were transferred to the new Statutory Corporation (LIC). Nationalization of the life insurance business in India was a result of the Industrial Policy Resolution of 1956, which had created a policy framework for extending state control over at least seventeen sectors of the economy. LIC began operations with 5 zonal offices, 33 divisional offices and 212 branch offices.

B. Objectives of Nationalization of LIC: Important objectives of nationalization of LIC are given below:

1. To spread life insurance cover widely in the country especially in the rural areas.
2. Spread life insurance to the socially and economically backward sections.
3. Providing adequate financial coverage against death at a reasonable cost.
4. Maximize the savings of the people through attractive schemes.
5. To meet the various life insurance need of the community.
6. Investing the people's savings in productive purposes.
7. To provide employment opportunities.

C. Dilution of Monopoly: The enforcement of new economic reforms in 1991 coupled with the formation of Insurance Regulatory and Development Authority Act (IRDA) of 2000 has diluted the monopolistic attitude commanded by LIC. The only insurance company belonging to the public sector now has to compete with several other corporate entities of its kind which often are heavyweight Indian as well as multinational life insurance companies themselves. Since the enactment of the IRDA Act in 1999, there has been tremendous growth in the number of insurance companies. The number of Life Insurance Companies in India increased from one at the end of September 2000 to 24 at the end of April 2012. During this period, IRDA granted registration to twenty new private life insurance companies, which commenced their operations.

D. Subsidiaries of LIC: LIC owns the following subsidiaries:

(a) Life Insurance Corporation of India International: Life Insurance Corporation of India International is a joint venture offshore company promoted by LIC which commenced operations in July, 1989 with the objectives of offering US$ denominated Policies to cater to the insurance needs of NRIs and providing insurance services to holders of LIC policies currently residing in the Gulf. LIC International operates in all GCC countries.

(b) LIC Nepal: A joint venture company formed in 2001 with the Vishal Group of Industries, Nepal.

(c) LIC Lanka: A joint venture company formed in 2003 with the Barleet Group of Companies, Sri Lanka.

(d) LIC Housing Finance: LIC Housing Finance was incorporated in 19 June 1989; its main objective is to provide long term finance for construction or purchase of houses or apartments.

(e) LICHFL Care Homes: A wholly owned subsidiary of LIC Housing Finance, it builds and operates "Assisted Community Living Centres" for senior citizens.

E. The Current Status of LIC: The Life Insurance Corporation of India began operations in 1956 with 5 zonal offices, 33 divisional offices and 212 branch offices has currently 8 zonal offices, 109 divisional offices, and 2048 branches located in different cities and towns in the country. LIC is now opening Satellite Offices attached to various branches. It has a network of 1.2 million agents for selling life insurance products. It also operates in 12 other countries, primarily to cater to the needs of Non Resident Indians. LIC still manages to be the largest player in the Indian insurance market, with the lion's share of 55 percent. The corporate office of LIC is in Mumbai.

9.2.3 General Insurance Corporation of India (GIC): Bombay Mutual Life Assurance Society was the first insurance company established in India, which opened its business in 1870. In 1905 following the Swadeshi Movement, many Indian entrepreneurs established banking and insurance institutions. The Indian Mercantile Insurance Ltd. formed in 1907 is considered as the first company to transact all types of general insurance business in India. Later many insurance companies sprung up like mushrooms. The area of operation of these institutions was mainly confined to cities and urban centres. There were also some banks in the thirties (General Insurance Bank of India Ltd. Mangalore) doing both banking and insurance business simultaneously. However, the business of these institutions did not survive for long for many reasons. The failure of insurance business was mainly due to lack of control over the business by the government because of the absence of legislative measures. Insurance business was conducted in India without any specific regulation for the insurance business. They were subject to Indian Companies Act (1866). In 1912, two sets of legislation were passed:

1. Indian Life Assurance Companies Act.
2. Provident Insurance Societies Act.

There are several striking features of these legislations. First, they were the first legislations in India that particularly targeted the insurance sector. Second, they left general insurance business out of it. The government did not feel the necessity to regulate general insurance. Third, they restricted activities of the

Indian insurers but not the foreign insurers even though the model used was the British Act of 1909.

9.2.4 India Reinsurer: GIC's supervisory role over its erstwhile subsidiaries was terminated by an administrative order; it was renamed as the Indian Reinsurer in 2000 by an Act of Parliament. GIC was to function exclusively as life and non-life re-insurer. Subsequently to the General Insurance Business (Nationalization) amendment Act of 2002, GIC ceased to be a holding company and its subsidiaries and ownership got vested with the Government of India.

9.3 Insurance Business in India after Independence

The entire general insurance business in India was nationalized by the General Insurance Business (Nationalization) Act of 1972. At the time of nationalization, about 100 small companies and a few large companies were operating in the field of general insurance. The Government of India, through nationalization took over the shares of 55 Indian insurance companies and the undertakings of 52 insurers carrying on general insurance business.

General Insurance Corporation of India was incorporated on November 22, 1972 under the Companies Act of 1956 as a private company limited by shares. GIC was formed for the purpose of superintending, controlling and carrying on the business of general insurance. As soon as GIC was formed, Government of India transferred all the shares it held in the general insurance companies to the GIC. General Insurance Corporation of India (GIC) was established in 1973.

The Insurance sector in India was organized as General and Life Insurance with the establishment of the Life Insurance Corporation of India (LIC) and General Insurance Corporation (GIC). After nationalization, one holding company named General Insurance Corporation of India (GIC) was set up with its Head Office in Mumbai. Subsequently all the existing companies were merged and reorganized into four fully owned subsidiaries of GIC viz.

1. National Insurance Company Ltd.
2. New India Insurance Company Ltd.
3. Oriental Fire and General Insurance Company Ltd.
4. United India Insurance Company Ltd.

These companies used to carry out the business of general insurance in India in a monopolistic manner up to1999 and in that year the insurance business was opened for private players also.

The next landmark happened on 19 April 2000, when the Insurance Regulatory and Development Authority Act, 1999 (IRDAA) came into force. This act also introduced an amendment to General Insurance Business (Nationalization) Act of 1972 and the Insurance Act of 1938.

9.4 Specialized Pubic Guarantee Institutions

The three important specialized public institutions in India are given below:

1. Export Credit Guarantee Corporation of India Ltd. (ECGC).
2. Deposit Insurance and Credit Guarantee Corporation (DICGC).
3. Agriculture Insurance Company of India Ltd. (AIC).

9.4.1 Export Credit Guarantee Corporation of India Ltd (ECGC): Export Credit Guarantee Corporation of India Ltd. (ECGC) is a company owned wholly by the Government of India. ECGC was set up by the government with the object of promoting Indian exports. ECGC is the fifth largest credit insurer of the world. It had initially set up as Export Risks Insurance Corporation (ERIC) in July 30, 1957. It was transformed into Export Credit Guarantee Corporation of India Ltd (ECGC) in 1964. ECGC has been registered with the Insurance Regulatory and Development Authority (IRDA) as an insurance company during September 2002. Registered office of ECGC is at Mumbai. ECGC has 5 Regional Offices and 52 branches.

A. Objectives of ECGC: The primary objective of setting up of ECGC is to promote Indian export by providing export credit insurance and other trade related services to Indian exporters. The corporation provides guarantee to financial institutions for the benefit of the exporters.

B. Management: Export Credit Guarantee Corporation of India Ltd. (ECGC) is controlled by the Ministry of Commerce and Industry, Government of India. It is managed by a Board of Directors comprising representatives of the Government, Reserve Bank of India, banking and insurance and exporting community.

C. Capital and Financial Resources: The present paid-up capital of the company is ₹ 900 crore and authorized capital ₹ 1000 crore. The Government of India instilled confidence in ECGC by establishing National Export Insurance Account (NEIA) with a corpus of ₹ 2,000 crore to be managed by ECGC.

D. Need for Export Credit Guarantee: Export credit insurance is essential for exporters to avoid the various risk factors connected with the export of goods and services. Payments for exports are prone to risks even at the best of times. The risks have assumed large proportions now a day due to the political and economic changes that are sweeping the world. Factors like a coup, an outbreak of a war, revolution or civil disturbances in the buyer's country, problems in balance of payment and such other risks can happen at anytime. In addition, the exporters have to face commercial risks of insolvency or protracted default of buyers. Export credit insurance is designed to protect exporters from the consequences of the payment risks, both political and commercial, and to enable them to expand their overseas business without fear of loss. To tackle all these risks and various other issues related to exports, it is very important to have an organization like Export Credit Guarantee Corporation to safeguard the interest of the exporter.

E. Functions: ECGC provides a wide range of credit risk insurance covers to exporters against loss in export of goods and services. Important functions of ECGC are the following.

1. It offers insurance protection to exporters against risk of payment.
2. It provides guidance in export related activities.
3. Offers guarantees to banks and financial institutions to enable exporters to obtain better facilities from them.
4. Makes available information on various countries with its own credit ratings.
5. Provides information on credit worthiness of the overseas buyer.
6. Helps to obtain export finance easily from banks and other financial institutions.
7. Assists exporters in recovering bad debts.
8. Provides overseas investment insurance to Indian companies investing in joint ventures abroad in the form of loan or equity shares.
9. Factoring services.

Besides the above ECGC now offers various products for the exporters and bankers. If readymade products are not suited to an exporter and the banker, then ECGC designs tailor made products. Tied-up with United India Insurance Company, ECGC offers marine insurance cover free for its policy holders as add-on benefit. Tied-up with National Small Industries Corporation (NSIC) ECGC offers refined and simplified policy to suit the requirements of small and medium enterprises spread over India.

ECGC has entered an agreement with Multilateral Investment Guarantee Agency (MIGA) an arm of World Bank. MIGA provides the following services.

1. Political insurance for foreign investment in developing countries.
2. Technical assistance to improve investment climate.
3. Dispute mediation service. Under this agreement protection is available against political and economic risks such as transfer restriction, expropriation, war, terrorism and civil disturbances etc.

9.4.2 Deposit Insurance and Credit Guarantee Corporation (DICGC): In India, deposit insurance scheme was introduced firstly in the year 1962. It was introduced as a means to provide protection to the depositors in the commercial and co-operative banks and RRBs. The scheme was introduced particularly for providing protection to the small depositors from the risk of loss of their savings arising from bank failures. The main object of deposit insurance scheme is to give a protection and to develop a confidence in the minds of public who contributes to the growth of banking system in the country.

A. Origin of DICGC: Bank failures in the 19th as well as the early 20th Century (1913-14) have serious consequences for the depositors and adversely affect the development of the banking system in the country. After the setting up of the Reserve Bank of India, the issue came to the fore in 1938 when the Travancore National and Quilon Bank, the largest bank in the Travancore region, failed. As a result, interim measures relating to banking legislation and reform were instituted in the early 1940s. The banking crisis in Bengal between 1946 and 1948, once again revitalized the issue of deposit insurance. It was, however, felt that the measures be held in abeyance till the Banking Companies Act of 1949 came into force and comprehensive arrangements were made for the supervision and inspection of banks by the Reserve Bank.

1960s and 1970s witnessed the establishment of several important institutions in the country. It was in 1960 that the failure of Laxmi Bank and the subsequent failure of the Palai Central Bank catalyzed the introduction of deposit insurance in India. The Deposit Insurance Corporation (DIC) Bill was introduced in the Parliament on August 21, 1961 and received the assent of the President of India on December 7, 1961.

The Deposit Insurance Corporation commenced its operation with effect from January 1, 1962. India was the second country in the world to introduce such a scheme, the first being the United States in 1933.

Deposit Insurance Corporation was promoted by Reserve Bank of India (RBI) with an authorized capital of ₹ 10 crore of which ₹ 2 crore have been fully paid up. The whole amount of capital has been subscribed by the RBI. Moreover, the corporation can also borrow up to ₹ 5 core from RBI. The management of the corporation is under the control of a Board of Directors consists five members. Board of Directors is entrusted with the task of supervising the functions of the corporation. Governor of the Reserve Bank of India is the chairman of the Board. One Deputy Governor and an officer of the RBI and two directors nominated by the Government of India in consultation with RBI are also members of the Board.

Following the establishment of Deposit Insurance Corporation (DIC) the Government commenced another institution called Credit Guarantee Corporation of India Ltd. (CGCI) in the year 1971. Credit Guarantee Corporation of India was established to encourage the banks to provide credit to the hitherto neglected sections and sectors of the economy without any excessive risk. The scheme covers the credit facilities extended by banks to certain categories in the neglected sectors and weaker sections of the society. The essential concern was to persuade banks to make available credit to not so creditworthy clients.

The credit guarantee scheme is extended to commercial banks, regional rural banks, co-operative banks, state financial corporations and other lending institutions. CGC introduced three schemes viz. (i) small loans guarantee scheme in 1971, (ii) small loans (financial corporation) guarantee scheme in 1971 and (iii) service co-operative societies guarantee scheme in 1971. A credit guarantee scheme for small-scale industries sponsored and formulated by the Government of India and administered by the Credit Guarantee Organization (Reserve Bank of India) had been in operations since July 1960. In pursuance of the recommendations of a Working Group constituted by the Government of India in 1979, it was decided to integrate all credit guarantee schemes under one organization. Accordingly, this scheme was cancelled by the Government of India in March 1981 and the Corporation, in its place introduced a new scheme with effect from 1 April, 1981 covering advances to small scale industries by commercial banks and other financial institutions.

In 1978, the Deposit Insurance Corporation (DIC) and the Credit Guarantee Corporation of India Ltd. (CGCI) were merged to form the Deposit Insurance and Credit Guarantee Corporation (DICGC). Consequently, the title of Deposit Insurance Act of 1961 was changed to the Deposit Insurance and Credit Guarantee Corporation Act of 1961. The merger was with a view to integrate the functions of deposit insurance and credit guarantee.

In July 1984, DICGC introduced small loans (co-operative banks) guarantee scheme with a view to extent the credit guarantee facility to the primary urban co-operative banks in respect of loans granted to transport operators, small business for professional and self employment. With the financial sector reforms undertaken in the 1990s, credit guarantees have been gradually phased out and the focus of the Corporation is veering back to its core function of Deposit Insurance with the objective of averting panics, reducing systemic risk, and ensuring financial stability.

The erstwhile Credit Guarantee Corporation of India Ltd., was operating three credit guarantee schemes pertaining to advances to certain specified categories of small borrowers and with the transfer of this undertaking to the Deposit Insurance Corporation in July 1978, the Deposit Insurance Corporation took over those credit guarantee functions also. The three credit guarantee schemes which were formulated by the Credit Guarantee Corporation of India Ltd. and continued by the Corporation, were intended to provide the necessary incentive to financial institutions for extending need based credit to small borrowers (including farmers) engaged in non-industrial activities.

B. Institutional Coverage: Deposit insurance scheme provides automatic coverage for deposits received in India by all commercial banks including regional rural banks. When the Deposit Insurance Corporation commenced operations in the early 1960s, 287 banks registered with it as insured banks. By the end of 1967, this number was reduced to 100, largely as a result of the Reserve Bank of India's policy of the reconstruction and amalgamation of small and financially weak banks so as to make the banking sector more viable. In 1968, the Deposit Insurance Corporation Act was amended to extend deposit insurance to eligible co-operative banks in the States and Union Territories. As a result, the DIC had to expand its operations very considerably. In terms of geographical coverage, the benefit of deposit insurance now stands extended to the entire banking system.

C. Extent of Coverage: Under the Scheme, in the event of liquidation, reconstruction or amalgamation of an insured bank every depositor of that bank is entitled to repayment of his deposits held by him in the same right and capacity in all branches of that bank up to a monetary ceiling of ₹ 1,00,000.

D. Payment of Premium: The insurance premium is collected by the corporation from banks at the rate of 5 paise per annum per hundred rupees at half yearly intervals. The banks are required to bear this fee so that the protection of insurance is available to the depositors at free of cost. In case of default in payment of the premium, the bank is liable to pay the overdue premium at a penal interest of 8 percent above Bank Rate.

9.4.3 Agricultural Insurance Company of India Limited (AIC): Agriculture Insurance Company of India Ltd (AIC) was a Company set up by Government of India to dispense insurance protection over agriculture and allied activities. AIC was incorporated under Indian Companies Act of 1956 on 20th December, 2002. The company was registered with an authorized share capital of ₹ 1500 crore and paid up capital of ₹ 200 crore. Thirty percent of the paid up capital of ₹ 200 crore has been subscribed by NABARD and the remaining by five public sector general insurance companies.

A. Promoters of AIC: Agricultural Insurance Company of India Limited (AIC) was promoted by General Insurance Corporation of India (GIC), NABARD and 4 public sector General Insurance Companies. The holding of shares by General Insurance Corporation of India and National Bank for Agriculture and Rural Development (NABARD) were 35 and 30 percent respectively. Balance 35 percent of shares was held by the four general insurance companies' (National Insurance Company Limited, New India Assurance Company Limited, Oriental Insurance Company Limited and United India Insurance Company Limited) in equal proportion.

Agriculture Insurance Company of India Ltd (AIC) is the largest agricultural insurance company in India and one of the biggest in the world, providing insurance cover to millions of framers. Popularly known as AIC, the company commenced its operation from April 1, 2003 by the Government of India. The main objective of AIC is to protect the interest of the farmers.

B. Administration: Agricultural Insurance Company of India Limited (AIC) is under the administrative control of Ministry of Finance, Government of India and under the operational supervision of Ministry of Agriculture. The Head Office of AIC is located at New Delhi. AIC has 17 Regional Offices spread across India.

C. Services Provided by AIC: AIC sells various agriculture and allied insurance products. A significant amount of business is derived out of National Agriculture Insurance Scheme, which was previously being implemented by General Insurance Corporation of India. The business is derived in the form of a compulsory nature of crop insurance at the time of an agricultural loan as per the directives of the Government of India. AIC offers area based and weather based crop insurance programmes in all most all districts in the country. Some important products are:

1. Weather Based Crop Insurance Scheme.
2. Plant Insurance Policy.
3. Wheat Insurance.
4. Mango Insurance.
5. Varsha Bima/Rainfall Insurance.
6. Coffee Insurance.
7. Rubber Insurance.
8. Rabi Weather Insurance.
9. Tree/Plant Insurance.
10. National Agricultural Insurance Scheme etc.

National Agricultural Insurance Scheme (NAIS) is implemented by AICI with the objective of protecting both the loanee and non-loanee farmers, without any ceiling on the land holdings, against losses suffered on account of crop failure due to natural calamities, etc., and restore credit worthiness for the ensuing cropping season.

All food crops (cereals, millets and pulses) oilseeds and eleven annual horticultural/commercial crops, viz., sugarcane, potato, cotton, ginger, onion, turmeric, chilli, jute, tapioca, banana and pineapple are covered under the scheme, at present. National Agricultural Insurance Scheme (NAIS) is implemented in 23 states and 2 Union Territories.

For an insurance coverage on crops, farmer can interact with a local Primary Agricultural Credit Societies (PACS) in his area or with a commercial bank branch directly. Three types of banks can participate: (i) Regional Rural Banks, (ii) District Central Cooperative Bank and (iii) Commercial Banks. One or two bank branches in every district in India would be chosen as a Nodal Bank, the bank would interact directly with AIC.

Short Answer Type Questions

1. What is UTI?
2. List out investment institutions in India.
3. What are the objectives of LIC?
4. Explain Specified Undertaking of UTI?
5. Name the specialized public guarantee institutions in India.
6. What are the objectives of ECGC?
7. Explain Indian reinsurer.
8. What is AIC?
9. What is ECGC?

Essay Type Questions

1. Explain the management and functions of ECGC.
2. Explain the objectives and functions of LIC.
3. What are the important functions of Unit Trust of India?
4. Give a brief history of LIC of India.
5. Explain the organization and functions of ECGC?
6. Write a note on history of general insurance in India.
7. What are the functions of Agriculture Insurance Company of India?
8. Give a brief history of the origin, development and objective of Unit Trust of India.
9. Explain the role played by ECGC in Indian export.

10

Regional Rural Banks (RRBs)

10.1 Introduction

The Regional Rural Banks (RRBs) is the major investors in different types of operations in the rural sector. The Regional Rural Banks (RRBs) in India are spread all across the country and have been playing an important role in the development and growth of the rural business and economy. The areas of operation of these banks are limited to a particular area or state and are required to provide credit facilities to the weaker sections in the rural areas.

RRBs are subsidiaries to the nationalized banks and their staff members are drawn mainly from the area of their operation. These banks are expected not only to provide credit but also to mobilize savings from rural households. RRBs are now occupying an important position in the rural institutional financing in terms of geographical coverage, clientele reach out and business volume as also in contribution to the development of the rural economy. Since their inception, regional rural banks (RRBs) have taken deep roots and have become a sort of inseparable part of the rural credit structure in India.

10.2 Objectives of RRBs

The main objective of regional rural banks is the "provision of credit and other facilities especially to the small and marginal farmers, agricultural labourers, artisans and small entrepreneurs in rural areas". RRBs were established "with a view to developing the rural economy by providing, for the purpose of development of agriculture, trade, commerce, industry and other productive activities in the rural areas, credit and other facilities, particularly to small and marginal farmers, agricultural labourers, artisans and small entrepreneurs, and for matters connected therewith and incidental thereto". These banks also provide assistance in the marketing of agricultural and other products through marketing organizations and help in the overall development of the villages. RRBs were expected to mobilize resources from rural areas and play a catalytic role in developing agriculture and rural economy by deploying such mobilized resources to rural sectors for the needy who are not covered by scheduled commercial banks in spite of their large network of branches.

10.3 Establishment of RRBs

Regional Rural Banks (RRBs) were established to meet the excess demand for institutional credit in the rural areas, particularly among the economically and socially marginalized sections. Although the cooperative banks and the commercial banks had reasonable records in terms of geographical coverage and disbursement of credit, in terms of population groups the cooperative banks were dominated by the rural rich, while the commercial banks had a clear urban bias. In order to provide access to low-cost banking facilities to the poor, a Working Group was appointed by the Government under the Chairmanship of Sri M. Narashimham (1975), to study the possibility of establishment of an alternative agency to provide institutional credit to landless labourers, rural artisans, small and marginal farmers.

The Narasimham Working Group proposed the establishment of a new set of banks, as institutions which "combine the local feel and the familiarity with rural problems which the cooperatives possess and the degree of business organization, ability to mobilize deposits, access to central money markets and modernized outlook which the commercial banks have". The decision to establish RRBs in India was taken by the then Prime Minister Smt. Indira Gandhi in 1975, with the primary objective of developing the rural economy for meeting the financial needs of the weaker sections of rural community.

Based on the report of the Working Group, the Government of India promulgated the RRBs Ordinance dated 26 September 1975. Accordingly on 2nd October 1975, the Government of India set up five Regional Rural Banks in four states. These five banks were sponsored by Syndicate Bank, State Bank of India, Punjab National Bank, United Commercial Bank and United Bank of India. The total authorized capital of each RRB was fixed at ₹ 1 crore which has since been raised to ₹ 5 Crore.

Regional Rural Banks were set up under the Regional Rural Banks Act of 1976. RRBs are meant to operate as State sponsored, region based and rural oriented commercial banks. In the year 1976, Regional Rural Banks Act was passed by giving legal form and status to the emergency ordinance. The Central Government is empowered, on the request of any bank called 'Sponsor Bank' to establish in a State or Union Territory one or more RRBs.

There are several concessions enjoyed by the RRBs from RBI such as lower interest rates and refinancing facilities from NABARD, lower cash reserve ratio, lower statutory liquidity ratio, lower rate of interest on loans taken from sponsoring banks, managerial and staff assistance from the sponsoring bank and reimbursement of the expenses on staff training. Regional Rural Banks are operating under the regulatory supervision of NABARD, which has the responsibility of laying down the policies, to supervise their operations, provide refinance facilities, to monitor their performance and to attend their problems.

The Sponsor Bank also assists the RRBs in several ways. The Sponsor Bank subscribes the share capital of RRBs to the extent of 35 percent of its paid up capital. It assists RRBs in its establishment, recruitment and training of personnel. The Sponsor Bank also provides managerial and finical assistances to RRBs.

10.4 Functions of RRB

Regional Rural banks (RRB) were created to provide sufficient institutional credit for agriculture to the rural areas of a state. The main function of RRB is to provide loans to the small marginal farmers and agricultural labourers. However, the functions of an RRB are limited to a specific area which is specified by the state. Important functions of RRBs are given below:

1. Granting loans and advances to small and marginal farmers, agricultural labourers for agricultural and other operations.
2. Granting loans and advances to primary agricultural credit societies, farmers societies, cooperatives farming and agricultural processing societies etc. for agricultural and other related purposes.
3. Granting loans and advances to artisans, traders and small entrepreneurs for trade, commerce or industry or other productive activities.

10.5 Capital Structure of RRBs

The authorized capital of each Regional Rural Bank shall be ₹ 5 crore divided into five lakh of fully paid-up shares of one hundred rupees each. The issued capital of each Regional Rural Bank should not be less than ₹ 1 crore. The equity capital of each RRB was contributed by the Central Government, the State Government concerned and the Sponsor Bank in the proportion of 50:15:35. There is a provision for increasing the issue capital by the Board of Directors of the RRB concerned, after consultation with the Reserve Bank of India and the Sponsor Bank and with the prior approval of the Central Government.

10.6 Management

Subject to the provisions of RRB Act, the general superintendence, direction and management of the affairs and business of a Regional Rural Bank shall vest in a Board of Directors who may exercise all the powers and discharge all the functions which may be exercised or discharged by the Regional Rural Bank.

10.7 Board of Directors

The Board of Directors of the Regional Rural Banks consists of a Chairman and eight directors. The chairman is appointed for a period not exceeding five. The Sponsor Bank shall appoint chairman in consultation with NABARD/Central Government. The Chairman shall devote his whole time to the affairs of the Regional Rural Bank and shall have, subject to the superintendence, control and direction of the Board, the management of the whole of the affairs of RRBs.

Two directors who are not officers of the Central Government, State Government, RBI, NABARD, Sponsor Bank or any other bank to be nominated by the Central Government. One director who is an officer of the Reserve Bank of India is nominated by that Bank. One director, who is an officer of the NABARD, is to be nominated by that Bank. Two directors, who are officers of the Sponsor Bank, to be nominated by that Bank and two directors, who are officers of the concerned State Government, to be nominated by that Government.

10.8 Growth of Regional Rural Banks

The basic objective of RRBs was to feel and get familiarized with local needs, and to remain a professionally managed alternative channel for credit dispensation to small and marginal farmers. From a modest beginning of 5 RRBs with 17 branches covering 12 districts in December 1975, the number grew to 196 RRBs in 26 states in 523 districts across the country (as on September-end 2011, the number of RRBs has declined significantly to 83 in 27 states). The number of branches of RRBs increased from 17 to 15,144 during the period December 1975 to June 2009. The State Bank of India was one of the major commercial banks having Regional Rural Banks. There were 30 Regional Rural Banks in India under the State Bank of India and it was spread in 13 states across India.

Even though these 196 RRBs were spread over twenty six States, most of them were located in seven States, i.e. Andhra Pradesh, Bihar, Karnataka, Madhya Pradesh, Maharastra, Rajasthan and Uttar Pradesh. Uttar Pradesh had the highest number of RRBs, i.e., 36 and Kerala has got only two amongst the major States of the country. The RRB branches alone constituted 20.87 percent of the total bank branches in the country and 79.5 percent of them were in the rural areas. Semi-urban and urban/metropolitan branches represented only 18.2 and 4.4 percent respectively of the total branches. The rural orientation of RRBs is formidable with rural and semi-urban branches constituting over 95 percent of their branch network.

RRBs have a large branch network in the rural area forming around 43 percent of the total rural branches of commercial banks. The rural orientation of RRBs is formidable with rural and semi-urban branches constituting over 97 percent of their branch network. The growth in the branch network has enabled the RRBs to expand banking activities in the unbanked areas and mobilize rural savings.

10.9 Financial Performance and Viability of RRBs

Regional Rural Banks established under the RRB Act of 1976 have rendered yeomen service for the economic upliftment of the rural people, especially those living below the poverty line. The involvement of RRBs in providing credit support to small and retail trade and other non-farm rural activities are better than that of co-operatives and commercial banks.

The RRBs as a group incurred a loss of ₹ 426 crore in the year 1995-96. The viability based categorization of RRBs as on 31 March 2002, showed that out of 196 RRBs, 86 RRBs wiped off their accumulated losses and in a way attained a sustainable viability whereas 89 other RRBs achieved a turn around and attained a current viability status leaving only 29 RRBs, which continued to incur losses. The viability-based review of RRBs has revealed that the loss making RRBs are concentrated in three states viz. Madhya Pradesh, Bihar and Orissa and in four sponsors viz. UCO Bank, State Bank of India, Bank of India, and Bank of Baroda.

Net profit of RRBs further increased to ₹ 769 crore during 2003-04. The net profits declined thereafter to ₹ 748 crore during 2004-05 and to ₹ 510 crore in 2005-06. The net profits of RRBs dwindled mainly because of reduction in the net margin and the payment of arrears. The overall financial strength of RRBs improved significantly over the last few years. The ratio of gross and net NPAs declined sharply during the year 2005-06 to 7.3 percent and 4.0 percent, respectively, enabled by improved recovery to the extent of 80 percent. The productivity of RRBs, both in terms of per branch and per employee, has increased significantly during the last 10 years.

10.10 Reasons for the Poor Performance of RRBs

Even though RRBs have succeeded in achieving their basic objectives, they are suffering from a number of maladies. In the wake of the introduction of financial sector reforms in 1991-92, the commercial viability of RRBs has become as the most crucial factor in deciding their desired role in the emerging economic scenario. However, the performance of most of the RRBs remains far from satisfactory. The financial health of RRBs gets weakened year by year. Various committees appointed by the Government and NABARD for the revivals of RRBs have identified the important reasons for the low profitability of RRBs:

1. Lack of commercial orientation.
2. Limited business flexibility.

3. Limited scope for expansion/diversification.
4. Wilful default due to weak monitoring and supervision.
5. Large number of defaulters.
6. Lack of legal and administrative support from the state government in the matter of recovery.
7. Smaller size of loans with higher exposure to risk-prone advances.
8. Professional inefficiency in financial deployment.
9. Branches have not been located at the right places.
10. Sponsoring banks are also running their branches in the same areas where RRBs are operating.
11. Political interference.
12. Low capital base.
13. Multiple ownership and divided responsibility.
14. Lack of adequate training for the RRB staff.
15. Low productivity, high transaction costs and lower CD ratio.

10.11 Restructuring of RRBs

The financial viability of RRBs has engaged the attention of the policy makers from time to time. In fact, as early as 1981, the Committee to Review Arrangements for Institutional Credit for Agriculture and Rural Development (CRAFICARD) addressed the issue of financial viability of the RRBs. The CRAFICARD recommended that 'the loss incurred by a RRB should be made good annually by the shareholders in the same proportion of their shareholdings'.

Though this recommendation was not accepted, under a scheme of recapitalization, financial support was provided by the shareholders in the proportion of their shareholdings. Subsequently, a number of committees have come out with different suggestions to address the financial non-viability of RRBs.

10.12 Reports of Various Committees for the Revival of RRBs

10.12.1 Kelkar Committee Report: Kelkar Committee (1986) made comprehensive recommendations covering both the organizational and the operational aspects of RRBs. The important recommendations of Kelkar Committee are listed below:

1. Enhancement of authorized capital of RRBs from ₹ 1 crore to ₹ 5 crore and paid-up share capital from ₹ 25 lakh to ₹ 1 crore.
2. Appointment of Chairman of RRBs by the concerned sponsor bank in consultation with NABARD.
3. Provision of assistance to RRBs in greater measure by sponsor banks in

training RRB staff and giving financial assistance to RRBs in the first five years of their existence.

4. Provision for amalgamation of RRBs in consultation with all the parties concerned.
5. Empowering the sponsor banks to monitor the progress of RRBs and also to arrange for their inspection, internal audit etc.

10.12.2 Khusro Committee: The Agricultural Credit Review Committee (Khusro Committee), 1989 pointed out that the weaknesses of RRBs, recommended for the merger of RRBs with the sponsor banks.

10.12.3 Narasimham Committee Report: The Committee on Financial Systems, 1991 (Narasimham Committee) also stressed the poor financial health of the RRBs. Of the 196 RRBs, 172 were recorded unprofitable with an aggregate loan recovery performance of 40.8 percent (June 1993). The low equity base of these banks (paid up capital of ₹ 25 lakh) did not cover for the loan losses of most RRBs. In the case of a few RRBs, there had also been an erosion of public deposits, besides capital. In order to impart viability to the operations of RRBs, the Narasimham Committee suggested that the RRBs should be permitted to engage in all types of banking business and should not be forced to restrict their operations to the target groups, a proposal which was readily accepted. This recommendation marked a major turning point in the functioning of RRBs.

10.12.4 Chalapathi Rao Committee: The Government of India set up a Working Group under the Chairmanship of Mr. M.V.S. Chalapathi Rao, Managing Director, NABARD in 2001 to examine various aspects of the functioning of RRBs and to make recommendations for RRBs to become an effective institution for the development of the rural economy. The Group submitted its report in August 2002 and suggested amendments to several provisions of RRB Act besides making a number of recommendations to improve the viability and performance of RRBs.

Subsequently, another committee under the Chairmanship of Chalapathy Rao in 2003 (Chalapathy Rao Committee) recommended that the entire system of RRBs may be consolidated while retaining the advantages of regional character of these institutions. As part of the process, some sponsor banks may be eased out. The sponsoring institutions may include other approved financial institutions as well, in addition to commercial banks.

10.12.5 Purwar Committee: Purwar Committee, 2004 recommended the amalgamation of RRBs on regional basis into six commercial banks, one each for the Northern, Southern, Eastern, Western, Central and North-Eastern Regions.

10.12.6 Advisory Committee: An Advisory Committee appointed by the Government under the Chairmanship of Shri V.S. Vyas "to improve the flow of credit to agriculture sector and other related activities" also recommended for the restructuring of RRBs. The Committee submitted its report in June 2004.

10.12.7 Report of the RBI's Internal Working Group: Following the recommendations of the Working Group, an Internal Working Group on RRBs was set up by the Reserve Bank. The Group examined various options available within the existing legal framework for the strengthening of RRBs. They suggested far-reaching measures including mergers and acquisitions of RRBs, change in sponsorship through involvement of private banks, appointment of chairman from the related sectors, minimum capital requirement and a host of new avenues of business to augment their fee-based incomes. The group proposed a change in sponsorship by which new banks both private as well as public to be involved with RRBs. With a view to improve the competitiveness, work culture, management and efficiency of RRBs a change in sponsorship may be considered. The committee also suggested to maintain the cash reserve ratio of RRBs at 5 percent and with the passage of time they are expected to align themselves with Basel-I norms. To increase the non-interest income of RRBs they may be permitted to act as agents for the distribution of products of mutual funds and insurance companies.

10.13 Recapitalization of RRBs

Government took several measures for reconstruction/recapitalization of the RRBs. Following the first phase of recapitalization i.e. in 1995-96 and 1996-97, the performance of RRBs was improved. However, by the introduction of prudential norms of asset classification, income recognition and provisioning for the RRBs did not produce the expected results. To strengthen the capital base of RRBs, the Government of India through budgetary allocations infused capital for the RRBs. The process of recapitalization initiated in 1994-95 continued up to the year 1999-2000.

In the fourth Phase of 1997-98, 90 RRBs were given capital support to the extent of ₹ 400 crore. This consists of 15 RRBs, which got capital support for the first time, and 75 RRBs that received assistance in the earlier phases and also got further amount allotted to strengthen their capital. A total sum of ₹ 2,188 crore had been infused as additional capital support to 187 out of 196 RRBs through six phases of recapitalization of the loss-making RRBs till January 2000. Out of 187 RRBs, 158 RRBs were fully recapitalized and 29 RRBs only partially. Further, while seven RRBs are yet to be taken up for recapitalization, two profit making RRBs do not need any capital support. During the year 2000-01, the Government of India did not take up recapitalization exercise and no budgetary allocation was made for the year 2001-02.

10.14 Restructuring of RRBs

Following the recommendations of the Internal Group, Reserve Bank examined various alternatives available within the existing legal framework for the strengthening of RRBs. The Group, in its Report submitted in June 2005, observed large variations in the number of districts covered and the branch network of RRBs. The Internal Working Group in its report stated that 47 RRBs covered only one district each, 111 RRBs covered 2 to 3 districts, 29 RRBs 4 to 5 districts and 9 operated in 6 to 9 districts. Similarly, 72 RRBs had up to 50 branches, 87 RRBs 51 to 100 branches, 21 RRBs 101 to150 branches and 16 had more than 150 branches. As many as six sponsor banks had only one RRB sponsored by them. While 11 sponsor banks had 2 to 4 sponsored RRBs, 3 sponsor banks had up to 10 RRBs and 8 sponsor banks had more than 10 RRBs sponsored by them scattered in different States. Of these, only 2 sponsor banks had more than 20 RRBs.

In order to improve the operational viability of RRBs and take advantage of their economies of scale by reducing transaction cost and taking into account, the route of merger/amalgamation of RRBs was suggested. The restructuring was to be a two-phased one as suggested by the committee:

1. Merger of RRBs of the same sponsor bank of the same State.
2. Merger of RRBs sponsored by different banks of the same State.

Amalgamation of RRBs would enable them to become bigger in size with a larger area of operation. It would also help them to function in a competitive environment more effectively by taking advantage of the economies of large scale and reduction in transaction cost. The process of pruning the number of RRBs would also make it more convenient for the sponsor banks to manage their affairs. The Group observed large variations in the number of districts covered and the branch network of RRBs.

As per the recommendations of the Committee, the Government of India in consultation with NABARD and the concerned State Government and sponsor banks initiated State-level amalgamation of RRBs. The process of sponsor bank-wise amalgamation of RRBs at the State level started on September 12, 2005 with a notification indicating the formation of 9 amalgamated entities. Till October 31, 2006, 137 RRBs were amalgamated to form 43 new RRBs, sponsored by 18 commercial banks spread over 15 States thus bringing down the total number of RRBs in the country to 102 from that of 196. The amalgamation process of phase-I is in the process of being completed. Due to reorganization and amalgamation of RRBs, the number of RRBs was reduced from 196 in March 2005 to 133 in March 2006 and dwindled to 83 at end of September 2011.

As part of financial strengthening of RRBs, the Union Budget 2007-08, had announced recapitalization by providing capital support to 27 RRBs, which had negative net worth as on 31 March 2007. Of the 27 RRBs, 11 were amalgamated and 16 were stand-alone. The funding requirement was ₹ 1,795.97 crore to be contributed by Government of India, the concerned State Governments and Sponsor Banks in the ratio of 50:15:35. As on 31 March 2009, 26 RRBs have been fully recapitalized and one RRB has been recapitalized partially, with total funding support of ₹ 1783.41 crore.

10.15 Special Package Announced by Government for Revitalizing RRBs

The process of amalgamation of RRBs gained further momentum only when the Finance Minister, Mr. P Chidambaram gave a nod for such a process in nine states. Accordingly, if a sponsor bank had more than one RRB in a State, all the RRBs in that State under a sponsor bank should be consolidated into one RRB. The Minister also stressed the need to provide adequate capital support to RRBs, which will enable them to have a net capital adequacy ratio of 5 percent. The share of sponsoring institutions in the capital structure of RRBs should be increased to make them a majority stakeholder. In the long run RRBs can be converted into vibrant and professional subsidiaries and area-specific Special Business Units (SBUs). Even co-operative banks can be merged with these SBUs subsequently. To revitalize and to improve the financial strength of RRBs, Reserve Bank of India announced a special package in December 2005. Following are the important proposals of the package:

1. Sponsor banks were advised to provide lines of credit to RRBs at reasonable rates of interest to strengthen their resource base.
2. RRBs were given access to inter-RRB term money/borrowings and to the repo/CBLO markets.
3. RRBs were permitted to set up off-site ATMs, issue debit/credit cards and to handle pension/Government business as authorized sub-agents of banks to conduct Government business.
4. Reserve Bank indicated that taking into account their financial position, requests from RRBs could be considered for opening of currency chests.
5. Reserve Bank to review the existing norms for the conduct of various types of foreign exchange transactions by RRBs with a view to allow them to undertake non-trade related current account transactions to release foreign exchange for certain specified purposes such as overseas education, business travel, medical treatment and private visits. The role of RRBs and their financial performance evolves in response to policy initiatives as well as changing business environment.

To strengthen RRBs and improve their performance, the Reserve Bank allowed RRBs to lend to non-target groups, deregulation of deposit and lending rates, and permitted investment of their surplus funds in profitable avenues. These measures were, supported with well-defined business plan preparation from the branches, time bound implementation for attaining profitability, human resource development programmes, and organizational development initiatives as an integrated tool for turnaround.

Reserve Bank of India in its notification on November 17, 2008 allowed greater flexibility to RRBs in opening new branches as long as they are making profits and their financials are improving. Accordingly, the conditions for opening of new branches for RRBs have been modified. Now RRB should fulfil the following conditions to become eligible for opening of new branch/es. (i) It should not have defaulted in maintenance of SLR and CRR during the last two years and (ii) The RRB should be making operational profits, its net worth should show improvement and its net NPA ratio should not exceed 8 percent.

Short Answer Type Questions

1. What do you mean by RRB?
2. What are the objectives of RRB?
3. What are the functions of RRBs?

Essay Type Questions

1. Give a brief history of the establishment of RRB
2. What are the reasons for the poor performance of RRBs?
3. Write a note on the restructuring of RRBs.
4. Critically examine the role and working of RRBs.
5. What are the reasons for the establishment of RRBs?
6. What is the special package announced by the Government for revitalizing RRBs?

11

Co-operative Banks

11.1 Introduction

The term co-operation is derived from the Latin word 'co-operari', where the word co means 'with' and *operari* means 'to work'. Thus, co-operation means working together. So those who want to work together with some common economic objective can form a society which is termed as "co-operative society". It is a voluntary association of persons who work together to promote their economic interest. It works on the principle of self-help as well as mutual help. The main objective is to provide support to the members. Nobody joins a co-operative society to earn profit. People come forward as a group, pool their individual resources, utilize them in the best possible manner, and derive some common benefit out of it.

11.2 Meaning of Co-operative Bank

Co-operative bank is a retail commercial banking institution which takes deposits and lends money. Co-operative banks are based on the co-operative values of "self-help, self-responsibility, democracy and equality, equity and solidarity" and the co-operative principles of "voluntary and open membership, democratic control, members' economic participation, autonomy and independence, education and training, co-operation among co-operatives, and concern for community". A co-operative bank is a legal entity owned and democratically controlled by its members. Members often have a close association with the enterprise as producers or consumers of its products or services, or as its employees.

A co-operative society can be formed under the Co-operative Societies Act of 1912, with a minimum of ten members. The co-operative movement is based on seven basic principles:

1. Voluntary and open membership.
2. Democratic control.
3. Members' economic participation.
4. Autonomy and independence.
5. Education, training and information.
6. Cooperation among co-operatives.

7. Concern for the community.

The co-operative banks in India started functioning almost 105 years ago. Credit co-operatives are the oldest and most numerous of all the types of co-operatives in India. Co-operative banks promote economic activity and provide banking facilities and services to the rural people. Thrift and savings is the fulcrum of the working of co-operative banks. Personalization of credit is the special feature of the co-operative banking system. Co-operative banks are deeply rooted inside local areas and communities. They are involved in local development and contribute to the sustainable development of their communities, as their members, management and board usually belong to the communities in which they exercise their activities.

11.3 Co-operative Societies Act

Co-operative banks in India started functioning almost 105 years ago. The first Co-operative Societies Act of 1904 was enacted by the Government of India to enable formation of "agricultural credit co-operatives". The basic objective of Co-operative Societies Act of 1904 was to establish 'co-operative credit societies' to encourage thrift and self help among agriculturists, artisans and weaker sections of the society. The co-operative credit movement in India recorded considerable progress after the passing of the Act of 1904.

The Co-operative Societies Act of 1904 was later repealed by Co-operative Societies Act of 1912. Co-operative Societies Act of 1912 recognized the formation of co-operative societies other than credit viz. marketing, farming, processing etc.

The Constitutional reforms which led to the passing of the Government of India Act in 1919 transferred the subject of "Cooperation" from Government of India to the Provincial Governments. As per the reforms each province was responsible for co-operative movement and its development. Accordingly the Government of Bombay passed the first State Co-operative Societies Act in 1925 "which not only gave the movement its size and shape but was a pace setter of co-operative activities and stressed the basic concept of thrift, self help and mutual aid." Other States also followed. This marked the beginning of the second phase in the history of co-operative credit institutions.

In 1942, the Multi-Unit Co-operative Societies Act was enacted by the Government of India with an objective to cover societies whose operations extended to more than one state. Later, in 1984, the Government of India enacted a comprehensive Act known as Multi State Co-operative Societies Act which also repealed the Act of 1942. On the recommendation of the Mirdha Committee and the "Model Co-operative Societies Act" the Government of India enacted the

Multi State Co-operative Societies Act of 2002 which provided for democratic and autonomous working of the Co-operatives. The Multi State Co-operative Societies Act, 2002 came into force with effect from August 19, 2002.

Co operative Banks in India are registered under the Co-operative Societies Act. The co-operative bank is also regulated by the RBI. Co-operative banks are thus often regulated under both banking and co-operative legislation. They are governed by the Banking Regulations Act of 1949 and Banking Laws (Co-operative Societies) Act, 1965.

11.4 Definition of Co-operative Bank

International Co-operative Banks Association (ICBA) has defined that "a co-operative bank is a financial entity which belongs to its members, who are at the same time the owners and the customers of their bank". Co-operative banks are often created by persons belonging to the same local or professional community or sharing a common interest.

Devine defined a co-operative bank as "a mutual society formed, composed and governed by working people themselves for encouraging regular savings and granting small loans on easy terms of interest and repayment".

11.5 Features of Co-operative Banks

In most countries, co-operative banks are supervised and controlled by banking authorities. Depending on countries, this control and supervision can be implemented directly by state entities or delegated to a co-operative federation or central body. Even if their organizational rules can vary according to their respective national legislations, co-operative banks share common features. The common features of co-operative banks are the following.

11.5.1 Customer Owned Entities: In a co-operative bank, the needs of the customers meet the needs of the owners, as co-operative bank members are both. As a consequence, the first aim of a co-operative bank is not to maximize profit but to provide the best possible products and services to its members. Some co-operative banks only operate with their members but most of them also admit non-member clients to benefit from their banking and financial services.

11.5.2 Profit Allocation: In a co-operative bank, a significant part of the yearly profit, benefits or surplus is usually allocated to constitute reserves. A part of this profit can also be distributed to the co-operative members, with legal or statutory limitations in most cases. Profit is usually allocated to members either through a patronage dividend, which is related to the use of the co-operative's products and services by each member, or through an interest or a dividend, which is related to the number of shares subscribed by each member.

11.5.3 Democratic Member Control: Co-operative banks are owned and controlled by their members, who democratically elect the board of directors. Members usually have equal voting rights, according to the co-operative principle of "one person, one vote".

11.6 Differences between Co-operative Banks and Commercial Banks

Co-operative banks differ from commercial banks by their organization, their goals, values and their governance. Service is the motto rather than profit in the case of co-operative banking. While commercial banks aim at earning maximum profits. The co-operative banks are associations of persons and not of capital. In the case of co-operative banking, the members enjoy the security of rights and status irrespective of the value of the shares held by them. The affairs of the co-operative banks are managed democratically based on the principle of 'one man one vote'.

In commercial banks the day to day work is carried on by well trained professional staff whereas in the co-operative banks the management is mostly in the hands of honorary secretary/president. Co-operative banks finance mainly for agriculture and other related activities whereas commercial banks finance mainly for trade, business and industries. In lending money, commercial banks emphasis mainly on three 'C's of customer's viz. character, capital and capacity of the borrowers to repay. Whereas in co-operative banks, promptness in repayment of loan is the main consideration for granting loans and advances. The procedure for sanctioning of loan is also different in the two types of banks. In co-operative banks loan is sanctioned by the managing committee whereas in commercial banks it is sanctioned by the paid employees or professionals. Systems and audit and inspection of co-operative banks also differ from those of commercial banks. Commercial banks can declare a high rate of dividend whereas in co-operative banks the rate of dividend is limited to a percentage fixed by the government.

11.7 Structure of Co-operative Banking

The Co-operative Credit Structure (CCS) of India was set up to serve the needs of short, medium and long term rural credit requirement. The structure of co-operative banking in India is federal or pyramidal in nature. The co-operative banking institutions in the country may be broadly classified into two:

1. Rural Credit Co-operative Banks, and
2. Urban Credit Co-operative Banks.

11.7.1 Rural Credit Co-operatives: The rural credit co-operative banks may be further divided into two namely:

1. Short-term Credit Co-operative Banks.

2. Long -term Credit Co-operative Banks.

A. Short-term Credit Co-operative Banks: Short term credit is supplied in rural India by three set of institutions. At the grass-root level there are Primary Agricultural Credit Societies (PACS) dealing directly with the individual borrowers. At the central level (district level) District Central Co-operative Banks (DCCB) function as a link between Primary Agricultural Credit Societies and State Co-operative Banks (SCB). State Co-operative Bank is the apex institution in the three tier co-operative credit structure, operating at the state level. Following are the co-operative banking institutions providing short term credit.

1. Primary Agricultural Credit Societies (PACS),
2. District Central Co-operative Banks (DCCB), and
3. State Co-operative Banks (SCB).

B. Long-term Credit Co-operative Banks: As against three-tier structure of short-term credit co-operatives, the long-term co-operative credit structure has two tiers in many States with:

1. Primary Co-operative Agriculture and Rural Development Banks (PCARDB) at the primary level.
2. State Co-operative Agriculture and Rural Development Bank at the state level.

11.7.2 Urban Credit Co-operatives/Urban Co-operative Banks: Urban Co-operative Banks provide banking and credit facilities to urban and semi-urban population.

11.7.3 Primary Agricultural Credit Societies (PACS): The co-operative movement in India is more than a century old. The movement recorded considerable progress after the passing of the first Co-operatives Act of 1904. By the twenties, the co-operative credit system emerged as the premier institutional agency in the country for the provision of agricultural credit, but witnessed a set back in the thirties with the onset of economic depression and mounting overdues. With the acceptance of the recommendations of the All India Rural Credit Survey Committee (1954), efforts were once again directed at the development of co-operatives. This position continued for long and until the closing years of the sixties. Meanwhile the review undertaken by the All India Rural Credit Review Committee (1969) found that the efforts of the co-operatives had to be supplemented. It recommended the adoption of a multi-agency approach for the provision of credit to the rural areas with a much larger role for the commercial banks so that the desired level of progress in agricultural production in the country could be ensured.

Primary Agricultural Credit Society at the grass root level constitutes the major retail outlet of short and medium term credit to the rural sector. The

Primary Agricultural Credit Society (PACS) is the foundation on which the whole co-operative edifice is built. PACS is supposed to be "an association of borrowers and non-borrowers who reside in a locality, know one another and take interest in one another's affair". A primary agricultural credit society can be started with 10 or more persons of a village.

The membership fee and share capital of PACS is nominal so that even the economically weakest sections of the society can become a member. The profit earned by the society is divided among the members in accordance with the by-law of the society. The area of operation of a PACS is restricted to a compact area, preferably a village or a group of small villages where every person knows every other person of the locality. Since the area of operation is generally confined to rural areas, they are known as Rural Credit Societies or Rural Banks.

Primary Agricultural Credit Societies are formed on the model of Raiffeisen Societies of Germany. In the case of Primary Agricultural Credit Societies, members contribute to the share capital and each member is required to purchase a minimum number of shares. It is also laid down that no member would hold shares beyond a maximum number of shares prescribed and each member has only one vote irrespective of the number of shares the member holds.

PACS acts as a link between the rural borrowers on the one side and the higher agencies on the other viz. District Co-operative Bank, State Co-operative Bank, Government and the NABARD. PACS provide short and medium term credit, supply agricultural and other production requirements and undertake marketing of agricultural produce. PACS supply production requirements like seeds, fertilizers, insecticides, agriculture implements and consumer goods etc.

A. Objectives of PACS: The objectives of PACS are:

1. To promote the habit of thrift, self help and co-operative attitude among members.
2. To increase agricultural production by providing credit facilities at low rate of interest and to guide them to the modern methods of cultivation.
3. To disseminate knowledge of the latest improvements in agriculture, handicrafts etc.
4. To help rural people in any other way.
5. To educate people about the values of co-operation.

B. Features of PACS: The important features of PACS are the following:

1. Limited area of operation.
2. Shares of small value.
3. Limited liability.
4. Loans only to its members.
5. Loans mainly for productive purposes.

6. Credit for relatively short period with facilities for repayment in instalments.
7. Absence of profit taking.
8. Payment of dividend is limited.

C. Sources of Funds: The important financial resources of PACS include the following:

1. Share capital.
2. Membership fee.
3. Reserve funds.
4. Deposits from members and non-members.
5. Borrowings from District Central Co-operative Banks.
6. Financial assistance from the government.

The share capital of a society is divided into units, called shares, contributed by the members. Primary societies issue only ordinary shares to its members. Deposits of savings of members are the most important source of finance of PACS. It is the primary duty of these societies to mobilize the savings of rural people. The primary credit societies depend largely on borrowings from. It is the most important element of their working capital. The borrowings of the society are based on some criteria which differ from State to State according to their liability.

D. Administration: The management of the society is vested in the Board of Directors. The general body of the society consisting of all the members elected the director board. The President and Secretary of PACS are elected from the director board.

E. Functions of PACS: Primary agricultural credit societies have been providing short and medium term credit to their members for productive purposes. The funds raised by PACS are utilized for providing loans to its members for productive purposes at low rates of interest with or without security. A co-operative society lends only to solvent and eligible members. The primary society does not advance loans to members limitlessly. It fixes limit for each and every member. Short term loans are given for seasonal agricultural operations, such as purchase of seeds, fertilizers, pesticides, small repairs etc. Medium term loans are given for purchase of cattle, pump-set and construction of cattle sheds etc. The main functions of PACS are the following:

1. Accepting deposits from members and non-members.
2. To provide short and medium term loan at right time concentrating on small and marginal farmers.
3. To distribute agricultural equipments, fertilizers, seeds, insecticides and other inputs to farmers.
4. To distribute food grains and other necessary goods.

5. To provide storage facilities to farmers for their agricultural produces.
6. To provide non farm credit to its members.

At the end of 31st March 2010, there were 94,647 Primary Agricultural Credit Societies in India covering more than 96 percent of the rural areas. Total members of PACS as on 31 March, 2010 aggregated 12.64 crore. The membership of these societies was 13.24 crore. The amount of deposit mobilised by PACS in the country stood at ₹ 35,286 crore as on 31 March, 2010 indicating a growth rate of 34 percent over the previous year.

11.7.4 District Co-operative Banks (DCB): The District Co-operative Banks (DCB) are in the middle level in the co-operative credit structure which links between the Primary Agricultural Credit Societies and the State Co-operative Bank. These banks play an increasingly important role in the co-operative credit field. The co-operative banks organized at the district level to finance, supervise and control the primary co-operative credit societies are called Central Co-operative Banks or District Co-operative Banks. The size and area of operation is very important for the successful working of the district co-operative banks. In 1915, the Maclagan Committee had expressed the view that "a central bank should cover as large an area as compatible with convenience and efficiency". Primary co-operative banks in compact areas federated themselves into banking unions and organized central banks to collect funds from the urban areas and divert to the village societies. The central co-operative banks are generally located at the district head quarters or some prominent town of the district. Branches can be opened in important centres of the district.

A. Objectives of District Co-operative Banks: Main objectives of District Central Co-operative Banks are stated below:

1. To act as a balancing centre of finance for the primary societies in the district by providing them funds when they face shortage.
2. To provide financial assistance to members at a low rate of interest.
3. To supervise and control the working of the primary societies.
4. To attract local deposits for strengthening co-operative activity.
5. To advise and guide the primary societies.
6. To develop and extent banking facilities in rural areas.
7. To act as a connecting link between primary societies and the apex bank.
8. To provide facilities for the healthy growth of co-operative movement.

B. Types of District Central Co-operative Banks: The district co-operative banks in India can be classified under three heads according to their constitution. Following are the three types of banks:

(a) Banks whose Membership is Open to Individuals: In this type of banks membership is given to individuals or societies are admitted as shareholders on exactly the same footings as individuals, without any special provision for their adequate representation on the board of management. Such banks stand in the same position as commercial banks. These types are now very rare in India.

(b) Banks whose Membership is Confined to Societies: The banks falling in this category are purely federal type of central bank consisting of primary societies only. These banks are registered under the Co-operative Act of 1912.

(c) Mixed Type of Banks Which Include both Individuals and Societies Members: The central banks falling in the third category are of the mixed type and have been organized on the lines suggested by the Maclagan Committee. These banks consist of societies and individuals both, in which societies are not only assigned certain portion of their shares but also given separate representation on the board of directors. A large majority of central banks today fall under this category.

C. Sources of Funds: The central co-operative banks derive their funds from the following sources:

1. Share capital,
2. Membership fees,
3. Reserve funds,
4. Accepting deposits from the public, primary societies,
5. Deposit of reserve funds of primary societies,
6. Loans from State Co-operative Banks, Government, NABARD, State Bank of India, and
7. Grants from Government.

The District Banks issue shares to individuals and society members. Certain restrictions and limits are generally imposed on the issue of shares to individual members. The value of the shares generally ranges from ₹ 50 to ₹ 100.

D. Lending by DCB: The functions of commercial banks and District Co-operative Banks are almost same. The main difference between the two is that commercial banks have the liberty to invest their funds at their choice. However District Co-operative Banks have to finance mainly to their own members and have no choice in the investment of their funds. These banks have to invest major portion of their resources in agricultural loans. The main function of DCB is to lend to primary credit society and apart from that, central co-operative banks have been undertaking normal commercial banking business also, such as attracting deposits from the general public and lending to the needy against proper securities. The central bank advance loans for cultivation expenses, purchase of seeds, fertilizers, land reclamation, building of cattle shed, digging of wells, purchase of cattle, purchase and installation of pump-set etc. In addition, they meet the credit needs of dairy, handlooms, sugar and such other affiliated co-operatives. They also lend directly to the public for non-agricultural purposes within the area of their operation.

The number of District Central Co-operative Banks at the end of March 31, 2010 was 370. Total borrowing of DCCBs was ₹ 28,188 crore as on March 31, 2010 as against ₹ 27,588 crore on March 31, 2009. The accumulated losses of DCCBs as on March 31, 2010 stood at ₹ 5276.67 crore as against ₹ 5204.07 crore on March 31, 2009.

11.7.5 State Co-operative Banks (SCB): State Co-operative Banks are the apex institutions in the three-tier co-operative credit structure, operating at the State level. State Co-operative Bank (SCB) is the keystone of the co-operative moment in the State. The co-operative bank established at the state level to finance, coordinate, and control the working of the credit co-operative banks are called Apex Bank or State Co-operative Bank (SCB).

State Co-operative Banks occupies a prominent position in the co-operative credit structured because it is only through them that the Reserve Bank of India provides finance to agriculture. State Apex Co-operative Bank is the federation of the District Co-operative Banks. Being the Apex Bank, it raises resources and channelises them through District Co-operative Banks for both agricultural and non-agricultural purposes.

It also channelises the refinance provided by National Bank for Agriculture and Rural Development (NABARD) towards short term and medium term agriculture and allied sector loans to District Central Co-operative Banks. It is the top most co-operative bank in a state. In each state, there will be a State Co-operative Bank.

Apex Banks do not deal directly with the primary societies but through the Central Co-operative banks. Similarly these banks do not deal directly with individuals. However, in practice Apex banks also deals with individuals and primary societies. State Co-operative Banks occupy a distinctive position in the co-operative credit structure because of the following reasons:

1. Apex banks provide a link through which the Reserve Bank of India provides credit to the co-operatives and thus participate in the rural finance.
2. They function as balancing centres for the central co-operative banks by making available the surplus funds of some central co-operative banks. The central co-operatives are not permitted to borrow or lend among themselves.
3. They finance, control and supervise the central co-operative banks.

A. Functions of State Co-operative Bank: State Co-operative Banks occupy a unique position in the co-operative credit structure. Borrowing and lending constitute the main functions of a State Co-operative Bank. Important functions performed by Apex Co-operative Banks are the following:

1. Providing financial assistance to the Central Co-operative Bank and other Apex Co-operative institutions in the state.
2. Coordinating and controlling the activities of the Central Co-operative Banks.
3. Formulating and implementing co-operative credit policies of the state.
4. Acting as a link between co-operative credits institutions in the state with RBI and NABARD.
5. Performing ordinary banking business like acceptance of deposits, lending money, collection of cheque etc.

B. Financial Resources of State Co-operative Banks: The Apex Bank raises financial resources from the following ways:

1. By issue of shares.
2. Borrowing from State Government, RBI, NABARD and State Bank of India.
3. Accepting deposit from the public.
4. Reserves and surplus.

State Co-operative Banks raise capital mainly from member co-operative societies and the central co-operative banks.

C. Administration: Like Central Co-operative Banks, the state co-operative banks are also of two types, one in which the membership is open to societies only and the other in which the membership is open to both individuals and societies. Apex bank is managed by a Board of Directors. Board of Directors consists of a few representatives of individuals elected by the general body, a few representatives of affiliated societies and urban co-operative banks, a representative each from State co-operative Agricultural and Rural Development Banks and representatives of the State Government. Secretary\Manager, assistant manager, accountant, several section heads and other staff are appointed for the day to day management of the office. The powers and duties of the Board, executive committee and other important offices are governed by the bye-laws. The sanctioning of loans and routine administration are done by an executive committee consisting of President, Vice President, Registrar and two or three directors of the board.

At the end of March 31 2010, there were 31 State Co-operative Banks in India with a network of 992 branches. The total loans advanced by these banks during the year 2009-10 amounted to ₹ 49,226 crore and the deposits amounted to ₹ 82,331crore.

11.7.6 Long-term Credit Co-operative Banks: The agricultural co-operative credit structure has two parts: one is engaged in short and medium term credit and consists of a three tier system viz. the State Co-operative Banks at the state level, Central Co-operative Banks at the district level and Primary Credit Societies at the base (village) level. The other part is engaged in long-term credit and consists of a two tier system, *viz.*, State Land Development Banks and Primary Land Development Banks.

A. Land Development Banks (LDBs): The long term requirements of the farmers were traditionally met by the money lenders. There was, thus a felt need in India for an institution specifically designed to cater to the long term credit needs of the agriculturists, which would offer long term funds at moderate rates and recover loans in annual or semi-annual instalments spread over a number of years. Hence the government set up its own machinery for giving long term loans to agriculturists from its funds under the Land Improvement Loans Act of 1883 and Agriculturist Loans Act of 1884. But the efforts taken by the government to advance long term loans under the above acts were failed due to many reasons. The co-operative credit movement started in 1904 advances money mainly for short term agricultural purposes and these societies were unsuitable to give long term loans to farmers.

Need for an institutional agency to address indebtedness of farmers led to the establishment of Land Mortgage Banks in the 1920's. First Co-operative Land Mortgage Bank was set up at Jhang in undivided Punjab in 1920. The second bank was established in the undivided Bengal in 1924 followed by two more banks in Madras Presidency (1925) and Bombay (1929). The movement of co-operative Land Mortgage Banks gradually spread to other states also.

The progress of Land Development Banks (LDBs) was rather slow in the beginning. In several states, Central Land Mortgage Banks did not exist for several years and it was the primary land mortgage banks that gave long term loans to farmers. A number of recommendations were made from time to time regarding organization and functioning of Land Mortgage Banks. The conference of the Registrars of Co-operative Societies held in 1929 recommended that Land Mortgage Banks should be organized on co-operative lines and should be registered under the Co-operative Societies Act. The Royal Commission on Agriculture (1926) and the Central Banking Enquiry Committee also made certain recommendations for the healthy growth of Land Mortgage Banks.

At the time of independence there were only 5 Co-operative Land Development Banks operating through 284 branches in the country. After independence these banks were assigned wider role of providing investment credit in agriculture and came to be known as Land Mortgage Banks, later with their shift in thrust to development of farm land these banks came to be known as Land Development Banks. It was however, the All India Rural Credit Survey Committee (1954) that recognized the importance and role of land mortgage banks and made several recommendations of far reaching significance which influenced to a great extent the organization and functions of these institutions.

The major recommendations were there should be a Central Land Mortgage Bank in each State and these banks should raise funds by issuing debentures with varying maturity periods. The banks should also issue special rural debentures to mobilize rural resources. The RBI and State Bank of India should take such steps as would make debentures issued by Central Land Mortgage Banks popular among the public by guaranteeing the payment of principal and interest. They further recommend that State Governments should also contribute the share capital of Central Land Mortgage Banks. Loans by the Land Mortgage Banks should be production oriented and for improvement in the agricultural sector.

A nine-member committee on Land Development Banks was constituted under Shri K. Madhava Das, Chairman in March 1973 to examine the structure of Land Development Banks and suggest measures to improve viability of the banks. The Committee made recommendations in regard to improving viability of Primary Land Development Banks by mobilizing rural savings tackles the problem of overdue, training of personnel of LDBs and project lending on schematic basis.

The Committee to Review Arrangements for Institutional Credit for Agriculture and Rural Development (CRAFICARD) recommended a bigger role for the Land Development Banks and recommended to incorporate development of agriculture and its allied activities including wastelands and non-farm sector development. The banks in due course diversified their activities with refinance support of NABARD which was established in the year 1982. However, late eighties and the beginning of nineties were the crucial period in which Land Development Banks adopted financing long term loans for more significant rural development activities like, village and cottage industries, rural artisans and rural housing etc. In view of broader role of Land Development Banks they are now known as State Co-operative Agriculture and Rural Development Banks (SCARDBs). Over a period of time the SCARDBs have made commendable progress in advancing long term loans for capital formation in agriculture.

B. Structure of Land Mortgage Banks: Land Mortgage Banks are exempted from the purview of Banking Regulations Act of 1949 they do not have to maintain the cash and liquidity reserves. As such these are not strictly banks but still are allowed to use the word "bank" in their name, an exemption from the above said Act. Legally these are registered under Co-operative Societies Act and are termed as Co-operative Credit Societies. Under the Banking Regulation Act 1949, only State Co-operative Apex Banks, District Central Co-operative Banks and select Urban Credit Co-operatives are qualified to be called as banks in the co-operative sector. In other words, only these banks are licensed to conduct full-fledged banking business.

The structure of Land Development Banks is not uniform in nature. It varies from State to State. But unlike the co-operative credit societies, LDB structure is not a three-tier system, but is federal in nature, with only two-tiers i.e. the Central Land Development Bank at the State level and Primary Land Development Bank at the district and important centres. In some states there are no primary LDBs, but the branches of the central LDBs act as primary LDBs.

11.7.7 Primary Co-operative Agriculture and Rural Development Banks (PCARDB): The Primary Co-operative Agricultural and Rural Development Banks (PCARDB) provide long term financial assistance to farmers with the period of repayment ranging from 5 to 15 years. They provide credit for developmental purposes like minor irrigation, cultivation of plantation crops and for diversified purposes like poultry, dairying and sericulture on schematic basis. They get requisite financial assistance from the State Co-operative Agriculture and Rural Development Bank. The Primary Co-operative Agricultural and Rural Development Banks (PCARDB) operate in important centres.

A. Functions: The Primary co-operative Agriculture and Rural Development Bank performs a number of functions like:

1. Granting loans to its members on the security of landed property.
2. Granting loans for making permanent improvement in agricultural lands.
3. Granting loans for the adoption of improved methods of cultivation.
4. Granting loans for purchase of land agricultural implements.
5. Liquidation of old debts.

In order to widen their scope of lending to compete with other financial agencies, the primary co-operative agriculture and rural development banks have been permitted to finance artisans, craftsmen and small scale entrepreneurs. They have also been permitted to issue loans to small road transport operators in rural areas for purchase of goods carriers and passenger vehicles.

B. Sources of Funds: Primary co-operative Agriculture and Rural Development Banks derive their funds from the following sources:

1. Issue of share capital.
2. Deposits from public.
3. Assistance from State Co-operative Agriculture and Rural Development Bank.
4. Grants and subsidies from the Government.
5. Borrowing from other agencies.

11.7.8 State Co-operative Agriculture and Rural Development Bank (SCARD): State Co-operative and Agriculture and Rural Development Bank (SCARD) is the apex institution for all Primary Co-operative Agriculture and Rural Development Banks (PCARDBs) constituted for issuing long term loans for the purpose of developing agriculture and allied activities. The Primary Co-operative Agriculture and Rural Development Banks located at Taluk and Block levels throughout the State are affiliated to the State Agriculture and Rural Development Bank. The main objective of the State Co-operative Agriculture and Rural Development Bank is to provide long term loans to primary agriculture and rural development banks.

A. Functions: The State Co-operative and Agriculture and Rural Development Banks perform the following functions:

1. Granting loans to primary co-operative agriculture and rural development banks for purposes approved by the National Bank for Agricultural and Rural Development and Registrar of Co-operative Societies.
2. Supervising and directing the working of primary banks.
3. To function as agent of any co-operative bank subject to such conditions as the Registrar of Co-operation may specify.
4. To develop, assist and coordinate the work of affiliated Primary Co-operative Agriculture and Rural Development Banks.

The bank issues long term and medium term loans towards agricultural and allied activities like construction of godowns, cattle shed, farm house, purchase of lands etc., and for minor irrigation purposes like construction of new wells, deepening of existing wells etc. In addition, long term loans are also sanctioned for animal husbandry, fisheries, plantation, farm mechanization, non-farm sector and other non-minor irrigation schemes. The loans are repayable in 15 to 20 years by annual instalment.

B. Sources of Funds: Debentures form the biggest source of finance. The State Co-operative Agriculture and Rural development Bank raises financial resources from the following:

1. Share capital and reserves.
2. Special development debentures.
3. Ordinary debentures.
4. Receiving deposits.

The State Co-operative Agriculture and Rural development Bank floats two types of debentures to raise funds required for issuing loans for developmental activities. Special development debentures are issued for a maturity period varying from 20 to 25 years guaranteed by the State government. These debentures are subscribed by co-operative banks, commercial banks, State Bank of India, Reserve Bank of India, National Bank for Agricultural and Rural Development and the Central and the State Governments. Ordinary debentures are generally issued for a period up to 7 years. These debentures are subscribed to by State Government, Government of India, Reserve Bank of India, other institutional investors, Local bodies and public.

C. Administration: The management of State Co-operative Agriculture and Rural development Bank is vested with the Board of Directors. In the Director Board three fourth of the directors can be from the representatives of Primary Co-operative Agriculture and Rural Development Banks. The Registrar of Co-operative Societies of the State is an ex-officio member. Representation is also given to the debenture holders. The representatives of debenture holders are generally nominated by the Registrar of Co-operative Societies. In practice a slight variation is found in the constitution of the Board of Directors of these banks from state to state. Secretary/Manager, Assistant Manager, Accountant, several section heads and other staff are appointed for the day to day management of the office. The powers and duties of the Board, executive committee and other important offices are governed by the bye-laws. The sanctioning of loans and routine administration are done by an executive committee consisting of President, Vice President, Registrar and two or three directors of the board.

11.8 Urban Co-operative Banks

Urban Co-operative Banks provide banking and credit facilities to urban and semi urban population. The term Urban Co-operative Banks (UCBs), though not formally defined, refers to primary co-operative banks located in urban and semi-urban areas. They mobilize deposits from the public and extend credit facilities for specified purposes. Their lending operations include provision of credit facilities to small traders, artisans and persons belonging to low and middle income group for purposes ranging from housing, business, education, consumer and other non-farm sector activities. The Urban Co-operative Banks are also popularly known as urban credit co-operatives. These banks, till 1996, were allowed to lend money only for non-agricultural purposes. This distinction does not hold today. Today, their scope of operations has widened considerably.

Urban Co-operative Banks (UCBs) are important part of the Indian financial system. There are about 1700 urban credit co-operatives and these societies together constitute for about 10 percent of the aggregate banking business and therefore regarded as an important segment of the banking system.

11.8.1 Origin of Urban Co-operative Banks: The origin of the urban co-operative banking movement in India can be traced to the close of nineteenth century. Inspired by the success of the experiments related to the co-operative movement in Britain and the co-operative credit movement in Germany such societies were set up in India. Urban co-operative credit societies, in their formative phase came to be organized on a community basis to meet the consumption oriented credit needs of their members. Salary earners' societies inculcating habits of thrift and self help played a significant role in popularizing the movement, especially amongst the middle class as well as organized labour. From its origin then to today, the thrust of Urban Co-operative Banks, historically, has been to mobilize savings from the middle and low income urban groups and purvey credit to their members.

The enactment of Co-operative Credit Societies Act of 1904, however, gave the real impetus to the movement. The first urban co-operative credit society was registered in Canjeevaram (Kanjivaram) in the erstwhile Madras province in October, 1904. The most prominent amongst the early credit societies was the Bombay Urban Co-operative Credit Society, sponsored by Vithaldas Thackersey and Lallubhai Samaldas established on January 23, 1906.

The Co-operative Credit Societies Act of 1904 was amended in 1912, with a view to broad basing it to enable organization of non-credit societies. The Maclagan Committee of 1915 was appointed to review their performance and suggest measures for strengthening them. The committee observed that such institutions were eminently suited to cater to the needs of the lower and middle income strata of society and would inculcate the principles of banking amongst the middle classes. The committee also felt that the urban co-operative credit movement was more viable than agricultural credit societies. The recommendations of the Committee went a long way in establishing the urban co-operative credit movement in its own right.

The first study of Urban Co-operative Banks was taken up by RBI in the year 1958-59. The Report published in 1961 acknowledged the widespread and financially sound framework of urban co-operative banks. The study emphasized the need to establish primary urban co-operative banks in new centres and suggested that State Governments lend active support to their development. In 1963, Varde Committee recommended that such banks should be organized at all urban centres with a population of 1 lakh or more and not by any single community or caste. The committee introduced the concept of minimum capital requirement and the criteria of population for defining the urban centre where UCBs were incorporated.

The Madhavdas Committee (1979) evaluated the role played by urban co-operative banks in greater details and drew a roadmap for their future role recommending support from RBI and Government in the establishment of such banks in backward areas and prescribing viability standards.

The Hate Working Group (1981) desired better utilization of banks' surplus funds and that the percentage of the Cash Reserve Ratio (CRR) and the Statutory Liquidity Ratio (SLR) of these banks should be brought at par with commercial banks, in a phased manner. While the Marathe Committee (1992) redefined the viability norms and ushered in the era of liberalization, the Madhava Rao

Committee (1999) focused on consolidation, control of sickness, better professional standards in urban co-operative banks and sought to align the urban banking movement with commercial banks.

11.8.2 Duality of Control: Primary Urban Co-operative Banks (UCBs) are registered as co-operative societies under the provisions of, either the State Co-operative Societies Act of the State concerned or the Multi State Co-operative Societies Act of 2002. They are regulated and supervised by the Registrar of Co-operative Societies (RCS) of State concerned or by the Central Registrar of Co-operative Societies (CRCS), as the case may be. The applicability of banking laws to co-operatives societies since March 1, 1966 ushered in 'duality of control' over Urban Co-operative Banks between the Registrar of Co-operative Societies/Central Registrar of Co-operative Societies and the Reserve Bank of India. In 1968, UCBS were extended the benefits of Deposit Insurance.

Large co-operative banks with paid-up share capital and reserves of ₹ 1 lakh were brought under the preview of the Banking Regulation Act 1949 with effect from 1st March, 1966 and within the ambit of the Reserve Bank's supervision. Banking related functions of urban co-operative banks viz. licensing, area of operations, interest rates etc. are governed by the RBI. Registration, management, audit and liquidation, etc. are governed by State Governments as per the provisions of respective State Acts. The Reserve Bank regulates and supervises the banking functions of UCBs under the provisions of Banking Regulation Act of 1949.

11.8.3 Functions of Urban Banks: Urban Co-operative Banks provide banking and credit facilities to urban and semi urban population. They mobilize deposits from the public and extend credit facilities for specified purposes. Their lending operations include provision of credit facilities to small traders, artisans and persons belonging to low and middle income group for purposes ranging from housing, business, education, consumer and other non-farm sector activities.

11.9 Role of Reserve Bank of India in Urban Co-operative Banks

The Urban Banks Department of the Reserve Bank of India is vested with the responsibility of regulating and supervising primary (urban) co-operative banks, which are popularly known as Urban Co-operative Banks (UCBs). RBI is regulating and supervising the activities of primary (urban) co-operative banks in India. Within the Reserve Bank, a separate department, viz. Urban Banks Department, has been entrusted with these functions. The Department performs these functions through its 17 regional offices. The Urban Banks Department performs three main functions viz.,

1. Regulatory Functions.

2. Supervisory Functions.
3. Developmental Functions.

11.9.1 Regulatory Functions: Regulatory functions include the following:

A. Licensing of New Primary (Urban) Co-operative Banks: For commencing banking business, a primary (urban) co-operative bank, is required to obtain a license from the Reserve Bank of India, under the provisions of Section 22 of the Banking Regulation Act, 1949 (as applicable to Co-operative Societies).

B. Licensing of Existing Primary (Urban) Co-operative Banks: Under this function all existing unlicensed primary (urban) co-operative banks in the country as on March 1, 1966, (when some banking laws were applied to UCBs), were required to apply to the Reserve Bank of India for a license.

C. Branch Licensing: Under the provisions of Section 23 of the Banking Regulation Act, 1949, primary (urban) co-operative banks are required to obtain permission from the Reserve Bank of India for opening branches.

D. Statutory Provisions: The regulatory functions of Urban Banks Department relate to monitoring compliance with the provisions of the Banking Regulation Act, 1949 (as applicable to Co-operative Societies) by urban co-operative banks. These provisions include:

1. Statutory provisions for maintenance of minimum share capital.
2. Maintenance of CRR and SLR.

E. Supervisory Functions: To ensure that the UCBs conduct their affairs in the interests of the depositors and also comply with the regulatory framework prescribed by the Reserve Bank of India, the department undertakes on site inspection of these banks with frequency ranging from one to two years depending upon the financial condition/status of banks. The thrust of supervision is to ensure that banks' affairs are not conducted in a manner detrimental to the depositors' interest and also to assess the solvency of the bank, besides examining the banks' compliance with the existing regulatory framework. The department also undertakes off-site surveillance of scheduled banks and non-scheduled banks with a deposit base of ₹ 100 crore and above based on a set of quarterly and annual returns.

F. Developmental Functions: With a view to extending institutional credit support to tiny and cottage units, the Reserve Bank of India grants refinance facilities to urban co-operative banks under the provisions of Section 17 of the Reserve Bank of India Act, 1934. The refinance is given at the Bank Rate. Training is imparted to the middle and top Management of Urban Co-operative Banks through College of Agricultural Banking, Pune.

11.10 Development of UCBs

Over the years, primary urban co-operative banks have registered a significant growth in number, size and volume of business handled. As on 31st March, 2009 there were 1,721 UCBs with a total network of 7,500 branches spread across the country. The membership of these banks was 20 million. Majority of the urban banks are 'unit banks' with out any branch network, while some of the large banks have established their presence in many states. Some of the banks are also authorized dealers in foreign exchange. A feature of the urban banks has been its heterogeneous character and its uneven geographical spread. In terms of geographical spread about 79 percent of urban co-operative banks are located in five states, viz. Andhra Pradesh, Gujarat, Karnataka, Maharashtra and Tamil Nadu. Further the UCBs in these five states account for approximately 82 percent of the total deposits and advances of the urban banking sector.

Short Answer Type Questions

1. What do you mean by a co-operative bank?
2. What is the meaning of co-operation?
3. What are the features of PACS?
4. Define co-operative bank.
5. What are the sources of finance of district co-operative banks?
6. What is state co-operative bank?
7. What is PACS?
8. What is a central co-operative bank?
9. What do you mean by land development bank?
10. What are the basic principles of cooperation?
11. What are the sources of finance of PACS?
12. What are the sources of finance of urban co-operative banks?
13. What is primary co-operative agricultural and rural development bank?
14. What are the objectives of PACS?
15. What are urban co-operative banks?
16. What are the objectives of urban co-operative banks?

Essay Type Questions

1. Explain the features of co-operative banks.
2. What are co-operative banks? What are the differences between commercial banks and co-operative banks?
3. Give a brief history of co-operative banking in India.
4. Critically examine the role and working of central co-operative banks.
5. What are the functions of state co-operative banks?

6. Outline the structure of co-operative banking in India.
7. What is meant by central co-operative bank? Explain the structure of central co-operative banks.
8. Discuss the category and features of co-operative banks.
9. Outline the structure and functions of state co-operative bank.
10. Outline the structure and functions of state co-operative and agriculture and rural development bank.
11. Explain the objectives, functions and financial resources of PACS.
12. Give a brief history of land development banks in India.
13. What are objectives and functions of district co-operative banks?
14. Explain the functions and administration of state co-operative banks.
15. Explain the administration and the functions of primary co-operative agricultural and rural development banks.

12

Non-banking Finance Companies

12.1 Introduction

The financial system comprises of financial institutions, financial instruments and financial markets that provide an effective payment and credit system and thereby facilitate channelising of funds from savers to the investors of the economy. The financial system in India comprises multiplicity of financial institutions. The commercial and cooperative banks and certain variants of non-banking financial institutions are among the oldest of the market participants. Apart from these two institutions, financial system also consists of a wide variety of institutions such as, all India financial institutions, specialized financial institutions, state-level development banks, investment institutions, capital market intermediaries such as mutual funds, market intermediaries viz. primary dealers, stockbrokers, moneylenders, insurance companies etc.

Non-banking Finance Companies (NBFCs) play a vital role in the Indian financial system because they supplement the activities of banks in terms of deposit mobilization and lending. NBFCs have attracted a large number of investors since the rate of return on deposits offered by these institutions are always higher than commercial banks. They are also flexible in lending money to the various clients according to their needs. Hence NBFCs play a very important role by providing finance to activities which are not served by the organized banking sector. NBFCs thus supplement the role of the banking sector in meeting the increasing financial needs of the corporate sector, delivering credit to the unorganized sector and to small borrowers. These institutions have a vital role in broadening the access to financial services, enhancement of competition and diversification of the financial sector.

12.2 Meaning of Non-Banking Finance Companies

Non-Banking Finance Companies (NBFCs) are heterogeneous set of financial institutions with differing financial intermediation. Non-banking financial companies (NBFCs) are the intermediaries engaged in the business of accepting deposits and delivering credit. NBFCs provide banking services, but do not hold a banking license. As compared to commercial banks, NBFCs are more quick and flexible in decision making and risk taking. Notwithstanding their diversity, by providing niche of financial services NBFCs have attracted a good number of customers. Their areas of operation are mainly confined to the local level and in response to the local requirements.

As per RBI guidelines a non-banking financial company (NBFC) is a company registered under the Companies Act of 1956 and is engaged in the business of loans and advances, acquisition of shares/stock/bonds/debentures/ securities issued by government or local authority or other marketable securities, leasing, hire-purchase, insurance business, chit business; but it does not include any institution whose principal business is agriculture activity, industrial activity, sale/purchase/construction of immovable property.

A non-banking institution which is a company and which has its principal business of receiving deposits under any scheme or arrangement or any other manner, or lending in any manner is also a non-banking financial company (residuary non-banking company).

12.3 Definition of Non-Banking Finance Companies

Reserve Bank of India (Amendment) Act of 1947 defined a non-banking company as:

1. A financial institution, which is a company.
2. A non-banking institution, which is a company and which has as its principal business the receiving of deposits under any scheme or lending in any manner.
3. Such other non-banking institutions, as the bank may, with the previous approval of the central government and by notification in the official gazette, specify.

This definition excludes financial institutions which carry on agricultural operations as their principle business.

12.4 Types of Non-Banking Finance Companies

Non-banking financial companies (NBFCs) encompass an extremely heterogeneous group of financial intermediaries. By employing innovative marketing strategies and devising tailor-made products, NBFCs have also been able to build up a clientele base among the depositors, mop up public savings and command large resources as reflected in the growth of their deposits from public, shareholders and directors. NBFCs consist of mainly eight categories of institutions, with differing financial intermediation which are given below:

1. Asset Finance Company.
2. Investment Company.
3. Loan Company.

4. Mutual Benefit Finance Company.
5. Equipment Leasing Company.
6. Residuary Non-banking Company.
7. Miscellaneous non-banking Company.
8. Housing Finance Company.

12.5 Non-Banking Financial Companies and their Principal Businesses

Table 12.1 provides a brief picture of the types of non- banking financial companies and the principal business conducted by each of the categories.

Table 12.1: Business Conducted by Non-banking Financial Companies

S.N	Type of Non-banking Finance Company	Principal Financial Services
1	Asset Finance Companies(AFC)	It is a company which carries on as its principal business as financing of physical assets supporting productive and economic activity, such as automobiles, tractors, lathe machines, generator sets, earth moving and material handling equipments, moving on own power and general purpose industrial machines. as hire purchase transaction or the financing of such transactions.
2	Investment Company (IC)	These companies are primarily engaged in the acquisition of securities and trading in such securities to earn a profit.
3	Loan Company (LC)	These companies are providing finance by making loans or advances, or otherwise for any activity other than its own, excluding equipment leasing, hire purchase and housing finance.
4	Mutual Benefit Financial Company (MBFC) (Nidhi Companies)	Mutual Benefit financial companies are NBFCs notified by the Central Government under Section 620 A of the Companies Act 1956. These companies are primarily regulated by Department of Company Affairs. These companies are exempted from the core provisions of NBFC directions relating to acceptance of public deposits. These companies are also exempt from the core provisions of the RBI Act viz., requirement of compulsory registration, maintenance of liquid assets and transfer of profits to reserve fund. Directions relating to ceiling on interest rate, maintenance of

		register of deposits, furnishing receipt to depositors and submission of returns to Reserve Bank of India are however applicable to these companies.
5	Equipment Leasing Company (ELC)	It is a company which carries on as its principal business leasing of equipments or the financing of such activity.
6	Residuary Non-Banking Companies (RNBC)	Residuary Non-Banking Company is a class of NBFC. Their principal business is receiving of deposits, under any scheme or arrangement or in any other manner and not being investment, asset financing, loan company. The functioning of these companies is different from those of NBFCs in terms of method of mobilisation of deposits and requirement of deployment of depositors' funds as per directions. Besides, prudential norms directions are applicable to these companies also. These companies do not belong to any of the categories as stated above.
7	Miscellaneous Non-Banking Company (MNBC) (Chit Fund Companies)	It is a company which collects money from specified number of subscribers periodically and in turn distributes the same as prizes amongst them. Any other form of chit is also included in this category. As per Miscellaneous Non-Banking Companies (RB) Directions, the companies can accept deposits up to 25 percent and 15 percent of the net owned funds from public and shareholders, respectively, for a period of 6 months to 36 months, but cannot accept deposits repayable on demand/notice. The Reserve Bank only regulates the deposits accepted by these companies, but it does not regulate their chit fund business, which is administered by the respective State Governments through the offices of Registrars of Chits.
8	Housing Finance Companies (HFC)	The financing of the acquisition or construction of houses including the acquisition or development of plots of land.

12.6 Regulatory Authorities of NBFCs

1. For regulatory purposes, NBFCs have been classified into 3 categories:
2. Companies accepting public deposits,
3. Companies not accepting public deposits but engaged in financial business,

and

4. Core investment companies with 90 percent of their total assets as investments in the securities of their group/holding/subsidiary companies.

The Reserve Bank of India is entrusted with the responsibility of regulating and supervising the Non-Banking Financial Companies by virtue of powers vested in Chapter III B of the Reserve Bank of India Act, 1934.

Reserve Bank of India is the regulatory authority for equipment leasing companies, hire purchase finance companies, loan companies, investment companies and residuary non-banking companies. The NBFCs that are registered with RBI such as equipment leasing company, hire-purchase company, loan company and investment company have been classified with effect from December 6, 2006 as follows:

1. Asset Finance Company (AFC).
2. Loan Company (LC).
3. Investment Company (IC).
4. Residuary Non-Banking Companies (RNBCs) .

The regulatory authorities for the different types of non- banking financial companies are given in Table 12.2.

Table 12.2: Regulatory Authorities for Non-banking Financial Companies

S.N	Type of NBFCs	Name of the Regulatory Authority
1	Equipment Leasing Companies (EL)	Reserve Bank of India
2	Asset Finance Companies (AFC)	Reserve Bank of India
3	Loan Companies	Reserve Bank of India
4	Investment Companies	Reserve Bank of India
5	Residuary Non-Banking Companies (RNBCs)	Reserve Bank of India
6	Miscellaneous Non-Banking Companies (Chit Funds)	Reserve Bank of India and Registrars of Chits of the concerned States
7	Mutual Benefit Finance Companies (Nidhis and Potential Nidhis)	Department of Company Affairs of Government of India
8	Micro Finance Companies	Department of Company Affairs of Government of India
9	Housing Finance Companies	National Housing Bank (NHB)
10	Insurance Companies	Insurance Regulatory and Development Authority (IRDA)
11	Stock Broking Companies	Securities and Exchange Board of India
12	Merchant Banking Companies	Securities and Exchange Board of India

12.7 Services Provided by Non-Banking Finance Companies

Non-banking finance companies are important financial intermediaries which are heterogeneous in nature in terms of their activity and are occupying an integral part in the Indian financial system. These companies are providing an extensive range of financial services which are divergent in nature. Important services provided by non-banking finance companies are the following:

1. Accepting deposits from public.
2. Advancing loans and investments.
3. Merchant banking.
4. Underwriting of shares and debentures.
5. Issue management and loan syndication.
6. Stock broking.
7. Portfolio management services.
8. Credit rating.
9. Factoring, forfeiting and discounting of bills.
10. Securitization of debts.
11. Leasing and hire purchase financing.
12. Venture capital financing.
13. Mutual fund.
14. Trading in money market instruments.
15. Depository services.
16. Advise companies in merger, acquisition, amalgamation and capital restructuring.
17. Financial engineering, advisory and consultancy services.

12.8 Fee Based Services and Fund Based Services

The services rendered by non-banking finance companies are either fee based or fund based. In fund based financial services, money in the form of cash is involved in the transaction. But in case of fee based financial services no money is directly involved but the subscribing non banking financial institution provide financial service to the customer taking probable risk and takes fee as a service charge.

The fee based services rendered by non-banking finance companies include portfolio management, stock broking, issue management, loan syndication, merger and acquisition, credit rating, depository services etc. Fund based activities include venture capital financing, housing finance, equipment leasing, hire purchase financing, underwriting, factoring, forfeiting, discounting of bills etc.

12.9 Registration of Non-Banking Financial Companies

A company incorporated under the Companies Act of 1956 and desirous of commencing business of non-banking financial institution as defined under Section 45 I (a) of the RBI Act, 1934 should have a minimum net owned fund of ₹ 2 crore. The company is required to submit its application for registration in the prescribed format along with necessary documents for Reserve Bank of India's consideration. The Reserve Bank issues Certificate of Registration after satisfying itself that the conditions as enumerated in Section 45-IA of the RBI Act, 1934 are satisfied.

12.10 Registration of Companies Accepting Public Deposits

Companies holding or accepting public deposits are required to comply with all the directions on acceptance of public deposits, prudential norms and liquid assets, and should submit periodic returns to the Reserve Bank of India.

12.11 Residuary Non-Banking Company

Residuary Non-Banking Company (RNBC) is a class of NBFC which has its principal business as receiving of deposits, under any scheme or arrangement or in any other manner and not being investment, asset financing and Loan Company. These companies are required to maintain investments as per directions of RBI, in addition to liquid assets. The functioning of these companies is different from those of NBFCs in terms of method of mobilization of deposits and requirement of deployment of depositors' funds. However, prudential norms directions are applicable to these companies also. RNBC can accept deposits for a minimum period of 12 months and maximum period of 84 months from the date of receipt of such deposit. They cannot accept deposits repayable on demand.

There is no ceiling on raising of deposits by RNBCs but every RNBC has to ensure that the amounts deposited and investments made by the company are not less than the aggregate amount of liabilities to the depositors. To secure the interest of depositor, such companies are required to invest in a portfolio comprising of highly liquid and secured instruments viz. Central/State Government securities, fixed deposit of scheduled commercial banks, certificate of deposits of scheduled commercial banks and financial institutions, units of mutual funds, etc.

12.12 Documents to be Submitted Periodically to RBI

The NBFCs accepting public deposits should furnish the following documents periodically to the Reserve Bank of India:

1. Audited balance sheet of each financial year and an audited profit and loss account in respect of that year as passed in the general meeting together with

a copy of the report of the Board of Directors and a copy of the report and the notes on accounts furnished by its Auditors.

2. Statutory annual return on deposits.
3. Certificate from the auditors that the company is in a position to repay the deposits as and when the claims arise.
4. Quarterly return on liquid assets.
5. Half-yearly return on prudential norms.
6. Monthly return on exposure to capital market by companies having public deposits of ₹ 50 crore and above.
7. A copy of the credit rating obtained once a year along with one of the half-yearly returns on prudential norms as at (5) above.

Companies not holding or accepting public deposits are regulated and supervised in a limited manner. They are required to comply only with prudential norms relating to income recognition, accounting standards, asset classification and provisioning against bad and doubtful debts. They are less frequently inspected. Such companies are presently not required to submit any returns to the Reserve Bank. Thus, market intelligence and auditors' exception reports constitute the important supervisory tools in respect of these companies.

12.13 NBFCs which are Exempted from RBI Registration

Insurance companies, stock broking companies, merchant banking companies, venture capital fund companies etc, which are covered by the generic term 'NBFC' but are regulated by other regulatory authorities, have been exempted from the RBI registration (under Section 45-IA of the RBI Act, 1934) in order to avoid duality of control. Stock broking companies, merchant banking companies and venture capital fund companies are regulated by the Securities and Exchange Board of India (SEBI). Housing finance companies are governed by the National Housing Bank. An insurance company holding a valid certificate of registration is regulated by the Insurance Regulatory and Development Authority (IRDA). Similarly, Chit Companies are regulated by the respective State Governments and Nidhi Companies are regulated by Ministry of Company Affairs, Government of India.

12.13.1 Merchant Banking Companies: A merchant bank is a non-banking financial institution primarily engaged in offering financial services and advice to corporations and to wealthy individuals. Merchant Banking Companies have been exempted from the Provisions of the Reserve Bank of India Act of 1934 relating to compulsory registration (Section 451A), maintenance of liquid assets (Section 451B), creation of reserve fund (Section 451C) and all provisions relating to deposit acceptance and prudential norms provided they are registered with SEBI. The Merchant Banking activity in India is governed by SEBI (Merchant Banking) Regulations, of 1992. All merchant bankers have to be registered with SEBI.

12.13.2 Chit Fund Companies: Non-banking finance companies primarily engaged in conventional chit fund business are exempted from the requirement of compulsory registration with RBI. The Registrar of Chit Funds concerned would be the authority for monitoring their activities. RBI under the Miscellaneous Non-Banking Companies (Reserve Bank) Directions, 1977, regulates the deposit taking activities of chit fund companies. The other provisions of directions are similar to those pertaining to NBFCs, in general. The requirement of credit rating has also not been made mandatory for these companies.

NBFCs are allowed to accept up to 25 percent of their net owned fund as deposits from public and up to 15 percent from their shareholders. However, these companies are exempted from the requirement of compulsory registration with RBI because they are primarily engaged in conventional chit fund business and the concerned Registrar of Chit Funds would be monitoring their activities.

12.13.3 Nidhi Companies: Nidhi Companies are non-banking finance companies which deal only with their own members. Since these companies are permitted to deal only with their own members they have been exempted from the core provisions of the NBFCs directions. The Department of Company Affairs, Government of India, (Section 620A of the Companies Act, 1956) has issued guidelines for the operation of Nidhi companies and deployment of their funds. However, the acceptances of deposits by Nidhi companies are under the jurisdiction of the Reserve Bank of India. RBI has prohibited these companies from advertising for acceptance of deposits and payments of brokerage. The quantum of deposits to be raised by them is also not co-related to their net owned fund.

12.13.4 Unincorporated Bodies: The deposit-taking activities of unincorporated bodies are governed under the provisions of chapter IIIC of the RBI Act. Under the pre-amended provisions of chapter IIIC, an individual was allowed to accept deposits from not more than 25 persons and a partnership firm/association of individuals of not more than 25 persons per partner/individual subject to a maximum of 250 persons, excluding relatives in all the cases.

Some of the unincorporated bodies, however, devised ingenious means to circumvent the above provisions and issued advertisements by offering attractive rates of return on deposits. Many of such unincorporated bodies failed to repay their deposits, once they mature. These provisions of Chapter IIIC were, therefore, amended by the RBI (Amendment) Act, 1997, which came into force from April 1, 1997. In terms of the amended provisions of Section 45-S, unincorporated bodies, whose principal business is that of receiving deposits or that of a financial institution, such as lending, investment in securities, hire purchase finance or equipment leasing, have been prohibited from accepting any deposits whatsoever. However, such an unincorporated body can collect deposits from relatives as specified in the Act and also borrow from banks, financial institutions, etc., for carrying on its activity. Unincorporated bodies have also been prohibited from issuing advertisement in any form soliciting deposits with effect from April 1, 1997. Unincorporated bodies, which accept deposits in violation of the provisions of Chapter IIIC of the RBI Act, are liable to prosecution under the provisions of Reserve Bank of India Act. The State Governments have been concurrently empowered to prosecute the offenders.

12.14 RBI Regulations on Non-banking Financial Companies

The Reserve Bank of India has been regulating and controlling the affairs of Non-Banking Finance Companies (NBFCs) from 1963 onwards. The entire gamut of regulation and supervision over the activities of NBFCs underwent a directional change in terms of both focus and thrust with the amendment of the Banking Regulations Act 1934.

The regulation of deposit acceptance activities of the Non-Banking Finance Companies (NBFCs) was initiated in the 'sixties with a view to safeguarding depositors' interests and to ensure that the NBFCs function on healthy lines. Accordingly, in 1963, a new Chapter III-B was inserted in the Reserve Bank of India Act of 1934 to effectively supervise, control and regulate the deposit acceptance activities of these institutions. Accordingly, the norms for classification of NBFCs into various categories were revised and redefined. However the regulations issued by RBI in 1963 were confined exclusively to the acceptance of deposits and do not cover their functional diversity and its growing financial intermediation. Later it was realised that, a regulation regarding the acceptance of deposits alone was inadequate for the RBI in controlling the affairs of NBFCs.

Since 1963, RBI appointed several committees in order to better align the NBFCs with the overall financial system. RBI in 1971 appointed Bhabatosh Datta Study Group, to examine the role and operations of NBFCs. The group recommended that NBFCs should be classified into 'approved' and 'non-approved' categories and the regulation should be cantered primarily on the 'approved' categories. 'Approved' categories of NBFCs are to satisfy certain additional requirements such as adequate amount of capital, reserves, liquid assets, etc. Later, James Raj Study Group (1974) appointed by the RBI recommended certain provisions related to the regulatory framework of NBFCs.

Subsequently, several experts/working groups, which examined the functioning of NBFCs, were unanimous about the inadequacy of the legislative framework and reiterated the need for enhancing the existing framework. The Chakravarty Committee, in its Report submitted in 1985, recommended for the introduction of a system of licensing (based on the level of business) of NBFCs in order to protect the interests of depositors.

Thereafter, the Narasimham Committee (1991) highlighted the growing importance of NBFCs in the financial intermediation process and outlined a framework for streamlining its functions. Such framework should include, in addition to the existing requirements of gearing and liquidity ratios, norms relating to capital adequacy, debt-equity ratio, credit-concentration ratio, adherence to sound accounting practices, uniform disclosure requirements and assets valuation. Further, the Committee argued that the supervision of these institutions should come within the purview of the proposed agency to be set up for this purpose under the aegis of the Reserve Bank of India. The Narasimham Committee highlighted the need for regulatory framework to govern these institutions.

The Shah Committee, in its report made wide-ranging recommendations for ensuring the functioning of NBFCs on sound lines and by vesting more powers to the RBI. An important recommendation of the Shah Committee implemented by the RBI, was the compulsory registration of NBFCs with a Net Owned Funds (NOF) of ₹ 50 lakh and above, with effect from April 1993. Based on the report, Reserve Bank initiated a series of other measures like the widening of the definition of regulated deposits to include inter corporate deposits, deposits from shareholders and directors and the borrowings by issue of debentures secured by immovable property.

In order to adhere strictly to the prudential norms viz. income recognition, asset classification and provisioning by non-banking companies, Reserve Bank constituted another expert group under the Chairmanship of Khanna in April 1995. The terms of reference of the committee were to suggest measures for the offsite surveillance and the on-site examination system for the NBFCs based on their asset size and the nature of business conducted by them.

In July 1996, the Reserve Bank introduced liberalization and rationalization measures for NBFCs which were registered, rated and were complying with the prudential norms. Under these measures, the eligible companies were given freedom to determine their own rate of interest on deposits, accept unrestricted amount of deposits and maintain lower level of liquid assets. In order to bridge the regulatory gap and in pursuance of the recommendations of the Shah Working Group and the observations made by the Joint Parliamentary Committee in 1992, the Reserve Bank prepared and forwarded to the Government a comprehensive draft legislation in 1994. The Government issued an Ordinance in January 1997 by effecting comprehensive changes in the provisions contained in Chapter III-B, III-C and Chapter V of the RBI Act, 1934. This was subsequently replaced by the Reserve Bank of India (Amendment) Act in March 1997. The amended Act provided:

1. Entry point norm for NBFCs as ₹ 25 lakh. Compulsory registration of NBFCs with a minimum net owned fund of ₹ 25 lakh and above. Reserve Bank is vested with the power of enhancing the minimum capital to ₹ 2 crore (raised to ₹ 2 crore w.e.f. April 21, 1999).
2. Maintenance of liquid assets in the form of unencumbered approved securities viz. Government securities/guaranteed bonds.
3. Creation of a reserve fund and compulsory transfer of at least 20 percent of the net profits to previously mentioned fund.
4. Authorizing Company Law Board (CLB) to direct a defaulting NBFC to repay deposits.
5. Vesting the Reserve Bank with the powers to:

- Issue directions to NBFCs regarding compliance with the prudential norms;
- Issue directions to NBFCs and their Auditors on matters relating to balance sheet and undertake special audit as also to impose penalty on erring auditors;
- Prohibit NBFCs from accepting deposits for violation of the provisions of the RBI Act and direct NBFCs not to alienate their assets;
- File winding up petition against NBFCs for violations of the provision of the Act/directions; and
- Impose penalty directly on NBFCs for non-compliance with the provisions of the Act.

12.15 New Regulatory Framework

The amendment to the provisions contained in Chapter III-B and Chapter V in the RBI Act in 1997, endorsed more powers to the RBI to regulate NBFCs. A new set of regulatory measures was further announced by the Reserve Bank in January 1998 through the amendment of the relevant provisions in the Act. The new amendment is to regulate those NBFCs which accept public deposits. As per the new amendment, NBFCs have been classified into 3 categories.

- NBFCs accepting public deposits.
- NBFCs which do not accept public deposits but are engaged in the financial business.
- Core investment companies, which hold at least 90 percent of their assets as investments in the securities of their group/holding/subsidiary companies.

The new sets of regulatory measures for NBFCs accepting public deposits announced by the Reserve Bank in January 1998 are the following:

1. The NBFCs having net owned funds of less than ₹ 25 lakh have been prohibited from accepting deposits from the public. In respect of new NBFCs (which are incorporated on or after April 20, 1999 and which seek registration with the Reserve Bank), the minimum net owned funds has been raised to ₹ 2 crore.
2. An NBFC intending to accept public deposit must have minimum prescribed credit rating from any of the approved credit rating agencies. The quantum of public deposits that can be raised by NBFCs has been directly linked to the level of credit rating.
3. Borrowings by way of inter corporate deposits, issue of secured debentures, bonds, deposits from shareholders by a private limited company and deposits from directors by both public as well as private limited companies have been excluded from the purview of public deposits. The Reserve Bank regulations on quantum, rate of interest, period of deposits, etc. will be applicable only with respect to public deposits.
4. The overall ceiling on borrowing by NBFCs has been removed and has been sought to be decided on the basis of capital adequacy requirements.
5. In order to streamline the working of NBFCs, which held public deposits in excess of their new entitlements, a period of 3 years has been allowed to these companies to reduce or regularize their excess deposits subject to the condition that at least 1/3rd of excess should be reduced every year commencing from the year ended December 1998 and to wipe out the entire excess by December 31, 2000.
6. For the first time, prudential norms pertaining to income recognition, accounting standards, asset classification, provisioning for bad and doubtful debts, capital adequacy, credit/investment concentration norms etc. have been prescribed for NBFCs for mandatory compliance.
7. Following the amendment of the RBI Act, the liquidity requirement for the NBFCs was enhanced. Accordingly, loan and investment companies, which were earlier maintaining liquid assets at 5.0 percent, were directed to maintain 7.5 percent and 10.0 percent of their deposits in Government and other approved securities to be effective from January 1 and April 1, 1998, respectively. For other NBFCs, the percentage of assets to be maintained by them as statutory reserves was increased to 12.5 percent and 15.0 percent of their deposits respectively, to be effective from April 1, 1998, and April 1, 1999, respectively. Besides, with a view to ensuring that NBFCs can have recourse to such liquid assets in times of emergency, the custody of these

assets with designated commercial banks was also prescribed.

8. The capital adequacy of NBFCs has been enhanced from 8 percent to 10 percent with effect from April 1, 1998, and further to 12 percent with effect from April 1, 1999.
9. As a move towards greater disclosure and transparency, NBFCs accepting public deposit have been asked to furnish certain essential information regarding their financial activities with regard to their applications for deposits and advertisement for soliciting deposits.
10. Statutory auditors of NBFCs are required to report by exception to RBI any irregularity or violation of the RBI regulations on acceptance of public deposits and prudential norms.
11. NBFCs, other than the core investment companies, not accepting public deposits have been exempted from the regulations on interest rates, period, and ceiling on quantum of borrowings. However, prudential norms, which have a bearing on the true and fair status of the financial health of these companies as reflected in their balance sheets, have been made applicable to these companies, except those relating to capital adequacy and credit concentration norms. The responsibilities of ensuring compliance of these regulations have been entrusted to the statutory auditors of these companies and the Reserve Bank has issued directions to the statutory auditors for this purpose.

The process of regulatory strengthening has been reinforced with the creation of an independent department, viz., Department of Non-Banking Supervision (DNBS), for focused attention to the supervision of NBFCs. To facilitate closer and continuous monitoring of NBFCs, the Department has opened 16 Regional Offices to supervise the NBFCs having their registered offices under their respective jurisdiction.

12.16 RBI Regulations Relating to Acceptance of Deposits by NBFCs

All NBFCs are not entitled to accept public deposits. Only those NBFCs holding a valid certificate of registration with authorisation to accept public deposits can accept/hold public deposits. The NBFCs accepting public deposits should have minimum stipulated net owned fund and comply with the directions issued by the Reserve Bank. Important Regulations Relating to Acceptance of Deposits by NBFCs are as under:

1. The NBFCs are allowed to accept or renew public deposits for a minimum period of 12 months and maximum period of 60 months. They cannot accept deposits repayable on demand.
2. NBFCs cannot offer interest rates higher than the ceiling rate prescribed by

RBI from time to time. The present ceiling is 12.5 percent per annum. The interest may be paid or compounded at rests not shorter than monthly rests.

3. NBFCs cannot offer gifts or incentives or any other additional benefit to the depositors.
4. NBFCs (except certain AFCs) should have minimum investment grade credit rating.
5. The deposits with NBFCs are not insured.
6. The repayment of deposits by NBFCs is not guaranteed by RBI. An unrated NBFC, except certain Asset Finance companies (AFC), cannot accept public deposits. An exception is made in the case of unrated AFC companies with CRAR of 15 percent with out credit rating and having net owned funds of more than ₹ 25 lakh but less than ₹ 200 lakh and they can accept public deposits, which are equal to their net owned fund.
7. AFCs with CRAR of 12 percent and having minimum investment grade credit rating and having net owned funds of more than ₹ 25 lakh but less than ₹ 200 lakh can accept deposit, which are equal to 1.5 times of the net owned funds.
8. Loan Companies/Investment Companies with CRAR of 15 percent and having minimum investment grade credit rating and having net owned funds of more than ₹ 25 lakh but less than ₹ 200 lakh can accept deposits which are equal to its net owned funds.
9. There are certain mandatory disclosures about the company in the application form issued by the company soliciting deposits.
10. If an NBFC defaults in repayment of deposit, the depositor can approach the Company Law Board or the Consumer Forum or file a civil suit to recover the deposits.

12.17 Comparison of Regulatory Norms for Commercial Banks and Non-banking Financial Companies

The regulatory norms for commercial banks and non-banking financial companies are as in Table 12.3.

12.18 Difference between Banks and NBFCs

Non-Banking Finance Companies (NBFCs) have in recent years grown sizably both in terms of their numbers as well as the volume of business transactions. The functions of commercial banks and non-banking finance companies are similar in many respects. The distinction between banks and non-banks has been gradually getting blurred since both the segments of the financial system engage themselves in many similar types of activities.

Table 12.3: Regulatory Norms for Commercial Banks and Non-banking Financial Companies

S.N	Particulars	Commercial Banks	NBFC
1	Minimum capital/Net Owned Fund	Minimum capital of not less than ₹ 200 crore is a pre-requisite for the registration of a commercial bank. It may be raised to ₹ 300 crore within three years of operation, in case of new banks. Promoters' minimum contribution is 49 percent of the paid-up capital.	Net owned fund of not less than ₹ 2 crore is a requirement for grant of certificate of registration for commencing the business of a non-banking financial institution.
2	Statutory Liquidity Requirement	Maintain in India, either in (i) cash, (ii) gold (at up to current market price), (iii) unencumbered approved securities valued at a price specified by the Reserve Bank, or (iv) net balances in current accounts with nationalized banks in India, at close of business on any day, an amount of not less than 25 percent of total of demand and time liabilities in India on fortnightly basis, or such other percentage not exceeding 40 percent, as the Reserve Bank, by way of notice, specifies from time to time.	To maintain in India in unencumbered approved securities valued at current market price, an amount at the close of business on any day, which shall not be less than 15 percent of the public deposits outstanding as at the last working day of the second preceding quarter.
3	Cash Reserve Ratio	Cash Reserve Ratio announced by the RBI from time to time is applicable.	CRR is not applicable to NBFCs.
4	Appointment of the managing directors.	Prior approval of Reserve Bank is necessary in the case of appointment of the managing directors, etc.	No such requirement
5	Control over appointment of auditors	Prior approval of the Reserve Bank for appointment, re-appointment or removal of the auditor is required.	No such requirement for NBFCs. These companies have freedom to appoint their auditors as per the Companies

			Act, 1956.
6	Payment system	Commercial banks are members of the RBI's payment and settlement system.	Not a member of the RBI's payment and settlement system.
7	Refinance facility	The Reserve Bank may grant refinance, rediscounting facilities and demand loans.	No such provision in the Reserve Bank of India Act, 1934.
8	Powers of amalgamation, and scheme of arrangement	The Reserve Bank has powers to sanction schemes of amalgamation, reconstruction, and arrangement approved by the requisite majority of shareholders of the bank.	No such provision
9	Winding up proceedings	Special provisions for winding up of a banking company under certain circumstances.	Winding up subject to the general provisions contained in the Companies Act, 1956.

Even though the functions of these institutions are almost same, there are few differences between commercial banks and NBFCs, which are given below:

1. Commercial banks accept demand deposits which are payable immediately on demand viz. current and savings bank deposits. But non-banking companies cannot accept demand deposits.
2. The minimum period for term deposit is generally less than one year in the case of commercial banks. However in the case of NBFCs the minimum period of term deposit is one year.
3. Commercial banks issue cheque book to their customers for withdrawing their demand deposits. Non-bank companies cannot issue cheque book to its customers.
4. Deposit insurance facility of Deposit Insurance and Credit Guarantee Corporation of India (DICGC) is available to commercial banks. But in Non-Banking Finance Companies no official agency guarantees the payment of principal or the interest on such deposits.
5. Leasing and hire purchase business in commercial banks is restricted to a maximum of 10 percent of their assets. However in the case of NBFCs there is no restriction on the volume of these businesses.
6. Licensing norms are tightly controlled and generally, it is perceived to be quite difficult to get a license for a bank. It is comparatively much easier to get registration as an NBFC.
7. 10 percent or above of the capital of a commercial bank can be acquired only with the prior permission of the RBI. In case of Non-banking Finance

Companies there is no limit on the acquisition of percentage of holdings.
8. In the case of commercial banks, 90 days past due leads to non performing asset (NPA) characterization and calls for provisioning as per international standards. In NBFCs as much as 12 months overdue is permitted in case of lease and hire purchase transactions and 6 months in case of loans and other exposures.
9. Reserve bank's strict regulations are applicable in the case of commercial banks. Whereas NBFCs have a much lighter regulation than that applicable to banks.
10. Foreign direct investments have restricted up to 74 percent of the capital in the case of commercial banks. Whereas in the case of NBFCs 100 percent of the capital can be held by foreign owners subject to minimum capitalization requirements under Foreign Direct Investment.

12.19 Reasons for the Growth of NBFCs in India

In India considerable growth has taken place in the non-banking financial sector in last two decades. Over a period of time they are successful in rendering a wide range of financial services. Initially intended to cater to the needs of savers and investors, NBFCs later on developed into institutions that can provide services similar to banks. The banking sector is financing only 40 percent to the trading sector and the rest is coming from the NBFC and private money lenders. At the same time 50 percent of the credit requirement of the manufacturing sector is provided by NBFCs. 65 percent of the private construction activities is also financed by NBFCs. In India they have become prominent in a wide range of activities like hire purchase finance, equipment lease finance, loans, investments, and so on. NBFCs also have greater reach and flexibility in tapping of deposits. Many of the NBFCs have entered into the domain of mutual funds and insurance. They have created a large customer base and the clientele of NBFCs ranges from small borrowers to established corporates.

The strong NBFCs have successfully emerged as 'Financial Institutions' in a short span of time and are in the process of converting themselves into 'Financial Super Market'. The NBFCs are taking initiatives to establish a self-regulatory organization (SRO). At present, NBFCs are represented by the Association of Leasing and Financial Services (ALFS), Federation of India Hire Purchase Association (FIHPA) and Equipment Leasing Association of India (ELA).

The growth of NBFCs in India has been rapid, especially in the 1990s. The number non-banking finance companies stood at 7,063 in 1981, at 15,358 in 1985 and increased to 24,009 by 1990 and to 55,995 in 1995 and then decreased to 54,167 in 2008 and further to 12,409 in 2011. The non-banking finance companies in India enjoy certain advantages compared to commercial banks and co-operative institutions. A number of factors have contributed to the growth of NBFCs in India which are listed below:

1. The rate of interest on deposits offered by NBFCs is higher than commercial and cooperative banks.
2. Easily accessible to borrowers.
3. Tailor-made services and charges according to the needs of the clients.
4. Relatively faster and prompt services than that of banks and financial institutions.
5. NBFCs companies assume greater risk than that of commercial and cooperative banks.
6. NBFCs have more organizational flexibility than that of banks.
7. High degree of their orientation towards customers and simplification of loan sanction procedures.
8. Quick decision-making ability.
9. Low transaction cost.
10. Absence or relatively lower degree of RBIs regulation over NBFCs.
11. Timeliness in meeting the credit needs of specified sectors like equipment leasing, hire purchase, housing finance and consumer finance, personal loans and marketing of insurance.
12. NBFCs able to cater to the needs of those borrowers who remain outside the purview of the commercial banks as a result of the monetary and credit policy of RBI.

Short Answer Type Questions

1. What are non-banking finance companies?
2. Define non-banking finance companies.
3. What is meant by fund based services?
4. Name the regularity authorities of non-banking finance companies.
5. Name any five fee based services.
6. What is meant by hire purchase finance company?
7. What is an investment company?
8. What is a loan company?
9. What is meant by fee based services?
10. What is asset financing company?
11. What are unincorporated bodies?
12. What are the functions of equipment leasing company?
13. What do you mean by mutual benefit finance company?
14. What are merchant banking companies?

15. Explain Nidhi companies.
16. Explain equipment leasing company.
17. What is residuary non-banking company?
18. Name the companies which are exempted from RBI's regulations.
19. Explain miscellaneous non-banking companies.
20. What is a housing finance company?

Essay Type Questions

1. What is meant by non-banking finance companies? Explain the services rendered by non-banking finance companies.
2. Outline the RBI regulations on non-banking finance companies.
3. Explain briefly the different types of non-banking finance companies in India.
4. Differentiate between commercial banks and non-banking finance companies.
5. Discuss the reasons for the favourable growth of non-banking finance companies in India.
6. Discuss the regulatory frame work on non-banking finance companies.

13

Merchant Banking

13.1 Introduction

Merchant Banker is an important financial intermediary provides wide range of financial services to the corporates and investors. Merchant banker may either be an individual or an agent, a financial institution, a bank, subsidiaries of commercial bank or by the private company. Merchant banking is basically non-banking and a non-funding financial institution. Merchant banker as a financial intermediary helps to transform capital from those possesses it to those who need it. The services provided by the merchant bankers help the growth of the corporate sector and ultimately reflects upon the overall economic development of the country.

The most familiar role of the merchant banker is stock underwriting. A large company that wishes to raise money from investors through stock market can hire a merchant bank to implement and underwrite the process. In connection with the fresh issue of securities, merchant banker will determine the number of securities to be issued, the price at which it is to be issued, the timing of the issue etc. The merchant banker also undertakes to file all the documents required by the various market authorities, and is also frequently responsible for marketing the new stock, though this may be a joint effort with the company but managed by the merchant banker. For large issue of stocks, several merchant banks may work together, with one acting as the lead underwriter.

13.2 Meaning of Merchant Banking

Since 18th century, the term merchant banker has considerably been broadened to mean composite of modern day activities. Merchant banks, now so called, are in fact the original bank. The term merchant banking has evolved in Europe and it pertained to an individual or a banking house. The term merchant banking is used differently in different countries. In banking a merchant bank is a financial institution primarily engaged in offering financial services and advice to corporations and to wealthy individuals. In America, merchant banking is concerned with mobilizing savings of people and directing the deposits to the business enterprises. In London, merchant banker refers to those who are members of British Merchant Banking and Securities House Association who carry on leasing, portfolio services, asset management, consultancy, advisory and other functions. The merchant banks are also known as "accepting and issuing houses" in UK and as "Investment Banks" in US.

13.3 Definition of Merchant Banking

It is difficult to define the term merchant banking because the modern merchant banking services involved varied activities. Hence there is no generally accepted definition for merchant banking. The definition of merchant banking has got changed drastically since the days of the earliest merchant banking family's viz. Rothschilds, Schroders, Warburgs. These great merchant banking families dealt with everything from underwriting bonds to originating foreign loans. Bullion trading and bond issuing were some of the specialties of the Rothschild family. The modern merchant banks, however, tend to advice corporations and wealthy individuals on how to manage their money. The advice varies from counsel on mergers and acquisitions to recommendation on the type of credit needed.

Merchant banker may be defined as an "institution which covers a wide range of activities such as underwriting of shares, portfolio management, project counselling, insurance etc. and they render all these services for a fee".

Securities and Exchange Board of India (SEBI) Regulations (Merchant Banker) 2006, defined a merchant banker as "any person who is engaged in the business of issue management either by making arrangements regarding selling, buying or subscribing to securities or acting as manager, consultant, adviser or rendering corporate advisory service in relation to such issue management."

The activities that merchant bankers are authorized to perform are listed by the SEBI. The activities that merchant bankers perform include wide range of activities and divergent functions like issue management, underwriting, portfolio management, venture capital financing, loan syndication, consultancy, advisory and a host of other functions.

13.4 History of Merchant Banking

Merchant bank is a traditional term for an investment bank. Merchant banks are in fact termed as the original banks. These banks were originally intended for the finance of long trading journeys and these methods were then utilized to finance the production of grain. The origin of merchant banking can be traced back to Italian grain merchants of the later medieval times. The Jews could not hold land in Italy, so they entered the great trading centres and halls of Lombardy, alongside the local traders, and set up their benches to trade in crops. The Jewish newcomers lent to farmers loans against crops in the field, a high-risk loan which would have been considered as usurious rates by the Christians. In this way, they could secure the grain sale rights against eventual harvests. They then began to advance loans against grains shipped to distant ports to be delivered. In both cases, they made their profit from the prevalent discount price against the future price. This two-way trade was time consuming and soon there arose a class of merchants, who were trading grain debt instead of grain.

The Jewish traders performed both finance and insurance functions. They derived income from the farmer by way of lending money to both develop and manufacture (through seeding, growing, weeding and harvesting) the annual crop. He would also underwrite (insure) the delivery of the crop to the merchant wholesaler who was the ultimate purchaser of the farmer's harvest. He would arrange to supply through alternative sources this buyer in the event of any particular farming district suffering a seasonal crop failure. He could also keep the farmer or other commodity producer in business during a drought or other crop failure, through the issuance of a crop insurance against the hazard of crop failure.

The medieval Italian markets were disrupted by wars and were limited by the fractured nature of the Italian states. Therefore, the next generation of bankers arose from migrant Jewish merchants in the great wheat growing areas of Germany and Poland. Many of these merchants were from the same families who were part of the development of the banking process in Italy. They also had links with family members who had fled from centuries before Spain to both Italy and England. Later, the centre for merchant banking got shifted from the Italian states to Amsterdam and then, in the eighteenth century, to London, where immigrants from France, Ireland, Russia, and the Italian states formed the core of early British merchant banking.

The term merchant banking originated in London in the late eighteenth century. The term merchant banking has evolved in Europe and it pertained to an individual or a banking house whose primary function was to facilitate the business process between a product and the financial requirements for its development. Merchant bankers also started financing foreign trade through acceptance of bills. In particular, the merchant banker acted as a source of capital whose primary activity was targeted towards a commodity trader/cargo owner who was involved in the buying, selling, and shipping of goods. Later they helped governments of underdeveloped countries to raise long-term funds.

In 1914, British merchants formed an association, which is now called Merchant Banking and Securities House Association. Like the Italian and Dutch houses these British houses were generally small, family-owned partnerships, and most of them continued to trade both for their own businesses and to finance others' trading. By the end of the eighteenth century, however, the British merchant houses had increased in their size and sophistication and began specializing in trade, marketing or finance. As the nineteenth century dawned, virtually no mercantile houses remained focused on both trade and finance. During the 19th century, foreign merchant bankers carried their operations in India through British East India Company.

However, during the 20th century, European merchant banks expanded their services. They became increasingly involved directly in the actual running of the business for which the transaction was conducted. Today, merchant banks actually own and run businesses both in their own account and that of others. Since 18th century, the term merchant banker has considerably been broadened to mean composite of modern day activities. These activities include those like that of an entrepreneur, a management advisor, a commercial and/or investment banker plus that of a transaction broker. The merchant banks are also known as "accepting and issuing houses" in UK and as "Investment Banks" in US.

13.5 Merchant Banking in United States

Merchant banking services in United States however, are undertaken by highly specialized "boutiques", which offer their own specialized services. They charge fees for each and every service and their transactions are oriented towards short- term deals rather than long-term relationships. Very few of them offer the complete range of services which are provided by traditional European merchant banks. In fact, most companies that approach US merchant bank for their services try primarily to either increase their financial stability or to meet a particular immediate capital need. There are many merchant bankers operating in North America today, both large and small, but only a subset of them offers a full range of services.

13.6 Merchant Banking in India

Merchant banking in India is of recent origin. Until 1969, merchant banker was alien to the Indian banking system. The merchant banking services in India were first started by foreign banks. It originated in India in 1969 with the setting up of Merchant Banking division by the Grindlays Bank to handle new capital issue. Later City Bank and Chartered Bank floated their own merchant banking divisions with the same objective. The Banking Commission in its report in 1972 indicated the requirement of merchant banking service in India. In view of the greater stress on industrialization in the Fifth Five Year Plan, the commission was in favour of a separate institution for merchant banking services in India.

State Bank of India (SBI) was the first Indian commercial bank to set up their merchant banking division in 1972 followed by the Industrial Credit and Investment Corporation of India (ICICI) in 1973. The merchant banking divisions of these institutions concentrated on only issue management and financial consultancy services. The year 1973 witnessed a boom in the capital market with the introduction of Foreign Exchange Regulations Act (FERA). With the introduction of FERA, many Indian commercial banks set up their own merchant banking division viz. Canara Bank, Syndicate Bank, Punjab National Bank, Bank of India, UCO Bank, Indian Overseas Bank, United Commercial Bank etc. and leading broker firms and foreign merchant bankers.

In the early stages, the role of merchant banking in India was confined mainly to the management of public issue of securities. Later, the scope of merchant banking got widened beyond the issue management to a wide range of other financial and related services to the customers.

The working of merchant banks in India is regulated by Securities and Exchange Board of India (SEBI) and Ministry of Finance, Government of India. SEBI issued the necessary rules and regulations relating to the working of merchant bankers. Merchant bankers in India are governed by the Securities and Exchange Board of India (Merchant Bankers) Regulations Act of 1992.

13.7 Difference between Merchant Banking and Commercial Banking

Both commercial banking and merchant banking have their roots that go beyond hundred of years or more. Merchant banks were actually the original banks, which were invented by Italian grain merchants in the middle ages. Commercial banking and merchant banking involve provisions for financial services and advice. The difference between commercial banking and merchant banking lie mainly in the services they provide, and to whom they are provided.

Commercial banking is generally accessible to anyone who approaches it for basic banking needs, whereas merchant banking serves only the large companies and very wealthy individuals. A merchant bank is said to be a wholesale bank or one engaged in the business of wholesale banking. A merchant bank does not have retail offices where one can do normal banking operations. A commercial bank has retail offices where one carry on all normal banking operations.

Commercial bank typically refers to a bank, which accepts deposits, and provides loans and advances to individuals and small businesses. It also purchases bonds from governments and corporate entities. Merchant banking, however, often focuses on investing a depositor's assets in a finance portfolio and managing these investments. Apart from investing and managing the assets of wealthy clients, merchant banks also offer counsel and advice to large corporations. All services of merchant bankers are fee based and fees constitute their major income. Commercial banks however focus mainly on accepting deposits and lending money for an interest with the objective of earning profit.

13.8 Merchant Banks and Investment Banks

Merchant banks and investment banks are two different types of financial intermediaries which involve the provision of various financial services. Both merchant banks and investment banks provide fee based corporate advisory services. The chief distinction between a merchant bank and an investment bank is that a merchant bank invests its own capital in a client company whereas an investment bank purely distributes the securities of that company in its capital raising role. Traditionally, investment banks focus on initial public offerings (IPOs), participated in underwriting and selling securities in large public and private share offerings.

Merchant banks tend to operate mainly in small-scale companies and offer creative equity financing, bridge financing, issuing letters of credit, transferring funds internationally, trade consulting and a number of corporate credit products. Investment banks however, tend to focus mainly on larger companies. Investment banks facilitate mergers and acquisitions through share sales and provide research and financial consulting to companies. Merchant banks provide services to wealthy individuals. Traditionally, investment banks did not deal with the general public. Merchant banks still offer trade financing products to their clients. Investment banks rarely offer trade financing because most investment banking clients have already outgrown the need for trade financing and the various credit products linked to it.

13.9 Registration of Merchant Bankers

The Merchant Banking activity in India is governed by SEBI (Merchant Banking) Regulations, of 1992. All merchant bankers have to register with the SEBI. No person shall carry on any activity as a merchant banker unless he holds a certificate granted by the SEBI under its regulations. SEBI has been vested with the power to suspend or cancel the authorization in case of violation of the guidelines. SEBI has the right to send inspecting authority to inspect books of accounts, records etc. of merchant bankers. Inspections will be conducted by SEBI to ensure that provisions in the merchant banking are properly complied with. Every merchant banker shall appoint a 'Compliance Officer' to monitor their observance of SEBI Merchant Banking Regulations.

13.10 Conditions for Grant of Registration as Merchant Banker

Before granting a certificate of registration as a merchant banker, SEBI takes into account several factors which are relevant to the activities of the merchant banker and in particular the factor that the applicant complies with the following requirements, namely:

1. The person applying for certificate of registration as merchant banker has to be a body corporate other than a non-banking financial company. Provided that the merchant banker who has been granted registration by the Reserve Bank of India to act as a Primary or Satellite dealer may carry on such activity subject to the condition that it shall not accept or hold public deposit.
2. The applicant has at least two persons in his employment with experience to conduct the business of a merchant banker.
3. The applicant has also to fulfil the capital adequacy requirements specified by the Securities and Exchange Board of India. The minimum capital adequacy requirement of merchant bankers depends upon the category.
4. The applicant, his partners, director or principal officer should not be involved in any litigation connected with the securities market, which has an adverse bearing on the business of the applicant.
5. The applicant, his director, partner or principal officer has not at any time been convicted for any offence involving moral turpitude or has been found guilty of any economic offence.
6. The applicant has the necessary infrastructure like adequate office space, equipments and work force to effectively discharge the activities of a merchant banker.
7. The applicant is fit and proper.
8. The applicant should possess the professional qualifications on finance, law or business secured from an institution recognized by the Government.

Every merchant banker should maintain copies of balance sheet, profit and loss account and statement of financial position. Half-yearly unaudited financial result should be submitted to SEBI with a view to monitor the capital adequacy of the merchant banker. Merchant bankers are prohibited from buying securities based on the unpublished price sensitive information of their clients. Every merchant banker shall preserve the books of accounts and other records and documents maintained for a period of five years.

13.11 Renewal of Certificate to a Merchant Banker

The SEBI may grant or renew a certificate to a merchant banker subject to the following conditions:

1. The merchant banker, in case of any change in his status and constitution, shall obtain the prior permission of the Board to carry on his activities as a merchant banker.

2. He shall pay the amount of fees for renewal, as the case may be, in the manner provided in the regulations.
3. He shall take adequate steps for redressal of grievances of the investors within one month from the date of receipt of complaint and keep the Securities and Exchange Board of India informed about the number, nature and other particulars of the complaints received.
4. He shall abide by the rules and regulations made under the SEBI Act in respect of the activities carried on by the merchant banker.

The certificate of registration or its renewal, as the case may be issued under rule 4 (SEBI Merchant Bankers Rules, 1992) and should be valid for a period of 3 years from the date of its issue to the applicant. The merchant banker may, if he so desires, make an application for renewal of registration 3 months before the expiry of the certificates.

13.12 Fee for Registration and Renewal of Certificate of Certification

Every merchant banker shall pay a sum of ₹ 10 lakh as registration fees at the time of the grant of certificate by the SEBI. A merchant banker to keep his registration in live shall pay a renewal fee of ₹ 5 lakh every three years beginning from the fourth year from the date of initial registration. The non-refundable fee payable along with an application for registration or an application for renewal of registration shall be a sum of twenty five thousand rupees. The merchant banker shall pay the fee within fifteen days from the date of receipt of intimation from the Board.

13.13 Classification of Merchant Bankers by SEBI

As per SEBI Regulations, merchant bankers are classified into four categories. The application by a person shall be made for any one of the following categories of the merchant banker:

13.13.1 Category I: This category of merchant banker can carry on the activities of issue management which consist of preparation of prospectus and other information relating to the issue, determining the financial structure, tie-up of financiers and final allotment and refund of subscription. The merchant banker can also act as an advisor, consultant, manager, underwriter and portfolio manager. The capital adequacy requirement in case of category I merchant banker shall be a networth of not less than ₹ 5 crore. Networth means the sum of paid up capital and free reserves of the applicant at the time of making application.

13.13.2 Category II: This category of merchant banker can act as an advisor, consultant, co-manager, underwriter and portfolio manager. The capital adequacy requirement in case of category II merchant banker shall be a networth of not less than ₹ 50 lakh. Category II merchant bankers are not permitted to carry out those activities which relates to the issue management.

13.13.3 Category III: This category of merchant banker can act as an underwriter, advisor and consultant to an issue but can not undertake portfolio management. Category III merchant banker must have a minimum networth of ₹ 20 lakh.

13.13.4 Category IV: This category of merchant banker can act only as an advisor or consultant to an issue. The minimum capital adequacy requirement is not insisted in case of category IV merchant bankers.

Merchant banking institutions in India are established mainly by the following types of institutions.

- Indian Commercial Banks.
- Foreign Banks.
- Private Firms and Stock Brokers.
- Merchant Banking firms established by Financial Institutions.

13.14 Functions of Merchant Banker

In the early stages, the role of merchant banking was mainly confined to the management of public issues of equity capital. Recently, merchant bankers are engaged for rendering a wide spectrum of financial and other related services to their customers. Besides the new issue management, modern merchant banker's role now starts rightly from the very promotion of the company. As a corporate advisor, merchant banker offers various services to the promoter i.e. for identification of the project, preparing feasibility report, selection of location of the project, size of organization, investment decisions, obtaining government approval and other legal formalities, pricing methods, resource mobilization, investment management, evaluation of financial alternatives, market survey, marketing strategy, cost reduction, cost control, working capital management, capital restructuring etc. All merchant bankers do not specialize on all these services. Different merchant bankers specialize in different services.

Before selecting a merchant banker, one should decide as to which of their services are required. Is it capital, general management consulting, supervision of an existing investment, a joint venture, or merger/acquisition assistance, a distribution, product or manufacturing opportunity that one requires? It is essential to know who in such an organization is best equipped to provide these services. Also, selection of the merchant banker depends on whether one needs to satisfy a short term or long-term objective, or both. The divergent services and functions rendered by merchant bankers in India are mainly the following:

1. Managing of public issue of securities.

2. Underwriting of public issue.
3. Portfolio investment management services.
4. Project counselling.
5. Advisory services relating to mergers and takeovers.
6. Loan syndication.
7. Investment services for NRIs.
8. Off shore finance.
9. Providing margin money for working capital.
10. Restructuring services.
11. Other services.

13.14.1 Managing of Public Issue of Securities: Managing of public issue of securities is one of the important functions of a merchant banker. At one time, management of issue of securities was perceived as the sole function of merchant bankers. Issue management function of merchant banking helps companies to raise money from capital market through the issue of various types of securities. Management of issues involves marketing of corporate securities i.e. equity and preference shares and debentures by offering them for public subscription. Merchant bankers assist the issuer for the completion of all formalities under the Indian Companies Act, SEBI Act and listing of shares in stock exchanges.

The appointment of the number of merchant bankers for a public issue depends upon the size of the issue. SEBI insists that at least one merchant banker functioning as the lead merchant banker should manage all issues. For an issue of 100 crore, a maximum of four merchant bankers can be appointed.

The success of an issue primarily depends upon the extent of care and due diligence exercised by the merchant bankers. Following are the services rendered by merchant banker as managers to the public issue of securities:

1. Preparing of prospectus and sending it to SEBI and then to file it with the Registrar of Companies.
2. Preparing and forwarding of application to Controller of Capital Issues (CCI) and in obtaining clearance from the CCI.
3. Deciding the size and time of public issue.
4. Appointment of bankers and registrars to the issue.
5. Selection of both individual and institutional brokers and underwriters.
6. Appointment of portfolio managers.
7. Preparation of advertising and promotional materials.
8. Selection of advertisement agencies.
9. To conduct meetings with company representatives and advertising agencies to decide upon the date of opening of an issue and its closing, launching publicity campaign etc.

10. Compliance of listing requirements of stock exchanges.
11. Help the companies to fix up the prices of their issues.
12. Collection of application forms.
13. Screening of applications.
14. Deciding procedure for allotment.
15. Posting of allotment letters, share certificates and refund orders.
16. To act as a coordinator of the company and other operators in the primary issue market.

Management of issue may be broadly classified into two stages viz. pre-issue and post-issue. (Pre-issue and post-issue functions of merchant bankers are given separately at the end of the chapter).

13.14.2 Underwriting of Public Issue: Underwriting of public issue is another important function of merchant bankers. Raising of external resources is easy for the issues backed by well known underwriters. Underwriting is an agreement whereby the underwriter undertakes to subscribe the unsubscribed portion of shares and debentures offered by a public limited company. This encourages the prospective issuers to offer shares and debentures to the public for subscription and they can raise fund from the public for implementation of their industrial activities. In respect of every issue to be managed, the lead merchant banker holding a certificate under category 1 shall accept a minimum underwriting obligation of 5 percent of the total underwriting commitment or ₹ 25 lakh, whichever is less. The outstanding underwriting commitments of a merchant banker shall not exceed 5 times of his net worth at any point of time.

13.14.3 Portfolio Investment Management Services: One of the important functions of a merchant banker is to provide portfolio management services to their customers. Merchant bankers provide services to both the issuers of securities and the investors in securities. Portfolio refers to investment in different kinds of securities such as shares and debentures issued by different companies. It is a combination of assets but a carefully blended asset combination. Portfolio management refers to maintaining proper combination of securities (equity and debt) in a manner that they give maximum return to the client. Generally most investors are interested in the safety, liquidity and profitability of their investment but they are not informed enough to choose the appropriate securities. Merchant bankers help investors in choosing different types of securities and the amount of investment in each type of security. Merchant bankers undertake the function of purchase and sale of securities for their clients. They also conduct regular market and economic surveys.

13.14.4 Project Counselling: Project counselling is another important service rendered by the merchant bankers to their clients. It refers to the technical appraisal of a project and providing of advisory services and it includes the following:

1. Development of an idea of a project.
2. Preparation of project reports.
3. Estimated cost of the project and the procedural aspects for its implementation.
4. Deciding upon the nature and type of financing pattern.
5. Appraisal of project on the basis of its technical, commercial and financial viability.
6. Filling up of application forms for obtaining funds from financial institutions.
7. Filling up of application forms for obtaining government sanction etc.

13.14.5 Advisory Services Relating to Mergers and Takeovers: Merchant bankers provide expert advice to their clients regarding takeovers, acquisitions and mergers. Merger is a combination of two or more companies into a single company where one survives and the other becomes extinct. Takeover is the purchase of one company by another company acquiring controlling interest of its share capital. Merchant banker acts as a middleman in between these companies. They negotiate the mode of payment and get approval from government and other statutory authorities. On behalf of their customers, merchant bankers comply with all the statutory and legal requirements for the mergers and acquisitions. These services include:

1. Assessing the pros and cons of financial reconstruction, mergers, takeover,
2. To render help in determining purchase consideration,
3. Negotiating the mode of payments,
4. Assistance in preparation and formulation of scheme of reconstruction,
5. Assistance in obtaining approval from shareholders, depositors, creditors, government and other agencies,
6. Implementation and monitoring of scheme of mergers and amalgamations,
7. Coordinating the activities of various parties involved in the mergers and acquisition such as solicitors, accountants, valuators and other professionals.

13.14.6 Loan Syndication: Loan syndication is an important service provided by a merchant banker. Under loan syndication, merchant bankers help their clients in raising loans from Indian and foreign countries for long-term requirements. Loan syndication involves preparation and submission of application form for raising short, medium and long-term finance from various financial institutions. Under this function, merchant banker performs the following activities:

1. Finalizing the cost of the project.
2. Estimating the financial requirements for plant, machinery, building etc.

3. Determining promoter's contribution.
4. Estimation of working capital requirements.
5. Provides assistance for obtaining loans from a single institution or consortium advance.
6. Selection of banks and other financial institutions in the case of participatory financing.
7. Assists the clients for preparation and submission of application form for loans from various financial institutions, government agencies etc.
8. Fulfilling the procedures for obtaining funds form All India financial institutions such as Industrial Development Bank of India (IDBI), Industrial Finance Corporation of India (IFCI), Small Industries Bank of India (SIDBI) NABARD, EXIM Bank of India etc.
9. Fulfilling legal formalities in connection with obtaining funds from different financial institutions.
10. To follow up the loan applications with banks and other financial institutions.
11. Managing Euro-Issues etc.

13.14.7 Investment Services for NRIs: Merchant banks provide various kinds of services to Non-Resident Indians. NRIs have to follow lots of complicated rules for investing in the shares in India. Merchant bankers encourage NRIs to invest their savings in Indian industries. Merchant bankers help them in choosing the shares and offer expert advice for fulfilling government regulations and thereby mobilizing more resources for the corporate sector. The services to NRIs include the following:

1. Supplying information regarding investment for the benefit of investors.
2. To render assistance to purchase and sell securities.
3. To provide information on market movements.
4. Securing approval from RBI for the purchase and sale of various securities.
5. To hold securities in safe custody.
6. Collection of dividend and interest on securities on behalf of customers.
7. Providing information on tax and filing of tax returns.
8. Evaluation of investment portfolio at the request of investors.

13.14.8 Off Shore Finance: Merchant bankers help their clients in obtaining offshore finance. These services include:

1. Obtaining long-term foreign currency loan like Eurodollar.
2. Managing and advising on international offerings of debt/equity i.e. Global Depository Receipts, American Depository Receipts.
3. Formation of joint ventures abroad.
4. Financing exports and imports.
5. To provide pre-shipment credit.

6. To arrange and negotiate foreign collaborations etc.

13.14.9 Providing Margin Money for Working Capital: Arranging working capital is another important function of a merchant banker. Merchant bankers assist in arranging working capital requirements of both existing and new enterprises. They also render assistance for obtaining working capital through debenture issues.

13.14.10 Restructuring Services: In order to obtain financial, marketing and production benefits merchant bankers assist their clients for the successful restructuring of various activities. Merchant bankers participate in different activities at various stages to attain the objectives behind restructuring. Restructuring services include the following:

1. Valuation of the financial proposals.
2. Assistance in financial restructuring.
3. Analyzing existing capital structure.
4. Determine the extent of capitalization.
5. Assistance in obtaining consent from the Controller of Capital Issue in case of bonus issue.
6. Advice the companies on the extent of and means for bringing fresh capital into the business.
7. Advice companies on disinvestment.
8. Examining the marketing strategies.
9. Help in seeking the right partner for strategic decisions.

13.14.11 Other Services: Besides the above-mentioned services, merchant bankers offer numerous other services which are listed below:

1. Offer services to the promoters of new ventures.
2. Assist existing companies in expansion, diversification and modernization.
3. Business valuation.
4. Private placement of securities.
5. Primary or satellite dealership of government securities.
6. Dealing in shares and stocks as market maker or stock broker.
7. Buy back assignments.
8. Share valuation.
9. Valuation of assets.
10. Corporate tax planning.
11. Financing hire purchase transactions.
12. Operating of mutual funds.
13. Dealing in commercial paper.
14. To maintain register of share holders and debenture holders.
15. Act as share transfer agent.

16. Debenture Trusteeship.
17. Acting as an agent for paying interest, dividend etc.

13.15 General Obligations of Merchant Bankers

Every lead merchant banker before taking up the assignment related to an issue should enter into an agreement with such body corporate setting out their mutual rights, liabilities and obligations relating to such issue and in particular to disclosures, allotment and refund. Merchant banker other than a bank or a public financial institution with a certificate of registration from SEBI should not associate with any business other than that of securities market. A merchant banker who has been granted certificate of registration to act as primary or satellite dealer by Reserve Bank of India may carry on such business as may be permitted by the RBI. A lead merchant banker shall not be associated with any issue if that merchant banker is not having a certificate concerning that issue.

No merchant banker or any of its directors, partner, or manager or principal officer shall either on their respective accounts or through their associates or relatives enter into any transaction in securities of body corporate on the basis of unpublished price sensitive information obtained by them during the course of any professional assignment either form the clients or otherwise. Every merchant banker shall submit to the Board complete particulars of any transaction for acquisition of securities of any body corporate whose issue is being managed by that merchant banker within fifteen days from the date of entering into such transactions.

The issue function of merchant banker may be broadly divided into two parts i.e. pre-issue and post-issue functions. In both pre-issue and post-issue of securities, merchant banker has to comply with all legal requirements and to coordinate a number of intermediaries associated with the issue of securities.

13.16 Number of Lead Merchant Bankers in Case of Issue of Securities

A merchant banker who is associated with the issuer company as a promoter or a director shall not lead manages the issue of the company. The appointment of number of merchant bankers to a public issue depends upon the size of the issue. At least one merchant banker functioning as the lead merchant banker should manage all the issues. Provided that, an issue of offer of rights to the existing members with or without the right of renunciation, and if the amount of the issue of the body corporate does not exceed ₹ 50 lakh, the appointment of a lead merchant banker shall not be essential. An issue of shares by way of rights by a company listed on a stock exchange and exceeding ₹ 50 lakh should be managed by an authorized merchant banker functioning as a lead manager. The appointments of maximum number of merchant bankers in a public issue are given below:

1. If the size of the issue is less than ₹ 50 crore, the maximum numbers of lead merchant bankers are restricted to 2.
2. If the issue size is between ₹ 50 crore and less than ₹ 100 crore the maximum number is restricted to 3.
3. If the issue is between ₹ 100 crore and less than ₹ 200 crore the maximum number of lead mangers shall be 4.
4. If the issue is between ₹ 200 crore and less than ₹ 400 crore the maximum number is restricted to 5.
5. If the issue is above ₹ 400 crore, five or more number of lead merchant bankers as agreed by the SEBI can be accommodated.

13.17 Fees Charged by Merchant Bankers

The fee payable to the managers to the issue for their services should not exceed 0.5 percent for issues of up to ₹ 25 crore and 0.2 percent for issues above ₹ 25 crore.

13.18 Pre-Issue Functions of Merchant Banker

All activities involved prior to the closure of issues are called pre-issue functions. Merchant banker acts as a link between the issuing company and other agencies related with the issue of securities. They have to coordinate the activities of the issuing company with different agencies such as Government, SEBI, Controller of Capital Issues, Registrar of Companies, Stock Exchanges, public bodies, professionals and private agencies. They are also required to fulfil all the statutory requirements under the Companies Act, Rules, Regulations and Guidelines of SEBI, Stock Exchange, Registrar of Companies etc. The pre-issue obligations of merchant bankers are listed below:

13.18.1 Drafting Memorandum of Understanding and Allocation of Responsibilities: No lead merchant manager shall agree to manage or be associated with any issue unless his responsibilities relating to the issue mainly, those of disclosures, allotment and refund are clearly defined. Each company issuing securities through public or rights issue has to enter into a Memorandum of Understanding (MOU) with the lead merchant banker, who specifies their mutual rights, liabilities and obligations relating to the issue. A statement specifying such responsibilities are to be furnished to the SEBI at least one month before the opening of the issue for subscription. Where there are more than one lead merchant banker to the issue the responsibilities of each of such lead merchant banker shall clearly be demarcated and a statement specifying such responsibilities shall be furnished to the SEBI at least one month before the opening of the issue for subscription.

13.18.2 Appointment of Other Intermediaries: The company in consultation with the lead merchant banker appoints other intermediaries such as Underwriters, Brokers, Bankers to the Issue, Registrars to the issue etc. Lead Merchant banker shall ensure that the other intermediaries being appointed are duly registered with the SEBI.

The issuer company and the lead merchant banker shall decide the number of underwriters. Similarly, the issuer decides the types of underwriters in consultation with the lead merchant banker. The lead merchant banker shall satisfy themselves about the competence of the underwriters to discharge their underwriting obligations. The lead merchant banker shall assess the overall exposure of underwriters belonging to the same group or management in an issue carefully. While selecting underwriters and finalizing underwriting arrangements, lead merchant bankers shall ensure that the underwriters do not overexpose themselves so that it may become difficult to fulfil the underwriting commitments.

The issuer company shall appoint Bankers to the Issue only in consultation with and the prior approval of the lead merchant banker. The issuer company can finalize the collection centres of the bank in consultation with the merchant banker. As per SEBI regulations, all Registrars to an Issue are required to enter into a legally valid agreement with the issuer company. In the case of a large issue, the issuer company and the lead merchant banker should decide the number of Registrar to the issue. In such a case, all the Registrars to the Issue shall execute the agreement and the issuer and the lead manager shall be a confirming party. A merchant banker acting as manager to the issue shall be responsible for the settlement of fees/commission due to various intermediaries appointed in connection with the issue of securities such as bankers to the issue, registrars to the issue, underwriters, advocates, solicitors, brokers, charges of printers and advertising agencies, stock exchanges etc.

13.18.3 Drafting Prospectus: The Lead Merchant Banker has to submit draft prospectus and draft offer document along with a due diligence certificate to the SEBI. The lead merchant banker shall simultaneously file copies of the draft offer document with the stock exchanges where the securities are proposed to be listed. The lead merchant banker shall make copies of offer document filed with the SEBI available to the public for a period of 21 days from the date of filing of the offer document with the SEBI. Twenty-one days after the draft offer document has been made public, the lead merchant banker should file a statement with the SEBI giving a list of complaints received, a statement as to whether it is proposed to amend or not the draft offer document and highlighting those amendments if any.

13.18.4 Payment of Requisite Fees to the SEBI: The lead merchant banker has to pay the requisite fee in accordance with the SEBI rules and regulations, along with draft offer document filed with the SEBI. Merchant Banker shall pay the fees as set out below:

S.N	Size of the issue including premium	Proposed fee per document
1	Up to ₹ 10 crore	₹ 25,000
2	More than ₹ 10 crore but less than ₹ 5,000 crore.	0.025 percent of the issue size.
3	More than ₹ 5,000 crore but less than ₹ 25,000 crore	₹ 1,25,000 + 0.00625 percent of the portion of the issue size in excess of ₹ 5,000 crore.
4	More than ₹ 25,000 crore	A flat rate of ₹ 3 crore.

In the case of rights issue if the issue size is more than ₹ 10 crore but less than ₹ 5,000 crore the fees shall be 0.005 percent of the issue size. If the issue size is more than ₹ 5,000 crore the fees shall be a flat charge of ₹ 5 lakh.

13.18.5 Filing of Due Diligence Certificate: The lead merchant Banker shall furnish to the SEBI the due diligence certificate. In addition to due diligence certificate, the Lead Merchant Banker shall also submit an undertaking to the SEBI with respect to the following matters:

1. Certify that all the amendments, suggestions or observations made by the SEBI have been incorporated in the offer document.
2. Furnish a new diligence certificate at the time of filing the prospectus with the Registrar of Companies.
3. Furnish a fresh certificate immediately before the opening of the issue that no corrective action on its part is needed in the offer document.
4. Furnish a fresh certificate after the issue has opened but before it closes for subscription as per the format specified at Schedule VI (Disclosure and Investor Protection Guidelines, 2000).

13.18.6 Appointment of Depositories and Compliance Officer: The lead manager should also ensure that the issuer company has entered into agreements with all the depositories for dematerialization of securities. The merchant banker has to appoint a compliance officer who will directly coordinate between the SEBI and the issuer company with regard to compliance of various laws, rules, regulations and other directives issued by the Board.

13.18.7 Despatch of Issue Material: The lead merchant banker shall also ensure that for public issues offer documents and other issue materials are despatched to the various stock exchanges, brokers, underwriters, bankers to the issue, investors association etc. in advance as agreed upon. In the case of rights issues, lead merchant banker shall ensure that the letters of offer are despatched to all shareholders at least one week before the date of opening of the issue.

13.18.8 Collection Centres and Authorized Collection Agents: The merchant banker in consultation with the issuing company decides the collection centres besides the four mandatory collection centres as specified by SEBI. The issuer company can also appoint authorized collection agents in consultation with the lead merchant banker subject to necessary disclosures including the names and addresses of such agents made in the offer document. The modalities of such selection and appointment of collection agents can be made by the lead merchant banker at their discretion.

13.19 Post-Issue Obligations of Merchant Bankers

The liability of the merchant banker will continue even after the completion of the issue process. The post-issue obligations of merchant bankers are given below:

13.19.1 Submission of Post-Issue Monitoring Report: Irrespective of the level of subscription, the lead merchant banker should ensure that the post-issue monitoring reports are submitted as per the format specified by the SEBI. In the case of both 'public issues' and 'rights issues' the due date for the submission of 3-day post-issue monitoring report shall be the 3rd day from the date of closure of subscription of the issue. The due date for the submission of 78-day post-issue monitoring report in the case of 'public issue' shall be the 78th day and in 'rights issues' 50th day from the date of closure of subscription of the issue. After the issue, the merchant banker should monitor the allotment, refund and dispatch and also redressal of investor grievances arising there from.

13.19.2 Co-ordination with Intermediaries: The post-issue lead merchant manger shall maintain close co-ordination with the 'Registrars to the Issue' and arrange to depute its officers to the offices of various intermediaries at regular intervals after the closure of the issue. The officers deputed will monitor the flow of applications from collecting bank branches, processing of applications including those accompanied by stock invest and other matters till the basis of allotment is finalized, dispatch security certificates and refund orders completed and securities listed. Any act of omission or commission on the part of any of the intermediaries noticed during such visits shall be duly reported to the SEBI.

13.19.3 Application Money: The post-issue Lead Merchant Banker shall also ensure that money received pursuant to the issue is kept in a separate bank (i.e., Bankers to an Issue). As per the provisions of Section 73 (3) of the Companies Act 1956, such money is released by the said bank only after obtaining the listing permission from all the stock exchanges where the securities were proposed to be listed as per the offer document.

13.19.4 Despatch of Allotment or Refund Orders: Lead Merchant banker shall ensure that the despatch of allotment letter/refund orders/share certificates is done by way of registered post/certificate of posting as may be applicable. Lead merchant banker shall ensure payment of interest to the applicants for delayed despatch of allotment letters, refund orders etc. as prescribed in the offer document. In the case of all issues, the advertisement should give details relating to oversubscription, basis of allotment, number, value and percentage of applications received along with stock invest, number, value and percentage of successful allottees who have applied through stock invest, date of completion of despatch of refund orders, date of despatch of certificate and date of filing of listing applications. Such advertisement shall be released within 10 days from the date of completion of various activities. The post issue lead merchant banker shall submit within two weeks from the date of allotment, a certificate to the SEBI certifying that the stock invests on the basis of which allotment was finalized, have been realized.

13.20 Code of Conduct for the Merchant Bankers

Merchant Bankers shall abide by the code of conduct specified by the SEBI, which are given below:

1. A merchant Banker in the conduct of his business shall observe high standards of integrity and fairness in all his dealings with his clients and other merchant bankers. He shall also abide by the provisions of the Act, rules and regulations, which may be applicable, and relevant to the activities carried on by the merchant banker.
2. A merchant banker shall render at all times high standards of service, exercise due diligence, ensure proper care and exercise independent professional judgment.
3. A merchant banker shall fulfil its obligations in a prompt, ethical, and professional manner.
4. A merchant banker shall endeavour to ensure that the investors are provided with true and adequate information without making any misleading or exaggerated claims or any misrepresentation and are made aware of the risks before taking any investment decision.

5. A merchant banker shall endeavour to ensure that copies of the prospectus, offer document, letter of offer or any other related literature are made available to the investors at the time of issue of the offer.
6. A merchant banker shall not make any statement or become privy to any act, practice, unfair competition, which are likely to be harmful to the interests of other merchant bankers or are likely to place such other merchant bankers in a disadvantageous position in relation to the merchant banker, while competing for or executing any assignment.
7. A merchant banker shall always endeavour to render the best advice to the clients having regard to the clients' needs and the environments and his own professional skill. A merchant banker shall also ensure that all professional dealings are carried on in a prompt, efficient and cost effective manner.
8. A merchant banker shall not divulge to other clients, press or any other party any confidential information about his client, which has come to his knowledge.
9. A merchant banker shall not be generally and particularly a party to or instrument for:

- Creation of false market.
- Price rigging or manipulation.
- Passing of sensitive information to brokers, members of the stock exchange, and other players in the capital market.
- Take any other action, which is detrimental to the interest of investors.

Short Answer Type Questions

1. Define merchant banking.
2. What do you mean by issue management?
3. What is a prospectus?
4. What is merchant banking?
5. What is post-issue management?
6. What is investment banking?
7. What do mean by margin money for working capital?
8. What is portfolio investment management service?
9. List out the restructuring services rendered by a merchant banker.
10. What do you mean by underwriting of public issue?
11. What is Project counselling?
12. What are the different types of merchant bankers in India?
13. What is credit syndication?
14. What is off shore finance?
15. What is meant by managing of public issue?

Essay Type Questions

1. Explain ʰe history of merchant banking in India.
2. What are the important functions of a merchant banker?
3. What are the post-issue services rendered by merchant bankers?
4. Explain the procedure for registration of merchant bankers in India.
5. Explain briefly the origin of merchant banking services.
6. What is the role of merchant bankers in the capital market?
7. What are the differences between merchant banking and a commercial banking?
8. Define issue management. What are the activities involved in the issue management?
9. What are the pre-issue functions of a merchant banker?
10. Explain the role of SEBI in connection with the registration of merchant bankers.
11. What are the general obligations of a merchant banker?
12. Write a note on merchant banking in India.
13. What are the services rendered by merchant banker as managers to the public issue of securities?

14

Venture Capital Companies

14.1 Introduction

Venture capital is a term used to describe financing for start-up and early stage businesses. It is invested generally in an unproven business venture. It is a very important source of funding for start-up ventures, especially those which do not have access to other sources of capital. Venture capital investments are relatively high-risk investments, but may offer the potential for above average returns. It is money provided, often by professionals who invest alongside innovative entrepreneurs in young, rapidly growing companies that have a reasonable, though not assured, potential to develop into significantly profitable ventures.

This form of raising capital is popular among new companies, or ventures, with a limited operating history that cannot raise capital through a debt issue or equity offering. Traditional debt financing is not always available to start-up and other emerging enterprises because they generally lack collateral securities and track record or earnings required for a loan. Since investing in an unproven business venture is highly speculative and risky venture capitalists generally target only those companies that have significant potential for growth and an opportunity to earn high rate of return within a relatively short period of time.

14.2 Definition of Venture Capital

Venture capital is money provided by professionals who invest and manage young rapidly growing companies that have the potential to develop into significant economic contributors. The concept of venture capital is defined in different ways. Definitions of venture capital are all very similar. Venture capital is defined as "an investment in a start up business that is perceived to have excellent growth prospects but does not have access to capital markets". Venture capital is defined in another way as "money provided by professionals who invest alongside management in young, rapidly growing companies that have the potential to develop into significant economic contributors". The OECD (1996) defines venture capital "as capital provided by firms who invest alongside management in young companies that are not quoted on the stock market. The main objective of venture capital is the expectation of high return from the investment. Value is created by the young company in partnership with the venture capitalist's money and professional expertise."

14.3 Features of Venture Capital

Investment made in venture capital generally involves the following features:

1. Venture capital or finance is generally provided to newly and rapidly growing high tech projects.
2. It provides seed capital to finance innovation even in the pre start up stage.
3. Undertakes higher risk.
4. Due to highly speculative nature of the investment, venture capitalist expects higher returns.
5. Generally long-term financing of more than five years.
6. Longer pay back period. The pay back period is generally 5-7 years.
7. Venture capitalist usually obtains a certain percentage of the equity ownership of the new company.
8. After obtaining reasonable returns, the equity is either sold back to the client company or offered to the public through a stock exchange.
9. Venture capitalist provides technical and operational guidance with active participation and control over management.
10. Venture capitalist adds value to the company through active participation.
11. Uncertainty regarding the success of the product or service in the market.

14.4 Functions of Venture Capitalist

Venture capitalist is involved in the following activities:

1. Providing funds for high risk and high return ventures.
2. Arranging additional financing from other sources.
3. Formulating the overall strategy of the company.
4. Assigning personnel to various key management positions.
5. Providing operational and technical guidance to enhance overall business efficiency.
6. Preparing the company for an initial public offering.

14.5 Venture Capital Fund

A venture capital fund is a pooled investment vehicle that primarily invests the financial capital of third party investors in enterprises that are typically too risky for typical investors or bank loans. Venture capital fund means a fund established in the form of a trust or a company including a body corporate and registered under these regulations which (a) has a dedicated pool of capital (b) raised in a manner specified in the regulations and (c) invested in accordance with the regulations.

According to SEBI regulations, venture capital fund means, "a fund established in the form of a company or trust, which raises money through loans, donations, issue of securities or units and makes or proposes to make investments in accordance with these regulations. The funds so collected are available for investment in potentially highly profitable enterprises at a high risk of loss".

14.6 Venture Capitalist

A venture capitalist is a person who makes such investments. Venture capitalists pool investors' cash and loans it to start-up firms and small businesses which entails high risk (high returns) with long-term growth potential.

14.7 Suppliers of Venture Capital

Venture capital may be provided by wealthy individual investors, mutual fund companies, government backed investment corporations, insurance companies, investment banking firms, professionally managed venture capital firms etc. Venture capitalists act as intermediaries between the investors with surplus fund and the innovative entrepreneurs seeking finance. They act as mentors to the enterprise. Besides providing finance (risk capital), the venture capitalists also provide technical and management expertise, networking and marketing support to highly innovative, prospective and risky business ventures.

14.8 Raising Finance

A venture capital fund may raise money from any source, whether Indian, foreign or non resident Indian by way of issue of units. No venture capital fund should accept any investment from any investor which is less than ₹ 5,00,000. However, this condition is not applicable to:

1. Employees or the principal officer or directors of the venture capital fund, or directors of the Trustee Company or trustees where the venture capital fund has been established as a trust.
2. The employees of the fund manager or asset management company.
3. Each scheme launched or fund set up by a venture capital fund shall have a firm commitment from the investors for contribution of an amount of at least ₹ 5 crore before the start of operations by the venture capital fund.

14.9 Categorization of Venture Capital Investors

Venture capital investors are categorized into four streams:

14.9.1 Incubators: An incubator is a hardcore technocrat who works with an entrepreneur to develop a business idea, and prepares a company for subsequent rounds of growth and funding.

14.9.2 Angel Investors: An angel investor is an experienced industry-bred individual with high net worth. Angel investors invest in his chosen field of technology and take active participation in day-to-day running of the company.

14.9.3 Venture Capitalists: Venture capitalists are organizations raising funds from numerous investors and hiring experienced professional mangers to deploy the same. They generally invest at second stage in proven ideas or businesses.

14.9.4 Private Equity Players: Private equity players are established investment bankers. They invest only in proven or established businesses.

14.10 Venture Capital Undertaking

According to SEBI Regulations (Venture Capital) 2000, venture capital undertaking means a domestic company (a) whose shares are not listed on a recognized stock exchange in India and (b) which is engaged in the business for providing services, production or manufacture of article or things or does not include such activities or sectors which are specified in the negative list by the SEBI with the approval of the Central Government by notification in the Official Gazette in this behalf. The negative list includes real estate, non-banking financial services, gold financing, activities not permitted under the Industrial Policy of the Government of India.

14.11 History of Venture Capital

Venture capital was predominantly an American phenomenon. It had its origin in North America in the late 19th and early 20th century. It emerged in other countries only in the late 20th century. The modern venture capital industry began taking shape in post-World War II which produced an abundance of technological innovations, primarily having military applications. The first modern venture capital firm namely American Research and Development (ARD) was created in 1946. It was formed in partnership with MIT, the Harvard Business School and local business leaders. The founder of ARD was General Georges Doroit, a French-born military man who is considered as "the father of venture capital."

In the mid-1950s, the U.S. Federal Government speeded up the development of advanced technologies. In 1957, the Federal Reserve System conducted a study which concluded that a shortage of entrepreneurial financing was a chief obstacle to the development of businesses in United States. As a response to this a number of 'small business investment companies' were established to "leverage" their private capital by borrowing from the federal government at below-market interest rates. Soon commercial banks were allowed to form small business investment companies and within four years, nearly 600 small business investment companies were in operation.

The 1960s saw a tremendous bull IPO market in USA that allowed venture capital firms to demonstrate their ability to create companies and produce huge investment returns. As a result, venture capital became a hot market, particularly for wealthy individuals and families. However, it is still considered too risky for institutional investors.

In the mid-1970s venture capital almost ceased to exist. It was mainly due to a red-hot IPO market which brought over 1,000 venture-backed companies to market their shares in 1968. The public markets went into a seven-year slump. It resulted in disappointment among the stock market and venture capital investors. Then in 1974, after U.S. Congress legislation against the abuse of pension fund money, all high-risk investments of these funds were halted. As a result of poor public market and the pension fund legislation, venture capital fund raising hit rock bottom in 1975.

Beginning in 1978, a series of legislative and regulatory changes gradually improved the climate for venture investing in USA. As a result of regulatory changes, funds flowing into the venture capital industry and the number of active venture organizations increased dramatically during the early 1980s. The important factors that leading to the increase in money flowing into the venture capital sector were the amendment of the 'Employment Retirement Income Security Act' and the reduction in the 'rates of tax on capital gains'. In 1979, the Department of Labour decided that portfolio diversification was a good thing and that allocating a small fraction of a portfolio in venture capital funds would not be seen as imprudent. This removed a major obstacle for flowing of huge amount of money into the venture capital industry. The late 1980s marked the transition of the primary source of venture capital funds from wealthy individuals and families to endowment, pension and other institutional funds.

The Israeli Government initiated two programmes to encourage venture capital funds in 1991, which led to increase in such funds. Singapore aggressively began promoting venture capital funds by providing tax incentives and through other measures in 1995, which led to a dramatic rise in investment activity in high technology research and development activity. Today venture capital financing has come to stay as a recognized model of financing innovative industries in a number of countries having capitalist economies.

14.12 Venture Capital in India: Historical Overview

Venture capital in India started in the late eighties and is still in its developing stage. In 1973, Committee on the Development of Small and Medium-sized Enterprises in India under the chairmanship of R.S. Bhatt emphasized the need to foster venture capital as a source of funding for new entrepreneurs and technology. The committee drew attention to the problems of new entrepreneurs and technologists in setting up industries.

The forerunner to venture capital financing in India was Industrial Finance Corporation of India (IFCI). In 1975, venture capital financing was introduced by IFCI with the introduction of a 'Risk Capital Foundation' (RCF). The objective of the fund was to encourage technologists and professionals to promote new industries. In 1976, the Industrial Development Bank of India (IDBI) introduced the 'Seed Capital' scheme for promoting new projects. However, the activity of venture capital did not gather momentum as the thrust was on high-technology projects. Until 1984, venture capital in India took the form of risk capital and seed capital.

In 1984, Industrial Credit and Investment Corporation of India (ICICI) decided to allocate funds for enterprises involving risk and high profit potential. In 1986, the Industrial Credit and Investment Corporation of India (ICICI) launched India's first venture capital company named 'Technology Development and Investment Corporation of India (TDICI). The company was established to encourage new technocrats in the private sector in emerging fields of high-risk technology.

To popularize venture capital financing, the government took an initiative and announced the creation of a Venture Capital Fund (VCF) in December 1985. Venture capital fund was set up by the Government of India for providing equity capital for projects that attempt the commercial application of indigenous technology. The fund which became operational in April 1986 is administered by IDBI.

The origins of modern venture capital in India can be traced back to the setting up of a Technology Development Fund (TDF) during 1987-1988, through the levy of a cess on all technology import payments. TDF was meant to provide financial assistance to innovative and high-risk technological programs through the Industrial Development Bank of India.

In 1988, IFCI sponsored Risk Capital Foundation (RCF) was converted into the Risk Capital and Technology Finance Corporation of India Ltd. In 1989, Unit Trust of India sponsored venture capital unit schemes. State Bank of India has a venture capital scheme operated through its subsidiary SBI Caps. ICICI flagged off a new venture capital company called Technology Development and Information Company of India (TDICI) with the objective of encouraging new technologies in the private sector to invest in high-risk areas. Canara Bank has set up a separate Asset Management Company (AMC) to undertake venture capital financing. During the same period, two State level corporations, viz., Andhra Pradesh and Gujarat also took initiatives to promote venture capital funds and could obtain World Bank assistance. Apart from these other public sector banks also participated in the equity share capital of venture capital companies and made in investments in schemes of venture capital funds.

The first attempt to frame comprehensive guidelines for governing venture capital funds was made in 1988-89. But these guidelines restricted the setting up of venture capital funds to either banks or financial institutions only.

The second phase in the growth of venture capital in India began with the issue of guidelines for venture capital funds issued by the Securities and Exchange Board of India (SEBI) in 1996. The guidelines allowed the entry of private overseas as well as domestic venture capitalists to make investments in India. These regulations also liberated the industry from a number of bureaucratic hassles. The move also paved the way for the entry of a number of foreign funds into India.

Indian venture funds, which operate under the SEBI guidelines, are set up either as trusts or as regular companies under either the Indian Trusts Act of 1882 or the Companies Act of 1956. Apart from the SEBI guidelines, domestic funds are subjected to other regulations of the Ministry of Finance under Government of India, the National Association of Software and Computers (NASSCO) and other task forces and standing committees, having power to intervene under various circumstances. The Union Budget for 1999-2000 stressed the need for higher investments in venture capital activity. Because it is difficult to access capital market to raise funds for technology development, especially for small and medium industries, venture capital fund can play a major role in this area.

In 2000, SEBI issued regulations aimed at creating an improved regime for investors in venture capital funds, alongside the government's creation of a much better tax environment. The National Venture Fund for Software and IT industry (NVFSIT) was launched in the year 2000 in this context. The Small Industry Development Bank of India (SIDBI) Venture Capital Ltd. (SVCL) manages NVFSIT, which is a wholly owned subsidiary of SIDBI.

In the backdrop of these developments, SEBI initiated a process of interaction with industry participants and experts to identify the various issues and key areas crucial for the development of the venture capital financing in India. The SEBI Committee on Venture Capital headed by Shri. K.B. Chandrasekhar, (Chairman, Exodus Communications, Inc.) set up in July, 1999, identified the impediments to the growth of venture capital financing and suggested several measures to facilitate the growth of venture capital activity in India. In order to obtain a global perspective, Indian entrepreneurs from the Silicon Valley were also incorporated with this Committee. The thrust of the Committee's recommendations was to facilitate, through an enabling regulatory, legal, tax and institutional environment, the creation of a pool of risk capital to finance idea-based entrepreneurship with a disproportionate potential reward–to-cost ratio.

Accordingly, all India public sector financial institutions, SBI and other scheduled commercial banks, foreign banks operating in India and the subsidiaries of the state bank of India were also eligible to start venture capital companies. Venture capital companies should have a minimum size of Rs. 10 crore and a maximum debt equity ratio of 1.5:1.

At present, several venture capital firms are incorporated in India, promoted mainly by All India Financial Institutions, public sector commercial banks, foreign banks and state financial institutions. Leading venture capital firms in India are Industrial Development Bank of India (IDBI's Venture Capital Fund), the Industrial Credit and Investment Corporation of India (ICICI), the Industrial Financial Corporation of India (IFCI), Small Industries Development Bank of India (SIDBI Venture Capital Fund), Unit Trust of India (UTI), ANZ Grindlays Bank, Canara Bank, SBI Capital Venture Fund, IL&FS Venture Capital Fund, Credit Capital Venture Fund (India) Ltd. etc. Many state governments have already set up venture capital funds for the IT sector in partnership with local state financial institutions and SIDBI. These include Andhra Pradesh, Karnataka, Delhi, Kerala and Tamil Nadu.

The Indian Venture Capital Association (IVCA), is the nodal centre for all venture activity in the country. The association was set up in 1992 and over the last few years, it has built up an impressive database.

14.13 Procedures in Venture Capital Financing

Venture capital is somewhat more difficult for a small business to obtain than other sources of financing, such as bank loans and supplier credit. Venture capital financing involves higher risk than conventional loans to industry and business. The applicant seeking finance may be a new entrepreneur or an established businessman. The project is to be innovative and has not been set up earlier. Before providing venture capital to a new or growing business, venture capital organizations require a formal proposal and conduct a thorough evaluation. Even then, they tend to approve only a small percentage of the proposals they receive.

For a business owner, the process of obtaining venture capital begins with a formal proposal. The most important element of this proposal is a detailed business plan about the company's goals and strategies. The proposal should also include projections of future growth, a brief history of the company, bio-data of key managers, the amount of money required, and a description of how the funds will be used.

On receiving a proposal of interest, a venture capital firm usually follows it up with a thorough investigation of the company's investment potential. This process might include analyzing financial statements, interviewing customers and suppliers, and meeting with the management team. If the venture capital firm remains interested following the evaluation phase, it usually responds with a proposal of its own, known as a term sheet. The term sheet acts as a blueprint for the investment deal, with provisions covering such issues as the valuation of the investment, voting rights, and liquidation options.

The final terms are decided through negotiations between the business managers and the venture capital firm. One of the most important factors in the negotiation process is agreeing upon the valuation of the business, which determines the amount of equity that is required in exchange for the venture capital. The venture capital firm usually hopes to achieve a return of three to five times the original investment within five years, by selling its equity either to the company's management or in the public stock markets.

14.14 Stages of Venture Capital Financing

Venture capital is a source of financing for new businesses. The venture capital funding varies across the different stages of growth of a firm. There are many stages in venture capital financing. The various stages are:

1. Seed Stage.
2. First Stage.
3. Second Stage.
4. Third Stage.
5. Bridge Stage.

14.14.1 Seed Stage: The first round of obtaining finance is referred as seed capital, seed financing, or concept stage financing. Seed capital refers to the provision of very early stage of finance to a company with a business venture or idea that has not yet been established. In this stage, the entrepreneur is in the stage of formation of an idea of a new product\service and the product or service is not fully developed.

In seed stage, modest amount of money is provided to the entrepreneurs to complete the product development and initial marketing formalities. Money may be utilised by the entrepreneurs for the product development and testing, market research, patent application and commence initial marketing formalities.

During this stage, the entrepreneur has to convince the firm why the idea/product is worth investing in. The venture capital firm will investigate into the technical and the economic feasibility of the idea. If the idea is not feasible at this stage, and the venture capital firm does not see any potential in the idea, the venture capital firm will not consider financing the idea. However if the idea is not directly feasible, but part of the idea is worthy of more investigation, the venture capital firm may invest some time and money in it for further investigation.

Early-stage finance is risky because it is often unclear how the market will respond to a new company's concept. However, if the venture is successful, the venture capitalist's return is correspondingly high.

14.14.2 First Stage: In first stage/early stage, finance is provided to the entrepreneurs to initiate full-scale commercial manufacturing and sales. First stage finance is generally provided only if the entrepreneur develops a new product and tests it fully. The funding from this stage is generally utilised by the entrepreneur for establishing a feasible production line, building infrastructure and developing a distribution system. At this point, the company is two to three years old.

14.14.3 Second Stage: In second stage the idea has been transformed into a product and is being produced and sold. The second round is referred as start up capital. In this stage, money is provided for hiring staff, renting office space, purchasing servers and other IT infrastructure, purchasing inventories and equipment and other activities involved in starting the business.

At this stage the management team is of proven capability to withstand competition. If the management team lacks in managing the company or does not succeed in competing with the competitors, the venture capital firm may suggest restructuring of the management team and extend the stage by redoing the stage again. In case the venture is performing badly due to a faulty management team or from fierce competition, the venture will cut the funding.

14.14.4 Third Stage: Third stage is the expansion or maturity phase of the previous stage. In third stage, funds are provided for a major expansion of the company. At this stage, future seems so bright and everything looks fine and good for the company. Sales are increasing and the customers are happy. The venture tries to expand market share they gained in the previous stage. In this stage, financing is used for increasing plant capacity, working capital, marketing, product improvement or purchase of new facilities.

14.14.5 Bridge Stage: Bridge financing is the last stage of venture capital financing process. It is otherwise called as mezzanine financing or later stage financing or pre public stage financing. It is the final round of financing which is provided just before the initial public offer. Bridge financing is a short-term form of financing used to prepare a company for its initial public offer. Companies sometimes seek this because they run out of cash before they receive long-term funding; sometimes they do so to strengthen their balance sheet in the run up to flotation. At this stage, the venture achieves a certain percentage of the market share. The company raises capital by issuing shares. Bridge finance are usually returned from the proceeds of public offering. Once a company's stock is publicly traded on a stock exchange, capital is raised by issuing shares.

14.15 Regulatory Authorities Involved in the Venture Capital Finance

In India presently there are three set of regulators dealing mainly with venture capital activity.

14.15.1 Reserve Bank of India: The investments and flow of foreign currency into and out of India is governed by the Reserve Bank of India (RBI).

14.15.2 Central Board of Direct Taxes: Central Board of Direct Taxes (CBDT) regulates the Income tax aspects of the venture capital funds in India. CBDT issued guidelines for tax-exemption purposes of venture capital companies in the year 1995 which was further modified in 1999. Venture capital funds which desire to claim exemption from income tax are required to follow rules given hereunder:

1. Registration with SEBI.
2. Claiming Income tax exemption in respect of dividend and capital gains income.
3. Not more than 40 percent of equity in a venture.

14.15.3 Securities and Exchange Board of India: Securities and Exchange Board of India (SEBI) is the nodal regulator for venture capital funds in India. As a part of its mandate to regulate and develop the Indian capital markets, SEBI issued 'Venture Capital Funds Regulations 1996' and Foreign Venture Capital Investors Regulations, 2000.

Indian venture funds, which operate under the SEBI guidelines, are set up either as trusts or as regular companies under either the (i) Indian Trusts Act of 1882 or the (ii) Companies Act of 1956. Apart from the SEBI guidelines, domestic funds are subject to other regulations of the Ministry of Finance under Government of India, the National Association of Software and Computers and other task forces and standing committees, which have the power to intervene in various circumstances.

14.16 Application for Grant of Certificate

Any company or trust or body corporate proposing to carry on any activity as a venture capital fund must apply to SEBI for grant of a certificate of carrying out venture capital activity in India. An application for grant of certificate must be made to the SEBI and must be accompanied by a non-refundable application fee of ₹ 25,000 payable to the Securities and Exchange Board of India. Registration fee for grant of certificate is ₹ 5,00,000.

If SEBI is satisfied that the applicant is eligible for grant of certificate, it will intimate the applicant of its eligibility. On receipt of intimation, the applicant must pay to SEBI, a registration fee of ₹ 5,00,000 and on the receipt of such fees, SEBI will grant a certificate of registration.

14.17 Conditions for the Grant of Certificate

1. The venture capital fund shall abide by the provisions of the SEBI Act.
2. The venture capital fund shall not carry on any other activity other than that of a venture capital fund.
3. The venture capital fund shall inform SEBI in writing of any information or details previously submitted to SEBI which have changed after grant of the certificate.
4. If the information or details submitted are found to be false or are misleading in any particular manner, suitable penal action can be taken.

14.18 Advantages of Venture Capital Financing

Venture capital offers several advantages over other forms of finance to a company. The important advantages of venture capital financing are the following:

1. Venture capital promotes technological innovations and entrepreneurship development.
2. Venture capital is likely to be available to start-up or concept businesses. For a start up company this frees up important cash flow that might otherwise be needed to service debt.
3. Venture capitalist injects long term finance which provides a solid capital base for the future growth of a company.
4. Venture capitalist provides operational and technical assistance to the management of the company.
5. Venture capitalist offers a number of value added services. They also help in the recruitment of key personnel, providing contracts in international markets etc. Venture capitalist has a network of contacts in many other areas that can add value to the company.
6. Venture capitalist acts as a financial partner and strategic advisor. They share both the risks and rewards.
7. The involvement of high profile investors may help a new company to increase their credibility.

8. Venture capitalists also identify potential acquisition targets for the business and facilitate the acquisition.
9. Venture capitalist equips the company for an initial public offering of its shares.

14.19 Disadvantages of Venture Capital Financing

The disadvantages associated with venture capital financing to a company include the following:

1. Compared to other sources of financing venture capital financing results in relatively higher costs over the long term.
2. Another important disadvantage of venture capital financing is that the venture capitalist become part owners of the business, and thus gains a say in business decisions.
3. The founders of companies face a dilution of ownership and control over the business over the long run.
4. Experts suggest that entrepreneurs should consider venture capital to be one financing strategy among many, and should seek to combine it with debt financing if possible.

14.20 Types of Venture Capital Funds in India

Generally there are three types of organized or institutional venture capital funds. They are:

1. Venture capital funds set up by angel investors.
2. Venture capital funds set up by high net worth individual investors.
3. Venture capital subsidiaries of corporations and private venture capital firms established by major corporations, commercial bank holding companies and other financial institutions.

14.21 Venture Capital Companies in India

List of important venture capital companies in India are given below:

1. Risk Capital and Technology Finance Corporation Ltd. (RCTC).
2. Technology Development and Information Company of India Ltd. (TDICI).
3. Technology Development and Information Company of India Ltd. (TDICI).
4. SIDBI Venture Capital Limited (SVCL).
5. Andhra Pradesh Venture Capital Limited (APVCL).
6. Gujarat Venture Finance Company Limited (GVCFL).
7. Canfina by public sector Canara Bank.
8. Grindlays India Development Fund.
9. Indus Venture Fund.

14.22 Venture Capital Funds in India

1. APIDC Venture Capital Limited, Hyderabad.
2. Canbank Venture Capital Fund Limited, Bangalore
3. Gujarat Venture Capital Fund, Ahmedabad.
4. Industrial Venture Capital Limited, Chennai.
5. Auto Ancillary Fund, Delhi.
6. Gujarat Venture Capital Fund, Ahmedabad.
7. Karnataka Information Technology Venture Capital Fund Bangalore.
8. India Auto Ancillary Fund, Mumbai.
9. Information Technology Fund, Mumbai.
10. Tamil Nadu Infotech Fund, Mumbai.
11. Orissa Venture Capital Fund, Mumbai.
12. Uttar Pradesh Venture Capital Fund, Mumbai.
13. SICOM Venture Capital Fund, Mumbai.
14. Punjab Infotech Venture Fund, Chandigarh.
15. National Venture Fund for Software and Information Technology Industry, Mumbai.

Short Answer Type Questions

1. Define venture capital.
2. What is meant by venture capital?
3. What is seed capital?
4. What do you mean by venture capital fund?
5. Who is a venture capitalist?
6. What is mezzanine financing?
7. Name the regulatory authorities of venture capital.
8. What is bridge financing?
9. Name the different stages of venture capital financing.
10. Who are the suppliers of venture capital?

Essay Types Questions

1. What is venture capital? What are the features of venture capital?
2. Define venture capital. Discuss the functions of venture capital.
3. Explain the different types of venture capital investors.
4. What are the advantages of venture capital financing?
5. Explain the procedure in venture capital financing.
6. Outline the recent developments in venture capital financing.
7. Explain the role of SEBI as regulator in venture capital funds.
8. Explain the procedure for registration of a venture capital company.

9. Give a brief history of the origin and development of venture capital.
10. Explain the different stages of venture capital financing.
11. Explain the regulatory framework in venture capital finance.
12. Explain the history of venture capital in India.
13. What are the disadvantages of venture capital financing?

15

Mutual Funds

15.1 Introduction

In the Indian financial sector, nearly eighty percent of the sources of funds are from the banking sector. Commercial banks in India as financial intermediaries are still in the forefront in mobilizing savings and investments to various sectors of the economy. A well structured and calibrated process of financial sector reforms, introduced in the early nineties has also resulted in creating competitive and resilient banking sector.

The Indian mutual fund industry is one of the fastest growing sectors of the Indian capital and financial market. As a result of the new economic policy built on the pillars of financial deregulation, liberalization, privatization and globalization, the mutual fund business in India gained a momentum and tempo. The year 1993, witnessed an impetus by way of the opening up of the industry to the private sector and later to the foreign mutual fund companies. Mutual fund industry is now emerging as one of the most vibrant segments of the Indian financial system. They play a very crucial role in an economy by mobilizing and investing the savings of the people in capital and money market.

15.2 Meaning of Mutual Fund

A mutual fund is a professionally managed form of collective investments which pools money from many investors and invest it in securities. It is an investment vehicle that is made up of a pool of funds collected from many investors for the purpose of investing in securities such as stocks, bonds, debentures and short-term money market instruments, or a combination of these assets. Mutual funds are managed by professional money mangers who invest the fund's capital and attempt to generate capital gains and income for the investors of the funds.

A mutual fund's portfolio is structured and maintained in such a way as to match the investment objectives stated in its prospectus. The pooled money in turn is invested in various securities depending on the objectives of the mutual fund scheme, and the profits and losses are shared by investors among themselves in proportion to their investments. The mutual fund is based on a simple concept i.e. the minimization of risk through the spreading of investments across multiple entities, which is achieved by the pooling of a number of small investments into a big bucket.

15.3 Definitions of Mutual Fund

Mutual fund is defined by SEBI as "a fund established in the form of a trust to raise money through the sale of units to the public or a section of the public under one or more schemes for investing in securities, including money market instruments".

Weston J. Fred and Brigham define mutual fund as "a corporation which accepts money from investors and uses the same to buy stocks, long term bonds and short-term debt instruments issued by issuers".

Generally, mutual fund is defined "as a diversified portfolio of securities invested on behalf of a group of investors and professionally managed. Individual investors own a percentage of the value of the fund represented by the number of units they purchase and thus share in any gains or losses of the fund".

In short, a mutual fund can be defined as "an investment company that pools money and invest in a variety of securities, including fixed-income securities and money market instruments".

15.4 History of the Mutual Fund Industry

Mutual funds are traced back to the times of the Egyptians and Phoenicians who used to sell their shares in caravans and vessels to spread the risk of these ventures. The mutual fund investment traces its origin in the 1800s. The foreign and colonial government Trust of London of 1868 is considered as the forerunner of the modern concept of mutual funds. Massachusetts Investors Trust (now MFS Investment Management) was founded on March 21, 1924, and after one year it had 200 shareholders and US$ 392,000 in assets. The entire industry, which included a few close ended funds, had only less than US$ 10 million in 1924.

The USA is, however, considered as the Mecca of modern mutual funds. By early 1930s a large number of close-ended mutual funds were in operation in the U.S.A. The stock market crash of 1929 slowed down the growth of mutual funds. In response to the stock market crash, Congress passed the Securities Act of 1933 and the Securities Exchange Act of 1934. These laws required that a fund be registered with the Securities and Exchange Commission and they were to provide prospective investors with a prospectus that contains all disclosures about the fund, the securities, and about fund managers. The Securities and Exchange Commission (SEC) helped to draft the Investment Company Act of 1940, which set forth the guidelines which all SEC-registered funds are to comply with now.

With renewed confidence in the stock market, mutual funds began to blossom. By the end of the 1960s, there were approximately 270 funds with US$ 48 billion in assets. In October 2007, there were 8,015 mutual funds which belonged to the Investment Company Institute (ICI) which was the national association of investment companies in the United States, with a combined asset of US$ 12.356 trillion.

15.5 Emergence of the Mutual Fund Industry in India

The development of Indian mutual fund industry passed through different stages, which are discussed below:

15.5.1 First Phase (1963-1987): The Indian mutual fund industry has a history that is about four decades old. During 1930s, the Central Banking Enquiry Committee recommended a need for the establishment and working of an investment type trust in India. The Shroff Committee appointed by the Government of India in 1954 also reiterated the desirability and the need for the establishment of UK type Unit Trust in India. Based on the recommendations of the Central Banking Enquiry Committee and Shroff Committee, the Central Government after consulting with Reserve bank of India (RBI) established the Unit Trust of India in 1963.

The foundation for the mutual fund business in India was laid by the parliament in 1963 with the enactment of the Unit Trust of India (UTI) Act. The then Finance minister Mr. T.T. Krishnamachari, who initiated the Act, made it clear to the parliament that UTI would provide an opportunity for the middle and lower income groups to acquire shares without much difficulty. Finally, in July 1964, UTI was set up with the twin objective of mobilizing household savings and investing the funds in the capital market for industrial growth. It functioned under the Regulatory and administrative control of the Reserve Bank of India.

The mutual fund industry was started in India in a small way with the UTI Act creating what was effectively a small savings division within the RBI. With this mission, UTI introduced its first fund which was an open ended one in 1964 and called unit scheme 64, which had managed assets at the end of 1988 totalling ₹ 67 crore. The first scheme launched by UTI was 'Unit Scheme 1964'. The Unit Trust of India from its very inception in 1963 was the only player in the field up to 1987. Over a period of 25 years UTI grew fairly well and gave investors a good return

In 1978, UTI was de-linked from the RBI and the Industrial Development Bank of India (IDBI) took over its regulatory and administrative control from RBI. The UTI grew in size by this time and attracted substantial investments. At the end of 1988 UTI had assets worth ₹ 6,700 crore under its management.

15.5.2 Second Phase (1987-1992): The second phase between 1987 and 1992 witnessed the broadening of the base of the mutual fund industry, consequent upon the Government carefully opening the door for more players to enter into the mutual fund business. Thus many commercial banks and public sector financial institutions entered into the field.

The period 1987-1993 saw the entry of seven public sector mutual funds which were set up by the public sector commercial banks and Life Insurance Corporation of India (LIC) and General Insurance Corporation of India (GIC). SBI Mutual Fund was the first non-UTI Mutual Fund to be established in June 1987. Following SBI Canara Bank set up 'Canbank Mutual Fund' in the same year. Subsequently public sector banks set up their own mutual funds viz. Punjab National Bank Mutual Fund (August '89), Indian Bank Mutual Fund (November '89), Bank of India (June '90), Bank of Baroda Mutual Fund (October '92). LIC established its mutual fund in June 1989 while GIC had set up its mutual fund in December 1990. At the end of 1993, all the seven mutual funds had assets worth ₹ 47,000 crore under their management.

15.5.3 Third Phase (1993-2002): The third phase is the most important phase, which saw the entry of private sector mutual funds in India. With the opening up of the industry to the private players in 1993, a new era started in the Indian mutual fund industry, giving the Indian investors a wider and better choice of fund families.

During this period, in addition to the private players foreign mutual funds also set up their mutual funds viz. Tatas, Birlas, ICICI, IDBI, Kothari Pioneer, Morgan Stanley etc. The erstwhile Kothari Pioneer (now merged with Franklin Templeton) was the first private sector mutual fund to be registered in July 1993.

The first of Mutual Fund Regulations in India also came into existence in the year 1993. Under SEBI's control and regulation, the financial sector was opened up for entry of more players of both domestic and foreign origin. All mutual funds, except UTI were to be registered and governed under this regulation. Franklin Templeton Mutual Fund started its operation in India in 1996, with the constitution of Franklin Templeton Mutual Fund as a trust and Franklin Templeton Asset Management (India) Pvt. Ltd. as an Asset Management Company. In 2002, it acquired Pioneer ITI Mutual Funds Pvt. Ltd. and Pioneer ITI AMC Ltd. to emerge as one of the largest private sector mutual funds in terms of assets and investor base and the range of mutual fund schemes.

15.5.4 Fourth Phase (2003-2011): In February 2003, following the repeal of the Unit Trust of India Act of 1963 UTI was bifurcated into two separate entities. One is the specified undertaking of the Unit Trust of India with assets under management of ₹ 29,835 crore at the end of January 2003, representing broadly, the assets of US 64 scheme assured return and certain other schemes.

The second is the UTI Mutual Fund Ltd, sponsored by SBI, PNB, BOB and LIC. It is registered with SEBI and functions under the mutual fund regulations. With the bifurcation of the erstwhile UTI which had more than ₹ 76,000 crore of assets under management in March 2000 and with the setting up of a UTI Mutual Fund, conforming to the SEBI Mutual Fund Regulations, and with recent mergers taking place among different private sector funds, the mutual fund industry has come of age and entered its current phase of consolidation and growth.

There were 1,131 mutual fund schemes as on March 31, 2011, of which, 679 were income/debt-oriented schemes, 376 were growth/equity-oriented schemes and 33 were balanced schemes. There were 727 open-ended schemes and 368 close-ended schemes as on March 31, 2011. In addition, there were 28 Exchange Traded Funds, of which 10 were Gold ETFs. The unit holding pattern of public and private sector mutual funds as on March 31, 2011 shows the dominance of private sector mutual funds in the number of investor accounts as well as share in net assets The private sector mutual funds had 65.4 percent of the total investors account compared to 34.6 percent in public sector mutual funds.

15.6 Working of Mutual Fund

A mutual fund is a trust that pools the savings of a number of investors with certain similar investment goals. A mutual fund cannot deviate from its stated objectives of the scheme at any point of time. Every mutual fund is managed by a fund manger. The fund manager pools money from different investors and invests in various types of capital and money market instruments.

The fund manager exercises his management skills and necessary research skills to ensure much better return than what an investor can manage on his own. The dividend or interest income earned from the investments and the capital gains realized or losses incurred are shared and ploughed back to the investors. The value of a share of the mutual fund, known as the Net Asset Value (NAV) per share, is calculated on a daily basis and is based on the total value of the fund divided by the number of shares currently issued and outstanding. The NAV of each scheme is calculated by dividing the net assets of the scheme by the number of units outstanding at the time of valuation.

15.7 Procedure for Investing in a Mutual Fund Scheme

Mutual funds normally come out with an advertisement in newspapers publishing the date of launch of the new schemes. Investors can also contact the agents and distributors of mutual funds who are present all over the country for necessary information and application forms. The filled in application forms can be submitted to the mutual funds through these agents/distributors etc. Now both post offices and commercial banks also distribute the units of mutual funds.

It is to be noted that the mutual funds schemes being marketed by banks and post offices should not be considered as their own schemes and they seldom give any assurance of returns. There is no restriction regarding the amount of maximum investment in a scheme of mutual fund. However, there are restrictions on the minimum amount of deposit in a scheme which are often decided by the fund managers.

15.8 Change in Asset Allocation

Taking into consideration the market trends, all prudent fund managers usually change the asset allocation i.e. they can invest a higher or lower percentage of the fund in either equity or debt instruments compared to what is disclosed in the offer document. It can be done on a short term basis and on defensive considerations i.e. to protect the NAV. Hence, the fund managers are allowed certain flexibility in altering the asset allocation in lieu of the interest of the investors. If the mutual fund desires to change the asset allocation on a permanent basis, they can close after informing the unit holders and giving them an option to exit the scheme at prevailing NAV without any load.

15.9 Procedure for Changing the Nature of the Scheme

For changing the format of the scheme e.g. its structure, investment pattern, etc from the one specified in the offer document it can be carried out only after sending written communication to each and every unit holder. It is also mandatory to publish an advertisement in English daily having a nationwide circulation and in a newspaper published in the vernacular language where the head office of the mutual fund is situated. The unit holders retain the right to exit the scheme at the prevailing NAV without any exit load if they do not want to continue in the scheme. The mutual funds are also required to follow the same procedure while converting the scheme from close-ended to an open-ended scheme and in case of a change in sponsorship.

15.10 Procedure for Redressal of Investor's Complaint

Investors can find with the offer document the name of the contact person to be approached for any query, complaints or grievances of the mutual fund scheme. Trustees of a mutual fund closely monitor the operations of the mutual fund. The names of the directors of the Asset Management Company and its trustees are also given in the offer documents. Investors can also approach the SEBI for redressal of any or all of their complaints. On receipt of complaints, SEBI takes up the matter with the concerned mutual fund and follows it up with the mutual fund until the matter is resolved amicably. Investors can send their complaints to the Mutual Fund Department of the Securities and Exchange Board of India.

15.11 Winding up of Mutual Fund Scheme

In case of winding up of a scheme, the mutual funds have to pay a sum to the investors based on the prevailing NAV after adjustment of expenses. Unit holders are entitled to receive a report with all necessary details on the winding up from the mutual funds.

15.12 Types of Securities where Mutual Funds are Invested

Mutual fund companies generally invest in three types. They are:

1. Stocks.
2. Bonds.
3. Money market instruments.

15.13 Structure of a Mutual Fund Company

A mutual fund is a company that brings together money from many people and invests it in stocks, bonds or other assets. A mutual fund is set up in the form of a trust. The structure of a mutual fund company consists of four parties. They are as under:

1. Sponsor.
2. Trustees.
3. Asset Management Company.
4. Custodian.

15.13.1 Sponsor: Either one sponsor or more than one who is like a promoter of a company usually establishes the trust. As per SEBI (Mutual Fund Regulations, 1996) guidelines, for the purpose of grant of certificate of registration, the sponsor has to fulfil the following requirements.

1. The sponsor should have a sound track record and reputation of fairness and integrity in all his business transactions and dealings.
2. The net worth is positive in all the preceding immediate five years.
3. The net worth in the first preceding year is to be more than the capital contribution of the sponsor in the asset management company.
4. The sponsor had profit in three out of the immediately preceding five years, including the fifth year.

The SEBI will normally grant registration to a mutual fund subject to the condition that the trustees, the sponsor, the asset management company and the custodian all comply with all the provisions of the SEBI Mutual Fund Regulations.

15.13.2 Trustees: A mutual fund shall be constituted in the form of a trust and the instrument of the trust shall be in the form of a deed, duly registered under the provisions of the Indian Registration Act of 1908, executed by the sponsor in favour of the trustees who are named in such an instrument. Trustees of a mutual fund closely monitor all the activities of the mutual fund. The trustees of the mutual fund hold its property for the benefit of the unit holders. The trustees are vested with the general power of superintendence and direction over the Asset Management Company (AMC). The trustees are to be responsible for the calculation of any income due to be paid to the mutual fund and also of any income received in the mutual fund for the holders of the units.

The mutual fund is required to have an independent Board of Trustees, i.e. two thirds of the trustees should be independent persons who are not in any way associated with the sponsors. An AMC or any of its officers or employees are not eligible to act as trustees of any mutual fund. In case a company is appointed as a trustee, then its directors can act trustees of any other trust provided that the object of such other trust is not in conflict with the object of the mutual fund. Additionally, no person who is appointed as a trustee of a mutual fund can be appointed as a trustee of any other mutual fund only if he is an independent trustee and prior approval of the mutual fund of which he is a trustee has been obtained for such an appointment.

The trustees are responsible for ensuring that no change is carried out in the fundamental attributes of any scheme of the trust or fees and expenses payable or any other change that would modify the scheme and affect the interest of unit holders, unless each unit holder is provided with a written communication of the same. The trustees are also required to ensure that an AMC has been diligent in empanelling and monitoring any securities transactions with brokers, so as to avoid any undue concentration of business with any broker. The Mutual Fund Regulations of SEBI further mandates that the trustees should prevent any conflicts of interest between the AMC and the unit holders in terms of deployment of net worth. They are obliged to make a quarterly review of all transactions carried out between the mutual funds, AMC and its associates.

15.13.3 Asset Management Company: The Asset Management Company (AMC) approved by SEBI manages the funds by making investments in various types of securities. The sponsor or the trustees are required to appoint an AMC to manage the assets of the mutual fund. Under the Mutual Fund Regulations of 1996 the applicant must satisfy certain eligibility criteria in order to be qualified to register with SEBI as an AMC.

1. The directors of the AMC should be persons having adequate professional experience in finance and financial services and related fields and are not

found guilty at any time of moral turpitude or convicted for any economic offence or violation of any laws relating to securities.

2. The sponsor must have at least 40 percent stake in the AMC.
3. The AMC has a net worth of not less than ₹ 10 crore.
4. The board of directors of such AMC has at least 50 percent directors, who are not associates of, or are associated in any manner with either the sponsor or any of its subsidiaries or trustees.
5. The Chairman of the AMC is not to be a trustee of any of the mutual funds.

A. Business Activities that can be Carried on by AMCs: The AMC shall not act as a trustee of any mutual fund. They are permitted to undertake only the following activities.

1. Portfolio management services.
2. Management and advisory services to offshore, pension, provident and venture capital funds.
3. Management of insurance funds.
4. Financial consultancy and exchange of research on commercial basis or any such activities are not in conflict with the activities of the mutual fund.

B. Obligations of Asset Management Companies: The AMC is required to take all reasonable precautions and exercise due diligence to ensure that the investment of funds pertaining to any scheme are not contrary to the provisions of the Mutual Fund Regulations and the trust deed. An AMC cannot, through any broker associated with the sponsor, purchase or sell securities, which is an average of 5 percent or more of the aggregate purchases and sale of securities made by the mutual fund in all its schemes. However, the aggregate purchase and sale of securities excludes the sale and distribution of units issued by the mutual fund and the limit of 5 percent shall apply only for a block of any three months. An asset management company shall not utilize the services of the sponsor or any of its associates, employees or their relatives for the purpose of any securities transaction its distribution and sale.

C. Custodian: Mutual Fund Regulations Act of 1996 specified that every mutual fund shall appoint a custodian to carry out the custodial services for the schemes of the fund. The mutual fund shall enter into a custodian agreement with the custodian. Only institutions with substantial organizational strength, service capability in terms of computerization, and other infrastructure facilities are approved to act as custodians. The custodian must be totally delinked from the AMC and must be registered with SEBI. The custodians, who are registered with the SEBI, hold the securities of various schemes of the fund in their custody. They monitor the performance of mutual funds and their compliance of SEBI Regulations.

Under the Securities and Exchange Board of India (Custodian of Securities) Guidelines, 1996, any person who proposes to carry on business of a custodian of securities must register with the SEBI and is required to fulfil the specified eligibility criteria. Additionally in a custodian in which the sponsor or its associates holds 50 percent or more of the voting rights of the share capital of the custodian or where 50 percent or more of the directors of the custodian represent the interest of the sponsor or its associates cannot act as a custodian for a mutual fund constituted by the same sponsor or any of its associate or subsidiary company.

The structure of a mutual fund company thus consists of a Sponsor, Trustees, an Asset Management Company and a Custodian. For example in the case of DSP Merrill Lynch Mutual Fund, DSP Merrill Lynch Ltd. is the 'Sponsor', DSP Merrill Lynch Fund Managers Limited is the 'Asset Management Company', DSP Merrill Lynch Trustee Company Private Ltd. as the 'Trustee' and Citibank NA as the Custodian. In the case of Reliance Mutual Fund, Reliance Capital Ltd. is the 'Sponsor' Reliance Capital Asset Management Ltd as the 'Asset Management Company', Reliance Capital Trustee Co. Ltd. as 'Trustee' and Deutsche Bank AG as the 'Custodian'.

15.14 Types of Mutual Funds

Mutual funds are of different types which are given below:

1. Equity Funds.
2. Money Market Funds.
3. Hybrid Funds.
4. Debt/Income Funds.
5. Gilt Funds.
6. Other Types.

15.14.1 Equity Funds: These are funds, which are considered more risky, but provide higher returns to their investors compared to other funds. There are different types of equity funds, which are given below.

1. Growth Funds.
2. Diversified Equity Funds.
3. Equity Index Funds.
4. Specialty Funds.

A. Growth Funds: Growth funds are those funds in which a mutual fund company invests its fund in the common stock of public limited companies with a high growth potential. Such funds have comparatively high risks. The investment objective of this type of scheme is capital appreciation of equity shares. The primary aim of growth funds is to produce an increase in the fund's NAV, which means that investors who buy growth funds are more interested in seeing the funds share price rise than in receiving income from their investment. For example, ICICI Prudential Growth Fund, Templeton India Growth Fund, HDFC Growth Fund, Reliance Growth Fund etc.

B. Diversified Equity Funds: Except for a small portion of investment in liquid money market, diversified equity funds are invested mainly in equities without any concentration in any particular sector. These funds are well diversified and reduce sector-specific or company-specific risks. However, like all other funds diversified equity funds too are exposed to equity market risks. One prominent type of diversified equity fund in India is Equity Linked Savings Schemes (ELSS). As per the mandate, a minimum of 90 percent of investments by ELSS should be in equities at all times. ELSS investors are eligible to claim deduction from taxable income (up to ₹ 1 lakh) at the time of filing the income tax return. ELSS usually has a lock-in period and in cases of any redemption by the investor before the expiry of the lock-in period it makes him liable to pay income tax on such incomes for which he may have received any tax exemptions in the past.

C. Equity Index Funds: Equity index funds have their objective to match the performance of specific stock market indices such as BSE Sensex, SP CNX 50, BSE BANKEX, NSE Nifty etc. Such funds are invested only in those shares that form a part of the benchmark index in exactly the same proportion so that the value of the index fund varies in proportion with the benchmark index. Index funds are expected to provide a rate of return over time that will approximate or match, but not exceed, that of the market which they are mirroring. NAVs of such schemes would rise or fall in accordance with the rise or fall in the index, though not exactly by the same percentage due to some factors known as "tracking error" in technical terms. For example SBI Magnum Index Fund, UTI Nifty Index Fund, Franklin India Index Fund, Reliance Index Fund etc.

D. Speciality Funds: Such funds are introduced with the object of taking the advantage of favourable conditions in a particular sector or in a specific income producing security. Speciality funds are comparatively riskier than diversified funds. For example DSP Merrill Lynch Opportunities Fund and Fidelity India Special Situations Fund etc. Following are the different types of speciality funds.

(a) Sector Funds: These are the funds which are invested in the securities of only those sectors or industries as specified in the offer documents. The exposure of these funds is limited to a particular sector i.e. information technology, auto, banking, pharmaceuticals or fast moving consumer goods etc. The returns from these funds are dependent on the performance of the respective sectors or industries. While these funds may give higher returns, they are riskier than diversified funds. For example Reliance Pharma Fund, JM Auto Sector Fund, ICICI FMCG Fund etc.

(b) Foreign Securities Funds: Foreign securities equity funds have the option to invest in one or more foreign companies. These funds have less risk than sector funds. Foreign securities equity funds are exposed to foreign exchange rate risk and country risk.

(c) Cap Funds: The term "cap" is shorthand for capitalization. The mutual fund investors generally inform their mode of investment in securities by stating the size of the company as 'All-Cap', 'Giant or Mega Cap', 'Large Cap', 'Mid Cap', 'Small Cap', 'Micro Cap' etc. These designations inform mutual fund investors about the investment focus of the fund in terms of company size.

Mutual funds that invests in equity securities without regard to the factor whether a company is characterized as small, medium or large is called 'all-cap fund'. In the case of all-cap fund, the portfolio manager has complete freedom to invest in companies of any size. Funds that are invested in companies having lower market capitalization than large ones are called mid-cap or small-cap funds. Market capitalization of mid-cap companies is less than that of big and blue chip companies (less than ₹ 2500 crore but more than ₹ 500 crore) and small-cap companies have market capitalization of less than ₹ 500 crore. Market capitalization of a company is calculated by multiplying the market price of the company's share by the number of its outstanding shares in the market.

15.14.2 Money Market or Liquid Fund: In the case of a money market fund, the company invests its funds in the money market instruments only. The investment objectives of such funds are to take advantage of the volatility in interest rates in money market. The typical investment options for liquid funds include treasury bills issued by governments, commercial papers issued by companies and certificates of deposit issued by banks. Such fund gives an opportunity to the investors to participate indirectly in the money market. These funds are appropriate for corporate and individual investors as a means to park their surplus funds for short periods. For example Templeton India Money Market Account Fund, IDBI-principal Money Market Fund 1997, JM Money Manager Fund etc.

15.14.3 Hybrid Funds: As the name suggests, hybrid funds are those funds whose portfolio includes a blend of equities, debts and money market securities. Hybrid funds have an equal proportion of debt and equity in their portfolio. Types of hybrid funds in India are given below:

A. Balanced Funds: The portfolio of balanced funds includes assets like debt securities, convertible securities, equity and preference shares held relatively in an equal proportion. The objectives of balanced funds are to reward investors with a regular income and moderate capital appreciation with minimum risk of capital erosion.

B. Growth and Income Funds: Funds that combine the features of growth and income funds are known as growth and income funds. These funds are invested in companies having potential for capital appreciation and those known for issuing high dividends. The level of risks involved in these funds is lower than growth funds and higher than income funds.

C. Asset Allocation Fund: Asset allocation funds adopt a variable asset allocation strategy that allows fund managers to switch over from one asset class to another at any time depending on their outlook for specific markets. In other words, fund managers may switch over to equity if they expect equity market to provide good returns and then switch over to debt if they expect debt market to provide better returns. The switching over decision is taken by the fund manager on the basis of his own judgment and discretion.

15.14.4 Debt/Income Funds: Debt or income oriented fund is a scheme in which the funds are invested mainly in debt instruments. The aim of income funds is to provide a regular and steady income to investors. The two important objectives of such a fund are ensuring safety of fund and regular income to its investors. These funds are not affected by fluctuations in equity markets. However, opportunities of capital appreciation are also limited in such funds. The NAVs of such funds are affected because of changes in interest rate in the country. When the interest rates fall, NAVs of such funds are likely to increase in the short run and vice versa. However, long term investors seldom bother about these fluctuations. The important investment avenues of such funds are fixed income securities such as bonds, debentures and other debt related instruments issued by private companies, banks, financial institutions and banks. For example Templeton India Income Fund, Franklin Templeton Monthly Income Plan, JM Income Fund etc. Based on different investment objectives, there are following types of debt funds.

A. Diversified Debt Funds: A debt fund is that invested in all the securities issued by entities belonging to all sectors of the market are known as diversified debt funds. The best feature of diversified debt funds is that investments are properly diversified into all sectors, which results in risk reduction.

B. Focused Debt Funds: The funds that are invested only on selective debt securities issued by companies of a specific sector or an industry is known as focused debt funds. Because of the narrow orientation of the fund, focused funds are riskier when compared to diversified debt funds. These funds are now not available in India.

C. High Yield Debt Funds: These are funds, which adopt a different strategy and prefer securities issued by those issuers who are considered as of below investment grade. The motive behind adopting this sort of risky strategy is to earn high interest returns from these issuers. These funds are more volatile and bear higher default risk. But they earn higher returns for investors occasionally or sometimes.

D. Assured Return Funds: These are debt funds, which provide lower risk to its investors. Assured return funds have a lock-in period and offer assurance of annual returns to investors during the lock-in period. But the asset management company suffers a shortfall in returns.

15.14.5 Gilt Funds: These funds are invested exclusively in government securities. Government securities have no default risk and provide safety of principal to the investors. NAVs of these funds fluctuate frequently. Interest rates and prices of debt securities are inversely related and any change in the interest rates results in a change in the NAV of the gilt funds in the opposite direction. For example ICICI Gilt Fund, DSP Merril Lynch Government Securities Fund, JM G-SEC Fund etc.

15.14.6 Other Types: Following are the other types of funds:

A. Commodity Funds: Those funds that focus on investing in different commodities or commodity companies or commodity future contracts are termed as commodity funds. A commodity fund is invested either in a single commodity or a group of commodities like metals, food grains, crude oils etc. Examples of commodity funds are gold fund, gold futures, precious metals fund, shares of crude oil producing companies, specified agricultural commodities fund etc.

B. Leveraged Funds: Leveraged funds are introduced with the aim of increasing the value of the portfolio and thereby to benefit the unit holders. These funds are invested mainly in speculative and risky investments. Investment companies obtain an advantage of the market by short selling when the market declines. Such funds are not common in India.

C. Hedge Funds: An aggressively managed portfolio of investments that uses advanced investment strategies such as leverage, long, short and derivative positions in both domestic and international markets with the goal of generating high returns are called hedge funds. Legally, hedge funds are most often set up as private investment partnerships that are open to a limited number of investors and require a very large initial minimum investment. Investments in hedge funds are illiquid, as they often require investors to keep their money in the fund for at least one year. The investment objectives of hedge funds are to hedge risks in order to increase the value of the portfolio. Such funds employ speculative trading principles i.e. to buy rising shares and sell those whose prices are likely to fall.

D. Exchange Traded Funds: Exchange traded funds provide investors with combined benefits of both close-ended and open-ended mutual funds. Exchange traded funds follow stock market indices and are traded on stock exchanges like a single stock at index-linked prices. The main advantage offered by these funds is that they offer diversification, flexibility of holding a single share at a time.

E. Fund of Funds: A mutual fund that is invested in other mutual fund schemes offered by different Asset Management Companies is known as fund of funds. Fund of funds maintain a portfolio comprising units of other mutual fund schemes and they maintain portfolio comprises debt, equity, money market instruments or non-financial assets. Fund of funds provide investors with an added advantage of diversifying into different mutual fund schemes with a small amount of investment, which further helps in diversification of risks. These funds are not available in India.

F. Tax Saving Funds: These schemes offer tax rebates to the investors under specific provisions of the Income Tax Act, 1961 as the Government offers tax incentives for investment in specified avenues. Pension schemes launched by the mutual funds also offer tax benefits. These schemes are growth oriented and are invested mainly in equities. Their growth opportunities and risks involved are like any equity-oriented scheme. For example, SBI Magnum Tax Gain, Reliance Tax Saver, Fidelity Tax Advantage Fund etc.

G. Domestic Funds: Domestic fund houses launch funds, which mobilize the savings of nationals residing within the country. These schemes can come under any one of the categories mentioned under portfolio classification and functional classification. Reliance Equity Fund, Franklin India Bluechip Fund, SBI Balanced Fund, ABN AMRO Equity Fund, JM Equity Fund, Tata Equity Opportunities Fund are examples.

H. Offshore Funds: Offshore funds or Overseas Growth Fund are invested in securities of foreign companies, after getting permission from RBI. The objective behind launching offshore funds is to attract foreign capital for investment in the country of the issuing company. These funds facilitate cross border fund flow, which is a direct route for getting foreign currency. From the investment point of view, offshore funds open up the domestic capital markets to international investors and global portfolio investments. For example Franklin India International Fund is an open-ended foreign securities scheme with an objective to provide returns by investing mainly in overseas mutual funds, which are primarily invested either in US Government securities or securities backed by the US Government.

I. Open-Ended Funds: Mutual funds are mainly of two types namely open-ended and close-ended funds. A good number of mutual funds are of the open-ended variety. There are divergent and conflicting rules and regulations governing open-ended and close-ended funds. However, as per SEBI's rule both open-ended and close-ended funds are required to get themselves listed immediately after closing of subscriptions.

Open-ended funds are perpetually open for investments and redemptions. Investors under this scheme are free to join the fund or withdraw from the fund at any time after an initial lock-in period. An open-ended fund is a mutual fund that does not have restrictions on the amount of shares it issues. In the case of open ended schemes, units can be purchased from or sold back to the fund at a Net Asset Value (NAV) based price on all business days. If demand is high enough, the fund will continue to issue shares irrespective of the number of investors. Open-ended funds also buy back shares when investors wish to sell. It should be noted that when a fund's investment manager(s) determine that a fund's total assets have become too large to effectively execute its stated objective, the fund will be closed to new investors and, in some extreme cases, be closed to all further new investments by the existing fund investors. By continuously selling and buying back fund shares, these funds provide to the investors a very useful and convenient investing vehicle. DSP Merrill Lynch Equity Fund, Lotus India AGILE Fund, Franklin InfoTech Fund, Reliance Vision Fund, SBI Magnum Balanced Fund are examples of open-ended funds.

J. Close-Ended Funds: Unlike the open-ended schemes, close-ended schemes do not issue units for repurchase or redemption on a periodic basis. Its units can be redeemed only on termination of the scheme, or through dealings in the secondary market.

A close-ended fund is a publicly traded investment company that raises a fixed amount of capital through an initial public offering (IPO). The fund is then structured, listed and traded like a share on a stock exchange. It is also known as a "close-ended investment" or "close-ended mutual fund." Despite the similarities in name, a close-ended fund has little in common with a conventional mutual fund, which is technically known as an open-ended fund. The former raises a prescribed amount of capital only once through an IPO by issuing a fixed amount of shares, which are purchased by investors in the close-ended fund as stock. Unlike regular stocks, close-ended fund stock represents an interest in a specialized portfolio of securities that is actively managed by an investment advisor and which typically concentrates on a specific industry, geographic market, or sector. The stock prices of a close-ended fund fluctuate according to market forces (supply and demand) as well as the changing values of the securities in the fund's holdings.

The facility for conversion of close-ended funds into open-ended funds is normally accepted and internationally permitted. In India, some of the mutual funds availed this facility. The restructured funds are called interval funds. UTI Infrastructure Advantage Fund, JM Agri and Infra Fund, Sundram BNP Paribas Energy Opportunities Fund are examples of such funds.

K. Incubated Funds: It is a fund that is offered privately when it is created first. Investors of this type of fund are usually employees associated with the fund and their family members. Incubation allows fund managers to keep fund's size small while testing different investment styles before the fund is made available to the public subject to rules and regulations. These types of funds are never officially called "incubated," but are instead called "limited distribution" funds.

L. Arbitrage Funds: These are funds, which provide capital appreciation and regular income for unit holders by identifying profitable arbitrage opportunities between the spot and derivative market segments as also through investment of surplus cash in debt and money market instruments. This type of funds are invested in equity and equity related instruments, derivatives including index futures, stock futures, index options, stock options, debt money market instruments etc. SBI Arbitrage Opportunities Fund is an example of this type of fund.

M. Blue Chip Funds: These funds offer a long-term growth in capital through an active management of investment in a diversified basket of equity of major corporations with a fairly stable record of earnings and dividend payments.

15.15 Distribution of Dividends

At the time of application, the investors can exercise their option for the mode of distribution of dividend. The investor may change options exercised at the time of application later by way of a communication to the Registrar of the scheme. Such changes would be effective only from a prospective date. Important dividend distribution Plans cr options are the following:

1. Growth Option.
2. Dividend Option.
3. Dividend Re-investment Plan.

15.15.1 Growth Option: Under the growth option or growth plan, the investor realizes only the capital appreciation on the investment (by an increase in NAV) and does not get any income in the form of dividend.

15.15.2 Dividend Option: Under the Dividend option, the investor realizes income in the form of dividend. However, his Net Asset Value (NAV) will fall to the extent of the dividend. Some companies offer daily, weekly, monthly, quarterly or half-yearly dividend pay out or reinvestment plan to its investors.

Dividend pay out options provide regular income to its investors. In the case of weekly dividend option, trustees are envisaged to declare weekly dividend for its unit holders by selecting a particular day of the week as record date. In the case of daily dividend option trustee envisages declaring daily dividend for unit holders on record as on each day. Certain companies insist that for dividend of less than a fixed sum say ₹ 500 will be automatic compulsory reinvestment and for dividend that is more than ₹ 500 will be paid out or reinvested as opted by the unit holders. However, actual distribution of dividends and the frequency of distribution are provisional and will be entirely at the discretion of the trustee. There is no guarantee or assurance regarding the rate of dividend or regular payment of the dividend.

15.15.3 Dividend Re-investment Plan: Here the dividend accrued on mutual funds is automatically re-invested in purchasing additional units in open-ended funds. In most cases, mutual funds offer the investor an option for re-investing the same.

15.16 Terms Frequently Used in Mutual Fund

15.16.1 Fund Manager/Investment Manager: Funds manager or investment manager is a person who is responsible for the implementation of a fund's investing strategy and managing its portfolios. A fund can be managed by one person, or by a team of two or more persons as co-managers. The individuals involved in fund management should have a high level of educational and professional qualifications and appropriate managerial expertise in investment to qualify for this position.

The whole question of investing in a fund is to be left to the investment management professionals. Therefore, the quality of the fund manager is one of the key factors to be considered when appraising the investment quality of any particular fund. Fund managers are paid a fee for their work which is a percentage of the fund's average assets under management.

15.16.2 Portfolio Manager: The person or persons who are responsible for investing in a mutual, exchange-traded or close-ended fund's assets, implementing its investment strategy and managing the day-to-day portfolio trading are known as portfolio manager. The portfolio management is one of the most important factors to be taken into consideration at the time of investing in funds.

15.16.3 Manager of Managers: Manager of managers are professional investment managers to oversee aspects of a client's investment fund. More specifically, the Manager of Managers (MOM) tracks the performance of each investment manager and has the power to fire ineffective managers and hire replacements on client's behalf. Using a MOM to handle investments funds is an alternative to hiring a single investment portfolio manager who makes all the asset management decisions. In the case of a teacher's union hiring a MOM to invest its pension fund then the manager of manager will hire a number of investment managers (such as a bond expert, a money market expert and a large-cap stock expert), each with the responsibility of managing the particular asset class in which he or she is a specialist. Because no single manager is an expert on investing in all asset classes, using a MOM allows clients to have an expert asset manager working on each aspect of an investment at all times.

15.16.4 Gunslinger: Gunslinger is a high-strung and adventurous portfolio manager who looks for high returns and invests in stocks which are of very high risk.

15.16.5 Net Asset Value (NAV): The value of a share of a mutual fund is known as the net asset value per share. In terms of accounting, Net Asset Value (NAV) or book value is the difference between the values of assets minus liabilities. In the context of mutual funds, the Net Asset Value of a particular scheme or fund is the current market value of a fund's holdings minus its liabilities. For example, if the market value of securities of a mutual fund scheme is ₹ 200 lakh and the mutual fund has issued 10 lakh units of ₹ 10 each to the investors, then the NAV per unit of the fund is ₹ 20.

NAV is usually determined and expressed on as per share amount. NAV per share is the value of a single unit, or share, of a fund. The NAV per share for a mutual fund is the price at which shares are bought and sold. For most funds, the NAV is determined daily, after the close of trading on some specified financial exchange, but some funds update their NAV multiple times during the trading day. Since market value of securities changes every day, NAV of a scheme also varies on day-to-day basis. It is calculated by dividing the total net asset value of the fund or company by the number of shares outstanding. It is calculated as follows:

Net Asset Value=Mutual Fund's Net Asset Value/Number of Shares Outstanding.

All mutual funds buy and sell orders which are processed at the NAV of the trade date. However, investors must wait until the following day to get the trade price. Mutual funds pay out (distribute) virtually all of their income and capital gains.

15.16.6 Load Funds: Mutual funds incur various forms of expenses in marketing, distribution, advertising, portfolio churning, fund managers salary etc. Many funds recover these expenses from the investors in the form of load. These are known as load funds. Those funds which do not recover any such charges from the investors are called no load funds.

15.16.7 Front-end Load: Load funds are sold through financial intermediaries such as brokers, financial planners, and other types of registered representatives who levy a commission for their services. The mutual fund and insurance companies generally charge a sales commission or sales load at the time of purchase of mutual funds and insurance policies, which are technically referred as front-end load.

Front-end load is a charge or a commission given to a broker by the mutual fund company when its shares are purchased. The value of the investment is reduced by the amount of the load and, as a result, it lowers the size of the investment. The justification for a load fund is that investors are compensating a sales intermediary (broker, financial planner, investment advisor etc.) for his or her time and expertise in selecting an appropriate fund. As such, these sales charges are not part of a mutual fund's operating expenses. For example, if you purchase ₹ 1,00,000 worth of a mutual fund with a front-end load of 2 percent, the amount actually invested in the fund is only ₹ 98,000. When there is no transaction cost to purchase a no-load fund then all the money invested will work for the investor.

15.16.8 No-load Fund: Mutual funds in which shares are sold without a commission or sales charge is called no-load fund. The reason for this is that the shares are distributed directly by the investment company, instead of going for a secondary party. This is the opposite of a load fund, which charges a commission at the time of the fund's purchase, at the time of its sale, or as a level-load as long as the investor holds the fund. Because there is no transaction cost to purchase a no-load fund, all the money invested works for the investor. For example, if you purchase ₹ 1,00,000 worth of mutual fund with a no-load ₹ 1,00,000 as a whole will be invested into the particular fund.

15.16.9 Back-end Load: In this type of fund an investor pays no sales charge at the time of purchasing shares, but will pay a commission out of the proceeds when shares are redeemed. It is also known as a contingent deferred sales charge or exit load. Back-end load or a deferred sales charge is a fee that the investors have to pay when they sell mutual fund shares within a specified number of years, ranging between five to ten years. The fee amounts to a percentage of the value of the share being sold. The load percentage is highest in the first year and decreases yearly until the specified holding period ends, when it drops to zero. For example, if one purchases ₹ 1,00,000 worth of mutual fund with back-end load of 1 percent then all ₹ 1,00,000 will be invested into the particular fund. However, when shares of the fund are sold for ₹ 1,20,000, the investor will be charged a fixed rate of sales proceeds (₹ 1,20,000) as sales commission or back-end load. The percentage of sales commission will be highest in the initial years and decreases on a yearly basis. Like other load, back-end load is also charged on the financial intermediary, and is not included in a fund's operating expenses.

15.16.10 Contingent Deferred Sales Charge: In some schemes, the percentage of exit load gets reduced, as the investor stays longer with the fund. This type of load is known as Contingent Deferred Sales Charge.

15.16.11 Level-load Fund: Another derivative structure is a level load fund, in which no sales charge is paid at the time of buying the fund, but a back-end load may be charged if the shares purchased are sold within a year.

15.16.12 Free Loading: It is a term used when mutual fund investors who have purchased load funds switch from one fund family to another family of funds without paying another sales charge. Not all funds families have freeloading procedures.

15.16.13 Tax-exempt Funds: Funds that are invested in securities free from tax liability are known as tax-exempt funds. All open-ended equity oriented funds are exempt from tax. Long-term capital gains and dividend income in the hands of investors are tax-free.

15.16.14 Non-tax-exempt Funds: Funds that are invested in taxable securities are known as non-tax-exempt funds. In India, all funds except open-ended equity funds are liable to pay tax on distribution of income. Profits arising out of sale of units by an investor within 12 months of purchase are categorized as short-term capital gains, which are taxable. Sale of units of an equity-oriented fund is subject to Securities Transaction Tax (STT). STT is deducted from the redemption proceeds of an investor.

15.16.15 Public Offer Price: Public Offer Price (POP) otherwise called sale price is the price at which an investor can invest in a particular scheme. The public offering price is usually determined by adding a sales load or entry load to the NAV of the particular fund. Open-ended funds sell their shares at POP and redeem shares at NAV, and process their orders only after the NAV is determined. Close-ended funds (the shares of which are traded by investors) may be traded at a higher or lower price than their NAV and this is known as either a 'premium' or a 'discount'. When a fund is divided into multiple classes of shares, each class will typically have its own NAV, reflecting differences in fees and expenses which are paid by the different classes.

15.16.16 Systematic Investment Plan (SIP): Here the investor is given the option of preparing a pre-determined number of post-dated cheques in favour of the fund. He will get units on the date of the cheque at the prevalent NAV.

15.16.17 Systematic Withdrawal Plan (SWP): As opposed to the Systematic Investment Plan, the Systematic Withdrawal Plan allows the investor the facility to withdraw a pre-determined amount or units from his fund at pre-determined intervals. The investor's units will be redeemed at the existing NAV as on that day.

15.16.18 Redemption Price: It is the price at which open-ended schemes repurchase their units and close-ended schemes redeem their units on maturity. Such prices are NAV related.

15.16.19 Repurchase Price: Repurchase Price is the price at which a close-ended scheme repurchases its units and it may include a back-end load. This is also called Bid Price.

15.16.20 Securities Transactions Tax: However, the mutual fund investors are liable to pay a Securities Transactions Tax (STT), under Chapter VII of the Finance (No. 2) Act, 2004. From 1-10-2004, the seller of an equity oriented mutual fund units has to pay an STT, currently 0.25 percent of the value of sale transaction, where value shall be the price at which the units are repurchased by the fund. The applicable STT of various securities transactions is given in Table 15.1.

Table 15.1: Securities Transaction Tax (STT)

S N	Nature of Transaction	Payable by	Rate of Tax (percent)
1	Purchase and sale of equity shares or units of equity oriented mutual funds on a recognized stock exchange on delivery basis.	Both purchaser as well as seller	0.125
2	Sale on stock exchange of equity shares or units of equity oriented mutual funds on non-delivery basis.	Seller	0.025
3	Sale of derivates on recognized stock exchange.	Seller	0.017
4	Sale of units of equity oriented mutual funds to the mutual fund	Seller	0.25

15.17 Mutual Fund Regulations in India

A number of regulations and guidelines issued by various agencies govern the mutual fund operation in India. Important agencies are the following.

1. Reserve Bank of India.
2. Ministry of Finance.
3. Securities and Exchange Board of India.

4. Indian Trust Act, 1882.
5. Indian Companies Act, 1956.
6. Income Tax Act, 1961.

15.18 Securities and Exchange Board of India

No uniform regulation of the mutual fund industry existed in India until 1996. SEBI as a regulator of the mutual fund industry has the responsibility to decide rules and regulations on mutual fund business. As far as mutual funds are concerned, SEBI formulates policies and regulates the operations of mutual funds to protect the interest of the investors. SEBI notified its regulations for the mutual funds in 1993. The rules for the formation, administration and management of mutual funds were clearly laid down in these regulations. Thereafter, mutual funds sponsored by private sector entities were also allowed to enter capital market. SEBI also issues guidelines to the mutual funds periodically to protect the interests of investors.

Mutual funds whether promoted either by the public sector or private sector or those promoted by foreign entities are all governed by the same set of Regulations. There is no distinction in regulatory requirements for these mutual funds and all are subjected to monitoring and inspections by SEBI. The risks involved in the schemes launched by the mutual funds sponsored by these entities are more or less of similar type.

During 1995-96, SEBI prepared a paper entitled "Mutual Funds 2000" and widely circulated it for extensive discussions and comments from the market participants, investors and other stake holders. The objective of the paper was to put forward suggestions for improvement in the working and regulation of the mutual fund industry, so that mutual funds could ensure better performance and service to all categories of investors and offer a range of innovative products on a competitive basis to match investor needs and preferences across various investor segments. Several proposals were put forward by different agencies to be incorporated in the regulations to improve the working of the industry.

Based on the comments, the recommendations made in the paper by market participants and investors and on the basis of discussions held with the Association of Mutual Funds of India (AMFI), the SEBI (Mutual Funds) Regulations, 1993 were revised and the new regulations were notified in December 1996. The revised guidelines tightened the accounting and disclosure requirements.

Presently, all mutual funds are regulated by SEBI. The operations of all mutual funds are regularly and closely monitored by SEBI.

15.19 SEBI (Mutual Funds) Regulations, 1996

The revised regulations embodied far-reaching changes in the regulation and functioning of mutual funds. The revised regulations are the following:

1. Enhanced level of investor protection.
2. Empowerment of investors.
3. Stringent disclosure norms in the offer documents, so that investors are better informed, better advised and are better aware of risks and rewards.
4. Standardization of norms for valuation of assets, computation of Net Asset Values (NAVs) of schemes of mutual funds and accounting standards and policies.
5. Complete freedom for asset management companies to structure schemes in accordance with investor preferences.
6. Removal of quantitative restrictions on investment by mutual funds and replacement through prudential supervision.
7. Replacement of vetting of offer documents by filing.
8. Guaranteed return schemes by mutual funds were permitted to provide returns including capital.
9. Indication of expected returns based on hypothetical portfolio permitted.
10. Better governance of mutual funds through higher responsibilities and empowerment of trustees as front-line regulators of mutual funds.
11. Closer scrutiny through off site and on site inspections.
12. Code of ethics for asset management companies.

The effect of the new regulations was felt immediately. Asset management companies framed several new schemes, influenced by the freedom provided to them by the new regulations. Not only did the number of schemes filed with SEBI increase significantly in a short period of time, but there was also a greater variety in the investment products offered. There was also a significant improvement in disclosures in the offer documents.

Another important development in the mutual fund industry was the issuance of Guidelines for Money Market Mutual Funds by RBI and the launching of Pension Schemes by mutual funds. The new regulations brought into greater focus the responsibilities of trustees of mutual funds who were uniquely positioned to promote the interests of the unit holders and to ensure that mutual funds are managed responsibly and ethically. The number of mutual fund houses proliferated with several foreign mutual fund companies setting up their funds in India and the industry is witnessing several mergers and acquisitions.

15.20 Advantages of Mutual Funds

Mutual funds are superior to other comparable investment avenues because of the following reasons. The important advantages of investing in mutual funds are the following:

15.20.1 Professional Management: One of the important advantages of mutual fund investment is that it is generally managed by a person called funds manager or by a team of two or more persons as co-managers with a high level of educational/professional qualifications and appropriate managerial experience. The fund manager appoints professionals who possess the experience and resources for analyzing the economy and financial markets thoroughly and spot good investment opportunities. The specialized investment expertise of the professional management would ensure greater achievements to the inexperienced investor who can not achieve the same on his own.

15.20.2 Credible Return: Mutual fund investments are invested mainly in capital market instruments. They offer greater returns at periodical intervals to its unit holders by way of capital appreciation and dividend income. The return on investment is comparatively higher than certificate of deposits and other forms of investments. This would also enable mutual funds to compete with banks and non-banking finance companies in mobilizing resources.

15.20.3 Liquidity and Convenience: Another advantage of mutual funds is the ability to enter and exit from them with relative ease. Mutual fund investments also facilitate easy encashment of the principal. There is only very little paperwork and it is very easy to track and monitor the flow of investments. Now most of the mutual fund companies offer facilities of direct credit of redemption\dividend proceeds\refunds etc and transfer them into to the investor's bank account instead of sending them cheque and demand draft. This method thus reduces the delay in getting the funds to the investors.

15.20.4 Transparency: Mutual funds provide updated information pertaining to the markets and the schemes to the investors. Their operations are transparent because the mutual fund companies supply adequate information to the investors on investment objectives, the allocation pattern of the scheme, load structure, investors strategy etc. The performance of a scheme is reflected in its net asset value (NAV) which is disclosed on a daily basis in case of open-ended schemes and on weekly basis in the case of close-ended schemes. The NAVs of mutual funds are also required to be published in two or more newspapers. The NAVs are available on the web sites of mutual funds and they are also required to put their NAVs on the web site of The Association of Mutual Funds in India (AMFI) www.amfiindia.com and thus the investors can know the NAVs of all mutual funds at one place. The account statement and annual financial results are also posted to the investors.

15.20.5 Low Transaction Cost: Due to the economies of a larger volume of the scale of operation, mutual funds pay lesser transaction costs. The transaction costs are divided among all the mutual fund shareholders, who are benefited by having a third party (professional fund managers) to use their expertise and dedicate their time to manage and research investment options.

15.20.6 Portfolio Diversification: Another important advantage of mutual fund investment is that it gives small investors access to professionally managed and diversified portfolios of equities, bonds and other securities, which would be difficult to obtain with a smaller amounts of capital.

15.20.7 Flexibility: The mutual fund investment plans are designed in such a way as to provide flexibility and convenience to its investors to suit their requirements. They are flexible and provide different features to its investors such as investors switching their holdings from a debt scheme to an equity scheme and vice versa, systematic investment plan, regular withdrawal plan, systematic transfer plan, dividend transfer plan, dividend reinvestment plan, etc.

15.20.8 Limited Risk: Another advantage of the mutual fund investment is that the investor takes only a minor risk than a direct equity investor. Even with a small investment in a mutual fund investors acquire a diversified portfolio of securities. Such investments in securities are spread across a wide sector of industries and other sectors and thus the risk is reduced considerably. Diversification reduces the risk because all the stocks will not move in the same direction, proportion and time.

15.20.9 Choice of Schemes: Mutual funds also provide to investors various schemes with different investment objectives. Investors have the option of investing in a scheme having a correlation between its investment objectives and their own financial goals. Now wide varieties of mutual fund schemes exist to cater to the varied needs of investors such as financial position, risk tolerance, return expectations etc.

15.20.10 Well Regulated: Mutual fund industry is part of a well-regulated investment sphere where the interests of the investors are zealously protected by the regulator. More over all funds are registered with SEBI and complete transparencies of transactions are also ensured.

15.20.11 Tax Benefits: Mutual fund schemes offer tax benefits under Section 80C. In addition, the returns from mutual funds, dividends and capital appreciations are also eligible for favourable tax treatment. The entire income of the mutual funds will be exempted from the income tax in accordance with the provisions of Section 10 (23D) of the Income Tax Act of 1961 which stipulated a condition for the registration of a mutual fund with the Securities and Exchange Board of India. The mutual fund will receive all the income without any deduction of tax at source under the provisions of Section 196 (iv) of the Act. In view of the exemption of income gained by the unit holders, no income tax is deductible at source, on income distribution by the Mutual fund from, 1st April 2003, under the Sections 194K and 196A of the said Act. Thus, the income received by the unit holders in respect of the units of the Mutual fund is exempt from tax under Section 10 (35) of the Act.

However, as per Section 196B of the Act, tax is required to be deducted at the rate of 11.22 percent from income payable in respect of units purchased in foreign currency from approved overseas financial organizations. This rate is inclusive of surcharge on income-tax at the rate of 10 percent and an additional surcharge by way of education cess at the rate of 2 percent on the amount of tax inclusive of surcharge. Where the total income of such organization does not exceed ₹ 1 crore, the above mentioned surcharge is not payable. The Finance Act of 2007 has levied an additional surcharge, called the 'Secondary and Higher Education Cess', at the rate of one percent of the income tax and surcharge (not including the education cess on income tax). This amendment came into effect on 1st April 2007.

15.21 Disadvantages of Mutual Fund

15.21.1 No Control on Cost: The investors have to rely on the integrity of the professional fund manager. They have also no control on the fund manager and pay investment management fees and fund distribution costs as a percentage of the value of the investments, regardless of the performance of the fund. Fund management fees may sometimes be unreasonable also for the services rendered.

15.21.2 No customized Portfolios: The portfolio of securities in which a fund is invested is a decision taken by the fund manager. Investors have no right to interfere in the decision making process of a fund manager, which will be a constraint to some investors in achieving their financial objectives.

15.21.3 Difficulty in Selecting Suitable Fund: Many investors find it difficult to select the right option which correlates with their investment objectives and goals from a plethora of available funds and schemes available. For this, they seek advice from financial planners enabling them to invest in the right fund to achieve their objectives.

15.21.4 Not Free from Risk: Despite the professional management, mutual funds are not free from risks. They have the same risks proportionate to the type of investments made. If the fund invests primarily in stocks, it is usually subject to the same ups and downs and risks as the stock market.

15.21.5 Fluctuating Returns: Unlike fixed income securities, mutual funds do not guarantee fixed return to its investors. Mutual funds generally experience price fluctuations and there is also the possibility of the value of the mutual fund getting decreased.

15.21.6 Mutual Fund Deposits are not Insured: Unlike bank deposits there is no deposit guarantee corporation to guarantee mutual fund deposits.

15.21.7 Difficulty in Evaluating Funds: Another disadvantage of mutual funds is the difficulty they pose to investors who are interested in researching and evaluating the different funds. Unlike stocks, mutual funds do not offer investors the opportunity to compare the P\E ratio, earnings per share etc. A mutual fund NAV gives investors only the total value of the funds portfolio minus liabilities.

15.22 Association of Mutual Funds in India

Association of Mutual Funds in India (AMFI) is a trade body of all the mutual funds in India. It was incorporated in August 1995 as a non-profit organization to promote and protect the interests of mutual funds and their unit holders, define and maintain high ethical and professional standards and enhance public awareness of and confidence in mutual funds. It serves as a forum where mutual funds are able to present their views, debate and participate in evolving their own regulatory frameworks. Today, AMFI is consulted on all matters long before regulations are framed, and it often initiates many regulatory changes to prevent malpractices that appear from time to time. All mutual funds in India are members of this association. AMFI works through a system of committees and working groups. AMFI works through a number of committees, some of which are standing committees to monitor areas where there is a need for constant vigil and improvements and ad hoc committees which are constituted to address specific issues. These committees consist of industry professionals drawn from among the member of mutual funds.

Over the years, AMFI has worked closely with SEBI in establishing international standards that match the best in the world. It has also played a significant role in introducing best practices to reinforce the growth of the industry on healthy lines and also to protect the interests of the investors.

One of the major initiatives of AMFI was the introduction of certification programme for agent distributors. SEBI has mandated that all those engaged in sales and marketing of mutual fund schemes will be AMFI certified and registered. AMFI has brought out a detailed workbook on mutual funds based on which it conducts computerized testing through National Stock Exchange test centres. It also organizes written examinations in different languages. Till date over 31000 agent distributors have passed the test. AMFI compiles and publishes data on a monthly and quarterly basis. It has a quarterly publication "AMFI update" which summarizes the major developments in the mutual fund industry and changes introduced in the regulatory framework.

15.23 Growth of Mutual Fund Business in India

The origin of mutual fund industry in India was with the introduction of the concept of mutual fund by UTI in the year 1963. However, its growth was slow, but it got accelerated from the year 1987 when non-UTI players entered the industry. Before, the monopoly of the market saw ending phase, the Assets Under Management (AUM) was ₹ 67 billion.

With the introduction of economic reforms particularly in the financial sector, the economy got opened up and many developments were taking place in the Indian money and capital market. Mutual funds have emerged as important mediums for channelising individual savings to the capital market, thereby facilitating small retail investors participation in the capital market. However, over the years, the corporate sector also invested heavily in units of mutual funds, influenced by tax benefits. The Indian mutual fund industry consists of mutual funds sponsored by banks and financial institutions and private and foreign sector mutual funds.

Short Answer Type Questions

1. What is meant by mutual fund?
2. What is meant by public offer price?
3. What is systematic investment plan?
4. What do you mean by net asset value?
5. What is AMFI?
6. Define mutual fund.
7. Explain load funds.
8. What is growth fund?
9. What is mean by dividend option?
10. What is meant by front end load?
11. Who is a portfolio manager?
12. What is diversified equity fund?
13. What are sector funds?
14. What is meant by growth option?
15. What is tax exempt fund?
16. What are the objectives of AMFI?
17. What is equity index fund?
18. What do you mean by an asset management company?
19. What is leveraged fund?
20. Name the different types of securities where mutual fund companies invest.
21. What is exchange traded funds?

22. What are the objectives of mutual fund?
23. What is offshore fund?
24. What do you mean by sponsor?
25. What is open ended fund?
26. What is liquid fund?
27. What do mean by balance fund?
28. Who are diversified debt fund?
29. What is money market fund?
30. What is close ended fund?
31. What is gilt fund?
32. What is hybrid fund?
33. List out the parties in a mutual fund company.
34. Who is a custodian?
35. Name the activities carried out by asset management companies.
36. What is hedge fund?
37. What is securities transactions tax?
38. What do you mean by investment manager?
39. What is equity fund?
40. What is debt fund?

Essay Type Questions

1. What is mutual fund? Distinguish between open ended funds and close ended funds.
2. Explain the organization structure of mutual fund schemes.
3. Define mutual fund. What are the advantages of mutual fund?
4. Explain briefly the mutual fund regulations in India.
5. What is mutual fund? Explain the procedure for investing in mutual fund.
6. Explain briefly SEBI guidelines on constitution and management of an asset management company.
7. Discuss the growth of mutual fund business in India.
8. Explain the concept of mutual funds. Give its disadvantages.
9. Discuss the origin of mutual funds in India.
10. Explain the need for setting up of mutual funds. Explain its role in the mobilization of savings.
11. Discuss the various mutual fund schemes prevalent in India.
12. What is AMFI? What are its objectives and functions?
13. Discuss the working of mutual fund scheme.
14. Explain the role of SEBI in the regulation of mutual funds in India.
15. What are the advantages and disadvantages of mutual funds?

16

Lease Financing Companies

16.1 Introduction

Lease financing is a type of financial intermediary service provided by specialized institutions to a firm or a person for the procurement of assets through lease. The firms can use the asset by paying periodic payments called lease rentals to the owner of the asset and without any lump sum payment. Leasing has emerged as a new source of financing capital assets. It is one of the important sources of intermediate and long-term finance to business enterprises to obtain various capital equipments. It enables a firm to avail the services of machinery and equipment without making investment for the same or incurring a debt. Leases have become more prevalent as businesses and consumers look for alternative source of finance for the acquisition of fixed assets. Leasing is an option for corporate enterprises to conserve capital because, in effect, they obtain 100 percent financing.

A lease is an agreement allowing one party to use another's property, plant, or equipment for a stated period of time in exchange for a consideration. Lease as a concept involves a contract whereby the ownership, financing and risk taking of equipments or assets are separated and shared by two or more parties. The lessee does not have to pay the cost of asset at the time of signing the contract of lease. Leasing contracts are more flexible so lessees can structure the leasing contracts according to their needs for finance. A great advantage to leasing is that it may be allowed to be "off the balance sheet." This means that leases can be disclosed as balance sheet footnotes. They do not appear as debt even though they represent an ongoing company liability.

16.2 Evolution of Lease Financing

Lease financing denotes procurement of assets through lease. Although leasing is often thought of as a modern day financing technique, the basic concept of leasing dates back to at least 1800 B.C., when the Babylonian king Hammurabi described the transaction in his code of laws stating its use. The basics of leasing have changed little since that time. Leasing has been employed in several countries for centuries in different forms and for different applications. Over the years, the strength of the leasing industry has been its resilience and its ability to attune itself to the changing business environment.

In USA in the early 1990s leasing was confined primarily to real estate rentals, although leasing was also used to finance cars and farm equipments. By the mid 1990s people and companies in USA were leasing everything from aero planes and oil rigs to televisions and office furniture. In fact, in the United States, leasing was the most common way to finance plant and equipment for manufacturing companies, and it was resorted to for a growing number of consumer purchases. Leasing is the most widely used method of personal property financing in the United States. Today leasing has evolved as a big industry in the USA and UK.

The practice of leasing evolved in other developed countries only during the early 1950s. As a result of several factors, including tax code changes and improved efficiency in the financial markets, leasing became a common financing tool after 1950. In the 1970s leasing developed as a convenient form of finance in other developing countries in Asia such as South Korea, Malaysia and Indonesia.

16.3 Growth and Development of Lease financing in India

Leasing, essentially a US-innovation, entered the country significantly in the early 80s, and was propagated as an alternative to traditional modes of industrial finance. In India, the concept of financial leasing was pioneered in the year 1973 when the First Leasing Company was set up in Madras by Farouk Irani, with industrialist A.C. Murtha. For several years, this company remained the only company in the country until 20th Century Finance Corporation which was established in the year 1979. The performance of First Leasing Company and Twentieth Century Leasing Company Limited forced many others to enter the leasing business. Eighties witnessed a rapid growth in the leasing business. Since then a number of companies and financial institutions entered into the filed of lease financing in India. By 1981, Shetty Investment and Finance, Jaybharat Credit and Investment, Motor and General Finance and Sundran Finance started leasing business.

During 1980s, International Finance Corporation (IFC) Washington announced its decision to open four leasing joint ventures in 4 metros in India. To add to the leasing boom, the Finance Ministry announced strict measures for enlistment of investment companies on stock-exchanges, which made many investment companies to turn overnight into leasing companies.

The Industrial Credit and Investment Corporation of India (ICICI) commenced leasing business in the year 1983. Another significant phase in the development of Indian leasing was the Dahotre Committee's recommendations based on which the RBI formed guidelines on commercial bank funding to leasing companies. The Banking Regulations Act (BRA) of 1949 was amended in the year 1986 to facilitate commercial banks to establish leasing subsidiaries. State Bank of India was the first commercial bank to set up its leasing subsidiary called SBI capital market followed by Can Bank Financial Services Ltd., BOB Financial Services Ltd. and PNB Financial Services Ltd.

Leasing business has a bright future in India. Due to certain tax concessions and benefits to the lessor, many leasing companies have been established. Today in India almost all types of fixed assets can be leased. The prospects of leasing in India are good due to growing investment needs and scarcity of funds with public financial institutions. Leasing in the sphere of land and building had been in existence in India for a long period of time, while equipment leasing has become very common in the recent times.

16.4 Meaning and Definition of Lease

Leasing is a form of renting of assets. A lease transaction is a commercial arrangement whereby an equipment owner or manufacturer conveys to the equipment user the right to use the equipment in return for a rental. In other words, lease is a contract between the owner of an asset (the lessor) and its user (the lessee) for the right to use the asset during a specified period in return for a mutually agreed periodic payment (the lease rentals). It is an arrangement that provides a firm with the use and control over the asset without buying and owning an asset. The important feature of a lease contract is separation of the ownership of the asset from its usage. Lease financing is based on the observation made by Donald B. Grant: "Why own a cow when the milk is so cheap? All you really need is milk and not the cow."

A lease is a legal contract that provides for the use of something, typically real estate or equipment in exchange for a payment. The lease contract is regulated by the terms and conditions of the lease agreement. It is an agreement that permits one party (the lessee) to use property owned by another party (the lessor).

International Accounting Standard-17 has defined a lease as "an agreement, whereby the lessor coveys to the lessee in return for rent the right to use an asset for an agreed period of time".

International Leasing Association of UK defined leasing as "a contract between lessor and lesse for the hire of a specified asset selected from a manufacturer or vendor of such assets by the lessee. The lessor retains the ownership of the asset. The lessee has possession and use of the asset on payment of specified rentals over the period".

16.5 Features of Lease Financing

Leasing industry plays an important role in the industrial and economic development of a country by providing financial intermediary service. Lease financing is particularly important for private sector concerns that face resource crunch. Commercial banks and financial institutions do not fulfil the financial requirements of these concerns. Important features of lease financing are the following:

1. The lessee does not have to pay the cost of asset or equipment at the time of signing the contract of lease.
2. Leasing contracts are more flexible and therefore lessee can frame the leasing contracts according to their needs for finance.
3. Outside securities or collaterals are not needed.
4. Documentation cost is very low.
5. Leasing can finance a higher percentage of equipment than bank loans.
6. Government allows lessees to deduct full lease payments from their income before tax.
7. The lessee can also pass on the risk of obsolescence to the lessor by acquiring those assets or equipments, which have high technological obsolescence.

16.6 Mechanism in Lease Financing

The following steps are involves in the mechanism of leasing:

1. The lessee normally selects the equipment and machinery they require and approach the leasing company.
2. The management of the leasing company evaluates the paying capacity and the financial stability of the lessee before offering leasing services.
3. The lessee then enters into a contract with the lessor known as lease agreement. The lease agreement contains the terms and conditions of the lease viz. type of lease, lease period, periodicity of rentals, amount of rent, details regarding payment of cost of maintenance and repairs, taxes, insurance and other expenses.
4. Lessor purchases the capital equipment in accordance with the requirements and specifications contained in the lesse agreement.
5. Lessor makes payment to the manufacturer or equipment dealer.
6. The manufacturer or equipment dealer delivers the asset to the lessee.
7. The lessor retains the ownership of the asset.
8. The lessee takes possession of the asset.
9. The right to the use of the asset is given to the lessee.
10. The right to use the asset is for a consideration known as lease rentals.
11. The lease rentals are predetermined and payable at fixed intervals of time

according to the mutual convenience of both the parties.

12. Lessee has no right to alter the physical shape of the asset leased.
13. In most of the leases, the lessor is generally responsible for the payment of taxes, insurance, and cost of maintenance and repairs of the asset leased.
14. The lessee continues to discharge the obligations till the end of the lease period.
15. Lease contract ends after the expiry of lease period.
16. At the end of the lease period, the assets leased are either returned to the lessor, renewed for a further period or sold to the lessee at a pre-agreed or at market price.

16.7 Parties in a Lease Agreement

A lease agreement involves at least two parties (a) lessor and (b) lessee.

16.7.1 Lessor: Lessor is the owner of the property or asset who gives it on lease. In lease agreement, the lessor has the legal or tax title to the equipment, grants the lessee the right to use the equipment for the lease term, and is entitled to the lease rentals. A lessor may be a leasing company, a manufacturer, a subsidiary company, a commercial bank, special purpose leasing companies, broker or a business organization conducting leasing business.

16.7.2 Lessee: Lessee is the party who uses the property owned by the lessor. A lessee may be an individual, partnership firm, a joint stock company, or government enterprises.

16.8 Types of Lessor

Lessor generally comes in one of the four varieties (a) commercial banks, (b) captive leasing companies, (c) independent leasing companies and (d) brokers.

16.8.1 Commercial Banks: Companies enter into leasing agreements with commercial banks with which already transact business or by other means. For bank lessors, leasing is another competitive product to satisfy the needs of bank customers. Leases may be safer than other bank products because the transactions are secured and leases are generally more profitable than commercial loans because of advantages inherent in their structure.

16.8.2 Captive Leasing Companies: These are usually subsidiaries of a parent company that manufactures the product being leased, e.g., IBM Credit Corp which leases IBM computers.

16.8.3 Independent Leasing Companies: These firms typically are unaffiliated with the manufacturer or the lessee and get most of their businesses from leasing to business firms.

16.8.4 Brokers: Leasing brokers act as intermediaries to link lessees and lessors. A broker is a company or person who arranges for a fee, transactions between lessees and lessor of an asset.

16.9 Legal Aspects of Leasing

As there is no separate statue for equipment leasing in India, the provisions relating to bailment in the Indian Contract Act govern the equipment leasing agreements also. Section 148 of the Indian Contract Act defines bailment as:

"The delivery of goods by one person to another, for some purpose, upon a contract that they shall, when the purpose is accomplished, be returned or otherwise disposed off according to the directions of the person delivering them. The person delivering the goods is called the 'bailor' and the person to whom they are delivered is called the 'bailee'.

Since an equipment lease transaction is regarded as a contract of bailment, the obligations of the lessor and the lessee are similar to those of the bailor and the bailee (other than those expressly specified in the least contract) as defined by the provisions of sections 150 and 168 of the Indian Contract Act. Essentially these provisions have the following implications for the lessor and the lessee.

- The lessor has the duty to deliver the asset to the lessee, to legally authorize the lessee to use the asset, and to leave the asset in peaceful possession of the lessee during the currency of the agreement.
- The lessor has the obligation to pay the lease rentals as specified in the lease agreement, to protect the lessor's title, to take reasonable care of the asset, and to return the leased asset on the expiry of the lease period.

16.10 Sources of Finance for Leasing Companies: Following are the usual sources of finance for a company leasing assets:

1. Issue of equity share capital.
2. Issue of debentures.
3. Terms loans from commercial banks and other financial institutions.
4. Accepting public deposits.
5. Inter-corporate deposits.

Of the various sources of finance, public deposits and inter-corporate deposits constitute the major sources of funds for a leasing company. The amount that can be raised through the issue of equity capital and debentures are inadequate for a leasing company. Due to certain restrictions imposed by RBI, availability of term loans from commercial banks and financial institutions are limited to a leasing company.

16.11 Important Terms

16.11.1 Lease Agreement/Contract: Lease agreement\contract is a contractual agreement between the lessor and the lessee that set forth all the terms and conditions of the lease. The lease agreement may be written either for a short term or for a long-term period. Once a lease is signed, its terms, such as the rent, cannot be changed unless both parties agree. A lease agreement is legally binding to both the parties, which means that in the violation of the agreement the concerned party will be held liable in a court. Lease agreement generally specifies the rights and obligations of the lessor and lessee. It contains mainly the following points:

- Name and address of the lessor and lessee.
- Description of the asset or equipment.
- Details regarding the time and place of delivery of the asset.
- Amount and periodicity of lease rental payments.
- Options for the renewal of lease rent if any.
- Lessee's responsibility regarding the maintenance of the asset.
- Lessee's obligations regarding the payment of insurance, repairs etc.
- Rights of lessor in case of default in payment of lease rentals.
- Arbitration procedure in the event of dispute.
- Option of renewal of lease agreement.
- Return of asset on expiry of the lease period.

16.11.2 Lease Rent: The periodic rental payment to the lessor for the use of an asset by the lessee is known as lease rentals. The lessor fixes the lease rentals after taking into consideration several factors such as purchase price of the asset, installation expenses, taxes, insurance, repairs and maintenance, expected return on investment, life of the assets, depreciation, scrap value of the asset etc.

The lease rental is predetermined and payable at fixed intervals of time. Lease payments are usually of an even amount. However, in certain circumstances lease rentals have gaps in the payment of amount as a result of seasonal fluctuations of lessee's income. Generally, leasing may provide for more flexibility in this regard than a loan. The lease can claim lease rentals paid as a tax deductible item. However, lease rentals received by lessor are taxable.

16.11.3 Primary and Secondary Lease Period: The period within which the entire cost of the asset leased recovered by the lessor is known as primary lease period. The remaining period of the asset is known as secondary lease period.

16.11.4 Peppercorn Rentals: During the primary lease period the lease rentals charged by the lessor would be higher and in the secondary period the lease rentals would be nominal or minimum so as to keep the asset alive. Such a minimum rent charged by the lessor in the secondary period is called peppercorn rentals.

16.11.5 Advance Lease Payments: One or more lease payments required to be paid by the lessee to the lessor at the beginning of the lease term is known as advance lease payments. Lease structures commonly require at least one payment to be made in advance.

16.11.6 End-of-term Options: Options stated in the lease agreement that give the lessee flexibility in its treatment of the leased equipment at the end of the lease term are called end of term options. Common options include purchasing the equipment, renewing the lease or returning the equipment to the lessor. Options are sometimes given as an amendment to the lease documents and are not made part of the actual lease document.

16.11.7 Fair Market Purchase Option: It is an option given to the lessee to purchase the leased property at the end of the lease term at its then fair market value. The lessor does not have the ability to retain title to the equipment if the lessee chooses to exercise the purchase option.

16.11.8 Lease Broker: Lease broker is an entity that provides one or more services in the lease transaction for its own portfolio. Such services include finding the lessee, working with the equipment manufacturer or dealer, securing debt financing for the lessor to use in purchasing the equipment and locating the ultimate lessor or equity participant in the lease transaction. The lease broker is also referred to as a packager or syndicator.

16.12 Types of Leasing

Lease as a concept involves a contract whereby the ownership, financing and risk taking of any equipment or asset are separated and shared by two or more parties. Thus, the lessor may finance and lessee may accept the risk through the use of it while a third party may own it. Alternatively, the lessor may finance and own it while the lessee enjoys the use of it and bears the risk. There are various combinations in which the above characteristics are shared by the lessor and lessee. Lease agreements are basically classified into two types (a) financial lease and (b) operating lease.

16.13 Other Types of Leases

1. Direct Leasing.
2. Leveraged Lease.
3. Sale and Lease Back.
4. First Amendment Lease.
5. Open-end Lease.
6. Straight Lease.
7. Modified Lease.

8. Domestic Lease.
9. International Lease.
10. Cross Border Lease.
11. Import Lease.
12. Foreign to Foreign Lease.
13. Net Lease.
14. Synthetic Lease.
15. In-House Lease.
16. Sales-type Lease.
17. Primary Lease.
18. Secondary Lease.
19. Sub-lease.
20. Wet Lease.

16.14 Financial Lease

Long-term, non-cancellable lease contracts are known as financial leases. A financial lease is a lease, which contains a condition whereby the lessor agrees to transfer the title of the asset at the end of the lease period at a nominal cost. In this type of lease only title deed of the asset leased remains with the lessor and the lease agreement is irrevocable. Under this type, the lessee is responsible for the payment of taxes and insurance and bears the cost of maintenance and repairs of the asset. Practically all the risks incidental to the asset ownership and all the benefits arising there from are transferred to the lessee. Since the financial lease is non-cancellable and for a long period, the lessee has to pay the rentals for the entire lease period even though the asset may become obsolete during the period of lease. Financial lease is also known as 'capital lease' or 'full payout lease' or 'long term lease'. A financial lease effectively allows a firm to finance the purchase of an asset, even if, strictly speaking, the firm never acquires the asset. Financial lease is a commercial arrangement whereby:

1. The lessee (customer) will select the asset.
2. The lessor (finance company) will purchase that asset.
3. The lessee will have use of that asset during the lease period.
4. The lessee will pay rentals at periodical intervals for the use of the asset leased.
5. The lessor recovers a larger part of the investment in the asset along with an acceptable rate of return during the period of the lease.
6. The lessee has the option to acquire ownership of the asset.

Typically, a finance lease will give the lessee control over an asset for a large proportion of the asset's useful life, providing them the benefits (and risks) of ownership. Under this lease, quite often, the lessor recovers 90 percent of the fair value of the asset as lease rentals and the lease period is 75 percent of the economic life of the asset. These leases are structured as equipment financing agreements with residuals of up to 10 percent.

The essential point of financial lease is that, it must give an option to the lessee to purchase the asset he has used at the expiry of the lease. It provides for a periodic rental payment during the period of lease, which are calculated on the basis of the amount of cost of the asset leased, duration of lease, periodicity of rental payments, return on original investment in the asset etc. The period of lease rental may either be monthly, quarterly, half-yearly or yearly. Usually the company may take an advance of the rental at the time of the lease which is adjusted at the end of lease. Finance leases are most attractive in cases where the lessee wants the tax benefits of ownership or expects the equipment's residual value to be high. In India, financial leases are very popular with high-cost and high technology equipments.

16.15 Features of Financial Lease

Following are the important characteristics of financial lease:

1. It is a non-cancellable lease.
2. The period of a finance lease tends to be longer, nearly covering the useful life of the equipment.
3. It must give an option to the lessee to purchase the asset at the expiry of the lease at a market purchase price or on a pre-agreed amount.
4. Lessee is responsible for the payment of taxes and insurance.
5. Lessee bears the cost of maintenance and repairs of the asset leased.
6. It provides the lease an option of renewing the lease for a further period for a nominal rent.
7. The cost of the asset and other expenses of the leasing company will be amortized during the period of the lease.

16.16 Operating Lease

An operating lease stands in contrast to the financial lease in almost all aspects. Operating lease is generally a short period lease or a period-to-period lease. In most operating leases, the term of the initial lease agreement is significantly shorter than the economic life of the property. An operating lease runs for less than the full economic life of the asset, and the lessee is not liable for the financing of its full value. In this type of lease, the lessee gets the asset for use sometimes along with other services. The lessor is responsible for the upkeep and maintenance of the asset. Operating lease has an option for revocation by serving a short notice and return of the asset leased before the expiry of the basic leasing agreement. An operating lease does not transfer the risk and benefits of ownership to the lessee. The lessor, as owner of the property, retains legal title. The lessor carries the risk associated with the residual value of the asset at the end of the lease.

An operating lease runs for less than the full economic life of the asset, and hence the cost of the asset and other expenses of the leasing company will not be amortized during the period of a lease. The lessee usually has an option of renewing the lease after the expiry of the lease period. But the lessor retains the right to the property's residual value at the end of the term. As it is for a short-term period, it implies higher risk to the lessor but the lease rentals will be higher. An operating lease is otherwise called service or true leasing.

16.16.1 Characteristics of Operating Lease: An operating lease has the following characteristics:

1. It is for a short period lease.
2. The lease usually runs for less than the full economic life of the asset.
3. An operating lease does not transfer the risk and benefits of ownership to the lessee.
4. Lessor is responsible for the payment of taxes, insurance, and cost of maintenance and repairs of the asset leased.
5. The lease agreement contains an option for cancellation by the lessee prior to its expiration by serving a short notice.
6. The lessor, as owner of the property, retains legal title.
7. The lessee is not given any support to purchase the asset at the end of the lease period.

Operating leases are particularly attractive to companies that frequently update or replace equipment and want to use equipment without ownership. An operating lease usually results in the lowest payment of any financing alternative and is an excellent strategy for by-passing capital budgeting restraints. Operating lease results in improved return on asset to an enterprise due to lower asset base. This type of lease is often used when the asset is likely to have a resale value and the rate of obsolescence is very high such as mines, computer hardware, communication equipments, aircraft and vehicles.

16.17 Difference between Financial Lease and Operating Lease

A financial lease differs from an operating lease in the following respects:

1. In a finance lease, the lessee uses the asset over most of its economic life. In an operating lease, the lessee only uses the asset for some of the asset's life.
2. In a finance lease, the lessor will recover all or most of the cost of the

equipment from the rentals paid by the lessee. In an operating lease, the lessor will have a substantial investment or residual value on completion of the lease.

3. Financial lease contains purchase option whereas operating lease does not contain such an option.
4. In a financial lease, the lessee is responsible for the upkeep and maintenance of the asset, whereas in operating lease the lessor is responsible for the upkeep and maintenance of the asset leased.
5. In a financial lease, the lessee selects the asset whereas in operating lease the lessor selects the asset.
6. The risk of obsolescence of the asset leased is assumed by the lessee in the case of financial lease. In operating lease the risk of obsolescence is assumed by the lessor.
7. A financial lease is a non-cancellable lease. An operating lease is generally cancellable.
8. A financial lease is a long-period lease whereas operating lease is short period lease.
9. In a finance lease, the lessee has the benefits and risks of economic ownership of the asset (e.g. risk of obsolescence, paying for maintenance, claiming allowances\depreciation). In an operating lease, the lessor has both the benefits and risks of owning the asset.

16.18 Direct Lease

It is a form of leasing under which a firm acquires the right to use an asset that it does not own previously. Under direct leasing, a firm acquires the right to use an asset from the manufacturer directly. A direct leasing may be arranged either from the manufacturer directly or through a leasing company. If the manufacturer leases the asset, then the manufacturer and the lessor are the same. The ownership of the asset leased out remains with the manufacturer itself. The major types of direct lessor include manufacturers, finance companies, independent lease companies, special purpose leasing companies etc. The lessor carries the risk associated with the residual value of the asset at the end of the lease.

16.19 Leveraged Lease

Leveraged lease is a specialized form of direct lease under which the lessor borrows funds for purchasing an asset from a third party usually a bank or a finance company (long-term lenders). In this type of lease, the lessor who purchases the property provides only a percentage (usually 20 to 40 percent) of the capital needed and the lender provides the balance on a non recourse debt basis. The asset or equipment so purchased is held as security against the loan. In this type of lease, the lessor acts as the owner of the asset as well as the borrower of loans from institutions.

Under leveraged leasing arrangement, besides lessor and lessee a third party is also involved. This type of lease thus involves at least three parties (a) a lessee, (b) a lessor and (c) long-term creditor or lender (the debt participant).

The borrowing is secured by a first lien on the property, assignment of the lease, and assignment of the lease rental payments. The lessor retains the residual value rights to the property at the end of the lease period. The lender is paid off from the lease rentals directly by the lessee and the surplus after meeting the claims of the lender goes to the lessor. The lessor who is the owner of the asset is entitled to depreciation allowance associated with the asset.

When the purchase price of the property is large, a leveraged lease may involve several lessors and debt participants. In such cases, an owner trustee generally holds title to the property and represents the lessors. Or an indenture trustee may hold the mortgage on the property on behalf of the debt participants.

This type of lease transaction is complex because of its size, the number of parties involved, legal demands, and the unique advantages to all parties. Because of the legal expenses and administrative costs involved, leveraged leasing usually finances only large capital property projects.

16.20 Sale and Lease Back

It is a sub-part of finance lease. Under this, the owner of an asset sells the asset to a party (the buyer), who in turn leases back the same asset to the owner in consideration of lease rentals. The seller gets the agreed selling price and the buyer gets the lease rentals. Under this transaction, the seller assumes the role of a lessee and the buyer assumes the role of a lessor. Repairs and maintenance cost, insurance etc. of the asset leased have to be born by lessee.

An important advantage of this type of leasing arrangement is that it enables a firm to receive cash from the sale of the asset which can be used for other purposes. It also enables the seller to retain the possession and economic use of the asset in consideration of periodic lease rentals. Another advantage of this method is that the lessee can satisfy himself completely regarding the quality of the asset and after possession of the asset convert the sale into a lease arrangement. Sale and lease back transaction is suitable for those assets, which are not subjected to depreciation but only to appreciation, i.e. land.

16.21 First Amendment Lease

The first amendment lease gives the lessee a purchase option at one or more defined points with a requirement that the lessee renew or continue the lease if the purchase option is not exercised. The option price is usually either a fixed price which is equivalent to approximate fair market value.

If the purchase option is not exercised, then the lease is automatically renewed for a fixed term (typically 1 or 2 years) at a fixed rental intended to approximate fair rental value, which will further reduce the lessor's end-of-term residual position. The lessee is not permitted to return the equipment on the option exercise date. If the lease is automatically renewed, then at the expiration of that initial renewal term, the lessee typically has the right either to return the equipment without penalty or to renew or purchase at fair market value.

16.22 Other Types of Lease

1. **Open-end Lease:** It is a conditional sale lease in which the lessee guarantees that the lessor will realize a minimum value from the sale of the asset at the end of the lease.
2. **Straight Lease:** Under straight lease, the lessor does not allow any modifications to the terms and conditions contained in the basic or original lease agreement. In straight lease, the lessee is required to pay lease rentals to the lessor over the estimated life of the equipment leased.
3. **Modified Lease:** During the period of the lease, if the lessor provides different options to the lessee for the modification of the basic lease agreement, such a lease is termed as modified lease.
4. **Domestic Lease:** Different parties involved in the lease contract are lessee, lessor and the equipment supplier or manufacturer. If these three parties are residing in the same country, then the lease agreement is considered as a domestic lease.
5. **International Lease:** When the lessor, lessee and the equipment supplier involved in the lease contract are residents of different countries, it is said to be an international lease. International lease may either be Cross Border Lease, Import Lease or Foreign to Foreign Lease.
6. **Cross Border Lease:** Cross border lease is a type of international lease. The lessor, supplying the equipment is domiciled in one country and the lessee is domiciled in another country. Such lease is considered as a cross border lease.
7. **Import Lease:** In this type of lease, both the lessor and lessee are residents of the same country but the equipment supplier belongs to a foreign country.
8. **Foreign to Foreign Lease:** In this type of lease there are three parties, the manufacturer residing in one country, lessor who belongs to another country and the lessee who belongs to a third country.
9. **Net Lease:** Net lease is a lease wherein payments to the lessor do not include insurance and maintenance. The lessee pays insurance, taxes, repairs and

maintenance relating to the asset leased separately.

10. **Synthetic Lease:** A synthetic lease is basically a financing structured lease for accounting purposes. Corporations that seek off-balance sheet reporting of their asset-based financing and who efficiently use the tax benefits of owning the financed asset use this structure.
11. **In-house Lease:** When an industrial house promotes a leasing company for the benefit of companies in the same group, that company is known as in-house leasing company. The in-house leasing company leases various assets or equipments to their sister group concerns. Instead of entering a lease agreement with an outside lessor, one or more of the group companies can obtain assets on lease basis from the in-house leasing company. Group companies can reduce the amount of taxable income by charging periodic lease rentals in their books of accounts. The in-house company which is the owner of the asset is entitled to the depreciation allowances associated with the asset. Thus, in-house leasing is beneficial to both the in-house leasing company and the group companies by way of savings in corporate tax.
12. **Sales-type Lease:** It is a part of finance lease. A sales-type lease is one that is structured so that the lessor (generally a manufacturer or dealer of property) not only obtains interest on income but also recognizes either a profit or a loss on the transaction. In this, type of lease the manufacturer or dealer directly extends the facility of leasing to its customers either by its own subsidiary leasing company or through a third party. It may be useful to see this type of transaction as equivalent to a sale. An agreement between an automobile dealers and a customer is a common sales type lease.
13. **Primary Lease:** Primary lease is otherwise called as front-ended lease. Primary lease is a type of lease in which the leasing company charges higher lease rentals for a fixed period of time (primary period) depending upon the useful economic life of the equipment. Under primary lease, the lessor thus recovers almost the total investment in the leased asset during the primary period itself. The first 5 years are generally called the primary lease period and the extended period is called the secondary lease period. The lease is non-cancellable during the primary lease period, that is, the lessee cannot return the asset.
14. **Secondary Lease:** Secondary lease is also known as back ended lease. If the asset leased is having a useful economic life after the expiry of the contract period (primary period), the lease contract is generally renewed for a further period of time. This is called secondary period. Secondary lease is a type of lease in which the leasing company charges only nominal rentals or 'peppercorn' rate for the secondary period. Thus, the asset will be enjoyed by

the lessee virtually for thc whole of its economic life.

15. **Sub-lease:** It is type of lease in which the lessee grants a sub lease to another person. In sub-lease the leased property is released by the original lessee to a third party. But the lease agreement between the two original parties will remain in effect.
16. **Wet Lease:** A wet lease is any leasing arrangement whereby a company agrees to provide an aircraft and at least one pilot to another company. 'Dry lease' on the other hand, refers to leasing only the aircraft.

16.23 Difference between Lease Financing and Bank Loan

Leasing and bank loan are the two different sources of finance available for acquisition of fixed assets. The comparative advantages of lease financing for an equipment loan from bank are given below:

1. Lease is a fixed rate financing. Lease rentals remain the same for the full term of the lease. Banks usually charge floating rates for equipment loans. Therefore, interest on loan will fluctuate frequently as prime lending rate changes.
2. Lease agreements are free from covenant restrictions and leasing procedures are simple and easy. Dealing with bank for an equipment loan requires several formalities and there is considerable delay in sanction of loans.
3. Lease offers 100 percent financing and may also finance the other expenses associated with the purchase of equipment. The lessee is not to provide or pay any margin money, as there is no down payment. Banks often require down payments of 20 percent to 30 percent or more and may limit terms to 36 months or less with floating rates.
4. Lease does not require any mortgage of assets because the ownership of the leased asset remains with the lessor and is not transferred to the lessee whereas a bank loan for the purchase of an asset, the bank insists upon the borrower to pledge the asset purchased as well as other assets as collateral security.
5. The term and frequency of lease payments can be tailored to suit the lessees own unique business requirements. Banks in general are not set up for step payments, delayed start payments or other unique structures.
6. Lease does not affect the borrowing capacity of the lessee. By leasing equipment, if structured properly, the lessee can maintain their credit worthiness, as the lease debt is not considered as a direct liability in the financial statements. An equipment loan from bank may limit the ability of the lessee to access working capital or other required finance from other lending sources.

16.24 Advantages of Leasing

There are several advantages of acquiring equipments or assets on lease:

1. **Saving of Capital:** Leasing covers the full cost of the equipment used in the business by providing 100 percent finance. The lessee is not to provide or pay any margin money, as there is no down payment. In this way the savings in capital or financial resources can be used for other productive purposes e.g. purchase of inventories.
2. **Flexibility:** The term and frequency of payments can be tailor made to the companies own unique business requirements. In a leasing agreement, it is easy to determine as to who will be responsible for the maintenance and servicing, how payments are to be arranged, how long the leased object will be available and how it will be further utilized at the end of the agreement period.
3. **Easy and Convenient Source of Finance:** Leasing is a convenient source of finance for the acquisition of fixed assets. Unlike the dealings with banks for loans and other alternative types of financing (equity and debt financing), leasing procedures are simple, easy and hassle-free.
4. **Lack of Restrictions:** Lease agreement is free from covenant restrictions and regulations that are generally associated with bank loans and debt financing. Leasing does not require any mortgage of assets because the ownership of the asset leased remains with the lessor and not transferred to the lessee.
5. **Leasing Provides Fixed Rate Financing:** Leasing is not subject to market fluctuations and interest rate increases. Lease rentals are not related to the success of the business. Therefore, no matter how well or not the business performs, the lease rate never changes.
6. **Leasing is a Hedge against Inflations:** Leasing is inflation-friendly. As the costs increase over the years, the lessee has to pay the same rate as and when the lease begins.
7. **Leasing Provides Options:** Leasing provides flexible end of lease options. Equipment at the end of the lease term can be returned, extended or purchased. There is a typical option to buy the equipment at the end of lease.
8. **Liquidity Advantage:** Since the leasing company is responsible for financing the capital investment, there will be no loss of liquidity.
9. **Leasing Facilitates Upgrading:** Leasing helps to maintain competitive edge by making possible equipment upgrades at any time. As new equipments become available, the lessee can upgrade or replace to the latest models of the same each time the lease ends.
10. **Leasing Increases Purchasing Power:** Leasing is an intermediate and long-term finance, which does not affect the borrowing capacity of the lessee. By

leasing equipment, if structured properly, the lessee can maintain their credit worthiness as the lease debt is not considered as a direct liability in the financial statements. This is advantageous, as it does not constrain the ability of the lessee to borrow from other lending sources.

11. **Leasing is a Good Strategy for By-Passing Capital Budget Constraints:** Leasing usually results in the lowest payment of any financing alternative and is an excellent strategy for bypassing capital budgeting restraints.
12. **Balance Sheet Advantage:** Since the lessor is the legal owner of the leased property and carries it on his balance sheet, the lessee does not incur a balance sheet extension. It is a hidden form of debt in the balance sheet of the lessee. This has positive effects on the debt equity ratio and is very important from the Basel II point of view.
13. **Ease of Budgeting:** When lease payments are fixed over the term of the lease, budgeting of cash flow is made very much easier.
14. **Planning Cash Flows Properly:** Leasing enables the lessee to plan his\her cash flows properly. The rentals can be paid out of the cash coming into the business from the use of the same assets.
15. **Tax Advantage:** While subject to regulatory guidelines, lease payments may be tax deductible. Leasing provides tax advantages to the lessee. Leasing instalments are considered as revenue expenditure and it will be able to deduct its lease payments from its taxable income immediately rather than deducting the cost of purchasing equipment as depreciation over time. The lessee can also arrange with the lessor to adjust lease rentals in such a way as to reduce the tax liability and thus can help him to plan tax payments.
16. **Supplementary Benefit:** Leasing companies offer many supplementary benefits such as maintenance, insurance, tax, fixed and floating rates etc.
17. **Avoidance of Upfront Cash Outlay:** Another important advantage of leasing is that it provides an alternative to ownership. Leasing facilitates the lessee to acquire the use of the asset without making an upfront cash outlay.
18. **High Return on Asset:** Since the leased items typically qualify for off-balance sheet treatment, it can result in improved return on assets due to a lower asset base.
19. **Avoidance of Risk of Obsolescence:** The lessee can easily shift the risk of obsolescence upon the lessor by acquiring the use of the asset on lease rather than buying the asset.
20. **Option for Purchase of Assets:** There is typically an option in financial lease to purchase the equipment at a substantially reduced cost at the end of the lease period.
21. **Leasing Conserve Working Capital:** Capital acquisitions reduce a

company's working capital. However, acquisition of assets through leasing conserves working capital, which can be used for other purposes.

16.25 Disadvantage of Leasing to the Lessee

Following are the shortcomings of lease financing to the lessee:

1. Interest cost of lease financing is generally higher than debt financing.
2. Lessee has generally no freedom to make substantial changes in the asset leased.
3. Typically, leases may not be terminated before the original term of the lease. Therefore, the lessee is responsible for paying off the lease. This can pose a major financial problem for the owners of a business when they experience an encounter in their business.
4. Even if the interest rate in the economy falls lease rentals remains fixed.
5. As the lessee does not become the owner of the asset, he is not eligible for depreciation and investment allowance.
6. Although lessee is not the owner, lessee is responsible for maintaining the equipment as specified by the terms of the lease. Failure to do so can prove costly.
7. Lessee is also responsible for the payment of miscellaneous expenses of the asset leased.
8. As the lessee does not become the owner of the asset, he loses the advantage of a potential capital gain in the case of certain assets such as land etc.
9. As the lessee does not become the owner of the asset, he cannot realize the salvage value at the expiry of the lease.
10. Leasing is a preferred means of financing for certain businesses. However, it is not for everyone.

16.26 Advantages to the Lessor

Compared to lessee, lease financing also benefits the lessor in several ways:

1. Lessor is able to acquire equipments at a low cost, liquidate it efficiently and can opt for acceptable financing terms. These advantages originate from various economies of scale, such as increased buying power of the sellers of equipments.
2. Lessor is better positioned to take advantage of certain tax laws, depreciation allowances, investment allowance etc.
3. In the case of in-house leasing, both in-house leasing company and the group companies are benefited by way of savings in corporate tax.
4. A shrewd lessor can make handsome profits by leasing of the asset.
5. The lessor gets return on investment in the form of lease rentals from the very

first year of investment.

6. During an inflation period when the demand for the property increases lessor may be benefited by way of potential capital gain.
7. In the case of captive leasing companies, lease financing helps them to increase sales of their parent companies.

16.27 Disadvantages of Leasing to the Lessor

Following are the disadvantages of leasing to the lessor:

1. If the lessee is not able to honour the obligations of the lease, the lessor usually suffer a loss.
2. Leasing is not subject to market fluctuations and interest rate increases. There is no provision in the lease agreement for enhancing the lease rentals in accordance with the increase in interest rates.
3. Problems may arise if the lessee decides to alter the physical shape of the asset leased.
4. The lessor generally carries the risk associated with the residual value of the asset at the end of the lease.
5. Leasing take a long duration period to recover the initial capital outlay.
6. Leasing has become highly competitive business because of the increase in the number of leasing companies.
7. Lease financing requires huge funds, which is often difficult to raise.

16.28 Challenges Facing the Indian Leasing Industry

16.28.1 Shortage of Funds: Most of the leasing companies are not deposit-taking institutions and they carry on their business on the basis of the equity capital that they have raised. The leasing companies have succeeded in raising enough equity capital from the market but have not been successful in raising enough loans from banks or public. Thus many companies are in trouble because of lack of enough funds and inability of management to raise funds.

16.28.2 Unhealthy Competition: Leasing companies are facing strong competition mainly from the banking sector. Bank subsidiaries and financial institutions have the competitive edge over the private sector concerns because of cheap source of finance. The leasing market has not developed commensurate with the growth of leasing companies. As a result, there has been an excess supply and low demand. This has led to severe competition and many of the leasing companies have closed down.

16.28.3 Lack of Trained Employees: Leasing is a specialized branch of financing and the managerial personnel should be expert in accounts, financial and legal matters and decision making must be sound. There has been a dearth of employees trained in leasing business. Most of the managers were not familiar with the workings of leasing business, which has created number of complicated problems.

16.28.4 Eroding Tax Benefits: The attitude of the government on tax benefits of leasing is not encouraging. Most people believe that lessees prefer leasing because of the tax benefits it offers. The lease becomes economically viable only when the transfer's effective tax rate is low. In addition, taxes like sales tax, wealth tax, additional tax, surcharge etc. add to the cost of leasing. Thus leasing becomes more expensive form of financing than conventional mode of finance such as hire purchase.

16.28.5 Inefficiency of Management: In India, the concept of leasing is of recent one and hence it is difficult to get right man to deal with leasing business. In many leasing companies the persons constituting the top management should not have enough knowledge of leasing business. On account of this, operations of leasing business are bound to suffer.

16.28.6 Delayed Payment and Bad Debts: The problem of delayed payment of rents and bad debts add to the costs of lease. The lessor does not take into consideration this aspect while fixing the rentals at the time of lease agreement. These problems would disturb prospects of leasing business.

Short Answer Type Questions

1. Define leasing.
2. What is lease rent?
3. What do you mean by lease financing?
4. Who is a lessor?
5. What is operating lease?
6. What is international lease?
7. What is direct lease?
8. Name the different types of lessor.
9. What is leverage lease?
10. Who are the parties in a lease agreement?
11. What is financial lease?
12. What is foreign to foreign lease?
13. What is primary lease period?
14. Explain straight lease.
15. What is sale and lease back?
16. What is meant by cross boarder lease?
17. What is in-house lease?
18. What is sub-lease?

19. What are peppercorn rentals?
20. What is wet lease?

Essay Type Questions

1. Define lease. What are the essential features of a lease agreement?
2. What is financial lease? What are the important features of financial lease?
3. Explain the functions of management of lease.
4. Explain the major types of leases in India.
5. State the benefits of leasing to the lessor?
6. What are the differences between lease financing and a bank loan?
7. Explain briefly the problems faced by leasing industries in India.
8. Define lease financing. What are its advantages to the lessee?
9. What is operating lease? What are the important characteristics of operating lease?
10. Differentiate between financial lease and operating lease.
11. What is cross boarder leasing? Explain its structure.
12. Explain the steps involved in the mechanism of leasing.
13. What are the disadvantages and disadvantages of leasing to the lessee?

17

Hire Purchase Companies

17.1 Introduction

The most common method of selling goods or property is the cash sales. The credit sale system is an alternative method of cash sale. The third system of selling goods is the instalment system. In instalment system, property is delivered to the buyer immediately but payment is made in periodic instalments such as monthly, half yearly or yearly. Hire purchase and Instalment purchase systems are two major parts of the instalment system.

17.2 Meaning of Hire Purchase

Hire purchase system allows a consumer to have the use of an asset before paying the full price. Hire purchase is a type of instalment credit under which the hire purchaser, called the hirer, agrees to take the goods on hire at a stated rental, which is inclusive of the repayment of principal as well as interest.

Under a hire purchase transaction, the hire purchaser acquires the property (goods) immediately on signing the hire purchase agreement but the ownership or title of the same is transferred only when the last instalment of hire is paid. The buyer gets the facility of paying the amount in instalments under this system and the seller is able to sell more goods under this system with the added security to repossess the goods in case the buyer makes any default in the payment of any instalments. This system is used mainly by small-scale firms and individuals who indented to acquire industrial machinery, office equipment, vehicles, etc., without making full payment.

17.3 Definition of Hire Purchase

The Hire Purchase Act of 1972 regulates the hire purchase system. Hire Purchase Act of 1972 defines a hire purchase as "an agreement under which goods are let on hire and under which the hirer has an option to purchase them in accordance with the terms of the agreement and includes an agreement under which:

1. Possession of the goods is delivered by the owner thereof to a person on condition that such person can pay the agreed amount in periodical instalments.

2. The property in the goods is to be passed to such person on the payment of the last of such instalments.
3. Such person can terminate the agreement at any time before the property so passes".

17.4 Origin and Development of Hire Purchase

Hire purchase is the legal term for a contract developed in the United Kingdom. The idea of hire purchase was developed in nineteenth century in United Kingdom by wagon companies as a means of enabling carriers to purchase wagons for use in their business. The wagon companies purchase the wagons and then let them out to collieries under hire purchase agreement. The hire purchase system was introduced first by Henry Moore, a piano maker in 1846. Later the Singer Manufacturing Company started selling sewing machines under hire purchase system. The Murphy radio dealers also started instalment facilities on hire-purchase basis to the customers of their products. Hire purchase system developed in the United Kingdom can also found in many countries like China, Japan, Malaysia, Australia, New Zealand etc.

The British concept of hire-purchase has, however, been there in India for more than 9 decades. The first hire/purchase companies in India were the Commercial Credit Corporation Ltd. and Motor and General Finance Ltd. which were set up to finance the transport sector. Commercial Credit Corporation Ltd. was based in Madras, where as Motor and General Finance and Instalment Supply Company was set up in North India. These companies were set up in the 1920s and 1930s.

With an increasing demand for better life, the consumption of property has been on the uprising scale. This has created the market for hire purchase system. Presently hire purchase transactions are done on a large scale by finance companies. Certain private banks and foreign banks have also entered this field through establishment of subsidiaries. Hire purchase is a preferred transaction for banks as it is a superior method than hypothecation. Banks are better placed in recovery of vehicle advances and borrowers would be benefited as more credit would be made available

17.5 Salient Feature of Hire Purchase System

The main characteristics of the hire purchase system are given below:

1. Like outright sale the buyer acquires the possession of the asset/equipments from the supplier immediately on payment of the first instalment.
2. The ownership of the asset remains with the seller till the payment of the last instalment.

3. The hirer is required to pay the value of the asset in instalments over a specified period of time.
4. The instalments are generally payable monthly in advance.
5. The ownership of the asset is transferred after the hirer has paid the last instalment.
6. When all instalments are paid, the seller has no right to repossess the property from the purchaser.
7. Each instalment will be treated as hire so that if default is made in the payment of even the last instalment the seller will be entitled to take back the goods without compensating the hire purchaser.
8. The terms and conditions relating to the usage of the asset, namely its maintenance insurance etc and the rights and obligations of the parties to the agreement are described in the hire purchase agreement.

17.6 Parties Involved in Hire Purchase System

Two parties are involved mainly in the hire purchase agreement. They are the following:

17.6.1 Hire Vendor: Hire vendor means the person who lets or delivers the possession of goods, to a hirer under a hire-purchase agreement and includes a person to whom the owner's property in the goods or any of the owner's rights or liabilities under the agreement has passed by assignment or by operation of law. Hire vendor is the manufacturer or retailer or owner who sells property to the hirer.

17.6.2 Hirer: Hirer means the person who obtained possession of goods from an owner under a hire purchase agreement. The hirer or hire purchaser is the buyer or customer who buys the asset or property.

17.7 Contents of Hire Purchase Agreement

Hire-purchase agreement means an agreement under which goods are let on hire and under which the hirer has an option to purchase them in accordance with the terms of the agreement. Hire purchase agreement set forth all the terms and conditions of the hire purchase. Hire purchase agreement must be in writing and signed by both parties. They must clearly set out the following information's:

1. Name and address of the both the hirer and the owner of the asset.
2. Clear description of the asset.
3. The hire-purchase price of the asset to which the agreement relates.
4. Cash price of the asset.
5. The date on which the agreement shall be deemed to have commenced.
6. Amount and date of monthly instalment and the number of instalments by

which the hire purchase price is to be paid.
7. A comprehensive statement of the parties' rights (sometimes including the right to cancel the agreement during a "cooling-off" period).
8. The right of the hirer to terminate the contract when he feels like doing so with a valid reason.

17.8 Mechanism in Hire Purchasing

Hire purchasing system involves the following procedures:

A hire purchase is an agreement drawn up and signed by the hirer and lending institution. It is an agreement whereby a buyer hires property for a period by paying instalments and can own the property after the payment of all instalments. Manufacturers or retailers often have an agreement with a finance company to provide the hire purchase finance. In such a case, a hirer makes the payments to the finance company not to the manufacturer or retailer. The name of the finance company will be included on the hire purchase agreement. As soon as the contract is signed, the hirer acquires possession of the property and therewith the right to use the property over an agreed period. However, the ownership of the property remains with the finance company until the hirer pays all instalments. Each instalment paid by the hirer is treated as hire charges for using the property or assets.

In case the hirer fails to pay any of the instalments, even the last one, the vendor or finance company takes back the hired property without any compensation to the hirer. This act of recovery of possession of the asset is termed as 'repossession of asset'. The repossessed assets are ultimately sold to other customers after repairing or reconditioning, if necessary. Then the hirer is called upon defaulter. The amounts received from the defaulter through down payment and instalments are treated as the hire charges by the vendor. The hirer, vendor or finance company may have the power to terminate the hire purchase agreement at any time on the non-compliance of the terms and condition of the agreement by any parties.

A guarantee under a hire purchase agreement applies in the same way as if property were bought outright. The manufacturer makes the guarantee. If there is a fault with the property, the hirer can choose to have the property repaired under the guarantee or to seek a full refund or exchange from the owner. The hire purchaser during that period when he is in possession of the goods, can not damage, destroy, pledge or sell such goods. In other words, the hirer has a duty to take reasonable care of the hired property. The vendor or finance company entitles to the cost of repairs if the property is damaged by the hirer and returned to the vendor or finance company.

17.9 Warranties to be Implied in Hire Purchase Agreement

Every hire purchase agreement usually contains warranties and certain implied conditions which are stated below:

1. The hirer will be allowed to enjoy the possession of the goods and no one will interfere with the hirer's possession during the period of the contract.
2. The properties will be free from any charge or encumbrance in favour of third parties.
3. The owner will be able to pass the ownership of the goods when the contract requires it.
4. An implied condition on the part of the owner that he has a right to sell the goods at the time when the property is to pass.
5. The goods are of merchantable quality and fit for their purpose.
6. Where the goods are let under a hire-purchase agreement by reference to a sample there shall be an implied condition on the part of the owner that:

- The bulk will correspond with the sample in quality, and
- The hirer will have a reasonable opportunity of comparing the bulk with the sample.

17.10 Rights of Hirer

The hirer usually has the following rights:

1. To buy the goods at any time by giving notice to the owner and paying the balance of the hire purchase price less a rebate.
2. To return the goods to the owner. The return of goods is subject to the payment of a penalty to reflect the owner's loss of profit but subject to a maximum specified in each jurisdiction's law to strike a balance between the need for the buyer to minimize liability and the fact that the owner now has possession of an obsolescent asset of reduced value.
3. With the consent of the owner, to assign both the benefit and the burden of the contract to a third person. The owner cannot unreasonably refuse consent where the nominated third party has good credit rating.
4. Where the owner wrongfully repossesses the goods, either to recover the goods plus damages for loss of quiet possession or to damages representing the value of the goods lost.

17.11 General Obligations of Hirer

The hirer usually has the following obligations:

- To pay the hire instalments.
- To take reasonable care of the goods.
- To inform the owner where the goods will be kept.

17.12 Obligation of Hirer in Respect of Care to be Taken of Goods

A hirer in the absence of a contract to the contrary shall be bound to take as much care of the goods to which the hire-purchase agreement relates as a man of ordinary prudence would, under similar circumstances, take of his own goods of the same bulk, quality and value shall not be responsible for the loss, destruction or deterioration of the goods. If the hirer damages the goods by using them in a non-standard way, he or she must continue to pay the instalments and, if appropriate, compensate the owner for any damage caused by failure to take care of the goods.

17.13 Obligation of Hirer in Respect of Use of Goods

If the hirer makes any use of the goods to which the hire-purchase agreement relates which is not according to the conditions of the agreement, the hirer shall be liable to make compensation to the owner for any damage arising to the goods from or during such use.

17.14 Right to Hirer to Terminate Agreement at any Time

The hirer may, at any time before the final payment under the hirer-purchase agreement falls due, and after giving the owner not less than fourteen days, notice in writing of his intentions so to do and re-delivering or tendering the goods to the owner, terminate the hire-purchase agreement by payment or tender to the owner of the amounts which have accrued due towards the hire-purchase price and not been paid by him, including the sum, if any, which he is liable to pay. Where the hirer terminates the agreement and the agreement provides for the payment of a sum named on account of such termination, the liability of the hirer to pay that sum shall be subject to the following conditions, namely:

"Where the sum total of the amounts paid and the amounts due in respect of the hire-purchase price immediately before the termination exceeds one-half of the hire-purchase price, the hirer shall be liable to pay the difference between the said sum total and the said one-half, or the sum named in the agreement whichever, is less".

17.15 Rights of the Owner of the Asset

The owner of the asset has the following rights:

1. The owner has the right to terminate the agreement where the hirer defaults in paying the instalments or breaches any of the other terms in the agreement.
2. In case of termination of agreement the owner has the right to forfeit the amount deposit by the hirer.
3. The owner has the right to retain the instalments already paid and recover the

balance due.

4. The owner has the right to repossess the goods.
5. The owner has the right to claim damages for any loss suffered.

17.16 Rights of the Owner to Terminate the Agreement

Where a hire purchaser makes more than one default in the payment of instalment as provided in the hire-purchase agreement, the owner shall be entitled to terminate the agreement by giving the hirer notice of termination in writing of not less than one week, in a case where the hire is payable at weekly or lesser intervals, and two weeks in any other cases. Provided that if the hirer pays or tenders to the owner the hire in arrears together with such interest thereon as may be payable under the terms of the agreement before the expiry of the said period of one week or, as the case may be, two weeks, the owner shall not be entitled to terminate the agreement.

17.17 Rights of Owner of Terminated Agreement

Where a hire-purchase agreement is terminated under the Hire Purchase Act, then the owner shall be entitled to the following rights:

1. Right to retain the hire which has already been paid and to recover the arrears of hire due.
2. Right to forfeit the initial deposit, if so provided in the agreements.
3. Right to enter the premises of the hirer and seize the goods.
4. Right to recover possession of the goods or by suit.
5. Right to claim damages for non-delivery of the goods, from the date on which termination is effective, to the date on which the goods are delivered to or seized by the owner.

17.18 Difference between Credit Sale and Hire Purchase

Hire purchase is a form of credit sale. But hire purchase is different from credit sale that in case of credit sale both ownership and possession of the goods is transferred immediately to the buyer. Where as in hire purchase system only the possession of the goods is transferred immediately but the ownership remains with the seller until the payment of last instalment.

17.19 Difference between Lease Financing and Hire Purchase

Hire purchase is of British origin. Where as leasing is essentially a US-innovation, entered the country significantly in the early 80s, and was propagated as an alternative to traditional modes of industrial finance. Hire purchase system originated much before leases became popular. Both lease and hire purchase provide a source for financing of assets. The assets usually subject matter of hire-purchase has been different from those generally leased out. Leasing has been used mostly for plant and machinery, while hire-purchase has commonly been used for vehicles, consumable durables etc.

The objectives of both hire purchase and leasing are almost the same but the workings of the two systems are entirely different. The following are the differences extracted from the point of view of the lessee and the hirer:

1. A lease transaction is a commercial arrangement, whereby an equipment owner or manufacturer conveys to the equipment user the right to use the equipment in return for a rental. Hire purchase is a type of instalment credit under which the hire purchaser agrees to take the goods on hire at a stated rental, which is inclusive of the repayment of principal as well as interest, with an option to purchase.
2. Lease rentals paid by the lessee are entirely revenue expenditure of the lessee. Only interest element included in the hire purchase instalments is revenue expenditure by nature.
3. Lease rentals consist of two elements (i) finance charge and (ii) capital recovery. Hire purchase instalments comprise three elements (i) normal trading profit (ii) finance charge and (iii) recovery of cost of goods/assets.
4. Under lease financing, generally there is no option to the lessee (user) to purchase the goods. However, in financial lease there is an option to purchase the equipment at a substantially lesser price at the end of the term of the lease whereas in hire purchase system, the ownership is transferred to the hirer on payment of the last instalment.
5. Lessee can not realize salvage value of the asset on expiry of the lease agreement or at the expiry of the life of the asset. However, hirer can realize the salvage value of the asset after payment of the last instalment and at the expiry of the life of the asset.
6. In lease financing depreciation on assets is not claimed by the lessee. However, in hire purchase system, the hirer can claim depreciation on asset purchased on hire purchase basis.
7. Under hire purchase system, the hire-purchaser is required to pay an amount (down payment), which is part of the hire purchase price at the time of signing of the contract. In the case of lease transaction, there is no such down payment.

17.20 Instalment System

Hire purchase should be distinguished from instalment system. Under the instalment system, the possession as well as ownership passes from the seller to the buyer immediately on payment of the first instalment. But in case of hire purchase (ownership remains with the seller until the last instalment is paid) buyer gets ownership after paying the last instalment. In instalment system if the buyer makes any default in the payment of any instalment, the seller has no right to repossess the goods.

17.21 Differences between Hire Purchase and Instalment System

The main differences between hire purchase and instalment system are the following:

1. Hire purchase is an agreement of hiring whereas instalment purchase system is an agreement of sale.
2. The two parties involved in hire purchase system are called hire purchaser and hire vendor whereas in instalment system the parties involved are called buyer and seller.
3. In hire purchase system the relation between hire purchaser and hire vendor is that of a bailee and bailor. Instalment system is a contract of sale and hence no bailment is involved.
4. In hire purchase system until the payment of the last instalment the hire purchaser has no right of disposal of goods. In instalment system the buyer can dispose of the goods as he likes.
5. In hire purchase system only the possession of the goods is transferred and not the ownership on payment of the first instalment. Under the instalment system, the possession as well as ownership passes from the seller to the buyer immediately on payment of the first instalment.
6. If the hire purchaser makes default in payment of instalments the hire vendor has the right to repossess the goods. On repossession, the hire vendor may not be required to refund part of money received by him. In the case of instalment system, the property in the goods passes to the purchaser immediately after the contract is signed and, if a default is made in the payment the remedy open to the seller is to sue the purchaser for payment of the instalments due and not to take possession of the goods.
7. The hire purchaser can terminate the hire purchase contract at any time after giving 14 days notice and returning the goods. Hire purchaser is free to return the goods without having to pay the instalments falling due after the return. In instalment system the buyer can not terminate the contract and escape the liability of the payment of the remaining instalments.
8. In hire purchase the hire purchaser has to take much care of the goods but he is not responsible for the loss of the goods. In instalment system as the buyer becomes the owner of the goods, any loss of goods will have to be born by the buyer.

Short Answer Type Questions

1. What do mean by hire purchase system?
2. Define hire purchase.
3. Who is hire vendor?
4. Who is hirer?
5. What is instalment system?
6. What are the obligations of hirer's?

Essay Type Questions

1. What is hire purchase system? What are the important characteristics of hire purchase system?
2. What are the differences between hire purchase and instalment system?
3. Differentiate between lease financing and hire purchase system.
4. State the warranties and implied conditions in the hire purchase agreement.
5. Explain the mechanism in hire purchase system.

18

Insurance Organizations

18.1 Introduction

Individual life and business operations are exposed to innumerable risks and accidents. In the case of an individual, he encounters a number of risks like serious ailments leading to indisposition, accidents and consequent disablements, premature and sudden death etc. On account of such and similar happenings, he may lose his income either temporarily or permanently leaving his dependents in the lurch or forcing them to search other means for their survival. In business concerns too, there are risks arising from fire, riots, theft, violence, loss in transit and various natural calamities like flood, earth quake, lightening etc. leading to heavy financial loss to the business. The risks inherent in life and business are varied and uncertain, causing tension, stress and strain and unbearable financial losses of grave consequences. The basic human trait is to be averse to the idea of taking risks. In order to encounter these innumerable risks, insurance has been introduced and it is capable of ensuring protection against almost all types of risks.

18.2 Meaning of Insurance

In legal sense, insurance is a contract between two parties, whereby one party covers the risk by paying a specified amount as premium and in return the other undertakes to indemnify the loss suffered by him. It is a contract of indemnity whereby the insurance company or the underwriter undertakes to indemnify the insured against the loss, which he may suffer in event of an uncertain happening. However, in the case of life insurance it is not strictly a contract of indemnity as it is an absolute undertaking to pay a certain sum of money on the death of the assured or on his attaining a certain age.

The person who covers his/her risks by insurance is called the insured, the person who undertakes to protect the risk is called the insurer, and the amount that is paid to insure the risk is called the premium. The insurer is a risk taker who accepts the risks of others and earns a profit by way of the difference between the total premium collected from the buyers of insurance and the total payment made on account of compensation for losses. Insurance is the means whereby the losses of a few are transferred to many. If a calamity were to be-fall on an individual, it would be difficult for him to bear it and maintain the standard of living or economic well being of his family and business concern. It would also be apparent that such losses and calamities would be far and few in between and would be-fall on only a minority. Thus, by everybody paying a small premium, a common fund can be created out of which losses that happen to the minority can be reimbursed or met.

Insurance thus involves the transfer of potential risk from the individual to a pool of the policyholders of the insurance company. The insurance company charges a fee called premium, for accepting the risk and 'pools' the premiums from a group of policyholders into a general corpus fund to extend the death benefits under contract. The pool combines all the potential losses and then transfers the cost of the predicted losses back to the exposures. Thus, insurance involves the transfer of loss exposures of several entities into a common pool, and the redistribution of the cost of actual losses among the members of the pool.

18.3 Definition of Insurance

In the finance dictionary insurance is defined as "for guarding against property loss or damage making payments in the form of premiums to an insurance company, which pays an agreed-upon sum to the insured in the event of loss". Insurance can be defined "as a social device whereby a large group of individuals who agree to make small contribution in order to reimburse those who suffer losses that may be foreseen and estimated". Wikipedia defines insurance as "the equitable transfer of the risk of a loss, from one entity to another, in exchange for a premium, and can be thought of as a guaranteed small loss to prevent a large, possibly devastating loss".

18.4 General Principles of Insurance

The business of insurance is based on certain basic and general principles. The general principles are the following;

18.4.1 Indemnity: All kinds of insurance except life insurance, personal accident and sickness insurance are based on the principle of indemnity. This means that the insured, in case of loss against which the policy has been issued, shall be paid the actual amount of loss not exceeding the amount of the policy, i.e. he shall be fully indemnified. The object of every contract of insurance is to place the insured in the same financial position, as far as possible, after the loss, as if the loss had not been taken place at all. It would be against public policy to allow an insured to make a profit out of his loss or damage.

The principle of indemnity does not apply to life insurance as it is not possible to place a monetary value upon human life and therefore one cannot determine the extent of the loss suffered by the death of a person. Under life insurance, therefore the sum insured is paid in the event of the death of the person or on the maturity of the policy, as the case may be.

18.4.2 Utmost Good Faith: A contract of insurance is based on the principle of utmost good faith. The principle of utmost good faith implies that the proposer must make a full disclosure of all material facts concerning the insurance. Any fact is material, which goes to the root of the contract of insurance and has a bearing on the risk involved. It is only when the insurer knows the whole truth that he is in a position to judge (a) whether he should accept the risk and (b) what premium he should charge. The withholding of any relevant information or mis-statement of any material fact may give the insurer the legal ground to declare the contract void. In such cases, the insurance company is under no consideration to pay compensation or to refund the amount of premium to the policy holder.

18.4.3 Insurable Interest: Insurable interest is a fundamental principle of insurance. A contract of insurance effected without insurable interest is void. It means that the insured must have an actual pecuniary interest and not a mere anxiety or sentimental interest in the subject matter of the insurance. The insured must be so situated with regard to the thing insured that he should have to be benefited from its existence and lose from its destruction. The following examples will make this point clear. A wife and a husband have insurable interest in each other. The death of husband or wife will result in financial losses. The owner of a ship runs a risk of losing his ship, the charter of the ship runs a risk of losing his freight and the owner of the cargo incurs the risk of losing his goods and profit. So, all these persons have something at stake and all of them have insurable interest. It is the existence of insurable interest in a contract of insurance, which distinguishes it from a mere watering agreement.

18.4.4 Proximate Cause: The rule proximate cause or causa proxima means that the cause of the loss must be proximate or immediate and not remote. If the proximate cause of the loss is a peril insured against, the insured can recover. The doctrine of causa proxima means that where two or more causes operate to produce a loss, only the proximate cause is to be considered and all other causes are to be disregarded. However, if the loss is brought about by any cause attributable to the misconduct of the insured, the insurer is not liable.

18.4.5 Mitigation of Loss: In the event of some mishap to the insured property, the insured must take all necessary steps to mitigate or minimize the loss, just as any prudent person would do in those circumstances. If he does not do so, the insurer can avoid the payment of loss attributable to his negligence. But it must be remembered that though the insured is bound to do his best for his insurer, he is not bound to do so at the risk of his life.

18.4.6 Doctrine of Subrogation: The doctrine of subrogation means that when an insured recovers a claim from an insurance company, he must pass over to the insurer any right of recovery that he may have against a third party. Doctrine of subrogation is a corollary to the principle of indemnity and applies only to fire and marine insurance. It must be clarified here that the insurer's right of subrogation arises only when he has paid for the loss for which he is liable under the policy and this right extend only to the rights and remedies available to the insured in respect of the thing to which the contract of insurance relates. For example a person has insured his property against fire. Through the negligence of a third party a fire arises and the property is damaged, the insurer pays the damage and is entitled to recover from the third party, whose negligence caused the damage. On the other hand, if the insured is allowed to have the insurance money as also to have the benefit of recovery from the third party, the total amount he will get from both the sources would be more than the actual loss suffered by him, and he will therefore make a profit out of his misfortune. This will be against the principle of indemnity. The doctrine of subrogation therefore gives the right of recovery from third party to the insurer so that he may reduce the amount of the loss suffered by him.

18.4.7 Contribution: Where there are two or more insurance on one risk, the principle of contribution comes into play. The aim of contribution is to distribute the actual amount of loss among the different insurers who are liable for the same risk under different policies in respect of the same subject matter. Any one insurer may pay to the insured the full amount of the loss covered by the policy and then become entitled to contribution from his co-insurers in proportion to the amount, which each has undertaken to pay in case of loss of the same subject-matter. In other words, the right of contribution arises when (a) there are different policies which relate to the same subject matter (b) the policies cover the same peril which caused the loss (c) all the policies are in force at the time of the loss, and (d) one of the insurers has paid to the insured more than his share of the loss.

18.4.8 Contract: The Insurance Policy is ultimately a contract and as such general law of contract would be applicable as modified by specific enactments in India such as Stamp Act, Insurance Act, etc. The basic aspects that exist for all contracts would also be relevant here such as:

A. Offer and Acceptance: There should be an offer by one of the parties to the contract with an acceptance by the other party. This is usually embodied by the proposal form and when this is accepted by the Insurer, the policy is issued which forms a valid contract, enforceable by law.

B. Capacity to Contract: Both the parties should be legally competent to enter into the contract. Mentally unsound persons, minors, etc. are generally deemed incapable of entering into a contract.

C. Flow of Consideration: Consideration should flow for both parties. In the insurance policy, the premium payment forms the consideration by the assured and the promise for indemnification, in the event of loss due to an insured peril, it forms the consideration by the Insurer.

D. Absence of Fraud: As in the case of normal contracts which can be rendered void due to any fraud or misrepresentation, the Insurance Policy or contract also would similarly be rendered void in the event of any fraudulent acts by either party. Misrepresentation may make it voidable at the instance of the insured party.

18.5 Functions of Insurance

Following are the important functions of insurance:

18.5.1 Insurance Spreads Risk: The primary function of insurance is to spread the risk to which human life and property are subjected. Insurance is a device to share the financial loss of a few by many. Insurance is the means whereby the losses of a few are transferred to many. All the insured contribute premiums towards a fund and out of which the persons exposed to a particular risk is paid.

18.5.2 Reduces Risk: Another important function of insurance is to provide protection by eliminating or reducing risks. A complete elimination of risk is not possible or feasible. However, it can be reduced by insuring life and goods and properties of human beings against accident, theft, fire and various natural calamities.

18.5.3 Provides Protection Against Risk: The primary function of insurance is to provide protection against future risk, accidents and uncertainty. Insurance can not check the incidence of risk, but can certainly provide for the losses of risk. Insurance is actually a protection against economic loss, by sharing the risk with others. The covering of risk and protection against loss creates a sense of security in the life of the individual as well as the businessman.

18.5.4 Provides Employment Opportunities: Insurance companies provide employment opportunities. A large number of people are directly employed in the insurance industry. It provides employment opportunities to individuals as agents, field officers, development officers, executive staff, lawyers, engineers, actuaries etc. Thus insurance business reduces unemployment problem to a certain extent.

18.5.5 Creates Savings Habit: Insurance creates the savings habit in the people. Policy holders are encouraged to save money and invest. Insurance is a compulsory way of savings and it restricts the unnecessary expenses by the insured.

18.5.6 Provides Benefit to the Community: Insurance is designed in such a way as to provide benefits to the particular individual and the community in general. It provides aid to the dependents of the insured in case of his demise. In the absence of insurance facilities, the dependents of the deceased person may be forced to seek public assistance which will become a burden in the community.

18.5.7 Facilitates Development of the Economy: Insurance helps to mobilize the savings of the people and in doing so, insurance renders a valuable service to the nation. Insurance provides development opportunity to industries by investing the huge amount received as premium for various productive purposes in divergent fields. Such investments cover a wide range of activities and thus a large number of people get its benefits both directly and indirectly. Thus, it performs a very useful function by mobilizing the savings of the people and investing them in productive fields.

18.6 Evolution and Growth of Insurance Business in India

Insurance in its modern form originated in the Mediterranean during the 13th century. The earliest references to insurance have been found in Babylonia and among the Greeks and Romans. Marine insurance is the oldest form of insurance followed by life insurance and fire insurance. India is not new to insurance business. It prevailed in India right from the 19th century i.e. with the arrival of British enterprises in India paving the way for a socio-economic transformation. Insurance in India has gone through two radical transformations. Before 1956, insurance was mainly a private enterprise with minimal government intervention. In 1956, life insurance was nationalized and a monopoly was created. Some of the companies that started later did provide insurance for Indians. As in the case of the history of banking in India, the history of insurance reveals that insurance industry evolved in India after passing through a number of trials and tribulations.

Life insurance in the modern form was first set up in India by a British company known as the Oriental Life Insurance Company in 1818 followed by the Bombay Assurance Company in 1823 and the Madras Equitable Life Insurance Society in 1829. Even though all these companies operated in India they did not insure the lives of Indians. They insured only the lives of Europeans living in India.

The first general insurance company, Triton Insurance Company Ltd., was established in 1850. It was owned and operated by the British. Bombay Mutual Life Assurance Society was the first insurance company established in India, which opened its business in 1870. In 1905 following the Swadeshi Movement, many Indian entrepreneurs established banking and insurance institutions. The Indian Mercantile Insurance Ltd. formed in 1907 is considered as the first company to transact all types of general insurance business in India. Later many insurance companies sprung up like mushrooms. The area of operation of these institutions was confined mainly to cities and urban centres. There were also some banks in the thirties (General Insurance Bank of India Ltd., Mangalore) transacting simultaneously both banking and insurance business. However, the business of these institutions did not survive for long for many reasons. The failure of insurance business was mainly due to lack of control over the business by the government because of the absence of legislative measures. Insurance business was carried on in India without any specific regulation concerning the insurance business. They were subject to Indian Companies Act (1866). In 1912, two sets of legislations were passed:

1. Indian Life Assurance Companies Act.
2. Provident Insurance Societies Act.

There are several striking features in these legislations. First, they were the pioneering legislations in India that specifically targeted the insurance sector. Second, they left general insurance business out of it. The government did not feel the necessity to regulate general insurance. Third, they restricted activities of the Indian insurers but not the foreign insurers even though the model used was the British Act of 1909.

Comprehensive insurance legislation covering both life and non-life business did not materialize for the next twenty-six years. The only significant legislative measure before the Insurance Act of 1938 was the Act of 1928. It enabled the Government of India to collect information on (a) Indian insurance companies operating in India (b) Foreign insurance companies operating in India and (c) Indian insurance companies operating in foreign countries. The last two provisions were missing in the 1912 Insurance Act.

The Indian Assurance Companies Act of 1912 was the first statute meant to regulate the life insurance business in India. However, insurance Act of 1938 was the first wholesome legislation in India intended to control comprehensively the business of insurance companies in India. In 1937, the Government of India set up a consultative committee. Mr. Sushil C. Sen, a well known solicitor of Calcutta, was appointed to chair of the committee. He made wide consultations with all stake holders including the insurance industry. Finally, in 1938, the Insurance Act was passed. This comprehensive legislation was the first of its kind in India. It covered the operations of both life and general insurance companies. It clearly defined as to what would come under the life insurance business, the fire insurance business and so on. It covered matters like deposits, supervision of insurance companies, investments, commission of agents, qualifications of directors appointed by the policyholders among others. This piece of legislation lost its significance after nationalization of insurance business. Life insurance was nationalized in 1956 and general insurance in 1972 respectively. However, the situation changed totally only after the country's independence and through a series of legislative and regulatory measures.

18.7 Insurance Business in India after Independence

The Insurance sector in India was organized as General and Life Insurance with the establishment of the Life Insurance Corporation of India (LIC) and General Insurance Corporation (GIC). LIC was formed after a take over and nationalization of the insurance business of Indian and foreign insurers and provident societies. The Life Insurance Corporation of India was established by an Act of Parliament, which received President's assent on 18th June1956. The Act came into force on 1st July 1956 and the Corporation became functional from 1st September 1956. When the life insurance business was nationalized in 1956, there were 154 Indian life insurance companies. In addition, there were 16 non-Indian insurance companies and 75 provident societies issuing life insurance policies. Most of these policies were of the metropolitan areas like Bombay, Calcutta, Delhi and Madras.

General Insurance Corporation of India (GIC) was established in 1973 after nationalization of general insurance companies in the country. At the time of nationalization, about 100 small companies and a few large companies were operating in the field of general insurance. After nationalization, one holding company named General Insurance Corporation of India (GIC) was set up. Subsequently all the existing companies were merged and reorganized into four subsidiaries of GIC viz. National Insurance Company Ltd., New India Insurance Company Ltd., Oriental Fire and General Insurance Company Ltd., and United India Insurance Company Ltd. These companies used to carry on the business of general insurance in India in a monopolistic manner up to 1999 and in that year the insurance business was thrown opened to private players also thereby creating a level playing field.

General Insurance Company's supervisory role over its erstwhile subsidiaries was terminated by an administrative order and it was re-designated as the "Indian Reinsurer" in 2000 by an Act of Parliament by which it was to function exclusively as Life and non-Life Re-insurer. Subsequently with the General Insurance Business (Nationalization) Amendment Act of 2002, GIC ceased to be a holding company of its subsidiaries and their ownership got vested in Government of India. The insurance industry in India has come a long way since the time when its operations were tightly regulated and concentrated in the hands of a few public sector insurers. Following the passage of the Insurance

Regulatory Development Authority Act in 1999, India abandoned public sector exclusivity in the insurance industry in favour of market-driven competition. This shift has brought about major changes in the industry. The inauguration of a new era of insurance development has seen the entry of international insurers, the proliferation of innovative products and distribution channels, and the raising of supervisory standards.

18.8 Insurance Regulatory and Development Authority (IRDA)

In order to provide better insurance cover to citizens, the government in its budget speech of 1998, pronounced its decision to open up the insurance sector and to set up a statutory Insurance Regulatory and Development Authority (IRDA). IRDA was an offshoot of the recommendations of Malhotra Committee. The Insurance Regulatory and Development Authority Act passed by the Indian Parliament came into force in the year 1999 and it opened the insurance business for the private sector also. IRDA was established with the object of protecting the interests of policyholders and to regulate, promote and ensure orderly growth of the insurance industry and for all other matters connected therewith and incidental thereto. The Insurance Act of 1938, the Life Insurance Corporation Act of 1956, and the General Insurance Business (Nationalization) Act of 1972 were also amended.

The IRDA consist of a chairman and not more than nine members of whom not more than five members are full-time members, to be appointed by the government from among persons of ability, integrity and standing who have knowledge and experience of insurance both life and general business and other related areas viz. actuarial service, finance, economics etc. The IRDA can constitute a 25 member Insurance Advisory Committee (IAC) to give representation to the interests of commerce, industry, transport, agriculture, consumer forum, member surveyors, agents, intermediaries, including brokers, consultants and loss assessors, organizations engaged in safety and loss prevention, research bodies and employees' associations in the insurance sector and to advise it on matters relating to making of its regulations and on such other matters as may be prescribed.

18.8.1 Salient Features of IRDA Act: The salient features of the 1999 IRDA Act are the following;

1. The IRDA Act, 1999, sets out detailed guidelines regarding the registration, renewal of registration, minimum capital requirement, equity and solvency requirement of both life and non-life insurance companies. The minimum capital requirement for direct non-life and life insurance business is ₹ 100 crore.

2. An applicant whose proposal for registration has been rejected should wait for a minimum of two years to make another proposal, which will have to be with a new set of promoters and for a different class of business.
3. For renewal of registration, the Act stipulates a fee of one-fifth of one percent of total gross premiums written direct by an insurer in India during the financial year preceding the renewal year.
4. For renewal of registration they are required to provide a detailed background of each of the key personnel viz. chief executive, chief marketing officer, appointed actuary, chief investment officer, chief of internal audit and chief finance officer. Details of the sales force, activities in rural business and projected values of each line of business are also required.
5. As per IRDA Act all insurers are required to provide some coverage for the rural sector. In respect of a life insurer, the share of premiums from the rural social sectors shall be (a) 5 percent in the first financial year; (b) 7 percent in the second financial year; (c) 10 percent in the third financial year; (d) 12 percent in the fourth financial year; and (e) 15 percent in the fifth year (of total policies written direct in that year). In respect of a general insurer, (a) 2 percent in the first financial year; (b) 3 percent in the second financial year; and (c) 5 percent thereafter (of total gross premium income written direct in that year).
6. In addition, each company is obliged to serve the social sector as follows. In respect of all insurers, (a) 5000 lives in the first financial year; (b) 7500 lives in the second financial year; (c) 10,000 lives in the third financial year; (d) 15,000 lives in the fourth financial year; and (e) 20,000 lives in the fifth financial year.
7. Further, the Act sets out the reinsurance requirement for (general) insurance business. For all general insurance a compulsory cess of 20 percent, regardless of the line of business, to the General Insurance Corporation (the designated national reinsurer) is stipulated.
8. The IRDA Act also prescribes guidelines and regulations on business conduct. It specifies the creation and functioning of an Insurance Advisory Committee (IAC) that sets out relevant rules and regulation.
9. Another important point in the Act is the appointment and the role of actuary. The actuary has to be a Fellow of the Actuarial Society of India. For life insurers, the appointed actuary has to be an internal company employee, but he or she may be an external consultant if the company happens to be a general insurance company. The appointed actuary is responsible for providing a detailed account of the company to the IRDA.
10. The Tariff Advisory Committee manages tariffs. General insurance business

lines that are subject to tariffs include fire, motor, marine hull, crop, engineering, industrial all risks, business interruption, personal accident and workers' compensation.

11. Life insurers have to observe the solvency ratio. The required solvency margin is based on mathematical reserves and sum at risk, and the assets of the policyholders' fund. The available solvency margin is the excess of the value of assets over the value of life insurance liabilities and other liabilities of policyholders' and shareholders' funds.
12. The life insurance companies are required to hold their assets in the following manner:

- Central government market securities of not less than 20 percent.
- Loans to National Housing Bank including (a) above should be no less than 25 percent.
- In state government securities including (b) above should be no less than 50 percent.
- In socially oriented sectors including the public sector, co-operative sector, house building by policyholders, own-your-own-home schemes including (c) above should be no less than 75 percent.

13. The guidelines for investment of General insurance companies was set out as follows:

- Central government securities of no less than 25 percent.
- State government and public sector bonds of no less than 10 percent.
- Loans to state governments, various housing schemes of no less than 35 percent.
- The remaining 30 percent investment could be in the market sector in the form of equity, long-term loans, debentures and other forms of private sector investment.

14. IRDA has mandated minimum educational qualifications for all agents, together with training and examination requirements.

18.9 Insurance Ombudsman

Through a Government of India Notification dated 11 November 1998, the Insurance Ombudsman was created to address grievances of the insured customers and protect the interest of policyholders. Twelve Ombudsmen have been appointed across the country to expedite disposal of complaints. They have jurisdiction in respect of personal lines of insurance where the contract value does not exceed ₹ 20 lakh. The Ombudsman is bound to pass a judgment within three months from the receipt of the complaint. It should be noted that the system is monitored and operated through a governing body of Insurance Council comprising of representatives of insurance companies. The IRDA deals with other disputes that fall outside the Ombudsman's jurisdiction.

Policyholder protection was enhanced through the enactment of the Protection of Policyholders' Interests Regulations, 2002. It stipulates the responsibility of insurance companies to spell out clearly the terms and conditions of insurance policies as well as other details. For example, in life insurance, details of any riders attached to the main policy have to be given to the policyholders.

18.10 Bancassurance

Bancassurance is emerging as an important new avenue of distribution of insurance in India. With the passage of the IRDA Act in 1999, banks were allowed to enter into insurance business. It was a milestone in the history of insurance business in India. The IRDA Act, 1999 has been enacted against the background of the widely recognized need for opening up of the insurance sector. Banks, with their wide net work of branches including in rural areas coupled with available work force can utilize this opportunity for mobilizing sizeable funds of long-term nature, which can finance infrastructure projects of long gestation periods.

In the 2001 "Report on Currency and Finance", the RBI laid down its views on bancassurance in more concrete terms. "The Reserve Bank, in recognition of the symbiotic relationship between banking and the insurance industries, has identified three routes of banks' participation in the insurance business, viz:

- providing fee-based insurance services without risk participation, i.e. distribution of insurance products as an agent of insurance companies.
- investing in an insurance company for providing infrastructure and services support iii) setting-up of a separate joint venture insurance company with risk participation.

Further, the bank has to maintain healthier distance relationship between its banking and insurance business. For banks entering into insurance business with risk participation, the prescribed entity (viz., separate joint-venture company) can avoid possible regulatory overlaps between the Reserve Bank and the Government/IRDA. The joint venture insurance company would be subjected entirely to the IRDA/Government regulations.

18.11 Guidelines by RBI for the Entry of Commercial Banks into Insurance Sector

With a view to assessing the scope, desirability and eligibility of institutions to take up insurance business, guidelines were framed for banks entering into insurance business with risk participation as also for permitting banks to undertake fee-based business as insurance agents. Reserve Bank issued final guidelines for banks' entry into insurance business along with the announcements in the Monetary and Credit Policy for the year 2000-2001. The guidelines are as under:

1. A scheduled commercial bank will be permitted to undertake insurance business as an agent of insurance companies on fee basis, without any risk participation. The subsidiaries of banks will also be allowed to undertake distribution of insurance product on agency basis.
2. Banks, which satisfy the eligibility criteria given below, will be permitted to set up a joint venture company for undertaking insurance business with risk participation, subject to safeguards. The maximum equity contribution such a bank can hold in the joint venture company will normally be 50 percent of the paid-up capital of the insurance company. On a selective basis, the Reserve Bank may permit a higher equity contribution by a promoter bank initially, pending divestment of equity within the prescribed period. The eligibility criteria for joint venture participant as on March 31, 2000 was as under:

- The net worth of the bank should not be less than ₹ 500 crore.
- The Capital to Risk Weighted Assets Ratio (CRAR) of the bank should not be less than 10 percent.
- The level of NPAs should be reasonable.
- The bank should have net profits for the last three consecutive years.
- The record of accomplishment of the performance of the subsidiaries, if any, of the concerned bank should be satisfactory.

3. In cases where a foreign partner contributes 26 percent of the equity with the approval of IRDA/Foreign Investment Promotion Board, more than one public sector bank or private sector bank may be allowed to participate in the equity of the insurance joint venture.
4. A subsidiary of a bank or of another bank will not normally be allowed to join the insurance company on risk participation basis. Subsidiaries would include bank subsidiaries undertaking merchant banking, securities transactions, mutual fund, lease finance, housing finance, etc.
5. Banks which are not eligible as joint venture participant, as above, can make investments of up to 10 percent of the net worth of the bank or ₹ 50 crore, whichever is lower, in the insurance company for providing infrastructure and services support. Such participation shall be treated as an investment and should be without any contingent liability for the bank.

Prior approval of the Reserve Bank is required for banks to enter into insurance business. The Reserve Bank would give permission to banks on a case-by-case basis, keeping in view all relevant factors including the position concerning the level of NPAs of the applicant bank to ensure that NPAs do not pose any future threat to the bank in its present or in the proposed line of activity, viz. insurance business. With a view to ensure insulation of banking business from any risks, which may arise from insurance business, there should be an 'arms length' relationship between the bank and the insurance outfit.

With the issuance of notification by the Government of India, specifying "Insurance" as a permissible form of business, applications were invited from banks with supporting documents for their entry into insurance business. During the year 2000-01, twelve banks expressed their intention to enter into insurance business by way of either joint ventures or agency arrangements. Of these, "in principle" approval was given to two banks, viz., State Bank of India and Vysya Bank Ltd. The State Bank of India was permitted to set up a life insurance subsidiary on risk participation basis with 74 percent equity holding, with Cardiff, France. ING Vysya Bank Ltd. was accorded approval to contribute 49 percent to the equity of insurance joint ventures on risk participation basis with ING Insurance, Netherlands.

With effect from October 2002, commercial banks were allowed to undertake referral business through their network of branches with the prior approval of the IRDA and the Reserve Bank. On a review of the matter of banks' entry into insurance business,(2004-05) it was decided that banks need not obtain prior approval of the Reserve Bank for engaging in insurance agency business or referral arrangement without any risk participation subject to their complying with IRDA regulations and certain other conditions. However, banks intending to set up insurance joint ventures with equity contribution on risk participation basis or making investments in the insurance companies for providing infrastructure and services support will have to obtain prior approval of the Reserve Bank.

In August 2003, a decision was taken to allow financially strong scheduled primary (urban) co-operative banks having a minimum net worth of ₹ 100 crore and complying with certain other norms to undertake insurance business as corporate agents without risk participation. In October 2004, Regional Rural Banks have been allowed to undertake, with prior permission of the Reserve Bank, insurance business as corporate agents without risk participation, subject to fulfilling certain terms and conditions such as positive net worth, compliance with prudential norms, NPAs not exceeding 10 percent, continuous profits in the last 3 years and with no accumulated losses.

18.12. Bancassurance in India

The nature of existing tie-up between insurance companies and commercial banks are given below:

18.12.1 Life Insurance Business:

1. HDFC Standard Life-Union Bank of India, Indian Bank and HDFC Bank.
2. ICICI Prudential Life-Federal Bank, ICICI Bank, Bank of India, Allahabad Bank, South Indian Bank, Citibank, Lord Krishna Bank.
3. Birla Sun Life-Citibank, Deutsche Bank, IDBI Bank, Development Credit Bank, Bank of Rajasthan, Bank Muscat, Catholic Syrian Bank Ltd, Andhra Bank, Karur Vysya Bank.
4. Tata AIG Life-HSBC, Citibank, IDBI Bank, Union Bank of India.
5. SBI Life- ING Vysya Bank.
6. Bajaj Allianz Life Insurance-Standard Chartered Bank, Syndicate Bank, Dhanalakshmi Bank, J&K Bank, Karnataka Bank, Canara Bank, Lakshmi Vilas Bank.
7. LIC-Corporation Bank, Oriental Bank of Commerce, Nedungadi Bank, Central Bank of India, Indian Overseas Bank, Vijaya Bank, The City Union Bank Ltd., Repco Bank.
8. Aviva Life Insurance-Canara Bank, ABN Amro Bank, American Express Bank, Punjab & Sind Bank.

18.12.2 Non-Life Insurance Business:

1. Bajaj Allianz-Bank of Punjab, Bank of Rajasthan, Jammu & Kashmir Bank, Karur Vysya Bank, Lord Krishna Bank, Punjab & Sind Bank, Karnataka Bank.
2. Royal Sundaram Alliance-Citibank, ABN Amro, Standard Chartered, American Express, Repco Bank, Lakshmi Vilas Bank.
3. Tata AIG-HSBC, IDBI, Development Credit Bank, Union Bank of India.
4. ICICI Lombard-ICICI Bank.
5. SBI-GE-Lakshmi Vilas Bank.
6. Reliance-Punjab National Bank; Andhra Bank, Dhanalakshmi Bank Indian Bank, South India Bank, Federal Bank.
7. New India-Union Bank of India, SBI, Corporation Bank, United Western Bank, Oriental Bank of Commerce, State Bank of Saurashtra.

18.13 Guidelines for Entry of All India Financial Institutions into Insurance Business

On account of the interest evinced by some All India Financial Institutions for entering into insurance business, guidelines regarding entry of All India Financial Institutions into insurance sector were issued in November 2001. The FIs are required to ensure that risks involved in insurance business do not get transmitted to the FI and that any risk that may arise from insurance business does not affect adversely its principal business.

1. **Insurance Business without Risk Participation:** An FI having a net owned fund of ₹ 2 crore is permitted to undertake insurance business as an agent of insurance companies on fee basis, without any risk participation.
2. **Insurance Business with Risk Participation:** An FI, which satisfies the eligibility criteria given below, is permitted to set up a joint venture company for undertaking insurance business with risk participation, subject to certain safeguards.

The maximum equity contribution that the FI can hold in the joint venture company will normally be 50 percent of the paid-up capital of the insurance company. On a selective basis, a higher equity contribution by a promoter will also be allowed.

The eligibility criteria for joint venture participant are:

- Owned fund of at least ₹ 500 crore.
- Minimum CRAR of 15 percent.
- Non-performing assets which are not more than 5 percent of outstanding loans and advances.
- The Financial Institution should have net profit for the previous three consecutive years. Further, performance of their subsidiaries, if any, should be satisfactory. There should be demonstrated compliance with the regulatory requirement of the RBI for raising of resources. If a foreign partner contributes 26 percent of equity with approval of Insurance Regulatory and Development Authority/Foreign Investment Promotion Board, more than one FI may be allowed to participate in the equity of the insurance joint venture. No Financial institution will be allowed to conduct business with risk participation departmentally. A subsidiary or a company in the same group of the FI or of another FI engaged in non-banking or banking business will normally be not allowed to join the insurance company on risk participation basis.

Financial Institutions, not eligible as joint venture participants, can make investments of up to 10 percent of the owned fund of the FI or ₹ 50 crore, whichever is lower, in the insurance company. Such participation is subject to certain eligibility conditions and will be treated as an investment and will be without any contingent liability for the FI. All FIs entering into insurance business as agents or investors or on risk participation basis have to obtain prior approval of the RBI.

18.14 Types of Insurance

During the formative days of insurance, the business of insurance coverage was confined to only a few categories of risks. Because of greater awareness of the usefulness of insurance, the people now extensively use it. On the basis of coverage of risk, insurance policies can be classified into two categories.

1. Life Insurance, and
2. General Insurance.

18.14.1 Life Insurance: As the name suggests, life insurance covers the risk involved in a person's life. Though human life cannot be valued, a monetary sum could be determined which is based on loss of income in future years. Life insurance products provide a definite amount of money to the dependants of the insured in case the insured person dies during his active income earning period or becomes disabled on account of an accident causing reduction/complete loss in his income earnings.

As per Section 2(11) of Insurance Act of 1938, life insurance business means the business of effecting contracts of insurance upon human life, including any contract whereby the payment of money is assured on death (except death by accident only) and the happening of any contingency dependent on human life, and any contract which is subject to payment of premiums for a term dependent on human life and shall be deemed to include (a) the granting of disability and double or triple indemnity accident benefits, if so provided in the contract of insurance, (b) the granting of annuities upon human life and (c) the granting of superannuation allowances and annuities payable out of any fund applicable solely to the relief and maintenance of persons engaged or who have been engaged in any particular profession, trade or employment or of the dependents of such persons.

The life insurance business was nationalized in 1956 with the establishment of Life Insurance Corporation of India (LIC). There were several reasons behind the nationalization of life insurance business. Major reasons for the nationalization are given below:

1. Channelise more resources to national development programmes.
2. To increase insurance market penetration through nationalization.
3. To avoid the number of failures of insurance companies. The government argued that the failures were the result of mismanagement and nationalization would help to protect policyholder's interests better. Thus, the post-Independence history of life insurance in India is largely the history of the LIC. The monopolistic status of LIC was revoked in 1999.

A. Types of Life Insurance Policies: There are a number of life insurance products, which offer protection and also coupled with savings. There is a variety of life insurance products to suit to the needs of various categories of people. In the past, the LIC had three commonly sold policies in the market for life insurance (i) whole life, (ii) endowment and (iii) money-back policies. Following the entry of the private insurers, there was a proliferation of products. According to IRDA, at present more than 120 life products are offered by life insurance companies in India. Of course, they were not all distinct products. Many products of different companies are similar. Some of the more popular products launched recently include creditor protection products like mortgage life, and unit-linked products. There are various types of life insurance policies which are given below:

1. **Endowment Assurance Policy:** An endowment policy provides for the payment of a stated sum of money either on the attainment of a certain age or at death, whichever occurs earlier. This policy covers risk for a specified period, at the end of which the sum assured is paid back to the policyholder, along with the bonus accumulated during the term of the policy.
2. **Whole Life Policy:** A whole life policy runs as long as the policyholder is alive. As risk is covered for the entire life of the policyholder such policies are known as whole life policies. A whole life insurance product provides a fixed amount of money on death. It is meant to give protection to the policyholder's family after his\her death. The premium on such policies is comparatively lower than other types of policies.
3. **Money Back Policy:** A money back assurance policy provides not only fixed amounts which are payable on specified dates during the period of contract, but also the full amount of money assured on death during the period of contract. A unique feature associated with this type of policy is that in the event of death of the insured during the policy term, the designated beneficiary will get the full sum assured without deducting any of the survival benefit amounts, which have already been paid as money-back components. Moreover, the bonus in such policy is also calculated on the full sum assured.
4. **Annuities/Pension Plans:** Pension plan is a unique insurance scheme designed for a salaried individual. Pension plans offered by different life insurance companies help in planning retired life in an effective manner. An annuity/pension fund product provides a series of monthly payments on stipulated dates provided that the life assured is alive on the stipulated dates. The premium can be payable as single lump sum or in instalments. The insured will receive back in return a specific sum periodically from a specified date onwards either for life or for a fixed number of years. The return can be payable either monthly, half yearly of annually. In case of death of the insured, or after the fixed annuity period expires for annuity payments, the invested annuity fund is refunded, usually with some additional amounts as per the terms of the policy. Annuities/Pension funds are different from all

other forms of life insurance as an annuity policy does not provide any life insurance cover but merely offers a guaranteed income either for life or a certain period. Main purpose of buying a pension plan is to keep the income continue after one gets retirement from service. Pension plan makes an individual feel ease and relaxed in the post-retirement life.

5. **Joint Life Policy:** This is a policy covering the risk on two or mores lives. Joint life policies are similar to endowment policies as they also offer maturity benefits to the policyholders, apart from covering risks like all life insurance policies. Joint life policy is also regarded as survivorship life insurance policy by which business partners, children and spouses can be benefited. If any one person dies, the survivor will get the entire proceedings of the joint life insurance policy. A joint life insurance is also helpful while one of the parents die unexpectedly in an accident or because of some other health reasons.
6. **Group Insurance Policy:** It is a type of life insurance where a group of individuals is insured by an insurer. Group insurance has gained popularity on account of the low cost of insuring the lives. Group insurance offers life insurance protection under group policies to various groups such as employees of companies, professionals, co-operatives etc. Group Life Insurance is quite affordable as an individual does not need to furnish any proof regarding the fact that he is insured. The premiums are paid either by the employer, employees or both. Each individual employee receives a certificate showing the amount of his insurance, the name of his beneficiary and the various rights and privileges under the policy.

   One of the most common features of the group insurance is that they need to be renewed after a year's span. An individual can avail the benefits of the group insurance only till the time the individual is related or associated to the company or the employer under which the person concerned has gained the insurance.
7. **Unit Linked Insurance Plan:** Unit linked insurance plan (ULIP) is a life insurance plan that provides for the benefits of risk protection and flexibility in investment. A linked product provides not only a fixed amount of money on death but also sums of money, which are linked, with the underlying value of assets on the desired dates. ULIPs are structured products and give choices to the policyholder. Introduction of unit linked insurance plans is perhaps the single praiseworthy innovation in the field of life insurance in India.

18.14.2 General Insurance: Insurance other than 'Life Insurance' falls under the category of General Insurance. General insurance or non-life insurance provides financial protection against unforeseen events, like accident, flood, earthquake, fire, burglary etc. General insurance also covers injury due to accident or hospitalization due to illness and surgery can also be insured. Unlike life insurance, general insurance is not meant to offer returns but is a protection against contingencies. Almost everything that has a financial value in life and has a probability of getting lost, stolen or damaged can be covered by a general insurance policy.

Along with the life insurance, non-life insurance business was not nationalized in 1956. Sixteen years later, i.e. in 1972, non-life insurance was finally nationalized (with effect from 1 January 1973). At that time there were 107 general insurance companies. They were mainly large city oriented companies catering to the needs of organized sectors especially trade and industry. They were of different sizes, operating at different levels of sophistication. Upon nationalization, these businesses were assigned to the four subsidiaries (roughly of equal size) of the General Insurance Corporation of India (GIC).

There were several goals in setting up this structure. Firstly, the subsidiary companies were expected to set up standards of conduct, sound practices and provision of efficient customer service in general insurance business. Secondly, the GIC was to help control the expenses of the subsidiaries. Thirdly, it was to help with the investment of funds for its four subsidiaries. Fourthly, it was to bring general insurance to the rural areas of the country, by distributing business to the four subsidiaries, each operating in different areas in India. Fifthly, the GIC was also designated as the national reinsurer. By law, all domestic insurers were to cede 20 percent of their gross direct premium in India to the GIC. The idea was to retain as much risk as possible domestically. This was in turn motivated by the desire to minimize the expenditure on foreign exchange. Sixthly, all four subsidiaries were supposed to compete with one another.

After the passage of the 1999 IRDA Act, the GIC was de-linked from its four subsidiaries. Each subsidiary, with their headquarters based in the four largest metropolitan areas, became independent. The only function the GIC retained was that of national reinsurer. However, the government still remains the sole owner of the four former GIC subsidiaries.

A. Non-life Products before and after Deregulation: Before deregulation in 1999, non-life products that were available in the market were rather limited and similar across the four GIC subsidiaries. Of these only some policies come under tariff regulations and others were not. Fire insurance, motor vehicle insurance, engineering insurance and workers' compensation etc. fell under the tariff regulations and burglary insurance, mediclaim, personal accident insurance etc did not fall under the tariff regulations. In addition, most specialized insurance (e.g. racehorse insurance) did not fall under tariff regulations. After the opening of the sector to private players, number of new products were introduced. They included products liability, corporate cover, professional indemnity policies, burglary cover, individual and group health policies, weather insurance, credit insurance, travel insurance and so on. Some of these products were completely new (e.g. weather insurance) while others were already available through the public insurance. Major insurance policies that are covered by general insurance are the following:

1. **Property Insurance:** Property insurance as the name suggests covers and compensates for the loss incurred to any property of the insured. Property insurance policy provides financial protection against any risk to property through natural hazard or theft or burglary. The loss incurred because of fire, theft, burglary or natural disaster is covered in by property insurance. A content of property covered includes (both movable and immovable) household appliances, furniture and fixtures, jewellery, cash, vehicle and other personal items at home.

   Property insurance includes various types of insurance viz. fire, boiler, flood, earth quake and home insurance. It assures the insured to lead a peaceful life and to get their hard earned money returned in case of any accident leading to loss of property. Under property insurance, the insurer insures the insured in two ways:

   - Open Perils: Under this property insurance policy, the loss of property incurred by any cause which is not excluded under the policy is covered or the loss is compensated. The exclusion includes loss of property due to earthquake, flood, terrorism or war and nuclear incidents.
   - Named Perils: Under this insurance policy of property the loss of property due to fire, explosion, theft, burglary and lightning are covered.

2. **Health Insurance:** Health insurance/ medical insurance is an insurance policy where the insurer assures the insured to compensate the loss incurred due to injury or illness. It offers compensation for medicine, hospitalization, doctors' fees, and other check up fees, room rent and medical expenses. Health insurance offered by non-life insurers mainly cover hospitalization expenses either on reimbursement or cashless basis. The cashless service is offered through Third Party Administrators (TPA) who have arrangements with various service providers, i.e., hospitals. The Third Party Administrators also provide service for reimbursement claims. Sometimes the insurers themselves process reimbursement claims. Health insurance plans can be done as group health plans, individual plans, workers' compensation and government health plans. Health Insurance Policies in India are sub-divided into the following types of insurance plans:

- Hospitalization plans: This insurance plan assures the insured of covering the hospitalization expense and frequent medical expenses. There is a varied pay structure and individual limit as per the plan for the various plans present under this category.
- Critical illness plans: This insurance plan cover expenses incurred in case of more serious and critical illnesses like heart attack, stroke, organ transplants and kidney failure etc. This medical plan covers infrequent and relatively higher medical expenses.
- Specific conditions coverage: These medical plans offer health insurance against health complications that might occur due to some disease. These medical plans often include disease management programs related to the condition or the illness.

3. **Travel Insurance:** Travel and tourism is one of the fastest growing sectors across the world. With the rise in standards of living, more and more people are embarking on journeys to new places. Travel insurance assures the insured to compensate for any loss incurred while travelling within national boundaries or outside national boundaries. Travel insurance also compensates medical expenses for injury or accident while travelling, loss of baggage, cancellation of bookings and delayed departures. Travel Insurances are of varied types and people can opt for any of the plans as per their requirements. The risks that are generally covered as a part of the travel insurance plans includes medical expenses for injuries or accidents during the trip, overseas funeral expenses, accidental death, injury or disablement benefit, curtail in the time of journey, loss, theft or damage of money or personal possessions, cancellation of bookings, delayed departure etc.
4. **Motor Insurance:** Motor insurance often referred to as vehicle or auto insurance covers the loss related to automobiles. Under this type of insurance both private and public commercial vehicles can be insured. The risk covered are damages to the vehicle due to accidents, loss of vehicle due to theft, personal injuries to the owner of the vehicle and injury or death of a third party due to an accident in which the vehicle of the insured is involved. If the policy covers all these types of risk, it is called a comprehensive policy. Legally, no motor vehicle is allowed to be driven on the road without valid insurance. Hence, it is obligatory to get the vehicle insured. Third party insurance covers not only the risk of injury or death of third party due to accident involving the vehicle of the insured, but also the risk of liability that may arise due to damage to the property of any third party.
5. **Agricultural Insurance:** The agricultural insurance policy helps the farmer against incurring any kind of loss due to crop failure. Agriculture insurance

provides protection against all kinds of damages which are caused by natural calamities like flood, excessive rain and hail storms, diseases and pests which wreak havoc on the crops. Agricultural insurance schemes provide the farmers financial support in case they are caught in any untoward situation which proves destructive to their crops.

6. **Marine Insurance:** Marine insurance is an insurance of ships and their cargos against damages and destruction during voyage. It is an arrangement whereby one party agrees to compensate the owner or of the cargo for complete or partial losses or destruction at sea. Marine insurance can be divided into two categories viz. (i) cargo insurance, which relates to the insurance of goods in export and import trade and (ii) hull insurance which relates to the insurance of vessels against damage by marine and other perils. The perils of the sea include loss resulting from sinking, capsizing, collision of ships, attack, storm, theft, fire, piracy jettison etc. Marine insurance is also a contract of indemnity.

B. Various Kinds of Marine Policies: There are various types of marine policies. These are:

1. **Time Policy:** It is a type of policy, which covers maritime loss for a definite period usually one year irrespective of the number of voyages. The insurer undertakes risks for a specified period.
2. **Voyage Policy:** This is a type of policy, which covers maritime loss in respect of a particular voyage. A policy insuring voyage from Calcutta to London is regarded as voyage policy. Under this policy the insurer undertakes the risks on a particular voyage.
3. **Mixed Policy:** Sometimes, time and voyage policies may be combined and a single policy called 'mixed' or 'time and voyage' policy may be obtained. This is a type of policy where the risks are undertaken for a particular voyage of limited period. This policy contains the essentials of time policy and voyage policy.
4. **Valued Policy:** This is a type of policy where the value of the subject matter is agreed between the insurer and the insured at the outset of the policy. The insurer will indemnify loss up to the declared value.
5. **Floating Policy:** A policy undertaken to cover several shipments is called a floating policy. The name of the ship of other particulars of the policy is made in a subsequent declaration.
6. **Employees Liability Insurance:** This type of insurance protect an employer against any liability that he may face as a result of death or physical injury sustained by his employees out of and during the course of employment.
7. **Fidelity Insurance:** This class of accident insurance is designed to give cover

to employees in respect of any monetary loss that they may suffer as a result of fraud or dishonesty on the part of their employees who are entrusted with handling money, securities etc.

8. **Commercial Insurance:** Commercial insurance offers products which suit the business and corporate needs of the insured and provides their commercial avenues both safety and security. The function of risk management is to provide safety against any kind of internal or external hazard. The value of premium for providing coverage to commercial ventures and corporate sectors is determined on the basis of a few factors which include nature of the commercial venture, size of the organization, type of the industry, strength of the employees, annual turn over of the business etc. The insurance companies are paid the premium on either monthly, quarterly, half-yearly or annual basis.

18.15 Difference between Life Insurance and General Insurance

1. Life insurance is not a contract of indemnity, whereas general insurance is a contract of indemnity.
2. Life insurance is a contract of guarantee. Payment is assured in the case of life insurance contract. Whereas in the case of general insurance, the amount insured is not guaranteed. The amount will be paid only on the occurrence of the event insured against.
3. In the case of life insurance the event insured against i.e. death or attaining a specific age is sure to happen. In the case of general insurance the event insured may or may not happen or occur.
4. Life insurance policies are issued for a much longer period. Whereas general insurance, policies are taken for one year.
5. A life insurance policy can be surrendered by the assured before maturity. Surrender of policy is not possible in the case of general insurance.
6. Life insurance contains both the elements of protection and investment whereas general insurance contain only the element of protection.

18.16 Factors Influencing the Growth of Insurance Business in India

Insurance sector plays a very important role in the economic development of a nation. Insurance companies enact different roles such as mobiliser of savings, promoter of investment activities, stabilizer of financial markets and as risk manager. While encouraging saving habits, it also provides a safety net to both enterprises and individuals. An ever-growing insurance sector is of vital importance for the economic growth. The insurance companies also renders some useful financial intermediary services like transferring funds from the insured to capital investment required for continued economic expansion and growth which in turn generates long-term funds for infrastructure development.

According to the latest research findings, nearly 80 percent of Indian population is without life insurance coverage while health insurance and non-life insurance continues to be below international standards. In fact, insurance products are unknown to millions of people in the country. The rural economy is yet to relish the benefits of life insurance on a wide scale. In the case of LIC, its businesses from rural areas still constitute only less than 50 percent. In spite of its best efforts, Life Insurance Corporation has not been able to penetrate more than 15 percent of the insurable population, which comes to more than 300 million people. India is the twenty-third largest markets for insurance business in the world with approximately US$ 7 billion of premium collected annually. It is at the 18th position among Life Insurance markets and 28th in non-Life Insurance markets in the world. This indicates that there is a huge untapped potential for insurance business.

Saturation of markets in many developed economies has made the Indian market even more attractive for global insurance companies. The insurance market in India has witnessed dynamic changes including entry of a number of global insurers in both life and non-life segment. With the entry of private sector players backed by foreign expertise, Indian insurance market has become more vibrant. Competition in this market is increasing with company's continuous efforts to lure the customers with new and diverse product offerings. Several other driving factors, which influence the growth on insurance business in India, are given below.

1. Growing per capita income.
2. Opening of the insurance sector for private players.
3. Entry of global insurers.
4. Rising demand for retirement provision among the ageing population.
5. Growing demand from semi-urban population.
6. The opening of the pension sector and the establishment of the new pension regulator.
7. Rising per capita incomes among the strong middle class, and spreading affluence.
8. Growing consumer class and increase in spending and saving capacity.
9. Bancassurance.
10. Public private partnerships in infrastructure development.
11. Dearth of innovative and buyer-friendly insurance products.
12. Success of auto insurance sector.

Short Answer Type Questions

1. Define insurance.
2. What is the meaning of insurance?
3. What is the meaning of utmost good faith?
4. What is the meaning of causa proxima?
5. What is whole life policy?
6. What is IRDA?
7. What is life insurance?
8. What is the meaning of indemnity?
9. What is doctrine of subrogation?
10. What is Bancassurance?
11. What is insurable interest?
12. What is health insurance?
13. What do you mean by money back policy?
14. What is endowment policy?
15. What do you mean by insurance ombudsman?
16. What is travel insurance?
17. What is joint life policy?
18. What do mean by general insurance?
19. What is marine insurance?
20. What is ULIP?
21. What is fidelity insurance?
22. What is agriculture insurance?
23. What is voyage policy?
24. What is time policy?
25. What is floating policy?

Essay Type Questions

1. What are the important functions of insurance?
2. Explain the evolution and growth of insurance in India.
3. What are the general principles of insurance?
4. What are the advantages of insurance?
5. What are the features of IRDA Act?
6. Discuss the growth of life insurance in India.
7. What are the factors influencing the growth of insurance business in India?
8. Give a brief account of RBI guidelines on entry of commercial banks in to insurance business.
9. What is Bancassurance? Discuss the recent development in the area of Bancassurance.

10. What are the different types of policies issued by life insurance companies?
11. Discuss the origin and growth of general insurance in India.
12. Explain the role of IRDA in connection with the development of insurance industry in India.
13. Define marine insurance. Discuss the various types of marine policies issued by general insurance companies.
14. What are the different types of policies issued by general insurance companies?
15. Explain the RBI guidelines on entry of financial institutions into insurance business.
16. What is general insurance? Discuss the different types of risks covered by general insurance companies.
17. Differentiate between life insurance and general insurance.
18. Discuss briefly the recent developments in the field of non-life insurance.
19. Explain the role of IRDA in the regulation of insurance business in India
20. Explain the concept of life insurance. Give its disadvantages.

Bibliography

Bibliography

Bank for International Settlements, *Supervision of Financial Conglomerates: A Report by the Tripartite Group of Bank, Securities and Insurance Regulators*, July 1995.

—*Electronic Banking Group Initiatives and White Papers*, Basel Committee on Banking Supervision, October 2000.

—International Banking and Financial Market Developments, *Quarterly Review,* September 2001.

Bartlett, J.W, *Fundamentals of Venture Capital*, Madison Book, London, 1999.

Basu, Durga Das, *Introduction to the Constitution of India* (New Delhi: Prentice-Hall of India Private Ltd., 1987).

Bhole L.M, *Financial Institutions and Markets: Structure, Growth and Innovations*, Tata McGraw Hill Co. Ltd., New Delhi, 2008.

Chander R., *Performance Appraisal of Mutual Funds in India*, Excel books, Mumbai, 2002.

Choubey B.N., *Principles and Practices of Co-operative Banking in India*, Asia Publishing Company, Mumbai, 1968.

European Central Bank, *Report on Electronic Money*, August 1998.

—*Opinion of ECB on e-money*, January 1999.

—*Issues arising from the Emergence of Electronic Money*, Monthly Bulletin, November 2000.

EXIM Bank of India, *Annual Report* (various years).

General Insurance Corporation of India, *Annual Report* (various years).

Ghosh, P.K. and Gupta, G.S., *Fundamentals of Leasing and Lease Financing*, Vision Book Pvt. Ltd., New Delhi, 1985.

Gopinath, S., Recent Development in Forex, Money and Government Securities Markets: Account and Outlook, *RBI Bulletin*, August 2005.

Government of India, *Banking Committee Report*, 1972.

—Ministry of Finance, *Budget Papers* (various years).

—*Economic Survey* (various issues).

—Ministry of Law, Justice, and Company Affairs, *Constitution of India.*

Gupta U.L., *Working of Stock Exchanges in India*, Thompson Press, New Delhi, 1972.

Hull J.C., *Fundamentals of Futures and Options Market*, Tata McGraw Hill Publishing Company Ltd. New Delhi, 2003.

Industrial Credit and Investment Corporation of India, *Annual Report* (various years).

Industrial Development Bank of India, *Annual Report* (various years).

Insurance Regulatory and Development Authority, *Annual Report* (various years).

International Monetary Fund, *World Economic Outlook*, September 2005.

—Currency Crises: The Role of Monetary Policy, *Finance and Development*, March 1998.

—*Guidelines for Public Debt Management*, 2001.

—*Debt Related Vulnerabilities and Financial Crises-An Application of the Balance Sheet Approach to Emerging Market Countries*, Policy Development and Review Department, 2004.

—*Global Financial Stability Report*, 2005.

Jadhav, Narendra, Partha Ray, D. Bose and Indranil Sen Gupta, The Reserve Bank of India's Balance Sheet: Analytics and Dynamics of Evolution, *RBI Occasional Papers*, 2003.

Jadhav, Narendra, Central Bank Strategies, Credibility and Independence: Global Evolution and the Indian Experience, *RBI Occasional Papers*, 2003.

—*Monetary Policy, Financial Stability and Central Banking in India* (New Delhi: Macmillan India Ltd.), 2005.

Jalan, Bimal, Finance and Development: Which Way Now? *RBI Bulletin*, January 2000.

—Development and Management of Forex Markets: A Central Banking Perspective, *RBI Bulletin*, February 2001.

—*Strengthening Indian Banking and Finance: Progress and Prospects*, Speech delivered at the Bank Economists' Conference at Bangalore, December 27, 2002.

Johnson H.J., *Financial Institutions and Markets*, McGraw Hill, New York, 1993.

Johri and Jauhari, *Role of Computers in Banking Operation Systems* (New Delhi: Himalaya Publishing House), 1994.

Kaveri, V. S., Loan Default and Profitability of Banks, *IBA Bulletin*, January 2001.

Khan, M.Y., *Financial Services*, Tata McGraw Hill Co. Ltd., New Delhi, 1997.

Khan, M.Y., *Indian Financial System*, Tata McGraw Hill Co. Ltd., New Delhi, 1996.

Kohli, S.S., *Indian Banking Industry: Emerging Challenge*, *IBA Bulletin*, March 2001.

Kohn Meir, *Financial Institution and Markets*, Tata McGraw Hill Co. Ltd, New Delhi, 2004.

Kulkarni, R.V., Changing Face of Banking from Brick and Mortar Banking to E-Banking, *IBA Bulletin,* January 2000.

Kumar. S.S.S., *Financial Derivatives*, Prentice-Hall of India Pvt. Ltd., New Delhi, 2007.

Life Insurance Corporation of India, *Annual Report* (various years).

Machiraju, H.R., *Working of Stock Exchanges in India*, New Age International Publishers, New Delhi, 1995.

Mahesshwari S.N. and Paul R.R, *Banking Theory: Law and Practice*, Kalyani Publishers, Ludhiana, 1997.

Malhotra, R.N., *Evolution of Financial System*, Nineteenth Frank Moraes Memorial Lecture, Chennai, September 1990.

Martinez, Jose de Luna and Rose Thomas A., *International Survey of Integrated Financial Sector Supervision*, World Bank Policy Research Working Paper 3096, 2003.

Metzer, S.R., Strategic Planning for Future Bank Growth, *The Banker's Magazine,* July- August 2000.

Mishra M.N, *Life Insurance Corporation of India*, RBSA Publishers, Jaipur, 1991.

Mohan, Rakesh, Transforming Indian Banking: In Search of a Better Tomorrow. *RBI Bulletin*, 2003.

—Globalisation: The Role of Institution Building in the Financial Sector: The Indian Case, *RBI Bulletin,* February 2003.

—Agricultural Credit in India: Status, Issues and Future Agenda, *RBI Bulletin,* 2004.

—Indian Banking and e-Security, *RBI Bulletin*, November 2004.

—Ownership and Governance in Private Sector Banks in India, *RBI Bulletin*, 2004.

—Financial Sector Reforms in India: Policies and Performance Analysis, *RBI Bulletin*, October 2004.

—A Decade of Reforms in Government Securities Market in India and the Road Ahead', *RBI Bulletin*, November 2004.

—Human Development and State Finances. *RBI Bulletin*, December 2005.

NABARD, *Annual Report* (various years).

Pathak V. Bharati, *Indian Financial System*, Pearson Education, New Delhi, 2003.

Pendharkar, V.G, *Unit Trust of India: Retrospect and Prospect*, UBS Publishers and Distributors, New Delhi, 2003.

Rangarajan, C., Activating Debt Markets in India, *Reserve Bank of India Bulletin*, Mumbai, October, 1997.

—*Issues in Monetary Management*, Presidential Address at the Indian Economic Conference, Calcutta, December 1988.

—*Autonomy of Central Banks*, Tenth Kutty Memorial Lecture, Calcutta, September 1993.

—Activating Debt Markets in India, *RBI Bulletin*, October 1997.

—*Dimensions of Monetary Policy*, Anantharamakrishnan Memorial Lecture, Chennai, February 1997.

—Some Critical Issues in Monetary Policy, *Economic and Political Weekly*, June 16, 2001.

Reddy Y.V., Future of India's Debt Market, *Reserve Bank of India Bulletin*, Mumbai, November, 1997.

—Financial Sector Reforms and RBI's Balance Sheet Management, *RBI Bulletin*, December 1997.

—Banking Soundness, Monetary Policy and Macro-economic Management: Random Thoughts, *RBI Bulletin*, February 1998.

—Development of Debt Markets in India, *RBI Bulletin*, November 1998.

—Development of Forex Markets: Indian Experience, *RBI Bulletin*, September 1999.

—Changing Role of RBI: Agenda for Attention, *RBI Bulletin*, July 2000.

—*Autonomy of the Central Bank: Changing Contours in India*, Speech Delivered at IIM, Indore, 2001.

—Implementation of Financial Standards and Codes: Indian Perspective and Approach, *RBI Bulletin*, April 2001.

—Issues in Choosing between Single and Multiple Regulator of Financial System, *RBI Bulletin*, June 2001.

—Developments in Monetary Policy and Financial Markets, *RBI Bulletin*, May 2001.

—Developing Bond Markets in Emerging Economies: Issues and Indian Experience, *RBI Bulletin*, March 2002.

—Managing Public Debt and Promoting Debt Markets in India, *RBI Bulletin*, June 2002.

—Banks and Corporates as Partners in Progress, *RBI Bulletin*, November 2005.

—The Road Map for Fixed Income and Derivatives Markets, *RBI Bulletin*, March 2005.

—Globalisation of Monetary Policy and Indian Experience, *RBI Bulletin*, June 2005.

—Monetary Co-operation in Asia, *RBI Bulletin*, October 2005.

—Implications of Global Financial Imbalances for the Emerging Market Economies, *RBI Bulletin*, November 2005.

—*Financial Stability: Indian Experience*, Speech at Zurich University Zurich. Switzerland, 2004.

Reserve Bank of India, *Functions and Working of RBI,* Fourth Edition (1983).

—*Reserve Bank of India: Fifty Years (1935-85)*, 1985.

—*Report of the Committee to Review the Working of the Monetary System in India* (Chairman: Sukhamoy Chakravarty), 1985.

—*Report of the Working Group on the Money Market* (Chairman: N. Vaghul), 1987.

—*Report of the Committee on Financial System* (Chairman: M. Narasimham), 1991.

—*Report of the Committee to Enquire into the Irregularities in Securities Transactions of Banks and Financial Institutions* (Chairman: R. Janakiraman), 1992.

—*Report of the High Level Committee on Balance of Payments* (Chairman: C. Rangarajan), 1993.

—*Report of the Expert Group on Foreign Exchange Market in India* (Chairman: O.P. Sodhani), 1995.

—*Report of the Committee on Capital Account Convertibility* (Chairman: S.S. Tarapore), 1997.

—*Payment Systems in India,* 1998.

—*Report of the Committee on Banking Sector Reforms* (Chairman: M. Narasimham), 1998.

—*Report of the Informal Advisory Committee on Ways and Means Advances to State Governments,* (Chairman: B.P.R. Vithal), 1998.

—*Report of the Technical Committee on State Government Guarantees* (Chairperson: Usha Thorat), May 1999.

—*Report on Repurchase Agreements* (REPO), 1999.

—*Core Principles of Effective Banking Supervision*, 1999.

—*Report of the Advisory Group on Transparency in Monetary and Financial Policies* (Chairman: M. Narasimham), 2000.

—*Report of the Working Group on Internet Banking* (Chairman: S.R. Mittal), 2001.

—*Report of the Working Group on Consolidated Accounting and Other Quantitative Methods to Facilitate Consolidated Supervision*, December 2001.

—*Reserve Bank of India: Functions and Working,* Reserve Bank Staff College, Chennai, 2001.

—*Report of the Working Group on Electronic Money*, 2002.

—*Risk-Based Supervision Manual*, 2003.

—*Report of the Group to Study the Pension Liabilities of the State Governments* (Chairman: B. K. Bhattacharya), 2003.
—*Report of the Advisory Committee on Ways and Means Advances to State Government* (Chairman: C. Ramachandran), 2003.
—*Report of the Working Group on Instruments of Sterilisation* (Chairman: Usha Thorat), 2003.
—*Report of the Working Group on Monitoring of Systemically Important Financial Intermediaries (Financial Conglomerates)*, 2004.
—*Committee on Flow of Credit to Agriculture and Related Activities from the Banking System* (Chairman: V.S. Vyas), 2004.
—*Report of the Internal Technical Group on Forex Market*, 2005.
—*Report of the Technical Group on Money Market*, May 2005.
—*Report of the Internal Technical Group on Central Government Securities Market*, July 2005.
—*History of the Reserve Bank of India* (Volume III), 2005.
—*Report on Trend and Progress of Banking in India (2004-05)*, 2005.
—*Report on Currency and Finance* (various years).
—*Handbook of Statistics on the Indian Economy* (various years).
—*Bulletins.*
—*Occasional Papers.*
—*Supplement on Finances of State Governments.*
—*Annual Report* (Various Issues).
Robert D Auerbach, *Financial Markets and Institutions*, Macmillan Publishing Company INC, New York, 1983.
Sadak H., *Mutual Funds in India*, Response Book, New Delhi, 2003.
Sahadevan K.G, and Thiripalraju, *Mutual Funds*, Prentice-Hall of India, New Delhi, 1997.
Securities and Exchange Board of India (SEBI), *Annual Report* (various years).
Sengupta A. K. and Kuvalekar S. V., *Factoring Services*, Skylark Publications, New Delhi, 1992.
Shekhar and Shekhar, *Banking Theory and Practice*, Vikas Publishing House Private Limited, New Delhi, 1999.
Tarapore, S.S., *Domestic Debt Management Policy and Monetary Control*, 18th SEANZA Central Banking Course Lectures, Reserve Bank of India, Mumbai, 1990.
—*Towards an Active Internal Debt Management Policy*, Speech at the Seminar on Management of Government Securities, UTI Institute of Capital Markets, October 1992.
—*The Role of an Active Debt Management Policy in the Economic Reform*

Process, Lecture at the Department of Economics, Mangalore University, September 1994.

—*Open Market Operations–Objectives and Techniques*, Inaugural Address at the Seminar on Strategies for Development of the Secondary Market in Government Securities and Public Sector Bond, Bankers Training College, December 1994.

—*The Government Securities Market: The Next Stage of Reform*, Valedictory Address at the Conference on Government Securities Market, Securities Trading Corporation of India, April 1996.

—Monetary Policy, Internal Debt and Autonomy of the Central Bank, *Macroeconomics and Monetary Policy–Issues for a Reforming Economy* (eds.) Montek S. Ahluwalia, Y. V. Reddy and S.S. Tarapore, 2002.

Thorat, U., Developing Bond Markets to Diversify Long-Term Development Finance: Country Study of India, *Asia-Pacific Development Journal*, June 2002.

Varshney, P.N. and Mittal, D.K, *Indian Financial System*, Sultan Chand and Sons, New Delhi, 2000.

Verma J.C., *A Manual of Merchant Banking*, Bharat Law House, New Delhi, 1989.

Vora N.D. and Bagri B.R., *Futures and Options*, Tata McGraw-Hill Publishing Company Limited, New Delhi,1998.

Websites

Ministry of Finance, Government of India
Ministry of Commerce and Industry
Planning Commission of India
Reserve Bank of India (RBI)
Securities and Exchange Board of India (SEBI)
Life Insurance Corporation of India
General Insurance Corporation of India
Insurance Regulatory and Development Authority

Index

Index